SHOCKING THE CONSCIENCE

Praise for *Shocking the Conscience*

"For three decades—from the dark days following the murder of Emmett Till in 1955 to the battles over busing and affirmative action in the 1970s—Simeon Booker was on the scene as a reporter, covering and commenting on the civil rights movement that transformed a nation. Now Booker has written a searing and eye-opening memoir that takes us back to that epochal time of struggle and sacrifice, when he and other brave journalists risked everything to record the death rattle of Jim Crow. Reading his eloquent words reveals the very soul of the struggle."
—**Raymond Arsenault,** the John Hope Franklin Professor of Southern History at the University of South Florida, St. Petersburg, and author of *Freedom Riders: 1961 and the Struggle for Racial Justice*

"*Shocking the Conscience* is an indispensable and overdue book that fills an important gap in the history of the coverage of race in America. As the Washington bureau chief for *Jet* and *Ebony* during five decades, Simeon Booker knew everyone who mattered, went everywhere that news occurred, and covered every major story in the struggle for racial equality. As a journalist, Booker had a front-row seat to the full sweep of the history of civil rights. Now, his insider's eyewitness account adds a crucial perspective to the history of American journalism. Picking up where *The Race Beat* left off, Booker shows us the challenges of covering race in America from the vantage point of the most important African American news media of the day. *Shocking the Conscience* will be required reading for anyone who wants a full understanding of this transformation in our nation's history."
—**Christopher B. Daly,** associate professor of journalism at Boston University and author of *Covering America: A Narrative History of a Nation's Journalism*

"I have not read a book on the history of the African American which I find more informative and enlightening than Simeon Booker's *Shocking the Conscience*. It is brilliantly written and will certainly become one of the valuable works in American history."
—**George W. Haley,** former U.S. Ambassador to The Gambia, West Africa

"*Shocking the Conscience* tells a story that needs to be told about the courage and determination of a black journalist during the civil rights era. Because of the relationship that developed with the family, Booker's coverage of the murder of Emmett Till in particular provides unique insights. Journalists, we often say, write the first draft of history; Booker's story behind the story holds up well."
—**Jacqueline Thomas,** former Washington bureau chief of the *Detroit News*

"Starting with his fascinating, inside account of the Emmett Till drama, Simeon Booker's *Shocking the Conscience* not only spans the civil rights movement, it serves as a testament to his role as a pioneer breaking color barriers in his own profession."
—**Curtis Wilkie,** author of *The Fall of the House of Zeus*

"Simeon Booker lived and breathed civil rights and politics. As *Jet* magazine's Washington bureau chief, Booker, as he was affectionately known, covered every major political event affecting African Americans. He told our stories to our readers but in his own way—with honesty and humility."
—**Linda Johnson Rice,** chairman, Johnson Publishing Company

"The black press was always first on the scene during the civil rights movement, and its dean, Simeon Booker, chronicled the battle from the very front lines of the struggle. From covering the Emmett Till murder and subsequent trial to daringly accompanying the Freedom Riders as they challenged the ramparts of segregation, Booker brought the story of the civil rights movement alive on the pages of *Jet* and *Ebony* magazines. His reporting informed and inspired millions of black readers. Now, in *Shocking the Conscience*, Booker's own eyewitness account of those years is told with the verve and passion of a young reporter and the reflective contemplative tones of an older man looking back over a half-century of pioneering journalism. This is a history not to be passed up by anyone wanting to learn the inside story on the critical role the black press played in the nation's most important and enduring fight for equality."
—**James McGrath Morris,** author of *Pulitzer: A Life in Politics, Print, and Power* and *Eye on the Struggle: Ethel Payne's Journey Through the Civil Rights Movement* (forthcoming)

"One of our nation's greatest journalists, Simeon Booker was a trailblazing reporter, radio commentator, author, and most of all, selfless and courageous advocate and defender of his people. I congratulate my dear friend, Simeon Booker, a preacher's son born in Baltimore, for another milestone in his career. In the pantheon of American journalism, he stands in the first tier."
—**Congressman Charles Rangel**

"Simeon Booker, renowned journalist, tells a riveting firsthand account of the civil rights movement. He vividly recounts the perils and violence he witnessed as civil rights leaders and organizers fought for the right of African Americans to vote and brings back to life the giants of the civil rights era. In the wake of renewed voter suppression efforts, and the continued fight for equality, *Shocking the Conscience* reminds us of how far we have come, and how far we have yet to go. This book is a must-read for our newest generation of leaders."
—**Congresswoman Barbara Lee**

"Simeon Booker deserves enormous and emphatic accolades for his outstanding insights and his courageous involvement in the American civil rights crusade. His vivid portrayals and inspiring portraits absolutely capture those times and clearly point us in the direction of these times that still beckon freedom fighters."
—**Congressman Bobby L. Rush**

SHOCKING THE CONSCIENCE

A Reporter's Account of the Civil Rights Movement

Simeon Booker

with Carol McCabe Booker

University Press of Mississippi / Jackson

www.upress.state.ms.us

The University Press of Mississippi is a member
of the Association of American University Presses.

First printing 2013
∞
Library of Congress Cataloging-in-Publication Data

Booker, Simeon, 1918–
Shocking the conscience : a reporter's account of the civil rights
movement / Simeon Booker with Carol McCabe Booker.
p. cm.
Includes bibliographical references and index.
ISBN 978-1-61703-789-4 (cloth : alk. paper) — ISBN 978-1-61703-790-0
(ebook) 1. Civil rights movements—United States—History—20th
century. 2. Civil rights movements—Press coverage—United States. 3.
Journalism—United States—History—20th century. 4. Booker, Simeon,
1918– 5. Journalists—United States—Biography. 6. African American
journalists—Biography. I. Booker, Carol McCabe, 1944– II. Title.
E185.61.B697 2013
323.0973—dc23   2012037033

British Library Cataloging-in-Publication Data available

"I tell you that the Negro will never rest until he gets his rights. . . . Why this discrimination against us when we enter public conveyances or places of public amusement? Why is a discrimination made against us in the churches; and why in the cemeteries when we go to pay that last debt of nature that brings us all upon a level? Gentlemen, I say to you this discrimination must cease."
—**Hon. Joseph Hayne Rainey (R-SC),** the United States House of Representatives, Dec. 19, 1873.

"No one shocked the conscience of the nation and the world like *Jet*."
—**Dick Gregory,** civil rights activist/entertainer, 1996.

Contents

Introduction

For decades, a pocket-size news magazine published in Chicago and distributed nationally, often by kids before and after school, kept black America informed about the turbulent events that were about to change the lives of black and white Americans alike throughout the country. In 1951, black mega-publisher John H. Johnson introduced *Jet* magazine to barbershops, beauty salons, doctors' and dentists' waiting rooms, and social centers, until it quickly became a staple in black homes in every Southern backwater and Northern ghetto in America. By 1955, *Jet* had become the national chronicler of the simmering civil rights movement, and with a single issue that cast aside all the niceties of the mainstream press, emerged as an undeniable force behind the nonviolent revolution that was building.

Throughout that decade and the next, young blacks sitting in at lunch counters, walking a gauntlet of taunting mobs to desegregate public schools, or riding interstate buses through the Jim Crow South to unjust prison sentences, would acknowledge that their defiance had been fueled at an early age by a photograph in *Jet* of the mutilated body of a fourteen-year-old black boy, dragged from his bed and murdered by white racists in the Mississippi Delta. Refusing to cave when Mississippi officials pressed for an immediate burial, Mamie Till Bradley had insisted on an open coffin funeral back home in Chicago, stating simply that she wanted to "let the world see" what she had seen.

The weekly magazine became the "bible" for news about the movement. "If it wasn't in *Jet*," they'd say, "it didn't happen." And if it did happen, *Jet*, the first national news magazine to feature a young Montgomery, Alabama, minister, the Reverend Martin Luther King, Jr., on its cover, would tell you the truth about it.

For the better half of a century, I was known more often as just "the man from *Jet*" than by my given name, as I reported on black America's march to freedom from two of the most divergent viewpoints: the protesters on the ground, converging upon the courthouses, state houses, and legislatures to peacefully demand their constitutional rights, struggling to win the battle before others might take up the fight in suicidal desperation; and the men in the White House, the succession of U.S. presidents confronted with an unstoppable movement, and for one reason or another irrationally wishing it would go away. I was one of a small but dedicated cadre of black reporters and photographers whose stories and photographs in the black press finally drew the attention of mainstream media—and the world—to incidents of state-supported terrorism, as cameras caught public officials turning their backs on white mob violence, police siccing vicious dogs on peaceful protesters, powerful fire hoses slamming down women and children, and police horses galloping over prone bodies. The stories and pictures brought such a hue and cry from around the world, an embarrassed White House was finally shamed into action.

As Washington bureau chief for *Jet* and its glossy sister, the monthly *Ebony* magazine, for more than fifty years, I reported on all the players, including ten U.S. presidents, until I retired in 2007. Since then, oceans away, the seeds of America's civil rights movement seem to have taken root in unexpected places, inspiring another generation of dreamers. A Saudi woman courageously driving a car in defiance of local law is called the "Rosa Parks" of the Arabian peninsula. Under the banner headline, "Apparent torture of boy, 13, sparks protests in Syria," *The Washington Post* reports a story that evokes the memory of young Emmett Till. In half-a-dozen or more Middle East countries, dreams of freedom erupt in nonviolent protests, and their message has a familiar ring: "Freedom—Now!" Just as the black American freedom movement gained tremendous momentum with the advent of network television, these protests have leapt continents via social networks and the Internet. Those movements, like ours, will spawn many heroes, most of them unsung, and tragically too many martyrs, most of them too young. It is to our heroes and martyrs that I dedicate this book.

SHOCKING THE CONSCIENCE

1

THE SLEEPING GIANT

Nothing in either my upbringing or training prepared me for what I encountered on my first trip to Mississippi in April 1955. I was a thirty-seven-year-old reporter for *Ebony* and *Jet*, two nationally circulated, black-owned magazines based in Chicago, and had worked previously on both Negro and white newspapers, including *The Washington Post*.

As a black man I had experienced the indignities of segregation in the border states of Maryland and Virginia, and even in the nation's capital. "Whites only" water fountains, bathrooms, and lunch counters, job and housing discrimination, and unequal schools were not new to me. But Mississippi in 1955 was like nothing I had ever seen. What I witnessed there was not only raw hatred, but state condoned terror. I quickly learned that you could be whipped or even lynched for failing to get off the sidewalk when approaching a white person, for failing to say "Yes, sir" and "No, sir" to whites no matter how young they were, or for the unpardonable crime of attempting to register to vote.

Jet photographer David Jackson and I arrived in Memphis after an early morning flight from Chicago. The Tennessee port on the Mississippi River would be the "jumping off" point for most of our future trips into the Delta. In an area known as the "mid-South," blacks considered the city a "turning point" in many ways, as suggested by the story of the black preacher from Chicago who was so scared on his first trip to the Deep South, he prayed, "Lord, please stay with me." And the Lord answered, "I'll stay with you, but only as far as Memphis!"

We had a contact at a car rental agency that rented to blacks, and would make sure we got a model so mundane and beat up it would never draw attention. Our destination was Mound Bayou, a small town in the Delta, that part of Mississippi that has been called the southern most place on Earth. That was one reason we were determined to get there before nightfall. We'd heard too many horror stories told and retold by the thousands of blacks who had fled North for us to take lightly our first venture into infamous territory. It wasn't just poor economic conditions that made Mississippi Negroes flee. It was a culture we would never fully understand until we experienced it ourselves.

We were journalists, and although still somewhat naive about the Deep South, we were savvy enough to know that our profession alone might be sufficient to cause us trouble. So we did our best to look like locals, an effort I soon discovered was futile in any situation where it might really count.

It didn't matter which of us took the wheel because Dave was every bit as cautious as I was, making sure we never exceeded the speed limit, or rolled through a stop sign. I was most comfortable trusting no one but myself, unless I was in an area where it was totally unsafe to get around without a savvy local, often a trusted contact, as a guide. But Dave, at thirty-three, with the skilled eye of a veteran photographer, was as adept as anybody at spotting trouble before it spotted us. He was also a pro at driving fast over back roads at night, even with headlights out when necessary to avoid detection.

In Chicago in those days, I used to wear a beret, but I knew it would be out of place in Mississippi, so I had stashed it along with an overcoat in a locker at Midway (still the Windy City's primary airport in the mid-'50s). When we deplaned in Memphis, I also took off my suit jacket and bow tie and stuffed them into my duffel bag. (Most people wore their "good" clothes when traveling on airplanes in those days, and for a black man particularly, looking right and hoping to be treated with a modicum of respect meant wearing a jacket and tie.) The rest of my attire was a white, short-sleeve shirt, black pants, and scuffed-up shoes. On trips such as this, I would leave at home my portable typewriter with the *Ebony* logo emblazoned on the scratched-up case, and rely on a pocket-size notebook to record thoughts, interviews, facts, and details, waiting until I got back to Chicago to type the story. In later days, I would carry a Bible in plain sight on the front seat of the car, hoping to pass for a poor country preacher, but on this trip, we were still feeling our way. Like me, Dave was dressed in the style of a rural black man out to do no harm to the status quo. But even though he tried to "blend in," his cameras were always a dead giveaway, and got him into trouble on more than one Dixie assignment.

The car had a radio, but it didn't keep a station very long, so for the most part, we rode in silence, each wondering what lay ahead. Down the highway was our destination, the first scheduled voting rights rally in Mississippi since the Supreme Court's landmark decision in *Brown v. Board of Education* (May 17, 1954) had sent shock waves across the nation. Nowhere was the shock felt more emphatically than in the Deep South, where politicians such as U.S. Senator James O. Eastland (D-Miss.), a plantation owner, were fiercely opposing the court's ruling that racial segregation in public schools was unconstitutional.

In the early 1950s, segregated public schools were the norm in most of the United States, and were mandated in the entire former Confederacy. Although all the schools in a given district were supposed to be equal, black schools were far inferior to their white counterparts. I had a close look at the disgraceful neglect of black education while working at the Cleveland *Call and Post*, a black weekly, where I reported in-depth on that city's shamefully neglected Negro schools, and won a national award for the series, the Wendell L. Willkie Award for Negro Journalism, sponsored by *The Washington Post*. Although the Supreme Court's decision required only the desegregation of public schools, and not other public areas such as restaurants and restrooms, Southern whites were worried that it signaled a threat to all racial segregation—and white supremacy.

While other manifestations of the South's Jim Crow system were bound to be mentioned, the primary focus of the rally we were about to cover was voting rights. Dave and I wondered whether there would be trouble, and specifically whether the local sheriff's men would hassle people heading to the rally, even try to break it up. Or was the local white power structure so secure it would ignore the event and continue with business as usual? We doubted it, but we were outsiders; we just didn't know.

Civil rights issues up to this time were argued in federal courts, mostly in litigation brought by the National Association for the Advancement of Colored People (NAACP). The bus boycotts, sit-ins, and mass marches came later. Voter registration drives were almost nonexistent except in this unlikely place, in the alluvial plain of the Mississippi Delta. The black town of Mound Bayou had hosted three in past years, but none since the *Brown* decision gave the state's minority white population cause for alarm. (Blacks far outnumbered whites in Mississippi.) And so we drove toward a town that had long ago been dubbed "The Jewel of the Delta," and wondered what really lay ahead.

One thing we knew was that there was nothing "antebellum" about the Delta. Framed by the Yazoo and Mississippi rivers, there wasn't much happening in the area until after the Civil War. Virgin forests and fields covered almost the whole area in 1870. Twenty years later, railroad tracks opened up new markets for King Cotton, the South's labor-intensive lifeblood. It was a life from which most of the blacks who'd fled North wanted to escape. The proliferation of tractors and other harvesting equipment in the 1940s left many of them little choice when the only work they'd had, as bad as it was, became insufficient to support their families. All along the highway, we could see evidence of the race-based system that kept white planters at the top and black workers, mainly sharecroppers, at the bottom. The shanties and rundown houses that lined the fields usually were not home to whites.

Outrageously racist sheriffs and judges rode roughshod over black people, wielding powers that became a brutal and intractable part of the system. Sometimes they left it to vigilantes to do the worst dirty work.

Despite this, or maybe because of it, a massive rally was scheduled in Mound Bayou on Friday, April 29, 1955. It was the state's largest civil rights meeting in almost fifty years. Whatever happened, we knew it would make news for *Jet*'s national readership. We only hoped we'd live to file the story.

"THE JEWEL OF THE DELTA"

We were headed for Bolivar County, where Mound Bayou lies just off U.S. Highway 61, halfway between Memphis and Vicksburg. The town was established in 1887 by former slaves as a place where blacks might work for themselves instead of for whites, providing for each other everything they needed, and feeling safe, even while surrounded by the white feudal system. The local joke—although it was more true than funny—was that Mound Bayou was "a place where a black man could run FOR sheriff instead of FROM the sheriff." From day one, Mound Bayou officialdom was black, from the mayor down to the cops. And although a dot on the map, with no more than 2,000 souls, the town had caught the attention of prominent Americans, including Booker T. Washington.

A renowned advocate of trade schools for blacks, and the founder of the Tuskegee Institute, Washington had impressed President Theodore Roosevelt, who invited him to the White House within weeks of taking office after President McKinley's assassination. They got along so well, Roosevelt invited him back for dinner. The next day the South erupted in fury when the Associated Press (AP) reported it on the wire. Diehard segregationists took the presence of a Negro as a guest at the White House as an insult to the South, and particularly threatening to the self-respect of any Southern woman. It always seemed to come back to the Southern woman. A Southern white man was not going to stand for any black man being in close proximity to a white woman unless the black was a servant. If proximity couldn't be avoided, it could never be on an equal basis.

According to historians, Roosevelt was disgusted by the outrageous attacks in the Southern press.[1] So, a few years later, he gave them some payback. On a bear hunting trip at the mouth of the Mississippi River after the 1904 elections, he had the train stop in Mound Bayou where he very pointedly crowned the black township, "the Jewel of the Delta."

Our contact person, and Mound Bayou's most prominent citizen, was Dr. T. R. M. Howard, a tall, broad-shouldered, bear of a man who was a gentleman planter, businessman, and home builder as well as a physician. (The "T. R.," coincidentally, was for Theodore Roosevelt and the "M" for Mason, which he added to his name out of appreciation for the white doctor, Will Mason, who had helped him acquire his medical education.) Born in Kentucky and educated in Nebraska and California, Doc Howard had begun his medical practice in Mississippi in the mid-'40s. By 1955, his civic activities (or more specifically, his *civil rights* activities) were having as much impact in the Delta as his medical practice, in which he performed as many as twelve operations a day and supervised a hospital where nearly 50,000 men, women, and children, most of them poor sharecroppers, could get treatment each year. After dark, however, his was a different world, in which he was warned repeatedly of a likely ambush if he ventured into the backwoods for nighttime speaking engagements. In the wake of *Brown v. Board of Education*, Mississippi was becoming even more inhospitable to anyone thought to be awakening "the sleeping Negro." And that was exactly what Dr. Howard was trying to do.

Among his non-medical activities, he was president of the Regional Council of Negro Leadership (the "Leadership Council"), an organization pledged "to guide our people in their civic responsibilities regarding education, registration and voting, law enforcement, tax-paying, the preservation of property, the value of saving and in all things which will make the black community stable."

The Leadership Council maintained that the poor schools attended by black children were what was driving their parents to pack up and head North. All the Council had been pushing for was parity—schools for black kids that were on a par with the ones white kids attended. Black kids, on average, attended school only four months a year, and spent the other months in the cotton fields, planting, hoeing, and picking to supplement their families' income. Putting the kids into the fields to help their parents was the only way these poor black families could make enough to survive. When they did go to school, the kids often walked for miles while busloads of white kids sped past them to better schools with better-trained teachers, and superior equipment, books, and supplies.

Dr. Howard's strategy for rousing and organizing the "grassroots" was to draw on the skills of blacks who had "made it" into leadership roles either in the business world, a profession, or the church. Working with the NAACP, the Leadership Council promoted civil rights, self-help, and business ownership. It made the white power structure nervous.

"Doc," as we called him, was expecting us, and put us up in a modest, two-unit guesthouse he owned across the road from his own home. It was considerably more comfortable than many of the accommodations we would find in the future, especially when reporting on lynchings. On those assignments, we would get a black undertaker to sneak us into the funeral home after dark so we could photograph the body and get an account of the murder. Sometimes we'd spend the night and slip out before dawn. Most blacks in the vicinity would be too frightened to be seen with us.

This rally would be the first to be covered by a national news outlet, because even though the previous years' rallies had each attracted around 10,000 participants, no one outside of Mississippi had taken any notice. This time, news of the rally would reach far beyond Mississippi. Chicago publishing pioneer John H. Johnson's *Jet* magazine, launched in 1951, was already a staple in black households and businesses nationwide, and every week, Johnson was fulfilling his promise to bring its readers "complete news coverage on happenings among Negroes all over the U.S."

Doc also had reason to believe that local reaction to this rally was likely to be different this year, because of the *Brown* decision. From the time the case was argued before the Supreme Court, and continuing ten-fold in the year since the decision had come down, racist tracts and pamphlets were being disseminated throughout the South, calling the school case Communist-inspired and supported. Meeting with us at his home the morning after we arrived, Doc handed me a yellow, five-by-seven-inch envelope, bearing an illegible postmark over four cents in cancelled stamps. It was addressed to:

T. R. M. Howard, negro
Mound Bayou, Miss.

Opening the metal clasp on the flap and removing the contents, I asked him who had sent them. Doc shook his head. "I have no idea," he shrugged, "but I don't think it was a friend."

There was no note inside, just a handful of documents, including two crude booklets on construction paper, three racist pamphlets, and a copy of an editorial, "NEW JERSEY NEGRO EDITOR WARNS HIS RACE OF THE DANGERS OF INTEGRATED SCHOOLS IN THE SOUTH," by Davis Lee, publisher and editor of the Newark *Telegram*. Lee's controversial argument was that if schools were desegregated, blacks would lose out in every way to whites, including, most significantly, the loss of teaching positions and income. Lee's preference was for "separate but equal." The problem was that in reality, despite the handful of examples of black success that he cited, separate was never equal and never would be. Lee's editorial had inspired a slew of racist tracts, some claiming to reflect the sentiments of other Negroes, arguing for maintaining the status quo. Mississippi's White Citizens' Councils had actually retained Lee to map a pro-segregation drive

A dog, kind and friendly when it's let alone,
Might turn in fierce anger to save its white bone.

Racist tracts, some containing cartoons such as this, warning Southern blacks of the dangers of desegregation and outsiders of the consequences of meddling in the South's affairs, proliferated throughout Dixie after the Supreme Court's school desegregation decision.

among the state's blacks,[2] but it was not clear whether he had any input into the two most creative, as well as particularly offensive, articles in the envelope which, using poor grammar and spelling and what was intended to look like Negro dialect, argued against desegregation. One was titled, "Mammy Liza's Appeal to Her People (On the Question of Integration in Southern Schools)," while the other was characterized as a "sequel," under the title "Uncle Ned Warns His People of the Dangers of Integration in Southern Schools." Both reduced Lee's arguments to minstrel-show perversions, as in the final couplet of Uncle Ned's five-page "verse:"

De angels in heaben each has deir own level.
Stay in yo' place . . . quit flirtin' wid de devil.

"Take a look at the back page, too," Doc suggested, pointing out that the booklet contained some not-so-subtle threats, as well.

Turning the pages, I found a cartoon depicting a fenced yard in which a bulldog stood warily eyeing his bone near a sign that warned "Keep Out." The caption explained, "A dog, kind and friendly when it's let alone, might turn in fierce anger to save its white bone." In case that was too subtle, Doc noted the booklet's opening lines:

Years ago, when ole Marse had a matter to settle,
Outsiders knowed well dat dey'd better not meddle.

It wasn't too subtle for Dave and me.

One of the formal pamphlets in the envelope was called "Research Bulletin No. 1," published in March 1954 under the title, "Negroes Menaced by Red Plot," by a group calling itself the Citizens Grass Roots Crusade of South Carolina. The objectives of the Communists in the South, according to the pamphlet, were to get the vote for Negroes, and then round them up under the "Red banner of the Socialist Planners." The group's Research Bulletin No. 2, issued in October, several months after the *Brown* decision, similarly purported to tell the "Truth About the Supreme Court's Segregation Ruling," setting the tone for the tract with a quote from FBI Director J. Edgar Hoover in an address to the Daughters of the American Revolution on April 22, 1954:

> To me, one of the most unbelievable and unexplainable phenomena in the fight on Communism is the manner in which otherwise respectable, seemingly intelligent persons, perhaps unknowingly, aid the Communist cause more effectively than the Communists themselves.

The pamphlet made good use of that quote to link any and all support for Negroes to a Red plot.

Although some blacks in Mississippi were either duped by this propaganda or too scared to do anything but continue with life as usual, there were many others who, like Dr. Howard, were intent on changing the system for the better for Southern blacks. They were the titans who would move the cause forward. Among them were Doc's colleagues in the Leadership Council, men whose names I'd been given by the NAACP as key contacts in the Delta. They were unknown to us then, but over the next decade, we'd be writing about them in *Jet* with such frequency, they would become household names in every black home in America.

The first was Amzie Moore, a broad-faced man who still walked with military bearing ten years after serving in the U.S. Army in Burma in World War II. Assigned to intelligence, he'd been ordered to inform African-American troops that conditions would be better for them when they returned from the war. Not only did that turn out to be untrue, but when Moore returned to his home state of Mississippi, he learned that a fanatic group known as the "home guard," a Civil War throwback related to the Ku Klux Klan, was killing a black person every week. After joining the NAACP, he uncovered the case of a man who had been whipped to death for stealing a saddle, even though witnesses supported his claim of innocence. The man's wife saw her husband killed, and three defendants even confessed to the lynching, but it took a grand jury less than ten minutes before releasing the accused slayers.

Moore opened a gas station, beauty shop, and grocery store in Cleveland, Mississippi, about a fifteen-minute drive south of Mound Bayou on U.S. 61, that would be used as a "revolving dormitory" and "safe house" for civil rights activists in Bolivar County during voter registration drives. Dr. Martin Luther King, Jr., the Reverend Andrew Young, and John Lewis would come to know his house well. Moore's gas station was the equivalent of an oasis in the desert; it offered the only restrooms for black travelers between Memphis and Vicksburg, a distance of more than 240 miles.

We also sought out Aaron Henry, who'd been described to us as "a conservative militant" among this group of Delta activists. He was a pharmacist who owned his own business—the Fourth Street Drug Store—in Clarksdale, Mississippi. As a business owner who was not dependent on the white power structure, Henry was in a strong position to agitate against it—and he risked his life repeatedly by doing so. In time, both his home and pharmacy would be bombed (once when Detroit Congressman Charles Diggs was a houseguest) and he would be jailed more than thirty times for his civil rights activities, which included serving as president of the state NAACP.[3]

Henry was a reliable contact for me in the Delta over the years, and our acquaintance alone would lead to a single reference to me in the secret files of the Mississippi State Sovereignty Commission, a misguided effort of the state government to spy on anyone active in civil rights. The state agency, established in 1956 in reaction to the *Brown* decision to provide financial and other support to the nefarious operations of the White Citizens' Councils, had spies—both black and white—all over the state. Teachers and civil servants were among those whose careers could be ruined by their identification as supporters of civil rights—even the basic right to vote—for blacks.[4] The Commission was abolished in 1977, and today its activities are reflected in an online database through which anyone can search for the names and files the Commission secretly maintained. In my case, my name, telephone number, and Johnson Publishing Company's Washington, D.C., address in the Keith-Albee Building show up in Aaron Henry's address book, the pages of which one of those spies apparently photographed and provided to the commission.

As president of the Leadership Council, Doc Howard also became a mentor to a young civil rights activist named Medgar Evers. A World War II combat vet, Evers moved to Mound Bayou to sell insurance for Dr. Howard's Magnolia Life Insurance Company after being refused admission to the University of Mississippi Law School. Evers and his wife, Myrlie, who worked as a typist for the insurance company, spoke of Doc as "kind, affluent, and intelligent," and "that rare Negro in Mississippi who had somehow beaten the system."

While selling insurance, Medgar Evers also promoted the Leadership Council and the NAACP, becoming its first field secretary in Mississippi. He would become well-known as a dogged investigator of civil rights violations—including lynchings—throughout the state. One of his biggest campaigns, however, was the organization of a 1952 boycott of service stations that failed to provide restrooms for blacks. As part of this effort, Medgar and Myrlie, supported by other members of the Leadership Council, distributed 20,000 bumper stickers with the slogan, "Don't Buy Gas Where You Can't Use The Restroom." Since most of the Negroes in the forefront of the Council were businesspeople and professionals, it was this group, as well as poor farmers who might support the campaign, that the white power structure targeted in response, freezing all local credit lines in order to force an end to the boycott.

To counter the economic squeeze, Dr. Howard helped to establish, and served on the board of directors of, an NAACP "war chest" at the black-owned Tri-State Bank in Memphis. The fund ultimately defeated the white credit squeeze, and lent muscle to the NAACP and the Leadership Council in their campaign to urge blacks not to leave Mississippi, but to stay and fight for their rights.

To me, as a northerner, for a black person to live day after day under the conditions I was seeing for the first time seemed second only to a death sentence. I was surprised, therefore, when young Evers told me that the lack of civil rights and even the dearth of job opportunities were actually accelerating black efforts to improve conditions rather than make plans to leave. "Because of the racial situation," he assured me, "Negroes are closer together." Implying that a lot more was going on than met the eye, he added, "A lot of our work is carried on underground."

When *Jet* ran my interview, the magazine's cover asked the question of the day: "Should Negroes Leave Mississippi?" Evers's answer was summed up in the headline: "DESPITE TERROR, MISS. NEGROES VOW TO STAY AND FIGHT RACISTS."[5]

In the same *Jet* issue, my weekly Ticker Tape USA column mentioned that Detroit Congressman Charles Diggs would make his first Dixie speech in Mound Bayou on April 29. On that day, under a sweltering tent with an audience overflowing into the streets of the town, Evers's call to stay and fight would be echoed by three powerful and moving speakers. One of them was Diggs, who would prove to be a staunch Congressional advocate for the disenfranchised blacks of Mississippi. Another would be forced to give up everything and flee North rather than risk his life any longer. The third would be shot dead before a new moon had risen over the Delta.

2

"TIME IS RUNNING OUT"

The voting rights rally proved to be, as expected, the largest ever in Mississippi, with an astounding 13,000 black men, women, and children in attendance—an assemblage unseen in the area since 1909, when Booker T. Washington dedicated the town's oil mill, the largest black business venture of the early 1900s. Despite the numbers, not one white reporter covered the event. In the racial climate at the time, the most an event of this magnitude would merit would be a line or two in "News From The Colored Community," normally located adjacent to the want ads section. But two black Mississippi weeklies covered the event: the *Jackson Advocate*, which had an editorial policy so conservative that it was often referred to as "neo-segregationist," and the *Southern Mediator Journal*, "The South's Progressive Negro Weekly," published in Little Rock.

David Jackson and I roamed through the crowd of sharecroppers, cotton farmers, schoolteachers, clergy, and businesspeople who came by truck, bus, cars, and even wagons from other parts of Mississippi, Arkansas, Tennessee, and Louisiana. In one interview after another, they confided that they'd come to the rally at the risk of being evicted from their homes, having their loans foreclosed, or finding their lives in jeopardy when they returned home. A large tent had been pitched, which could only accommodate 5,000 people, while some 8,000 others sat or stood in the warm sun. The two-mile-wide town could barely handle the overflow. Townsmen rerouted vehicles and blocked highway traffic in order to accommodate 5,000 additional folding chairs brought from the Tri-State Fair Grounds. They built temporary wood-plank seating facilities on two wings of the tent to hold 2,000 additional people.

Some fifteen soft drink and candy stands were set up. During the day, visitors consumed a ton of hot fish, three tons of barbecued chicken and ribs, 500 cases of soda pop, and 300 gallons of ice cream—and took home 13,000 voter registration forms. In the evening, Dr. and Mrs. Howard entertained some 1,000 guests at a buffet supper at their showplace country home.

In his opening remarks at the rally, Dr. Howard's booming voice announced that more blacks had been registered to vote in Mississippi during the past twelve months than in any previous year. Pledging a state-wide drive to further increase black voter registration and end a wave of police brutality, he emphasized the importance of the vote as the best way of unseating vicious sheriffs, cops, and judges. The crusade against police brutality was almost as much a priority for Dr. Howard as the voting rights drive. He introduced me to a woman whose family had considerable real estate in the Delta, but she refused to buy a family car for fear one of her sons would be arrested while driving it and roughed up by police for no reason. This kind of fear reached every Negro, including children.

Dr. Howard also called for increased contributions to the NAACP supported "war chest," which now totaled $300,000, to help militant blacks denied loans or credit by white institutions, a tactic supported by the White Citizens' Councils. Fourteen white Democrats had formed the first White Citizens' Council almost a year earlier, in the nearby Delta town of Indianola in Sunflower County. They were reacting to the activities of Dr. Howard and the Negro Leadership Council, but the *Brown* decision was another big concern.

The White Citizens' Councils quickly attracted some 5,000 members in Mississippi alone, before spreading to all the other Deep South states, and swelling to tens of thousands of members. They drew their membership from among the town leadership, which often proudly erected a billboard announcing, "The White Citizens' Council of . . . Welcomes You." Their members were different from the Klan in that they dressed like everyone else, and claimed to be non-violent, although that, too, soon appeared to be an unsupportable claim. The Councils kept lists of "militant" Negroes who were urging blacks to vote, as well as those who tried to register, and went after them where it hurt most: in the wallet, evicting them from their homes, denying them credit, refusing them farm services. To underscore his point, Dr. Howard quoted directly from the Citizens' Councils' credo:

The Negro who insists upon registering and voting and who insists upon integration in Mississippi is to be classed as a troublemaker in his community and is to be relieved of his job, asked to move out of the house that he lives in, if he does not own it. If he is a farmer, the gins will not gin his cotton, and his credit rating will be taken away from him. His notes are not to be renewed and the lending agencies in his community are not to make loans to him.

Then, citing a comment by a leader of the Citizens' Councils movement that "a few killings now might save much blood later on," Dr. Howard grimly predicted, "When it is realized that the economic pressure has been a flop, the next round will be a well-organized wave of violence."

One of the reasons the regional Negro Leadership Council rallies had been so popular (each drawing more than 10,000 participants in the past three years) was the high quality of the speakers. At an earlier rally, U.S. Rep. William L. Dawson, a Democrat who represented Chicago for 27 years, became the first black congressman to speak in Mississippi since the nineteenth century. Chicago Alderman Archibald J. Carey, a judge as well as a religious leader who used his influence in support of civil rights, was another speaker. Perhaps the greatest draw had been Thurgood Marshall, then general counsel for the NAACP and the architect of the *Brown v. Board of Education* case. The grandson of a slave, Marshall was considered by many to be the star quarterback in the early days of the civil rights movement, when the action was in the federal courts. He was preparing, at that very moment, to argue before the Supreme Court in a series of cases known as *"Brown II"* that the court should set a date certain—like, immediately—for the dismantling of segregated public school systems. I would come to know him well during the four decades when I covered his succession of civil rights victories in the courts, and his historic rise to the top of the legal profession, ultimately becoming the first African-American on the Supreme Court.

Freshman Congressman Charles C. Diggs, Jr., a Democrat from Detroit, was this year's keynote speaker. With his election in 1954, Diggs became the third black in Congress, joining Chicago's Dawson and Harlem Rep. Adam Clayton Powell, Jr.

Although born in Detroit, Diggs had roots in Mississippi. His father, Charles C. Diggs, Sr., was born in Issaquena County, population just 2,000, the smallest county in Mississippi. Located in the Delta, it also had the second lowest per capita income in Mississippi and the 36th lowest in the United States.

Leaving Mississippi as a boy, the elder Diggs migrated to Detroit where he founded the House of Diggs Funeral Home. His business survived the Great Depression, and he became interested in politics. In 1936, he ran for the state senate and was elected, becoming the first black state senator in Michigan—and the only one in the country at the time. After rising to prominence at the state level, in 1948 he was charged with accepting a $150 bribe from lobbyists, convicted, and sent to prison. When he was released less than two years later, he ran for and won his former senate seat, but Republican leaders in control of the legislature refused to seat him because of his prison record. Diggs argued unsuccessfully that whites with prison records had been reseated, and that his was a clear case of discrimination. In the end, the younger Diggs ran for his father's seat in a special election in

1951, and won, becoming at twenty-nine the youngest member of the Michigan state senate. Taking up the elder Diggs's fight against racial discrimination in Michigan, especially Detroit, he successfully sponsored the first Fair Employment Practices Commission, and spearheaded other measures to foster black equality in his home state.

In 1954, Charles Diggs, Jr., ran for Congress, first winning the Democratic primary against an incumbent who had been in office fourteen years, and then trouncing his Republican opponent, Landon Knight, whose father, John Knight, was the editor and publisher of the *Detroit Free Press*, the second largest daily in the state.

Diggs Sr. and Jr. visited Issaquena County before the rally, and when they arrived in Mound Bayou, they were followed by a contingent of white state policemen, ostensibly for their protection. Dr. Howard and other council members suspected, however, that the troopers were there to monitor the event, and report back to their superiors in Jackson. It was disturbing, but not unnerving, since the troopers didn't appear to be anything other than spies. As the rally would be reported in the black press anyway, there didn't appear to be cause for undue concern.

The congressman was an eloquent speaker who, like Dr. Howard, had a deep voice that stirred the crowd. Urging a coast-to-coast boycott of firms that engaged in the "economic freeze" against blacks seeking civil rights, Diggs vowed, "We won't permit company officials to grin in our faces in the North while slamming the door in your face in the South."

Even with state policemen within earshot, Diggs, like Dr. Howard, didn't hesitate to bring up the sensitive subject of the White Citizens' Councils. He told the crowd the economic pressures applied by the Citizens' Councils, as well as incidents of police violence against black activists, were "on the lips of people halfway around the world, who judge America not by what she preaches but by what she practices."

"Fight with growing confidence," the young legislator exhorted his audience, warning others who would stop them, that the clock was ticking. "Time is running out in Mississippi," he roared, ". . . it's two minutes to midnight."

The audience shouted back its approval. They believed what he was saying. In this meadow, at least, the dream was very much alive, like a fire burning in the human breast. And the young legislator from Detroit was stoking it.

3

THE RALLY ENDS;
THE KILLING BEGINS

Known paradoxically as both the most hated and the best loved man in Mississippi, Dr. Howard, along with other civil rights leaders in the state, was on a white racist death list. Doc hired gun-toting bodyguards to protect himself and his family around the clock. He kept a small arsenal of weapons in his home, including a .45-caliber Thompson submachine gun. Death threats against him and his family became increasingly common.

During my stay in Mound Bayou, Doc introduced me to another prominent civil rights leader on the Klan's death list, the Reverend George Washington Lee of Belzoni, Mississippi. Located in Humphreys County, the Delta town was named for the nineteenth century Italian archaeologist and explorer Giovanni Batista Belzoni.

Lee, 51, who was also a speaker at the Mound Bayou rally, was a vice president of the Leadership Council. He told the massive audience, "Pray not for your mom and pop. They've gone to heaven. Pray that you can make it through this hell." I was impressed by him and the way his down-home talk and sense of political timing electrified the crowd. A co-founder of the Belzoni branch of the NAACP, Lee was the first black person to register to vote in Humphreys County since Reconstruction. It didn't make him popular with the White Citizens' Councils, especially in Belzoni, which enjoyed a particularly bad reputation for the way it dealt with blacks "who didn't know their place."

In addition to being pastor of four churches, Lee ran a grocery store. A black-owned grocery store in Mississippi often served more than the obvious purpose. One almost legendary story originating in the Delta involved a Negro grocery store operator who frequently posted signs out front bearing misspelled words. Whites passing by laughed at the weird phonetics, but in the end, the blacks had the last laugh—the store was owned by the local NAACP president, whose civil rights activities went undetected.

Lee and his wife, Rose Bud, also set up a small printing business, successful enough to provide the resources to enter the battle for civil rights. He was able to register nearly all of the county's black voters, despite resistance from the white power structure and reactions ranging from indifference to outright hostility on the part of many ordinary blacks and fellow preachers who didn't want to alienate that powerhouse.

He also had to watch his back against another group, the ones he called "Judas niggers." Nothing new in the South, these blacks were cut from the same cloth as black slave drivers and plantation overseers. Now, almost 100 years after the Civil War, they still curried favor with the white power structure by informing on other blacks.

By all accounts, the top dog in Humphreys County was Sheriff Ike Shelton. A rabid segregationist, he aggressively worked with the local White Citizens' Council to purge blacks from the voting rolls through intimidation and economic pressure. While many potential voters backed down, Rev. Lee and Gus Courts, another black grocer, stood their ground. Even after white officials offered Rev. Lee protection on the condition that he halt the voter registration efforts, he steadfastly refused.

As head of the town's NAACP chapter, Gus Courts was ordered by his banker to turn over all NAACP books, and when he refused, was told to leave town. He refused to do that either. Once a Citizens' Council member handed him a list of ninety-five blacks registered in Humphreys County, warning that anyone whose name was not removed from the voting list would lose his or her job.

Both Courts and Rev. Lee had tried for years to pay poll taxes in order to vote and were finally allowed to sign the register only after Sheriff Shelton, fearing federal prosecution, gave the go ahead. Actually casting a ballot, however, required a separate fight.

After the rally, David Jackson and I hung around Mound Bayou a few more days to interview Rev. Lee, Gus Courts, Medgar Evers, Amzie Moore, and Aaron Henry, before flying back to Chicago to file several articles for *Jet*. Under the circumstances, we didn't trust any courier but our own hands to get our copy and photos there safely. I was excited by what I'd seen in Mound Bayou—the raw courage of the local activists, the spirit of the people who responded to them, the hopes for the future. But I was also uneasy. Despite all of our foreboding as we had headed toward this assignment, everything seemed to have turned out too well.

THE FIRST TO FALL

A week after my return from Mississippi, on Sunday, May 8, 1955, I received word from the Delta that Rev. Lee had been murdered. He was returning from a Leadership Council board meeting in Mound Bayou and had just

Jackson Advocate

Link Belzoni Preachers Death To Howard Meeting

DEATH OF REV. G. W. LEE IN
BELZONI SATURDAY NIGHT
PUTS SPOTLIGHT ON RACE
RELATIONS IN MISSISSIPPI

Say Victim in Mystery Death Was
On Citizens Council Black List

SOUTHERN MEDIATOR JOURNAL

"We Lift As We Serve"

PREACHER'S MOUTH SHOT OFF, TONGUE SHOT INTO, ALLEGEDLY, BY WHITE MEN

| Mrs. R. Lee Being Consoled By Sister | Improved Housing, Suggested Project By Rockefeller | Picken Black Dies At His Blackville Home | Ambushed Last Saturday Night | Bystanders Accuse Whites Of Shooting Rev. Willie G. Lee |

The murder of Rev. George W. Lee was front-page news in the black press, including the conservative *Jackson Advocate* and out-of-state papers such as the progressive *Southern Mediator Journal* in Little Rock, but not a single white-owned newspaper reported on the first civil rights-related murder since the Supreme Court's school desegregation ruling a year earlier. I vowed my coverage of the next lynching would make it harder for them to ignore.

gotten his pants pressed at a tailor shop in readiness for preaching on Sunday. As he drove along Church Street, a car pulled in behind him. A rifle shot punctured the right rear tire of the minister's Buick. Then a Ford convertible pulled parallel, and two shotgun blasts were fired at near point-blank range into Rev. Lee's vehicle.

The clergyman's car careened across the dirt road, swerved fifty feet across a walk, and crashed into a shanty house, knocking the structure from its foundation. His face almost blown off and badly bleeding, Rev. Lee groped his way from the wrecked car, staggering blindly. Two black taxicab drivers ran to him and helped him into one of their cabs. He tried to speak, but was unable to do so before he died on the way to the hospital. Called to investigate, Sheriff Ike Shelton took one look at the lifeless body and pronounced the death due to concussion from a traffic accident.

Rev. Lee's widow, Rose Bud, was unconvinced, and resisted the sheriff's attempts to persuade her to turn the body over to a black funeral home for embalming, without an autopsy. Instead, Mrs. Lee summoned two of her husband's closest friends, Dr. Cyrus Walden, a Yazoo City surgeon, and Dr. Clinton Battle, a twenty-eight-year-old physician from Indianola, to conduct a postmortem examination. Dr. Battle, also a civil rights activist, had enraged the White Citizens' Council by urging blacks to vote in nearby Sunflower County, the birthplace of the Councils and home of Senator James Eastland, where blacks outnumbered whites by more than 2-to-1. The postmortem uncovered a number of lead pellets, identified as buckshot, about the minister's face and head. One shot had passed through his neck at the throat; his jugular vein was severed, the lower part of his mouth shot off, and his tongue shot in two.

After the autopsy results were made public, Dr. Battle, the first Negro to vote in Indianola in fifty years, was even more unpopular with the White Citizens' Council, and after receiving a number of threats, he fled with his family to North Carolina.

Sheriff Shelton tried to explain away the pellets by saying that they were dental fillings torn loose by the impact of the crash. When this explanation was scorned, the sheriff theorized that Rev. Lee was a "ladies man" who had probably been killed by a rival. Again, this far-fetched explanation satisfied no one, as it was patently untrue. It was much more likely that Rev. Lee's death resulted from white outrage over his speech in Mound Bayou. He had made Belzoni look bad, and the racists couldn't stand that.

A few years earlier, the sheriff's lame explanation might have been the end of the incident, but Dr. Howard, Evers, and others had different ideas. They demanded a thorough investigation. Mississippi Gov. Hugh White rebuffed their demand, a spokesman announcing that the governor "pays no attention to NAACP requests." But the U.S. Attorney General ordered the FBI to investigate the murder to determine whether any federal laws were violated. Dr. Howard was one of the people FBI agents interviewed at length about Rev. Lee's murder. While they were questioning him, his telephone rang. It was a death threat.

Shaken but also incensed, I decided that I had to return to Mississippi. More aware now of the dangers we faced than on our first foray weeks earlier, David Jackson and I again flew to Memphis, where we rented a car from the same fellow we'd been sent to just weeks before. He would come to know us well over the next few years. We took turns at the wheel and had no problem until we neared Belzoni, and had to stop several times for directions to the site of the funeral. I removed my trademark bow tie, and carrying a Bible, we attempted to pass ourselves off as a couple of itinerant preachers who were lost. Our ruse, which we would use many times in the tumultuous years during which we covered the South, was only partially successful. One white woman looked at my horn-rimmed glasses and remarked, "You're not from around here. Niggers around here don't wear glasses like that."

I reported in *Jet* that even while the FBI was probing the shotgun murder of Rev. Lee, seven other Mississippi Negro leaders had been marked for death by white supremacists: in addition to Dr. Howard, state NAACP president Dr. A. H. McCoy, NAACP state secretary Medgar Evers, undertaker T. V. Johnson, grocer Gus Courts, Dr. James Stringer, former NAACP state president, and Dr. Clinton Battle. All had spoken out in support of immediate integration of public schools and had participated in voter registration drives.

A black newspaper, the *Southern Mediator Journal* of Little Rock, carried a front-page story under a banner headline with a picture of Rev. Lee lying in his open casket. A similar picture appeared in the *Chicago Defender*, a well-regarded black weekly. Mrs. Lee insisted that the casket remain open during the funeral, so that everyone could see how brutally her husband had been martyred.

REQUIEM FOR A WARRIOR

The little town of Belzoni seemed oddly dark on the day of the funeral, as though the black cloud that hovered over it had been sent by an angry God. High in the distant heavens thunder rumbled, while below on the flat, stone-flecked plot of rich Delta soil, two husky cotton workers went through the grim routine of digging a grave. The mound of earth prevented the diggers from watching, but they could hear the low, dirgeful spirituals and occasionally the hysterical sobs of members of the bereaved family.

A good 100 feet away, across a churchyard path, lay the body of the Reverend George W. Lee, high in a metal casket in full view of the two thousand Negro men, women, and children who had converged on the Delta town to pay final tribute. Dressed in overalls and tattered work clothes, and wearing shoes that had seen many years of tramping through rows of cotton, the Delta citizens crowded into every available chair, leaving many standing in the aisles. Some men sat on the tailgates of work trucks, and both men and women perched on the church windowsills. In striking testament to the minister's widespread leadership, the autos, trucks, and buses jammed into the parking lot bore license plates from every Mississippi county as well as nearby states.

As we made our way to the chapel, we ran into another black reporter, Moses Newson, 28, with the *Tri-State Defender*, a weekly based in Memphis. Moses and I became lifelong friends as we crossed paths again and again on the road to freedom, covering the marches, the trials, and atrocities. Our next encounter would come just a few months later at a bizarre trial in Sumner, Mississippi. Years later, we were just an hour apart on the first two buses of the Freedom Ride, when the Klan waylaid and burned his Greyhound bus. Moses was one tough newsman.

Behind the makeshift wooden pulpit, draped with white and black crepe paper, sat the state's leading black Baptist ministers, some of whom came from rural areas and wore the work clothes of poor backwoodsmen. Backing up the deep voiced preachers were two gospel choirs.

As the rich strains of Negro spirituals faded into the background, a small, weather-beaten preacher edged to the rostrum. "We all wonder why the good brother is laying here," he said in a soft, compelling voice. "We all ask the question as to why he was taken away. We all beg to God for courage and faith in this dark hour." Tears edged down the rough cheeks of the cotton workers, the tractor operators, and the nimble-fingered domestics. Even the preachers bent their heads and wiped away tears. It was a sad day in Belzoni.

When Dr. Howard ascended the rostrum to pay his last respects to his fallen comrade, a ray of sunshine suddenly skittered across the congregation. His eulogy was as passionate as any I'd ever heard, and he spared no one. Pumping his fist in the air, he shouted, "There are still some Negroes left in Mississippi who would sell their grandmas for fifty cents. But Rev. Lee was not one of them. Rev. Lee was a warrior. Rev. Lee was murdered because he refused to put down his arms in this civil rights battle. He was murdered because there are people in this state who oppose our having every advantage of citizenship. Rev. Lee died not as a cringing coward but as a hero. His death will be long remembered in this Delta land. He did not die in vain."

An old, ebony-skinned woman leapt to her feet and shouted in affirmation, but if that was the consensus, it was not unanimous. I heard others in the congregation whisper that Rev. Lee "did wrong" and "shouldn't have tried to go against the white man." Others expressed fear that he'd stirred up something he shouldn't have, and had "got this white man evil." One man actually mumbled that he was glad Rev. Lee was gone. I felt whipsawed between the outpouring of grief over a martyr for the cause, and the murmured expressions of relief that a troublemaker was gone. When I left Mound Bayou just weeks earlier, I thought I left behind a promising civil rights campaign. Now I was discouraged. I had thought the stories of Negro acquiescence to the myth of white supremacy were unbelievable. But here at Rev. Lee's funeral, they suddenly appeared well founded.

Following Dr. Howard to the pulpit, Roy Wilkins, only recently elected executive secretary of the NAACP, promised that the organization would do everything in its power to bring the murderers to justice. The crowd chorused, "Amen." Then the mourners followed the casket and pallbearers to the graveyard, where a white detective walked through the throng without touching a soul. A pathway seemed to open automatically as if the Negroes, even those with their backs turned, could feel the presence of an approaching white man, although no Negro would ever look one in the eye. Beyond the graveyard, there wasn't a white man on the streets anywhere near the chapel during the funeral.

Standing by her husband's freshly dug grave, Mrs. Lee, who had been sick in bed when he was gunned down, broke down in tears. A burley cotton worker attempted to comfort her. With the faith of generations, he soothed, "Don't cry, Rose Bud. Rev. Lee's not really dead." I wondered, however, if Belzoni's voting rights movement was.

As Dave shot pictures for *Jet*, an old woman lumbered across the church grounds and, slipping up to him, said, "Son, you better get out of town. The sheriff's done recognized you." For Dave, shooting with one camera, with a back-up in a bag slung over his shoulder, there was no hiding. But he wouldn't run. There was no way he'd give up such an assignment. As soon as the funeral ended, we began a circuitous route from one safe house to another before finally slipping out of town, hoping anyone looking for us would have given up by then. It wasn't until later that I realized the gnawing in my gut the whole time had been fear. I'd never felt anything like it before in my life.

"BLIND JUSTICE?"

Although no one was ever charged with Rev. Lee's murder, the FBI focused its inquiry on two individuals, Peck Ray and Joe David Watson, Sr., members of Belzoni's White Citizens' Council. Ray, a local handyman, and Watson, a gravel hauler, were suspected from the start because of their reputations for violence. Before Rev. Lee's murder, Watson had been arrested, but not convicted, for randomly shooting into a black sharecropper's home.

In addition to Dr. Howard and Medgar Evers, the federal investigators were assisted by Ruby Hurley, the NAACP's tireless and courageous southeast regional director, who built the region into the largest and strongest in the NAACP organization. She quickly got on the trail of the witnesses, who had disappeared when they realized what they had seen. One eventually was located in East St. Louis, Illinois. A second was found in another far-off Northern locale. They told a chilling murder story involving two white men and a black who rode in the convertible that overtook Rev. Lee. They also pointed the finger at Ray and Watson.

Federal agents turned over their evidence to the local prosecutor, Stanny Sanders, who declined to convene a grand jury. The agents held Watson's 20-gauge double-barrel shotgun and shells for possible use in a federal civil rights trial, but that never happened, because the Justice Department said it could not substantiate allegations that the minister was murdered because of his voting rights activities.

A month after the murder, Tom Ethridge, a columnist for the race-baiting white daily, the Jackson *Clarion-Ledger*, wrote a column condemning the federal involvement: ". . . just let a couple of Southerners whip a colored person, or let a Negro get himself killed under unusual circumstances and every pressure group in the land promptly howls for FBI action, plus rigid laws that would destroy our basic liberties. Whoever said 'Justice Is Blind,' certainly knew the score." Ethridge's paper consistently ignored the evidence and blatantly pandered to prejudice.

The case received extensive impartial coverage in a number of black weeklies in the South, while in the North, it would be months before a white newspaper even mentioned Rev. Lee's gangland-style murder. It was a grievous omission that I found hard to rationalize. Lee's shooting was the first civil rights murder in the South since the Supreme Court struck down school segregation. Yet not a word appeared in the nation's major newspapers. It made me wonder how many casualties it would take to arouse white press attention to the brutality against blacks in Mississippi. But it did not surprise me. Before going to work for *Jet*, I had been a newspaperman, working for Negro newspapers in Maryland and Ohio as well as one of the great bastions of the white press, *The Washington Post*. Even from childhood, I was aware of the difference between how the black press and mainstream newspapers treated news about black folk. It was as striking as the difference between night and day—or black and white.

4

BORN TO DREAM

Baltimore molded many giants in the freedom movement, including that great "quarterback" of the civil rights team, Thurgood Marshall, and my first mentor, Carl Murphy, crusading publisher of the *Afro-American* newspapers. I never want it forgotten that I was born there, although I grew up in Youngstown, Ohio.

In 1917, the year before I was born, my father, Simeon S. ("S. S.") Booker, General Secretary of the Colored Branch of the Baltimore YMCA, was tasked with raising funds for a new building, after a recent segregation ordinance required the organization to abandon its site at McCulloh and Dolphin Streets. The *Crisis*, the NAACP's historic chronicle of Negro life, reported in December that property on Druid Hill Avenue had been secured and "a four-story building will be erected at a cost of $100,000." The figure was important because it meant the Y had met the requirement for a grant from Julius Rosenwald, the leading Jewish philanthropist of the time. Rosenwald believed in the social mission of the YMCA, and didn't quarrel with its practice of bowing to local customs when it came to racial segregation. The YMCA established whites-only and black Y's in many cities, even though the national organization officially opposed segregation. Rosenwald helped to build both, including about two dozen "colored" YMCA buildings, by offering the sum of $25,000 to communities that raised $75,000. The black Y's brought many opportunities to blacks that they would not have received from any other source. The Druid Hill branch of the Y, for example, was the first facility in Baltimore with an indoor pool available to the black community. (After forming a lasting friendship with black educator Booker T. Washington, whom he met at a YMCA dinner in Chicago in 1911, Rosenwald also provided seed grants to build almost 5,000 Negro schools in the South, based on a model on which he and the Tuskegee Institute founder collaborated.)[1]

My maternal grandfather, Dr. James Henry Nelson Waring, a medical doctor as well as a renowned educator, was involved in YMCA work during

World War I. He wrote my mother in May 1918 (four months before I was born) of his visit to Boston's Soldiers Welfare Club, a colored women's group, to arrange for their presentation of a flag to the YMCA unit of which he was a member at Camp Devens, a temporary cantonment established in 1917 for training soldiers for battle. The Y had moved in immediately, constructing fourteen buildings, including an administrative center, an auditorium, and nine "huts," long, single-story buildings, spread out throughout the camp to serve as church, theatre, and fraternal meeting place for young soldiers.

Normally, the Y would have respected local custom and designated the huts by race, but my grandfather wrote that "on account of the scattering of the colored soldiers around different parts of the cantonment," the team's leaders had abandoned the idea of having a separate hut for black soldiers and decided instead to admit them to all huts on the grounds. The members of Dr. Waring's staff (that is, the Y unit's Negro staff members) were to be assigned one to a hut in "neighborhoods" where there were colored troops, and he had been asked to be the Camp Supervisor of the colored work. Such a decision was novel and not without risks, so he had sent to Jesse Moorland, the Y's General Secretary and coordinator of colored units, for approval of this departure from the norm, which he realized was a pretty big deal. As Dr. Waring wrote my mother:

> Putting a colored man on a regular staff and admitting colored men to all huts, if we can get the colored men to take advantage of this, is of course the biggest thing yet and puts the work on a fine theoretical basis—democratic and American.

Camp Devens was also the site of the base hospital for the Division of the Northeast, and housed about 50,000 men in August 1918 when an influenza epidemic broke out, developing rapidly and stalling all routine work at the encampment, as well as prohibiting all assemblages of soldiers, who were dying at an average rate of 100 a day. Ironically, a white doctor wrote a friend, the darkening of the victim's facial skin caused by the infectious disease "made it hard to distinguish colored men from the white."[2] Called the "Spanish influenza," the epidemic eventually killed more Americans than the war.

When I was seven years old, the Y sent my father to Youngstown, Ohio, to replicate his fundraising success in Baltimore. With Rosenwald's challenge grant of $25,000, my father raised the rest of the funds for "Steel Town's" first colored YMCA branch from some 100 individuals and corporations. Located on West Federal Street, the building, according to the program for its dedication ceremony, was constructed at a cost of $190,000 by an Italian

The YMCA Secretaries Summer Conference at Bordentown (NJ) Military Institute was an annual destination for our family, Reberta and S. S. (2nd row, light clothing), and me and my siblings, James, Ray and Carolyn (front row, l-r). (Courtesy of author.)

Catholic contractor, "to serve the 15,000 negro [*sic*] citizens of this city." ("Negro" was not capitalized in those days.) A Tudor Gothic, residence-type building, it was described as "reminiscent of the English manor house at a period when the forbidding feudal spirit had changed to one of welcoming hospitality." In less literary terms, it also was considered "state of the art" and "the finest of its kind erected in America."

The dedication on Sunday afternoon, August 16, 1931, was a grand affair, attended by a list of dignitaries that included Ohio Governor George White. The ceremony was broadcast live over WKBN of the Columbia Broadcasting System by "remote control," as the program put it, from the WKBN Studio in the Central Branch of the Y. Just two weeks short of my thirteenth birthday, even I had a small but memorable role in the event. My assignment was to wait on the roof with a delegation headed by my father as a small plane flying overhead dropped a ceremonial wreath which I was supposed to carry downstairs in a procession to the audience waiting on the ground floor. The only problem was the wreath was bigger and heavier than we expected and when I tried to catch it, it knocked me off my feet. With some help, I managed to get it downstairs. The impressive building still stands today, but no longer belongs to the YMCA, which sold it a few years ago for $1 to the city's rescue mission.

The Depression years in Youngstown took their toll on my family, but we fared much better than many. My father and mother, Reberta ("Bert") Waring Booker, were resourceful, at one point moving the family out of our house at 310 West Myrtle Avenue and renting it out, while we lived in rooms on the top floor of the Y.

My father was an alumnus of Virginia Union University in Richmond and a lifelong officer of Alpha Phi Alpha, the first intercollegiate, black Greek letter fraternity. The fraternity's membership, including such monumental figures as Martin Luther King, Jr., and Thurgood Marshall, is a roster of black men who have made lasting contributions to our country.

Born the descendant of slaves in rural Prince Edward County, Virginia, S. S. Booker, a serious Baptist teetotaler for whom life was a mission, rose from poverty by his hard work, perseverance, and social conscience. An outspoken crusader, my father was publicly critical of Youngstown's black clergy, declaring the church "too tame" in its activities, as well as neglectful of black youth and the broader community. He called on ministers to take on the social problems of the urban black population, instead of acting as if the next life, not this one, were all that mattered. His criticism gave rise to suggestions that he take on the cloth himself, which he ultimately did. After a thirty-five-year career with the YMCA, S. S. was ordained a minister, becoming pastor of Youngstown's Third Baptist Church.

THE WARINGS

My mother, a graduate of Howard University and Columbia Teachers College, could trace her love of teaching back through two generations of nationally-known educators, and her auburn hair back even further than that. Reberta Waring's side of the family has been documented back to Captain Billy Waring, a Virginia plantation owner who reportedly earned his rank in the Revolutionary War, and Arrica Vessels, his mulatto slave, who bore him several children, the first when he was forty-six and she only fourteen years old. His name would be anathema to their descendants but for two things—he freed (manumitted) Arrica and the children in 1806, and when he died in 1815, left them a large inheritance of $5,000 each, which they used wisely to make their way in the world despite the loss of their white "protector."

One of their sons, William Waring II, cut a path west as a businessman, winding up in Chicago, where he died in 1854, a victim of cholera. He'd been so successful, his inheritance, according to his son, was still intact when he died. The second of his eleven children, William Waring III, my

Renowned educator Booker T. Washington (center) was president of the Negro Business League when he joined my maternal grandparents, educator/physician Dr. James H. N. Waring (left), then principal of Colored High and Training School in Baltimore, and Caroline Brown Waring (front-center), and other friends for a photo at the League's Ninth Annual Convention, August 19–21, 1908, in Baltimore, Maryland. (Courtesy of author.)

great-grandfather, was active in Negro causes in Ohio and Michigan before the Civil War, during which he served as chaplain to the 102nd Regiment USCT (originally the 1st Michigan Colored Volunteer Infantry Regiment), an African-American infantry unit of the Union Army. After the war, he went to Washington, D.C., where he worked as a government clerk, a prestigious position for a Negro at the time, studied law at Howard University, and was one of its first graduates. Ordained a Baptist minister, he was a founder and first pastor of Washington's Berean Baptist Church, organized in 1877. He and his wife, Amanda Fitz-Allen Hill, lived at 1930 12th Street NW, in an area of Washington populated by more African-Americans than lived in Harlem at the time, and considered a black cultural center long before the Harlem Renaissance of the 1920s and '30s.

Their son (my maternal grandfather), James H. N. Waring, was born before the couple moved to Washington, in Berrien County, Michigan, in 1861, and was educated in the public schools of Oberlin, at Howard University, and Western University in Pennsylvania. For eleven years he was supervising principal of the colored schools of the District of Columbia. He also studied medicine at night, and earned an MD degree from Howard, where, like his father, he later served on the board of trustees, which he joined at the same time as his friend, Booker T. Washington.

Dr. Waring was recruited from his post with the District of Columbia schools to Baltimore's colored public schools, which he helped to build into one of the best school systems in the country, administered by Negroes instead of whites for the first time since the Civil War. Thurgood Marshall, a product of Baltimore's Colored High and Teacher Training Schools, proudly referred to himself as "one of Dr. Waring's boys!"

My mother, a charter member of the Kappa chapter of Phi Delta Kappa sorority at Columbia, continued to teach school in Baltimore after marrying my father, but gave up the classroom when they started a family (eventually, three sons, of whom I was the second, and a daughter). After they moved to Youngstown, she helped S. S. manage the new YMCA, including, among other things, running the Y's cafeteria, an enterprise I eagerly joined in when I was old enough to become her assistant pastry chef. Having lost three of her six siblings to illnesses at young ages (including her twin sister, Regendia, our "Aunt Gen"), she was no stranger to tragedy, and when my older brother, James, died of pneumonia while still in college, she was the rock who supported the family through our grief.

Together my mother and father made a difference in the lives of young Negroes in Youngstown. They organized outreach and enrichment programs, including an annual forum on current social issues; promoted education and personal responsibility through "Go-to-high school, Go-to-college" drives (a national program of the Alphas); and sponsored tennis matches and other sports activities. Tall and gangly throughout my teen years, I played center on the Y's undefeated State Championship basketball team. (I even tried high school football briefly—until a guy tackled me and the football went one way and my helmet another. I never engaged in contact sports again.)

When S. S. died in 1960, the *Chicago Defender* described him as "one of Youngstown's outstanding Negro leaders." Alpha Phi Alpha, in which he had served as national president (1921–23) and remained active his entire life, acknowledged that he had embodied the fraternity's highest and noblest ideals: "manly deeds, scholarship, and love for all mankind." His death came four years after a horrendous automobile accident had taken my mother's life, and left him badly injured. They'd been driving from Youngstown to Cleveland to attend a state convention and visit my brother, Ray, and sister, Carolyn, when their car, driven by my father, collided broadside with a tractor-trailer. My mother, 69, died almost immediately, as an ambulance rushed her to St. Luke's Hospital in Shaker Heights. An article on the accident in the *Chicago Defender* noted Reberta Waring Booker's many contributions to black life, particularly the programs she and my father had initiated for youth in the city of Youngstown.

For me, the biggest "happening" at the Y during my teenage years was the night "De Lawd" himself came to dinner. In 1932, the Pulitzer Prize–winning Broadway play, *The Green Pastures*, came to Youngstown on a national tour, and the all-black cast stayed with us. (While the Y is mainly thought of today in connection with its recreational and fitness facilities, in the early part of the twentieth century it often provided the only decent, safe, and affordable accommodations for young blacks traveling through or newly arrived in a city.) The play depicted well-known Bible stories as they might be imagined by blacks in Louisiana, acting them out in Southern black dialect amid familiar scenes such as a fish fry. It had revolutionized the theatre by not only daring to present an actor as God, but making God black! The Lord—or "de Lawd," as he was known in the dialect of the play—was Richard B. Harris. Even without his sudden aura of stardom, the actor was a stunning figure, almost six feet tall, with light tan skin, and a mane of smooth, gleaming white hair flowing from his high forehead to the base of his neck. Born in 1864 in Ontario, Canada, he was the son of fugitive slaves who had escaped North via the Underground Railroad.

At dinner, I had a continuous stream of questions for Harris after learning that we shared three of the same passions—baseball, fishing, and poetry, which I liked to write, and he had won prizes, even as a boy, for reciting. His half-century climb to the "Great White Way" had been, as poet Langston Hughes would have said, "no crystal stair." The actor had supported himself for decades as a bellhop, waiter, or porter, while somehow finding the means to put on one-man shows and poetic recitations before finally being "discovered" for the Broadway role. Having balanced his answers to my questions so as neither to dampen my youthful enthusiasm nor throw stars in my eyes, Harris at the end of the evening looked at me from beneath his dark, bushy eyebrows, and said soberly, "Never give up, son. It took me fifty years to win a name in the theatre. I didn't make it to Broadway until a few years ago, but I never gave up."

From an early age, I knew I wanted to be a writer, although there was little inspiration for that, and certainly no role models, for a black kid in the white press. When I was just a youngster, the *Vindicator*, the daily newspaper serving Youngstown and adjacent counties, hired a Negro to write a column which the paper descriptively titled, "News Notes for Colored Folks." Into this column went everything about the city's "colored folks"— weddings, church items, obituaries, and even a few two-line ads. The man was considered one of the "bridges" between the black and white communities, since the column turned out to be of interest to white folks, too, helping them keep track of a maid or chauffeur by taking note of who was attending gospel meetings and other functions. There was a comic aspect to the column, as well, inspired not only by its odd variety of items, but also the unfortunate affliction of the reporter. The man drank heavily and often, even while he was writing, and frequently garbled his facts, sometimes making the column all the more enjoyable. Nevertheless, he was for years the Negro representative in Youngstown's daily press.

It's easy to understand why my father was not impressed by my ambitions to be a journalist. He told me to make sure that my bylines always included "Jr." so that no one would think he was responsible for the articles I would write. He also began appending "Sr." to his name. If there was one trait my father and I had in common, it was probably a crusading spirit; beyond that, our personalities were like oil and water, and he knew I would chart my own course. While he clung to teaching and preaching as the most promising ladders for black advancement, I saw my future as a member of the fourth estate.

Black Americans' image in the daily press changed very slowly over the years. The first step was to get newspaper editors to capitalize the word *Negro*. Then came the campaign to remove that word from personal descriptions in news stories. That was followed by the struggle for inclusion in general news columns and equal opportunity in hiring. It was a long haul, during which the black citizen's image was shaped, blighted, and blemished. To many segments of the press, the Negro was not a citizen at all, but a casualty, an outsider, a migrant, or (as writer Ralph Ellison described him) an "invisible man." Tragically, too many white Americans shared this view because of the white press.

To its credit, the *Vindicator* also had an exception to the norm, Esther Hamilton, a white reporter who saw beyond a person's skin color. Esther took an interest in me in my teen years, becoming both a friend and early booster when I pitched news items or poetry to the paper. She had been a reporter in Youngstown since 1918, and became such a cherished fixture at the *Vindicator* that when she finally retired to Florida, the paper let her continue writing her column about happenings in Youngstown—from the Sunshine State.

My first published piece was a four-line poem in the *Vindicator*, an achievement my mother celebrated by baking a cake. I have no recollection of that poem, or, with one exception, any of the others that were published in weekly newspapers and magazines, including the NAACP's *Crisis*, or later, in an *Anthology of American Verse*, compiled by Clement Wood, a very interesting fellow. Born in Alabama in 1888, he practiced law and was a judge there before being dismissed for jailing the lieutenant governor for contempt. Wood then bought a one-way ticket to New York to begin a new career, at which he did quite well, becoming a prolific writer of novels, poetry anthologies, and other books, while teaching at prestigious schools, including New York University. He was also way ahead of many people from his state on racial issues. One of his novels, published in New York in 1922, although titled *Nigger*, was considered an enlightened treatment of the racial drama playing out in America.

Wood came to Richmond for a speaking engagement while I was attending Virginia Union. The forum where he was speaking was, like all of the Old Dominion, segregated, but I still hoped to meet him. I wrote him a letter in advance of his visit, telling him of my intense interest in all things literary, and his work in particular, and asking if it would be possible for a classmate and me to hear him speak. He wrote back that we should meet him before the event and he would see that we were admitted. He did, and as Professor Wood's guests, we had no problem. In fact, no one even seemed to look at us.

In high school I was sports editor for the *Buckeye Review*, Youngstown's small, black weekly—about eight pages—with circulation of about 1,000, and a motley crew that solicited ads. The publisher, attorney J. Maynard Dickerson, printed the paper in his basement. I also freelanced for the *Afro-American* newspapers. My mother's brother, James (Uncle Jamie) H. N. Waring, Jr., had introduced me to the publisher, Carl Murphy, his former Harvard classmate. At the time, the *Afro-American* was the nation's largest black newspaper chain, with editions in five eastern seaboard cities. Between my uncle and Murphy, I began to visualize how my dream of becoming a reporter might one day come true.

Uncle Jamie took me to Ivy League football games and a couple of times we rode the train to the annual Harvard/Yale boat races, America's oldest collegiate athletic competition. He inspired my dream that, like him, I might attend Harvard someday. Ironically, he was also the one to douse that dream a few years later, when he threw me out of the Downingtown Industrial and Agricultural School, in Chester County, Pennsylvania, where he had succeeded my grandfather as principal.

Dr. James H. N. Waring, Sr., had survived the influenza epidemic at Camp Devens (this particular strain of the virus struck young adults the hardest), and after the war, was living in Hopkinton, Massachusetts, in semi-retirement when, in September 1921, he received a telegram offering him the principalship of Downingtown, which had been left without a headmaster upon the death of its first principal and co-founder, the Reverend William A. Creditt. The school's student body was primarily urban and similar in background to the others with which my grandfather had years of successful experience. "So thoroughly was school work in [Dr. Waring's] blood," newspapers later reported, he took the post, despite the pleas of his wife and children that it would be too much for him. Dr. Waring must have known that his heart would soon give out, because at his last meeting with his son and namesake, my Uncle Jamie, he pleaded with him to resign his professorship of German at Howard University and come to Downingtown. "I have come to feel about the school," the senior Waring told his son, "as I feel toward my own sons and daughters. I know that a heart attack is likely to snatch me away at any moment. I would be content to go, if I knew that I were leaving Downingtown in the hands of one of my children." A few months later, while on a vacation trip to Boston, Dr. Waring suffered a fatal heart attack and died without knowing that Uncle Jamie had accepted his call to Downingtown.

I lasted less than a year at the state-supported, semi-military boarding school. Modeled after Alabama's Tuskegee Institute, the school was established in 1905 on a 110 acre campus, to provide academic and vocational training to African-American teenagers, mostly from Philadelphia, fifty miles away, some of whom were neglected, under-achieving, or otherwise considered "at risk." In part because the school offered a wealth of extracurricular activities for its boys and girls, including sports teams, most, if not all, of Uncle Jamie's nephews and nieces clamored for the chance to spend at least a year there, enjoying the freedom that came with living in a dormitory with other kids the same age. But the experience had its downside as well. Being a city kid, albeit neither an underachiever nor one who had ever gotten into any trouble, I was never comfortable with the school's odd mixture of rural life (it ran its own dairy farm, for example) and regimentation.

Uncle Jamie ran a tight ship—lights out from 10:00 p.m. to 7:00 a.m., no "hangin' around" on campus, and regimented marching to and from meals, which were served family-style in a building across campus from the two dormitories. Still, there were some things that went on that the very proper and strict principal must have known about, even if he pretended not to. One of them was hazing, which in retrospect was pretty mild, but probably contributed to my decision a few years later not to pledge to any fraternity—not even the Alphas, in which my own father had been a national officer—because the initiation included unrestricted hazing.

The upperclassmen's pranks were far from the worst aspect of boarding school at Downingtown. Food at the state-supported school was so bad, the 100 or so students did whatever we could to fill our stomachs outside the dining hall, including raiding nearby fruit farms and returning to the dorm with bags of apples or pears. All the meals seemed unimaginative, but the one I most detested was breakfast because it was always warm mush, presumably oatmeal, which came just short of making me gag. Even worse was getting up at the crack of dawn and standing outside our rooms in the hallway of the dorm, waiting for the command to march across the campus to eat. I could have returned home, but life with all the other kids, despite the regimentation and bad food, gave me more "liberty," more sense of independence, and more opportunities to have fun than living at home under the close supervision of a YMCA executive whose greatest aspiration was to become a Baptist preacher.

My cousin, Percy Steele, who like me was given no special treatment by Uncle Jamie, also detested the morning "mush." One morning, we awoke before sunrise so hungry our empty stomachs seemed to vibrate like drums. We put our heads together and devised a plan. Slipping out of the dorm in the darkness before anyone else appeared to be awake, we ran across the campus to the kitchen, where the bakery delivery man had already left his large metal basket of bread at the door. Snatching one of the hot loaves, we ran back to the dorm, scooped it out, coated the inside of the crust with creamy peanut butter we'd bought from a little store across the back road from the school, and then stuffed the soft bread back inside. This delicious concoction was called a "jug 'n' loaf," and whatever we couldn't eat immediately we stowed in a dorm trunk for future consumption. Unfortunately, we got caught, and Uncle Jamie had no choice but to banish his own blood from the school in shame. There was no way he could give his nephews another chance and still keep order at the school. With that, I thought I had lost forever any chance of seeing Harvard from the inside looking out.

RE-CHARTING THE COURSE

I finished high school in Youngstown, and a year later, my matriculation at Youngstown College, a YMCA sponsored institution, also came to an early and abrupt end when I was tossed out for protesting the denial of activity cards to Negro students. At my father's urging, I swallowed my inclination to chart my own course and enrolled in his alma mater, Richmond's Virginia Union University.

Virginia Union was my first experience in the South, and my first adult view of real segregation. Although it was no preparation for my later foray into the Mississippi Delta, Richmond was nevertheless an eye opening experience for a kid from "Steel Town." Black high schools in Richmond, for example, had formal dances. This was the first time in my life I had ever seen formal attire. Furthermore, I had never seen so many educated blacks as were at Union. When it came to finances, however, Union was a poor school. The buildings were in disrepair, the cafeteria menu resembled a relief diet, and few professors earned as much as $5,000 a year, although they were very dedicated to their jobs. Yet on our campus in the heartland of Virginia, students could speak on any issue and discuss any problem, even though we could not enjoy freedom of expression in the city. This was not the case on the campuses of state-supported schools, which had larger facilities and more numerous buildings. The joke at the time was that before a Negro became president of a state college, he had to know how to say, "Yes, sir," to bow low, and to chauffeur a governor around the campus.

Union was a place where students not only expected but demanded respect, even from visitors. I recall one time when a white man failed to remove his hat when he entered the president's office. Students nearby in the hallway took it not only as a discourtesy, but perhaps even a sign of supremacy, which they were not about to tolerate. When the man emerged, they booed and warned him that if he didn't take off his hat, they would. Red faced, he obliged. This was the spirit of the student body, defiant and determined.

An English major, I worked my way through college handling publicity for Virginia Union's football and basketball teams. The experience helped me get similar work back in Youngstown during the summer, where I was well paid—at least $100 a game—for promoting the baseball games of the Homestead Grays. Team owner Cumberland ("Cum") Posey and manager/player Vic Harris took an interest in me, probably because my enthusiasm made up for my initial lack of knowledge of the sport. Cum, who began as a player and wound up owner of the team, was its locomotive, driving the Grays to eight of nine Negro National League pennants between 1937 and 1945, including three world titles. I like to think his giving me a break had something to do with his recognized ability to pick and develop talent, a skill usually mentioned in connection with the more than ten Negro League Hall of Famers who played on his squads. Harris, a great player sometimes known for an equally explosive temper, was never anything but kind to me.

My two promotion items were signs and free tickets. Anyone who would put a sign in their window or front yard announcing a game would get a free ticket. After the game, I'd write up the story and take it down to the *Vindicator*'s sports editor, Frank "Doc" Ward. Doc reigned over that desk for almost four decades, from 1911 to 1950, earning a national reputation. He was generous both with space and professional advice, often as basic as "make sure you get all the facts." Sometimes I'd also do an advance piece. I was probably the youngest promoter in the country, and by the time I moved on, I knew how to write a pretty good baseball story.

I didn't save any of my sports stories, but my wife recently found a few on the Internet. One from the *Chicago Defender* (national edition) describes the "thrilling" action on the basketball court in varsity and jayvee contests between the "fighting Virginia Union Panthers" and the "scrappy Hampton Institute Pirates," during which the Panthers, "like a house afire," apparently whipped some butt so bad it's a wonder no one in the stands had a heart attack. Another article retrieved from the May 10, 1941, *New York Amsterdam Star-News* promotes an upcoming baseball game:

Homestead Grays Battle
Baltimore at Richmond
By Simeon Booker, Jr.

The article recaps performance to date of the "hammering Homestead Grays," 1940 National Negro League champs, and the "crack, hard-hitting Baltimore Elite Giants" at Mayo Island in Richmond, with so much sizzle only a fool wouldn't want to be there. Those were the days.

When I finished Virginia Union in 1942, I was so eager to start my job at the Baltimore *Afro-American* that I didn't even wait for graduation. I was about to earn $18 a week—and go in the hole for $20 after every payday. I had found a place to sleep in the Baltimore Y that my father used to manage, and I sometimes borrowed money from my parents to keep going. (I was so grateful for their support, I privately vowed to pay off the mortgage on their home on Myrtle Avenue when I had "made it," and eventually I did, just a few years before the 1956 automobile accident that ended my mother's life and badly injured my father.)

The *Afro-American's* publisher was my hero. No black publisher was a greater believer in providing his readers firsthand reports from throughout the country and the world. Carl Murphy encouraged "frontline" reporting as well as crusading journalism, and I carried both preferences with me for the rest of my career. The youngest reporter in the newsroom, I was called "Skeezix" by the staff, after the *Gasoline Alley* comic strip character readers watched grow up in real time. I was also the only male reporter on the city side, and therefore the only one permitted to witness executions at the Maryland penitentiary, where I covered nine or ten hangings. After a couple of years of this, I'd had enough of crime and seen more than enough bodies swinging from scaffolds. I was also thoroughly broke.

I worked briefly in an ordnance plant in Baltimore, and then in the fall of 1944, I landed a job with Cleveland's black weekly, the *Call and Post*. The Ohio paper was published by William O. Walker, an ardent Republican, who was more interested in marketing and promotion than in the news content of his paper. He gave his editors and reporters a relatively free rein, except during campaign season, when we were given stories trumpeting Republicans running for office. We were almost a Republican propaganda sheet. Still, my journalistic career flourished at the *Call and Post*. After only a few months, I took over the duties of city editor from Charles H. Loeb, while he served for a year as a war correspondent for the National Newspaper Publishers Association in the Pacific Theatre, covering the surrender of Japan aboard the USS *Missouri*. (I would later seek the pool reporter assignment myself at the outbreak of the Korean War.) I was also the first black reporter at the *Call and Post* to win a Page One Award, sponsored by the Cleveland Newspaper Guild, for a series on exploitation of slum housing. In a letter supporting my first application for a Nieman Fellowship in 1948, Loeb credited the series with exposing "numerous housing profiteers," resulting in "tenants winning back thousands of dollars in refunds," as well as "improvement of many substandard and unsanitary conditions." I also won the Willkie Award, sponsored by Agnes Meyer, Katherine Graham's mother, for a series on the racial inequality of Cleveland's public schools. The judges were all Harvard Nieman Fellows: Alan Barth, editorial writer for *The Washington Post*; Grady E. Clay, Jr., *Louisville Courier-Journal* reporter; David B. Dreiman, science writer for the *Minneapolis Star*; and E. L. Holland, Jr., editorial writer for the *Birmingham News*. They served under the chairmanship of Louis M. Lyons, curator of the Nieman Fellowships.

Although I racked up awards, some of which were "firsts" for the *Call and Post*, ironically, Walker was also the only employer who ever fired me—for trying to organize a Newspaper Guild chapter at the paper. While appealing my dismissal to the National Labor Relations Board (NLRB), I managed to stay afloat pumping gas at a filling station operated by a friend, Herman Burrell, an enterprise we both abandoned to travel cross-country in the summer of 1947. Herman, a sociologist, and his wife, Eleanor, had decided to relocate to Hawaii, which even in the late '40s enjoyed a much more harmonious, multiracial society than most of the mainland.

My own purpose for the trip was an "affair of the heart." I was living in a multiracial co-op house at Western Reserve University, and had fallen in love with another co-op member, a pretty Japanese-American woman named Ruby, who had recently returned to her parents' home in Hawaii, where I intended to ask her father for her hand in marriage. I paid my travel expenses by freelancing articles for *Ebony*, the full-size, black-oriented magazine founded by John H. Johnson in 1946. My topics included an African-American cowboy living in Wyoming and black Mormons in Utah. My final article was a feature on Schofield Barracks at Pearl Harbor, the first U.S. military base to integrate during World War II. After a couple of weeks, I flew home, dejected by a note from Ruby implying that her wealthy father had no interest in her marrying a poor Negro reporter, and might kill me if I came anywhere near his home. I never even saw her while I was on the island. Sixty years later, my closest friend from the co-op, Janet Nakashima, also a Hawaiian, laughed when she heard that story. "Booker," she chuckled, "it wasn't her father. Ruby was as fickle as she was pretty." My male ego still clung to my version.

Back in Cleveland, I embarked upon a project that would almost kill me. I moved into dilapidated slum housing to gather material for a book about the lives of the city's poorest. The flat I was in was so run down, I could see the family living downstairs through cracks in the floorboards. Conditions were so bad that I caught pneumonia and wound up in the hospital. I never finished that book.

Fortunately, the National Labor Relations Board ruled in my favor on my firing, and I returned to the *Call and Post* with an award of two weeks back pay. By now, I was more determined than ever to pursue an opportunity I had dreamed about for years—the Harvard Nieman Fellowship in Journalism. Established in 1938, pursuant to the bequest of Agnes Wahl Nieman, widow of Lucius Nieman, founder of the *Milwaukee Journal*, the Nieman administers the oldest mid-career sabbatical program for journalists from all over the world for a year of study and exploration at Harvard. Since its inception, the mission of the foundation has been "to promote and elevate the standards of journalism and educate persons specially qualified for journalism."

Approaching thirty-one, I also got married. Thelma Cunningham was a pharmacist. My father performed the nuptials on June 12, 1949, at Youngstown's Third Baptist Church. Unfortunately, ours was a mismatch from the beginning, with our differences becoming more pronounced under the stresses and tensions of the next two decades. After a long separation, we divorced in 1973.

A SECOND CHANCE

My applications for the Nieman Fellowship were unsuccessful in 1948 and '49, but on Wednesday, June 14, 1950, my fingers couldn't work fast enough to open a telegram from Nieman curator Louis M. Lyons. It stated simply: "CAN YOU SEE NIEMAN COMMITTEE SUNDAY PALMER HOUSE CHICAGO 930 DAYLIGHT OUR EXPENSE." I could barely think of anything else for the rest of that week. Since I had little money, I took a Greyhound bus from Cleveland around midnight on Saturday, wearing my "Sunday best." Arriving in early morning, I sat in the deserted hotel lobby, too nervous to eat anything, and repeatedly checking my hands to make sure my palms weren't sweating. Shortly after 9:00 a.m., I went upstairs to the interview. When it was over, the panel told me to submit a bill for my expenses. I told them the total was $8.00. I later learned that other candidates had flown to Chicago and stayed at the Palmer House overnight. The candidate who was interviewed before me had run up a bill of $100. I still wonder if that had something to do with my getting the fellowship! Five days after my interview, I received another telegram with the panel's decision: "FELLOWSHIP AWARDED. CONFIDENTIAL UNTIL ANNOUNCED. LYONS."

For a few weeks, I was walking on air. I was going to Harvard, not just as a student, but as a Nieman Fellow, one of journalism's chosen few. It was hard to believe, but the news clips and congratulatory cards and letters kept coming in, as friends and family forwarded reports of my selection from dailies and weeklies around the country. Then, suddenly, I was faced with what could be the most important decision of my career. As fate sometimes has it, another opportunity I had long dreamed of also materialized in mid-summer. *AFRO* newspaper chain president Carl Murphy had selected me to replace Albert Hinton as a pool representative for the combined Negro press in the Far East Command. On July 27, Hinton was killed when the C-47 transport plane carrying him and other correspondents crashed into the sea off the coast of Japan. He was the first black war reporter to lose his life in a theater of operations. The letter from the army approving my selection was dated the next day. The United States had been at war with North Korea for a month, and the letter directed me to complete and return the enclosed forms so that my clearance could be expedited. Just nine days earlier, Murphy had sent me a letter congratulating me on the Nieman Fellowship.

Whatever I was going to do, I had to decide fast. Would it be Cambridge or Korea? With Carl Murphy's encouragement, I decided to pass up the Korean opportunity and accept the Nieman Fellowship, which I'd craved for so long. I also suspected that this would not be my last chance to cover Americans at war. The Korean conflict was following closely behind World War II, in which I had not been able to serve after being classified 4-F due to poor eyesight. It was likely our troops would be fighting again somewhere in the world, and I would have another opportunity to follow them and report on how well the armed forces were dealing with integration. I telegraphed Louis Lyons with my decision, and he wrote back saying he was glad that I valued the fellowship enough to pass up a chance at Korea. But he also suggested that, if it wasn't too late, I could postpone my Nieman fellowship for a year, and thus "have your cake and eat it, too." "A fellowship," he counseled, "has its value only to assist in a journalistic career. It is not a substitute for one." But I had made up my mind, and have never regretted my decision. From the start, Louis Lyons not only gave me good advice, but lived up to his reputation as a "godfather" in the profession. Upon learning, for example, that I was the lowest paid member of the class, he doubled my cash allowance.

I was the second black accepted into the Nieman program. The first was my good friend Fletcher Martin, a reporter with the *Louisville Defender*, a Kentucky weekly, who went on to the *Chicago Sun-Times*, and later the U.S. Information Agency. Fletcher offered to help us find a place to stay in Cambridge, which we quickly did, in the comfortable home of a gracious black woman, Mrs. Leah Gilmore, at 69 Dana Street, within walking distance of Harvard Yard.

The Nieman year was a life-changing experience for me. Nieman Fellows choose a field of study for a year, and I chose government, state, and national, focusing particularly on why some cities succeed while others constantly seemed besieged by turmoil. (My real interest was race relations, but in those days such studies were considered exotic.) Harvard had some of the very best instructors in the field of government in America. Among them was Arthur Schlesinger, Sr., who took a personal interest in me, and was generous with both his time and advice.

The program included a smorgasbord of lectures on a broad array of subjects, as well as luncheons and cocktail parties where the Fellows were exposed to top national movers and shakers. One of Louis Lyons's innovations after becoming the program's second curator (the first was Archibald MacLeish) in the 1940s was a weekly seminar on Tuesday afternoons, at which various professors would discuss developments in their fields of study, while the Fellows asked questions in press conference style. Under Lyons, the program also began publication of the *Nieman Reports*, a quarterly magazine with contributions from all over the country on the state of journalism in America. It was a heady experience—even more so than I had dreamed during the football trips with my uncle as a youth. Moreover, relationships formed with other Nieman scholars were invaluable and served me well in the years ahead.

The newspapers of ten states were represented in the Class of 1950–51, which included a city editor (Malcolm Bauer, 36, *Portland Oregonian*), telegraph editor (Bob Eddy, 33, *St. Paul Pioneer Press*), state capital correspondent (Emery Hugh Morris, 35, Louisville *Courier-Journal*), two editorial writers (Sylvan H. Meyer, 28, *Gainesville* [Georgia] *Times* and Wellington Wales, 32, Auburn [NY] *Citizen-Advertiser*), a small daily editor (Dwight Sargeant, *Portland Press Herald*), Associated Press news editor (Angus MacLean Thuermer, 33, Chicago bureau), foreign correspondent (Dana Adams Schmidt, 34, *New York Times*), city hall reporter (Roy M. Fisher, 31, *Chicago Daily News*), and two other general reporters besides myself. One was Edwin Guthman, 30, a Pulitzer Prize winner on the *Seattle Times*, who later became press secretary to Attorney General, and then Senator, Robert F. Kennedy. The second was Hoke Norris, 36, of the *Winston-Salem Journal*. Among the dozens of congratulatory letters I received was one from A. A. Morisey, a colleague of his on the North Carolina daily, who accurately predicted that I would be glad to meet Norris at Harvard. Morisey had joined the Winston-Salem *Journal* and Twin City *Sentinel* the previous December (1949), becoming the first Negro reporter to work in the newsroom of a Southern daily. He wrote that it was "a wonderful experience," and that he had "made front page several times." His given names were Alfred Alexander, but he always used A. A. professionally to avoid being addressed by his first name, as Southerners usually did to Negroes at the time, no matter what the black person's age, gender, or station. After six years in the Twin Cities, A. A. returned to public relations, first in Philadelphia, then at Howard University in Washington, D.C., and ultimately New York, where he was public relations manager for the *Times*. His letter meant a lot to me, and was one of many from black colleagues who saw my achievement as not just a personal victory, but a source of pride and hope for other members of the black press.

By far the best experience of my professional life, the Nieman year taught me what real power was, how to use it, and how to expose its abuses. It also instilled in me a determination to do something meaningful to help my race after I completed the program. Under the Nieman rules, a Fellow is supposed to return to the organization from which he came. For me, there was no question of going back. At the *Call and Post*, there would be no opportunity to utilize all I had learned and experienced at Harvard. I decided to ignore the rules and apply at a white-owned, daily newspaper. I typed out forty letters seeking employment and sent them to forty publishers. The only answer that came back to me was from Philip Graham, publisher of *The Washington Post*. Graham, a Harvard Law School graduate, wrote that he didn't have an opening at the moment, but if I would move to Washington and take a job, any job, he would offer me the first reporter's slot that opened up on his newspaper.

I got a job shelving books at a federal government library, and about three or four months later, true to his word, Graham offered me a slot on the paper.

THE WASHINGTON POST

Washington in 1951 was still a very Southern and very segregated city. I couldn't eat lunch downtown, even in some federal agency cafeterias, including, ironically, the Interstate Commerce Commission, where I might be covering a story related to segregation. White taxi drivers usually didn't stop for me, and even the police treated me more like a suspect than a reporter when I covered a crime scene or a fire. I lived briefly with my aunt, Dorothy Waring Howard, until I found an apartment where Thelma and our children could join me. Blue-eyed and fair skinned, Aunt Dorrie could pass for white when she chose to do so, but that was only when it was more convenient, as on the sultry night in August of 1918 when she rode the train from Washington, D.C., to Baltimore to help her sister with her newborn son, and give me my first bath. After the death of her husband, Dr. William J. Howard, in 1945, she had continued the nationally recognized nursery school she started in 1929 in her townhouse at 1728 S Street NW. The school, which she named The Garden of Children, grew out of her interest in early education, as well as her need for suitable day care for their own young daughter, Carolyn. Over the years, the school's alumni included many of Washington's top black achievers in every profession, and Aunt Dorrie continued to run it until her retirement in 1961. For me, in the early 1950s, Aunt Dorrie's home was a haven from the daily grind of dealing with Washington's segregation.

Black nightlife centered around the U Street corridor with its colored movie theaters and clubs. It was very different from Cleveland, even in the mid-'40s, where I had lived in Roosevelt Co-Op House near Western Reserve University. The multiracial, multicultural cooperative was home to twenty-three young men and women, including two Negroes, five Japanese, one Chinese, and fifteen whites—seven Gentiles and eight Jews—from all over the country, and as far as Hawaii. No such integration was going on in Washington, D.C., in 1951. In fact, during the last years of the Truman administration and the early part of Eisenhower's, several prominent Negroes would turn down high government jobs rather than move their families from Northern communities to the stifling segregation of Washington, D.C.

Phil Graham knew that I would need moral support in those early days and told me, "Don't hit anybody. If you get mad, just come up to my office and sit down and cool off." It was clear from the beginning that most of the *Post*'s staff wasn't ready for me. It was all new to them, having a black reporter in the newsroom. It was even suggested—in fact, recommended—that I use only the bathroom on the fourth (editorial) floor. But at least I could eat in the cafeteria, and I was thankful for that, since I didn't always have time to walk to Aunt Dorrie's house for lunch.

The stories I covered spanned the gamut of urban and federal news. One of the first, on November 21, 1951, ran under the headline, "Senate Group Issues Negro Status Report." A Senate labor subcommittee had found that "in almost every significant economic and social characteristic that can be measured" including life expectancy, employment, education, and income, Negroes were on the bottom of the pile. No more than a summary of the study, it was the kind of story I would have liked to pursue, to dig deeper, to explain how the system worked, how institutions affected people's lives, and how government variously helped or failed the most needy. Although I suggested investigative pieces about race relations and other urban topics during my two years on the paper's staff, most were shunted aside. Some of my assignments were interesting, but others, such as a short, August 14, 1952, front-page piece on the year's first sighting of ragweed pollen in the capital, left me feeling my training—my experience in Cleveland, as well as my year as a Nieman—was being wasted. Moreover, I felt the chances of ever moving up in the paper's hierarchy were nil given the racial climate (not only in the newsroom, but in the city), and the types of assignments I was given, although they included many front-page stories.

Some thirty years later, after reading an account of what I went through at the *Post*, Ben Gilbert, a longtime, senior editor at the paper, sent me a very kind letter, recalling that there were a number of staffers at the time who were "out of step with the times and the paper's policies." Had he known about it, he wrote, it would not have been tolerated. Gilbert drew upon his three decades at the *Post* (1941 to 1970) for an essay, "Toward a Color-Blind Newspaper; Race Relations and *The Washington Post*," in which he included my experiences as the paper's first black reporter, noting that hostility had replaced the support usually volunteered to newcomers. Outside the newsroom, there'd been even worse incidents, such as when the capital's overtly racist police chief physically threatened me.

Gilbert recounted that the city editor had assigned another reporter, sympathetic Murray Marder, to act as a "buddy" to guide me through what was for me an extremely cold work environment. Marder thought that a black reporter needed to have an awfully thick hide to survive, and he concluded that I did not. He later described me as "an extremely shy, gentle fellow, propelled into the doubly hostile Washington police reporting atmosphere." I'll admit to being "gentle" if by that he meant that I never did hit anybody. I never had to "cool off" in Phil Graham's office either. But as for being "extremely shy," I don't know how I would ever have gotten to the *Post* if that were true.

John Russell Wiggins, the paper's managing editor in the early 1950s, also sent me a very touching letter in the mid-1980s in which he observed that it was inconceivable that racial antipathies could have been as serious as they were back then. He said he'd never forget the flap the first time the paper put the engagement of a Negro couple on the society page. Shortly after that, there was a big stir over publication of a photo panel of Korean

War casualties, some of whom were black and some white. He recalled that the feeling was so high in Washington when the paper did such things that management arranged to have the telephone complaints answered at his desk. While dismayed by the complaints, he found it encouraging that after a few minutes discussion, the caller usually agreed that the paper had done the right thing. The world in 1984 was, in many respects, a better place, and he said he was glad he and I could make a small contribution to this change for the better. I'd say amen to that.

I did my best to tough it out at the *Post*, although it was quite a comedown from the equality and cordial collegiality I had experienced in Cambridge as a Nieman Fellow, and I got to know only a few of the paper's reporters. I struggled so hard to succeed that friends thought I was dying; I looked so fatigued. Trying to cover news in a city where even pet cemeteries were segregated was overwhelming. I set a goal and decided to leave the *Post* if I ever got a banner headline. After two years at the paper, that day came. I don't even recall what the story was.

Looking back, I give Phil Graham credit. He hired me. The newspaper may or may not have been ready. They had no standards or policies regarding the integration of their ranks, such as the military had developed. If it was a social experiment, I think I passed the test—although it damn near killed me.

MOVING ON

Driving a used car I bought for $150, I headed to Chicago. Thelma would join me later, after I'd found a place for us. (We now had two children, Theresa and Simeon, and Jimmy would be born in March 1954.) I was leaving Washington with very mixed emotions. On one hand, I felt I'd be regarded as a loser, someone who failed the chance, who couldn't make it as a daily journalist on a white paper. But I was also excited as hell to be joining the magazines started by publisher John H. Johnson—*Ebony* in 1946 and *Jet* in 1951, which were gaining in popularity like nothing else in the black community.

Eye-catching and glossy, *Ebony* was wildly successful in black households, quickly drawing comparisons to Henry Luce's *Life* magazine. It reflected in full, vibrant color the good life everyone aspired to and a few blacks had attained. The covers featured movie stars such as Harry Belafonte, Sidney Poitier, Lena Horne, and Josephine Baker. Inside, as John H. Johnson later described it, the magazine was 80 percent orange juice and 20 percent castor oil, the latter being the less glamorous accounts of the Negro's struggle against segregation, discrimination, and poverty. A savvy entrepreneur, Johnson also founded other magazines over the years including *Negro Digest*, *Black Stars*, and *Ebony Jr.*, but none of these was as popular or as long-lived as *Jet*, a pocket-size compendium of news, photographs, and both serious and entertaining features.

Every *Jet* issue, with few exceptions, had an African-American beauty on the cover, while inside there were substantive stories, as well as outrageously funny accounts of both black and white foibles. It was not uncommon for kids to pocket $5 a week peddling the magazines to barber shops, beauty parlors, shoeshine stands, and other black-owned businesses before going to school in the morning when shift workers were heading home. They earned five cents a copy for each fifteen-cent *Jet*, and ten cents a copy for each thirty-cent *Ebony* they sold to businesses or their patrons. As one such entrepreneur (now a senior citizen) told me recently, selling the magazines was considered a very lucrative enterprise.

I was also glad that John H. Johnson had no particular political persuasion or journalistic bias, unlike my earlier publisher at the *Call and Post*. "Mr. J.," as longtime staff called him, was aware of me from my days as a freelancer for *Ebony*, and with the Nieman Fellowship and my stint at *The Washington Post* now on my resume, he was happy to add me to the editorial staff, which he had decided would consist of those he considered the best and the brightest Negro journalists.

My name was added to the masthead of the August 6, 1953, issue of *Jet*, and I immediately began writing articles on the issues I longed to cover, the serious issues affecting black people. The spectrum spanned race relations in all major news categories from politics to employment, the military, federal government, foreign affairs, and so on, but not sports or entertainment, in which I had no interest. The magazine still covered its customary fun and froth, and there's no denying that the readers loved it. But Mr. J. agreed that it was time to increase the ratio of "castor oil" by including more of the serious news and features that a loyal readership would not find in any other nationally circulated publication, certainly not any white-owned ones.

I worked out of the Chicago headquarters until 1956, when Mr. J. sent me to Washington to open the first JPC news bureau in the nation's capital. Shortly before leaving the Windy City, I joined in the formation of a predominantly black press club, much like the Capitol Press Club in Washington, D.C., founded in 1944. Led by *Jet*'s managing editor, Vincent Tubbs, we put a lot of effort into it, and succeeded where earlier attempts had failed. Mayor Richard J. Daley swore in the officers of the new Windy City Press Club at a fancy Loop restaurant, and the club received a huge boost from a lavish cocktail party and dinner hosted by rising calypso star Harry Belafonte, at which he was made an honorary member. While the club was mainly Negro, it did not discriminate on the basis of race (as neither did Chicago's other press clubs at the time), and it had white members as well. The rationale behind establishing the club, however, was the belief that there were some serious problems and situations peculiar to the press on Chicago's South Side that could be better addressed by such an organization. The group quickly established an impressive program, including a scholarship fund to aid a deserving high school graduate interested in pursuing a journalism career, an awards dinner to honor an outstanding citizen, and nominations for an annual "newsman's newsman" award. The club also hosted off-the-record briefings on sensitive subjects of the day, such as civil rights campaigns.

As chairman of the program committee, I introduced Mississippi civil rights leader Dr. T. R. M. Howard at one of the club's first events, to talk about that state's White Citizens' Councils' growing campaign against desegregation. Over the next decade, I would report frequently on Dr. Howard's civil rights activities in Ticker Tape USA, a weekly *Jet* column that carried my byline for the rest of my fifty-plus years with the magazine. Making its debut in April of 1955, just weeks before my first assignment in the Deep South, the column was a compendium of newsy tidbits with national relevance, and even an occasional tip about a job opportunity. It was also a vehicle for focusing immediate, national attention on significant events ignored by the white press, as well as the efforts and accomplishments of blacks at the local, state, and federal level, including the black members of Congress, whose ranks had just grown to three with the election of thirty-one-year-old Detroit Congressman Charles Diggs. The next month, the freshman congressman and I crossed paths at the rally organized by Dr. Howard near his home in the Mississippi Delta where 13,000 black men and women launched the last long push to freedom that came to be known as "the civil rights movement." It was, for me, the assignment of a lifetime.

5

"LET THEM SEE
WHAT I'VE SEEN"

On Saturday afternoon, August 17, 1955, three months after the assassination of the Reverend George Lee in Belzoni, Mississippi, I received a call from a source in the Delta informing me that another civil rights activist in the state had been murdered. Like Rev. Lee, Lamar Smith, a sixty-year-old farmer and World War I vet, was an organizer of black voter registration. Moreover, he had actually voted, along with his wife and other family members, in a primary election eleven days earlier. A close friend of Dr. T. R. M. Howard, he also had been present at the massive Mound Bayou rally organized by Howard's Leadership Council and the NAACP in April.

Smith was killed in mid-morning right outside the Lincoln County courthouse in Brookhaven, in the southwest corner of Mississippi. Brookhaven's most famous son at the time was a rabidly racist judge named Tom Brady, best known as the author of *Black Monday*, a no-holds-barred attack on the Supreme Court's *Brown* decision that pulled out all the sexual bugaboos about golden-haired Southern belles being forced to sit next to not only subhuman creatures, but forms of life at the bottom of the food chain with cockroaches. The tract was very popular in his hometown and elsewhere, and was even given to schoolchildren.

The courthouse was busy as usual at ten o'clock on a Saturday morning, when a number of people saw Smith arguing with three white men before he was felled by a single shot fired at close range from a .38-caliber pistol. The bullet entered his chest under his right arm, sending an explosion of blood from the wound as he collapsed. The sheriff, who also happened to be at the building at the time, reported seeing a white man covered with blood leaving the scene. The sheriff also later claimed that no witnesses could be found.

When NAACP Mississippi representative Medgar Evers investigated the murder, he learned that the Negro farmer had received threats several weeks earlier warning him to quit local politics or "be killed two days prior to the August 2 primary or two days afterwards." A few hours after receiving word that Smith had been killed, State NAACP President Dr. A. H. McCoy received an anonymous phone call at his home in Jackson, warning, "We got that nigger at Brookhaven and you're next."

Despite a lack of cooperation from local officials, a courageous district attorney ultimately charged a white farmer, Noah Smith, with the murder. Then two more white men were identified and arrested. Surprisingly or not, depending on your viewpoint, in the end no one was indicted by the grand jury when it met the following month.

As usual, Smith's murder was not mentioned in the Northern daily press. I debated making a third trip to Mississippi, and decided against it. However, I made up my mind that if there was another white-on-black murder down there, I'd personally see to it that it was well publicized.

As it turned out, I had only two weeks to wait. The victim this time wasn't a civil rights activist. He was a fourteen-year-old Chicago boy, Emmett Till, who was visiting relatives in Mississippi. His alleged offense was disrespecting a white woman. In the Mississippi Delta of the 1950s (and more than a decade later), that would have been considered by some a capital crime, punishable by unspeakable acts, up to and including death. Even considering the boy's young age, his kidnapping and murder, as heinous as any, might have gotten little coverage in the nation's mainstream press, were it not for two horrifically contrasting photographs, and the eruption of visceral, agonized emotions when *Jet* published them. One was a portrait I borrowed from his mother when her son went missing. It showed a boyish face still so young it was more that of a beautiful child than a handsome young man, with clear, creamy skin and light hazel eyes sparkling with the confidence of a kid who knows he's his mama's heart and soul. The second photo was of his unrecognizable, mutilated corpse, lying in a casket, exposed to the flash of the camera, as his mama insisted, so all the world could see what they'd done to her boy. Some people said it looked like a nonhuman alien.

The horrifying photograph of the murdered boy was never forgotten by the hundreds of thousands of blacks who saw it, passing around the pocket-size magazine in the barbershops, the beauty parlors, the projects, sharing their shock, as well as their anger. In the early 1960s, some of the up-and-coming generation would cite that picture as having made them want to grow up faster so they could demonstrate with other students, sit-in at lunch counters, and do whatever else it was going to take to tear down the system that not only made white men believe they could get away with such crimes, but actually let it happen.

I was one of the first reporters on the story. Some of the details I learned from the boy's family, especially the mother whose bold decision assured that out of her son's death would come the strongest impetus for the civil rights movement to date.[1]

MAMIE'S LITTLE "BO"

Emmett Till was born at Chicago's Cook County Hospital to Mamie and Louis Till on July 2, 1941. He was their first, and as it turned out, their only child, for the marriage that had started out as hopeful, if not promising, soon deteriorated as Louis became not only difficult but abusive. Mamie went to court for a protective order, but even then, he was incorrigible and kept violating it. Judges don't like their orders disobeyed, but this judge gave Louis a break. He allowed him to enlist in the army instead of going to jail.

Several months later, looking sharper than ever in his uniform and claiming he'd mended his ways, Louis showed up again, asking Mamie to take him back. She was tempted, but before she'd made up her mind, military police were at the door. Louis hadn't changed at all. He was AWOL. They took him and locked him up until shipping him out to the European front. Over the next two years Louis sent Mamie money from his gambling winnings, supplementing her regular military spousal allotment. His middle name might have been "Trouble," but at least he was helping to support their son. In 1945, when Emmett was just four years old, the money suddenly stopped coming. Then Mamie received an official telegram from the government. Louis was dead, killed in Italy, the result of "willful misconduct." That was it. No details. The military said she did not qualify for survivor's benefits, but wouldn't explain why not. Ten years later she would learn why in a most public way.

During the summer that he turned three, little "Bobo" or "Bo," as Emmett's family called him, contracted polio. The disease was a real menace in those days, especially in summertime, causing parents to keep their children out of swimming pools and away from beaches where they thought it might spread. No one knew how or exactly when it had stricken Emmett, but he was much luckier than the thousands of kids who wound up in wheelchairs, unable to walk. Emmett was not left paralyzed or brain damaged. His only lasting vestige of the illness was a pronounced stutter. After years of practice, he all but overcame it, except when he was nervous. Mamie came up with a trick for dealing with that. She taught him to stop and blow out through pursed lips, in effect whistling. When Emmett did it, the sound was like a wolf-whistle, and it helped him get out the word he was trying to say.

When I first met Mamie in 1955, she still used the name Mamie Till Bradley (sometimes hyphenated), although her marriage in 1951 to another poor choice named Pink Bradley had ended in divorce after just two years. She was working for the U.S. Air Force, and had a new man in her life, a calm, affable, and very hardworking fellow named Gene Mobley, who held two jobs—one at the Ford Motor Company plant and the second cutting hair as a barber.

Gene Mobley hit it off with Emmett even before he won over Mamie. Emmett was an industrious kid and enjoyed running errands for Gene. Gene, in turn, enjoyed making sure Emmett always had spending money. Standing about five feet three inches and weighing in at a chubby 160 pounds, Emmett seemed big for his age, and liked to think of himself as the man of the house, helping his mama keep the place up, and even cooking dinner when she worked late. He could be mischievous at times, but he was also good-natured, and enjoyed making people laugh, especially his mother.

Mamie and Gene were planning to take Emmett on a month-long road trip to Detroit and then on to Omaha in late August, but those plans were shelved after Mamie's uncle, Moses Wright, came up to Chicago from tiny Money, Mississippi, to attend the funeral of a relative. Uncle Mose, as he was called, had been a minister at one time, until giving it up in 1949, but the sharecropper was often still called "Preacher" or "Reverend." Uncle Mose obviously preferred country life over living in Chicago, and shared with Emmett the kind of stories—many of them fish stories—that made a city kid want to pack up and go back to Mississippi with him. Emmett was hooked like a small perch snapping on a worm, especially when he learned that his cousin, Wheeler Parker, Jr., who was like an older brother to him, was going to spend the rest of his summer vacation with Uncle Mose and their other cousins in the Delta. Emmett just couldn't see how anything in Detroit, much less Omaha, could compete with that.

He begged his mother to let him go with his great uncle. Mamie wouldn't have denied Emmett anything she thought was good for him, but this trip was not on that list. Everything about it made her inclined to say no. She had been born right there in Tallahatchie County, Mississippi, and although she had moved North when she was only two, she had been back, and had heard her share of horror stories about how black people suffered under the heel of the white power structure in the Delta. She also read the black press, which never failed to report on the horrible things going on in the South, including the lynchings, said to number more than 500 and still counting in Mississippi alone since 1882.

Ultimately, Mamie gave in. Uncle Mose assured her that he would personally look out for Emmett and keep him safe. But before her son left for Mississippi, Mamie still tried to make him understand that he had to act differently in the South. She later recalled that she had drilled Emmett on the "code of behavior" for Negro survival in the Delta. Speak only when spoken to. Always put a "handle" on your answer: not just "Yes," but "Yes, sir," or "Yes, ma'am." And as humiliating as it might seem, get off the sidewalk and step into the street if necessary when a white person is approaching. Lower your head; avoid eye contact. If it's a woman, never turn around and look at her after she passes. Mamie recited from the same unwritten rulebook I had to memorize a few months earlier when I made my own "maiden voyage" into the Delta. I can imagine how this strange code must have seemed to a fourteen-year-old Chicago kid. Emmett couldn't believe it, but his mother insisted that was the way it was in Mississippi. Later, she would recall that she had been especially specific about the "white woman" issue. She had told Bobo he shouldn't be caught even glancing at a picture of a white woman, let alone looking one in the face.

Mamie hated to tell her son all this stuff, and she did it only to protect him. Whether he understood that or not, he assured her he did, and would know how to act.

A few days before the City of New Orleans pulled away from Chicago's 63rd Street Station with Emmett and his uncle aboard, the boy put his late father's silver ring on the middle finger of his right hand, after wrapping tape around the back so it wouldn't slip off. On the face of the ring the letters "L. T." and the date "May 25, 1943" were engraved. It was one of the few personal effects the army had forwarded to Mamie after notifying her of Louis Till's death. The ring would later become a major piece of evidence.

Gene Mobley did his part to give the boy a good send-off, making sure his hair was neatly cut, and slipping him some pocket money, even more than usual. He also added his own admonition to Mamie's about that code of conduct for Negroes in the South, which Gene, also a native Mississippian, knew all about.

For the first three days after Emmett arrived in Mississippi on August 21, 1955, things went pretty much as Uncle Mose had expected. Emmett joined his great uncle and his cousins in the cotton fields, where they taught the city kid the arduous routine of picking and bagging cotton. As big as he was, the work was too hard for someone not used to it. Although it may have seemed like Emmett wasn't trying hard enough to keep up with his cousins, Uncle Mose cut him more slack than he'd ever allow them, since this was Emmett's "vacation" and he had promised the boy a good time. At least Emmett had tried, and he was a good kid, a nice kid to have around.

THE INCIDENT

On August 24, 1955, a fun summer evening turned really bad. With Mose's son Maurice behind the wheel, Emmett and four other boys, including his cousins Wheeler Parker and Simeon Wright, loaded into Mose's battered 1946 Ford and drove three miles into Money, an unincorporated village in Leflore County with one street at the center of a population of one or two hundred, depending on whom you asked. They were headed to Bryant's Grocery and Meat Market, a two-story country store with a porch and the usual Coca-Cola sign out front. It sold things poor black sharecroppers needed for everyday living, as well as the things their kids liked to have, such as candy and bubblegum.

Although they were white, the Bryants, Roy, 24, and Carolyn, a pretty, twenty-year-old brunette, were almost as poor as their clientele. Even by Mississippi standards, the couple and their two young boys were pretty bad off, lacking even an automobile. While Carolyn ran the store, Roy and his half brother, J. W. Milam, carted shrimp by truck from the Gulf Coast to Texas.

Seventeen-year-old Wheeler Parker told me that he, Emmett, and the others were watching some boys play checkers in front of the store when somebody mentioned that there was a "pretty lady" inside. Bobo said he was going in to buy some bubble gum. According to Simeon Wright, his cousin was alone in the store with Carolyn Bryant no more than a minute before Simeon joined him, and a few minutes later he and Bobo left together. After that, Carolyn left the store, and that was when Bobo whistled at her.[2] Over time there would be a number of embellishments on the incident, some contradictory, and one, Carolyn Bryant's, outrageously self-serving. Bryant's version was so inflammatory, the judge wouldn't let the jury hear it. It's likely, however, that the whole town had heard it by then. She claimed Emmett had come on to her, while showing her a wallet picture of a white girl. Many of us, myself included, doubted the boy would have been so bold after the warnings his mother had drilled into him less than two weeks earlier. Mamie said she even doubted that Emmett's whistle had anything to do with Carolyn Bryant, but was the same whistle he used to control his stutter when he got stuck on a word. Simeon disagrees with that, recalling it as a loud wolf whistle, and says he thought Bobo was just trying to be funny.[3] One thing there is no disagreement about is that whatever happened, it did not justify what Roy Bryant and his half-brother later set out to do about it.

According to Wheeler, after the boys exited the store, someone hollered, "She's getting a gun!" The kids ran to the car and sped away as Carolyn Bryant supposedly went to get a pistol from her sister-in-law's car. Although one of the kids predicted that there'd be trouble when Roy Bryant got back to town, they never mentioned it to Uncle Mose, who probably would have sent Emmett back to Chicago.

The boys playing checkers had their own version of what happened and the incident became a subject of town gossip. Emmett reportedly was worried enough that he considered going back to Chicago, but as two and then three days passed without incident, he figured it had blown over.

Roy Bryant, 24, returned home at 5:00 a.m. on Friday, but didn't learn about the incident until some time later, from one of the black men who had been outside the store. (Some blacks called snitches like that "Judas niggers.") He asked Carolyn about it, and she filled in the details. As a Southern white male, particularly one with little education and less money, Bryant obviously felt he had to retaliate, or be shamed in the eyes of the entire rural community. More than just a question of Southern womanhood (which would have been serious enough), this was a challenge to his own manhood. He found his tough guy half-brother, J. W. Milam, more than willing to help him.

Nicknamed "Big," thirty-six-year-old John William (J. W.) Milam stood a strapping six feet two inches tall and weighed 235 pounds. He'd dropped out of school in the ninth grade with little to show for it except a big chip on his shoulder. Milam's size and tough talk, reinforced by his reputation from service in World War II, convinced people never to cross him. He'd come home from the war with decorations for bravery and a battlefield commission. It was said that he'd taken down a large number of Germans in hand-to-hand combat, and that his weapon of choice was a .45-caliber Colt semi-automatic pistol, useful not only in combat, but for pistol-whipping prisoners as well. There was something very ugly about J. W. Milam.

Roy Bryant had been just a kid while his half-brother fought in the war, but he served for three years as an army paratrooper when he was old enough.

Milam was enraged on Saturday night when Bryant told him what had happened. A white woman—his own sister-in-law—had been insulted by some nigger kid from Chicago. It had to be dealt with. He told Roy he'd pick him up in the truck the next morning. But it was too much to try to sleep on. After thinking about it, he decided this couldn't wait. He picked up his .45-caliber pistol and drove back to Bryant's house.

It's hard to imagine the fear and confusion in Moses Wright's unpainted cabin when Milam pounded on the door with his pistol around 2:30 Sunday morning. Calling the old man "Preacher," Roy announced, "This is Mr. Bryant." Then one of the men demanded that he give them "the boy from Chicago, who did the talking." Although his nephews hadn't told him the full story, Moses knew enough to suspect why they wanted Emmett. He pleaded that the kid was from up North and didn't know how to act around white people in the South. In fact, the boy had been to Mississippi only once before, and that was with his mother when he was nine years old. Whatever he had done, why not give him a good whipping right then and there and leave it at that?

The commotion had woken Aunt Lizzy, who, immediately figuring out what this was all about, wanted to waken Bobo and get him out of the house so he could hide somewhere. But the men (she thought there were three) were too quick and stormed into Emmett's back bedroom after searching other bedrooms. She begged them to leave Emmett alone, but one of them said if she didn't go back to bed he'd "beat the hell" out of her. Then they ordered Emmett to get dressed and follow them.

As the men dragged Emmett from the house, Milam threatened Moses, concluding with, "How old are you, preacher?"

"Sixty-four," he replied.

If Moses were to identify them, "Big" warned, "You'll never live to be sixty-five."

Uncle Mose later testified that two black men, who never said a word and never entered his house, had accompanied Bryant and Milam on the truck. He figured they were the ones who led the half-brothers to his house, and although their identity has been suspected, it's never been established. They held Emmett on the back of Milam's green Chevy pick-up truck as it drove away with the lights off.

Several hours later, Lizzy was inconsolable, telling Moses she would not stay in that house another night. She had long wanted to move her family to Chicago, but Moses had insisted on staying in Mississippi. He drove her to the home of her brother, Crosby Smith, in Sumner, and a few days later put her on a train to Chicago. She would never return to Money.

A MISSING BOY . . . AND A MURDER

According to Simeon Wright, his father then notified Leflore County Sheriff George W. Smith about what had happened. The sheriff was a friend of Bryant and Milam. He drove to Money about 2:00 p.m. and found Bryant sleeping in the back of his store. Bryant said he and Milam had taken the fourteen-year-old out of the "preacher's" cabin and brought him back to the store, where Bryant's wife said it wasn't the right boy, so they had released him unharmed. The sheriff didn't make notes, although Bryant had voluntarily admitted to committing a crime.

When Sheriff Smith obtained a similar story from J. W. Milam, and there was no sign of Emmett, both half-brothers were arrested and jailed without bond in Greenwood, Mississippi, charged with kidnapping.

When Mamie was told of her son's abduction, she wanted to go to Mississippi immediately to look for her boy, but family members persuaded her to stay put in Chicago.

JET

Vol. VIII   No. 18
September 8, 1955
A Johnson Publication

Business 23
Census 16
Crime 56
Education 19
Entertainment ...59
Foreign 14
Labor 26
Medicine 25
Modern Living ...38
Mr. and Mrs......17
National 3

People 58
Press Digest 50
Radio-TV Guide ..66
Religion 22
Society World 41
Sports 51
Ticker Tape 13
Weekly Almanac...27
Week's Best Photos 29
Words of the Week 24

NATIONAL REPORT

Chicago Boy, 14, Kidnaped By Miss. Whites

A 14-year-old Chicago junior high school student, Emmett (Bobo) Till, who was kidnaped by a trio of three gun-toting whites early Sunday morning while visiting relatives in Money, Miss., was feared a lynch victim because he "whistled at a white girl."

Leflore County authorities admitted that "we are afraid some harm has been done to the boy." Sheriff George Smith told JET that the boy's disappearance was being investigated and that one of the white men, Money grocer Roy Bryant, was being held in jail without bond for questioning.

Meanwhile, the sheriff ordered the family of 64-year-old Rev. Moses Wright, a retired Church of God in Christ minister and the boy's uncle, to "take his family from the town for their own safety." The minister, however, refused to leave his home after making arrangements to hide

Emmett Till

Published weekly by Johnson Publishing Co., Inc., at 1820 S. Michigan Avenue, Chicago 16, Illinois New York office at 55 West 42nd Street, Los Angeles office at 1127 Wilshire Blvd. Entered as second class matter at the Post Office at Chicago, Ill., under the Act of March 3, 1879. Entire contents copyright 1955, by Johnson Publishing Co., Inc. Subscriptions: $7 one year, Canada $9, Foreign $10.

Mamie Till Bradley gave me photos of her missing son when I interviewed her for my *Jet* article on his kidnapping, and promised I would stay on the story. (*Jet*, Sept. 8, 1955.)

A short article from the Associated Press in one of the Chicago dailies reported that a local boy visiting relatives in Mississippi was missing and two suspects were in custody. I looked up Mamie Till Bradley's name in the phone book and arranged to talk to her.

Several distraught friends and relatives were in Mamie's living room when I arrived. Sitting in the kitchen so we could talk, I let her know that I'd had firsthand experience with the backwoods culture of Mississippi during my recent trips there. I understood why she feared the worst, even while she prayed her boy would come home. She showed me three photos of Emmett, taken the previous Christmas. One showed him all dressed up in a dress shirt and tie, a fedora framing his beaming, boyish face; another was a mother-and-son pose; and the final one had Emmett leaning against a television set mugging for the camera. *Jet* would be the first magazine to publish these pictures. Before I left, I arranged to keep in close touch with her.

On August 31, three days after he had disappeared, Emmett's body surfaced in the Tallahatchie River, several miles upstream from Money, after it became snarled in tree roots in the swampy river. A teenaged fisherman reported his gruesome discovery to Leflore County Deputy Sheriff John Ed Cothran. It took a half-dozen men in two boats to get the naked and battered body out of the river, which ran about twenty feet deep at this point.

A seventy-five-pound cotton gin fan had been attached to Emmett's neck with barbed wire, weighing the body down to keep it from surfacing. Mud clogging the circular fan probably doubled its weight. Had the murderers also weighted down Emmett's feet, his body might have remained submerged.

The body was as ghastly a sight as most people will ever see. It looked as if someone had set about to destroy any vestige of its humanity. The tongue was swollen and grossly distended from the mouth. The left eyeball had been gouged out, and the right eyeball was hanging from the socket, held only by an optic nerve. On top of all that, a bullet hole was apparent on the right side of the head slightly behind the temple. Moses Wright was summoned to identify the body. His heart sank when he saw the silver ring inscribed with the initials "L. T." and the date "May 25, 1943." It was Emmett.

Reaction to the murder was instantaneous. Dr. Howard and NAACP Executive Secretary Roy Wilkins sent telegrams to Illinois Governor William Stratton and Mississippi Governor Hugh White asking for assistance. Another request for aid was made to J. Edgar Hoover, but the FBI director was reluctant to get involved. Calling it "a local murder case," he refused to commit any of his agents to the Till investigation. The U.S. Department of Justice announced that it lacked jurisdiction to enter the case. Mayor Daley, who presided over Chicago's Democratic Party, sent a telegram to President Eisenhower asking that "all the facilities of the federal government be immediately utilized so that the ends of justice may be served." Eisenhower, a Republican who was viewed as indifferent toward civil rights, took no action. Mamie herself sent a telegram to the president asking for federal intervention in the case. The FBI would tell the White House the boy's mother was being used by the Communist Party, and should not get a response, not even a letter of condolence, from Eisenhower. Over the years of the ensuing, tortuous civil rights movement, Hoover would claim that others who grieved publicly over the murders of their loved ones were also tools of the Communists.

In Mound Bayou, Dr. Howard saw it differently after two of his colleagues in the movement, Dr. George Lee and Lamar Smith, and now a fourteen-year-old child, were slain in quick succession in the Delta. The government, he suggested, had good reason to take action. "If this slaughtering of Negroes is allowed to continue, Mississippi will have a civil war," he warned. "Negroes are going to take only so much." Before long, he would be on Hoover's list of lowlifes, too.

At this point, a controversial character emerged to assert jurisdiction over the case. Tallahatchie County Sheriff H. C. Strider insisted that since the body was discovered in Tallahatchie County, that's where jurisdiction lay, although Emmett was abducted in Leflore County and may well have been killed in Sunflower County. Of the three counties, Tallahatchie had the reputation of being the toughest on blacks, which was somewhat surprising since Sunflower was the birthplace of the White Citizens' Councils.

Strider was the quintessential stereotype of a loudmouthed, racist Southern sheriff. An obese, obnoxious man, he got both kicks and kickbacks (the latter mainly from bootleggers) from the job, as well as a share of all fines and a cut of local tax collections. Besides that, he owned a large cotton plantation, on which more than thirty black families lived and worked as sharecroppers, buying all they needed from his store. He was an ugly man, inside and out.

THE BODY OF A BOY

Sheriff Strider ordered Moses to bury Emmett in Mississippi without delay, but Mamie wasn't having it. She dug her heels in and insisted that her son's body be returned to Chicago for burial. The body was released, and Mamie's other uncle in Money, Crosby Smith, accompanied it on the train to Chicago, where arrangements would be handled by the A. A. Rayner Funeral Home, one of the largest and most highly respected black funeral establishments in the area.

On Friday, September 2, *Jet* photographer David Jackson and I waited all night at the train station on Twelfth Street in Chicago with Mamie Bradley and the funeral director for the train carrying Emmett's body to arrive. The story was being reported as it unfolded in the *Chicago Defender* and other black newspapers, as well as in *Jet*, and a crowd of about a thousand onlookers milled about the station waiting for the train from Mississippi. By then I had spent hours talking with Mamie, and I was deeply impressed by the strength and resolve she'd shown as the terrible scenario developed, and the horrific details were communicated to her by family members in the Delta. But when the box containing her son was being unloaded from the freight car, all the weight of the world seemed to come down on her shoulders. Crying out to God, she collapsed in the arms of Gene Mobley and two clergymen.

Mississippi officials had stipulated that the body could be released only on the condition that the casket would not be opened. Later, in the funeral home, A. A. Rayner made it clear to Mamie (and the rest of us) that the box was locked up and had the seal of the State of Mississippi embossed on it to make sure that the order was followed. Rayner told her that, because of the seal, "We can't open that box." It appeared that Emmett would have to be buried without his mother seeing her son one last time. Mamie looked stunned and asked him to explain what he was saying.

Promises had been made just to get the body out of Mississippi, Rayner reiterated, adding, "I had to sign papers, the undertaker had to sign papers, your relatives had to sign papers."

Mamie was suddenly unbending. She looked the undertaker in the eyes and told him that if necessary she would take a hammer and open the box herself. He hesitated, trying to figure out what to do, but Mamie finally prevailed. Rayner said if she was that determined, he would get the body ready and let her view it.

The box was opened, and an overpowering stench of death permeated the funeral home. Everyone seemed to stop breathing or put a sleeve or handkerchief to his nose while Rayner sprayed aerosol cans of disinfectant into the air, which was of little help. He commented that the body had been packed in lime to make it deteriorate faster. We would later learn during the trial that certain people in Mississippi were determined to make the body as difficult to identify as possible.

When the funeral attendants removed the body from the shipping case, a chunk of skull fell off. We all stood as if frozen in time, until *Jet* photographer David Jackson calmly reached over and replaced the slice of bone, skin and hair.

Although the body was badly bloated, it did not appear to be bruised below the neck, and Emmett had not been castrated, as his mother had feared. What perplexed her was the gunshot wound, on top of all the other horrendous abuse. "Did they have to shoot him?" she exclaimed. Surely the torture must have been enough to kill him.

She studied the body so carefully, trying to find the beautiful features that once made Emmett such a good-looking kid. The hazel eyes—but one was now gone and the other lay on his cheek. I didn't know how she could do it. I had to look away. I had never seen anything so gruesome, so hideously unspeakable in my entire life. And this was the woman's son. Gene Mobley stood beside her the whole time, and added to her positive identification, saying that he recognized the haircut he'd given Emmett before the boy left with Uncle Mose. Mamie and Gene were two incredibly strong people. I just wanted it to end.

Finally, Mamie declared with absolute certainty, "That's Bobo." Gene, just as confidently, quietly agreed.

first

NATION HORRIFIED BY MURDER OF KIDNAPED CHICAGO YOUTH

Aroused by America's first lynching in four years — the kidnaping and murder by three Mississippi white men of chubby, 14-year-old Chicagoan Emmett Louis (Bobo) Till because he whistled at a white woman —leaders of both white and Negro groups demanded "stern and immediate" action against the "barbarians."

Mrs. Mamie Bradley and slain son, who was slated to enter 8th grade in Chicago this fall. He was her only child.

NAACP executive secretary Roy Wilkins wired Mississippi Governor Hugh White: "We cannot believe that responsible officials of a state will condone the murdering of children on any provocation." Swamped with hundreds of similar protesting telegrams, Gov. White answered: "Mississippi does not condone such conduct." Calling the Mississippi white people "horrified by the act," white Greenwood newspaper editor Tom Shepherd described the killing as "nauseating" and "way, way beyond the bounds of human decency."

The kidnaping episode came to a stark and shocking end when the youth's nude body, weighted with a 200-pound iron gin mill fan, was discovered by a fisherman in the shallow waters of the Tallahatchie River. The fan was wired around his neck.

Recovering the body, law officers found a "bullet hole one inch above his right ear." The left side of his face was crushed to the bone.

Meanwhile, Leflore County police continued to hold

two white men (Groce Roy Bryant and his half-brother, J. W. Milam) and pushed a search for the other members of the "lynch party," Mrs. Roy Bryant (who was whistled at) and another unidentified man. FBI officials said in Washington that they could not enter the case because it was "a local murder."

Greenwood Sheriff John Cochran examines 200-pound gin fan that was wired to neck of boy's nude body.

Recounting the boy's kidnaping from the home of his grandfather, 64-year-old Rev. Moses Wright, in Money, 17-year-old Wheeler Parker, one of the three Chicago cousins who were visiting in Mississippi, but

Saddened by boy's murder are cousins, Simeon, 12, and Maurice Wright, 16, (l.) and 64-year-old grandfather Rev. Moses Wright. He was not told about "incident" in town.

Boys Never Told Grandfather About 'Incident'

who escaped after the crime, told JET:

"When the men came, swearing and all, grandma tried to awaken Bobo and hide him outside, but the men stormed in and told her to get back in bed and shut up before they beat 'hell' out of her.

"Grandma knew about the 'incident' because we'd told her and not Grandpa, who would have gotten angry at us. We'd gone into town Wednesday and were watching some boys playing checkers in front of the store. Somebody said there was 'a pretty lady' in the store and Bobo said he was going inside to buy some bubble gum.

"After a while, we went in and got Bobo but he stopped in the doorway and whistled at the lady. She got angry and followed us out, then ran toward a car. Some one hollered, 'She's getting a gun' and we ran."

Mrs. Bradley got first look at brutally battered son in undertaker's morgue. More than 600,000, in an unending procession later viewed body (r.).

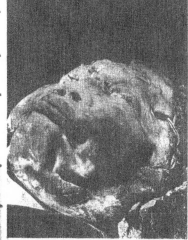

Close-up of lynch victim bares mute evidence of horrible slaying. Chicago undertaker A. A. Raynor said youth had not been castrated as was rumored. Mutilated face of victim was left unretouched by mortician at mother's request. She said she wanted "all the world" to witness the atrocity.

Horror, anger, rage, and ultimately determination were some of the emotions wrought by *Jet's* weekly coverage of the Till murder case. (*Jet*, Sept. 15, 1955.)

And then she seemed to stun the funeral director again, telling him that she wanted an open-coffin funeral. Rayner by then knew better than to argue. He asked her if she wanted him to work on her son, to make him more presentable.

"No," she said. That was the way she wanted him presented. "Let the world see what they did to my boy." Then, after a pause, she added, "Let them see what I've seen."

Despite Rayner's promise not to touch the body up, the mortician stitched the eyelids shut, removed the tongue, closed the mouth and refastened the back of the skull using some coarse thread. These repairs did little to lessen the ghastly appearance of the corpse. With Mamie's permission, David Jackson shot a picture of Emmett's head. We never doubted that John H. Johnson would publish it in *Jet*. When he did, David Jackson's photograph of Emmett Till's tortured remains ignited a firestorm.

THE FUNERAL

There were then about one million black people living in the Chicago area, a large number of them refugees from Mississippi. Many of them still had family there. Many had also experienced the cruelty of the sick feudal structure firsthand or knew someone else who had. Emmett's brutal murder caused a powerful, visceral reaction.

Tens of thousands of people lined up at the funeral home for four days to view Emmett in his open casket. The *Chicago Defender* estimated the number who came to pay their respects to be as high as 250,000. Many fainted. Some screamed. So many eyes wept.

Bishop Louis Henry Ford officiated at the funeral service at Roberts Temple of God in Christ at 41st and State Streets. A capacity crowd of several thousand mourners was inside, with another five thousand outside the church. Bishop Ford based his sermon on Matthew 18:6. "But who so shall offend one of these little ones which believe in me, it were better for him that a millstone were hanged about his neck and that he were drowned in the depth of the sea."

Illinois State Senator Marshall Korshak was there to represent Governor Stratton. He called Emmett "a young martyr in a fight for democracy and freedom, in a fight against evil men."

Emmett was buried at Burr Oak Cemetery. The same day, September 6, a Tallahatchie County grand jury indicted J. W. Milam and Roy Bryant for kidnapping and murder. Both men pleaded not guilty and were held in jail until the start of the trial, which would be held without delay, and, as soon became evident, without either the opportunity or the resources for the prosecution to establish an adequate case.

6

THE TRIAL

The trial of J. W. Milam and Roy Bryant began on September 19, 1955, less than two weeks after Emmett Till was buried in Chicago. Judge Curtis M. Swango would preside, having insisted that the trial be held during the court's current session, due to expire shortly, rather than in the next session in the spring. The courthouse was in Sumner, one of Tallahatchie's two county seats, the other being Charleston.

Sited appropriately in the town square, the three-story courthouse had all the trappings of respectability: Gothic-style architecture, a clock tower, and a manicured lawn with a Confederate statue on which was inscribed, "The cause that never failed." We thought it had. We found the town's slogan disputable as well, particularly from a black perspective: "Sumner—a good place to raise a boy," although many of its 450 residents probably thought it was true.

Bryant and Milam would be tried in a second floor courtroom designed to accommodate about 150 spectators, but packed "to the rafters" for this trial with close to 300, including those leaning against the walls or perched on the windowsills, which turned out to be pretty good seats. Two fans hanging from the ceiling dispersed the cigar and cigarette smoke, my own included, to every corner of the room and only occasionally out the tall, open windows. The outdoor temperature hit the mid-nineties by midday, while inside the humidity made it less than comfortable. Except for the lawyers and the black newsmen, every man in the room seemed to be wearing an open-neck, white, short-sleeve shirt. Like the lawyers, the black newsmen wore suits and ties—in my case, my usual bow tie. The few women in the courtroom usually wore tailored, cotton dresses. Everybody was hot as hell, but the rows of white men seemed accustomed to it. If they were hot, it was not from the weather.

Just over a week before the trial, *Jet* had published Dave's unedited, close-up photo of Emmett's mutilated face. The reaction was electrifying. The magazine quickly sold out, and for the first time, Johnson Publishing

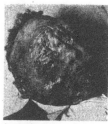

Because the gang-fashion May slaying of Rev. George W. Lee in Belzoni and the court-house yard August slaying of Lamar D. Smith in Brookhaven have both remained unsolved, the Urban League's usually soft-spoken Lester Granger has roared that he expects the murderers to go "unpunished," despite Mississippi Governor Hugh White's assurances that "the courts will do their duty" in the wolf-whistle lynching of

"I hope you haven't died in vain," boy's mother cried at graveside.

Savage lynchers crushed boy's skull, shot him, mutilated his face.

WILL MISSISSIPPI WHITEWASH THE EMMETT TILL SLAYING?

As the horribly mutilated body of 14-year-old Emmett Louis Till was lowered into the cold ground of a Chicago cemetery many days and many miles away from the watery Mississippi grave his kidnap-murderers intended for him, his distraught mother screamed to the world that his death be avenged. But as time wore on and southern justice began to bear its strange fruit, national leaders, the heartsick mother and thousands of other Americans began to wonder if Mississippi will whitewash its latest and most fiendish atrocity when the accused kidnapers go on trial September 19.

Chicago youth Emmett L. Till was plump, handsome.

At grand jury hearing, accused men John Milam (c.) and Roy Bryant (r.), admitted kidnaping but denied harming Till.

Mamie Till Bradley's insistence that the world see what racists had done to her fourteen-year-old son resonated throughout the nation. My coverage of the murder in *Jet* in the weeks leading up to the trial was hard-hitting and relentless, and has been credited with galvanizing a movement that would change the nation forever. (*Jet*, Sept. 22, 1955.)

Co. did a second printing. When that sold out, too, thousands more copies were run off the press. The *Chicago Defender* published a similar photo two days later.

Although *Jet* and the *Defender* had primarily black readerships, numerous white daily news organizations saw the ferment over the story and decided to cover the trial as well, as did the three television networks, transforming it into an international media event. It was probably the first time television cameras were present for anything like this, and at first I thought they were a distraction that would do little to help people understand what this trial was all about. What I didn't realize was the impact that the footage alone would have on the American psyche as it filled television screens in living rooms across the country. Newspapers and magazines had their audiences, but television news was now bringing living images—and in this case, the dead—to the same screen that Americans were looking to for entertainment—and they would be shocked by what they saw. It was the beginning of the end for Jim Crow, but we didn't know it yet.

JPC sent four of us to Sumner. I covered for *Jet*, while Cloyte Murdock was there for *Ebony*. In addition to David Jackson, we had a second photographer, Mike Shay, who was white. Sending Shay was a savvy decision on the part of *Jet* managing editor Robert Johnson (no relation to the publisher), because it gave us access in some instances where Jackson was barred because of his race.

While Sumner's white residents obviously resented the descent of the mainstream press on their little town, they had less use for the dozen or so black journalists. It was clear that somebody would have to lay down the law as far as any racial mixing was concerned, and Sheriff Strider couldn't wait to do that. He informed us right off the bat, "I ain't having no nigger reporters in my courtroom."

Strider also spread the rumor that as many as 1,000 carloads of Chicago Negroes were en route to Mississippi to seek revenge. As proof, he added that one such car with Illinois plates had just forced female members of the Milam family off the highway. No wonder we started to notice more and more sidearms strapped to the hips of white men in and around the courthouse. All the blacks who entered the courtroom were checked for concealed weapons, while some of the white spectators carried guns in full view. Even before the trial started, Strider was telling people that the body pulled from the Tallahatchie River was not Emmett's, but one that had been planted by the NAACP. (He later testified that he was "continuing the search for Till's body," and complained that the trial was holding him up.) The mere mention of the NAACP was enough to get a reaction out of most white Mississippians.

"ORDER" IN A MISSISSIPPI COURT

With support from a handful of white journalists, we appealed to Judge Swango, and he overruled the sheriff and allowed us into the courtroom. But the judge was no liberal and, like Strider, he had his limits, although not nearly as narrow. A year after the Supreme Court's *Brown* decision had struck down school segregation (in theory, at least), separate and unequal was still an okay arrangement in Judge Swango's courtroom. He made space for the black press along a side wall, behind rows of spectators, where it was at best difficult to hear the testimony. At first we didn't even have a table to write on, but another protest got us a folding table set up under the window. There wasn't enough room for all of us, even with the photographers standing against the wall, so we had to rotate seating at the table. The one good thing about the arrangement, we all agreed, was that if things went really bad and we had to get out fast, we had a window exit, albeit from the second floor of the building.

The original "Negro press table" at the Till murder trial was a folding card table not even large enough to accommodate the first of us in the segregated courtroom: Clotye Murdock (*Ebony*), me, L. Alex Wilson of *The* (Memphis) *Tri-State Defender*, and Steve Duncan of the *St. Louis Argus*. (Courtesy of author.)

Sheriff Strider, demonstrating that he bore no resentment at being over-ruled by the judge, greeted us every morning at our press table with a cheery, "Good morning, niggers." It was humiliating, and his way of reminding us that although we might be able to cover the trial over his objections, he was still the boss.

Strider also made clear that any mixing between black and white report-ers, either in the courtroom or outside, would get us kicked out of the trial and the town. He also prohibited all reporters from hanging around Sumner after dark, as if we might hold up a convenience store or something.

We managed to make room at the Jim Crow table for Mamie Till Brad-ley, who would be called to testify, and was joined at times by her father, John Carthan, and cousin Rayfield Mooty. Another notable observer at the trial was Congressman Charles Diggs who thought his presence might ensure some integrity in the proceedings. Or at least that's what he said, whether he really believed it or not. The rest of us didn't. He had sent the judge a telegram, and got one back saying he was welcome to observe the trial. But when he arrived, he was refused admission to the courtroom. He asked Jimmy Hicks, who was covering the trial for the National Newspaper Publishers Association (NNPA) and was probably the brashest of our group, to intercede.

Hicks tried to take Diggs's card to the judge, but was blocked by a deputy who asked, "Where you going, nigger?"

Hicks replied that he was going to see the judge. The deputy told him that wasn't going to happen. Hicks persisted, telling the deputy there was a Negro congressman outside who'd asked Hicks to give his card to the judge, who had already agreed that the congressman could observe the trial. He had to repeat his story for a succession of deputies, including one who was really incredulous.

"A nigger congressman? It ain't possible. It ain't even legal!"

Sheriff Strider came up to see what was going on, and Hicks ran through his story again, this time getting Strider to take the card to the judge.

When Strider came out of the judge's chambers, he strode up to the Jim Crow press table and informed us of the decision as if it were his own.

"You got a nigger congressman down here who is here to observe the trial. I'm going to bring him and sit him down with y'all." After another protest, a second folding table was added to our press table to accommodate Diggs and other blacks at the trial.

If we were amazed at Strider's lack of respect for Diggs's office, we were really appalled by Judge Swango's. Later, some white reporters called the judge "even-handed." While he was undoubtedly better trained and better behaved than many judges in the South in those days, I didn't see how you could call a segregationist "even-handed."

The usual carved wooden railing across the front of the courtroom separated the players from the spectators. To no one's surprise, the white reporters, with some necessary rotation due to their numbers, got to sit in the "well" of the courtroom with the judge, jury, lawyers, and defendants, along with the defendants' families. They would have no trouble hearing the testimony, except perhaps when the young Milam or Bryant children, playing with water pistols while sitting on their daddies' laps, got restless and started wandering around.

All five members of the Tallahatchie County bar who were in private practice represented Bryant and Milam. Friends and neighbors had raised nearly $10,000 for their defense.

The lead prosecutor was Gerald Chatham, district attorney for more than a decade. Assisting him was Robert B. Smith III, a Marine officer during World War II, who had also been with the FBI for four years. Largely in response to all the publicity, Mississippi Governor Hugh White had assigned

Smith to the case as a special prosecutor, but gave him no resources. The final member of the team was James Hamilton Caldwell, Jr., whose recent heart attack left him in bad shape.

The first day was taken up with jury selection. It was during that tedious piece of business that Judge Swango set the pattern for what would be acceptable courtroom conduct when he uncapped a Coca-Cola and began sipping it as the lawyers ran through their *voir dire*. The gesture of informality seemed to delight two spectators who promptly opened cans of beer and drank them down without any rebuke from the judge or the bailiffs. Several young peddlers were also allowed to roam the courtroom hawking Cokes and box lunches, which, as it turned out, was lucky for the white press because they had a bigger problem getting food during the day than we did. Sumner's only cafe was operated by and for blacks. Our white colleagues either had to bring something from Clarksdale, where they stayed, miles away from Sumner, or buy whatever the vendors were hawking in the courtroom. There was no water fountain in the courthouse for "Colored" folk, and some of the young vendors flatly refused to sell their wares to the Jim Crow press table. We were also out of luck when it came to sanitation. The only facilities available to Negroes were three blocks away. The two defendants, however, were allowed to use the toilet in the judge's chambers.

With no blacks registered to vote in Tallahatchie County, there would be none on the jury, even though blacks constituted more than 60 percent of the population. Women were kept off juries by state law. A number of men in the jury pool acknowledged knowing Bryant and/or Milam and were disqualified for that reason, as were others who had contributed to the defense fund. In the end, two carpenters and an insurance agent were seated on the twelve-man jury with a complement of farmers.

There was no doubt in our minds that the State faced seemingly insurmountable odds. No autopsy had been conducted. No ballistics comparisons had been made between the bullet that was still in Emmett's skull and Milam's .45-caliber pistol. The prosecution didn't even know where Milam's pistol was. Basic chemical tests of possible bloodstains in the back of Milam's pick-up truck and on the floor of an equipment shed where it was most likely that Emmett had been beaten had not been performed, because the prosecution was given no funds for these tests. On top of that, they could not say for sure in what county Emmett had actually been murdered.

SOCIAL ORDER, MISSISSIPPI STYLE

There was little likelihood of reporters of different races running into each other by chance outside of Sumner because while the whites stayed overnight in Clarksdale, we stayed an hour's drive away in Mound Bayou with Dr. Howard or with other families in that all-black enclave. Dave and I again shared one of the rooms in Dr. Howard's two-room guesthouse across the highway from his home.

On the first night of the trial, we had a pleasant surprise when two white reporters defied the state's segregation laws and breezed into Mound Bayou to pay us a visit. One of them was Clark Porteous, a reporter for the *Memphis Press-Scimitar*, who, like me, also happened to be a former Nieman Fellow. As they saw it, the trial was already "fixed." The State had lined up only two witnesses, Uncle Mose and his twelve-year-old son, Simeon, who'd shared the bedroom with Emmett the night his cousin was kidnapped. The reporters predicted the entire trial wouldn't take more than two days, adding that the State didn't even know where Emmett was killed. They also thought there was hardly enough circumstantial evidence of a killing, but having seen the body myself, I disagreed with that. Moreover, they warned us that Strider was waiting for us to make one false move so he could pitch us all out of the trial—and out of Sumner as well.

We were still digesting all of that when the phone rang. Dr. Howard had learned that two Negro workers had vanished on a Milam-owned plantation. One of them reportedly had knowledge of the crime. The next day, Jimmy Hicks shared some information that dovetailed with that. He'd been given a tip about two black men, both of whom worked for Milam, who were said to have been in the truck when Emmett was kidnapped. According to several locals, these men had been picked up by Strider and were being held in jail, presumably under aliases, in Charleston, Tallahatchie's other county seat. We decided that this information was too important to sit on. Hicks told prosecutor Gerald Chatham that two witnesses might be in the Charleston jail, and Chatham promised to look into it. A third black man whom some witnesses had identified by name as also on Milam's truck the day of the kidnapping was never found. For all we knew, he, too, might be at the bottom of the Tallahatchie River.

Then we heard reports that other Negroes were being "jailed" or whisked away from area plantations to keep them from testifying. It was not only difficult but dangerous to try to track down some of these stories, with such high hostility in the area to "outside agitators." Even driving from Mound Bayou to Sumner could be a hazardous proposition. A day before the trial began, David Jackson and I had gotten lost when I took a wrong turn. I slowed down to stop and check our map, when a pickup truck suddenly pulled alongside, and we heard a command from the passenger seat.

"Stop, ya damn niggers."

Glaring down at us from the truck were five white men, armed to the teeth with shotguns. We had no choice but to stop. At first I thought they might be deer hunting, but we later learned the season hadn't opened yet. Their prey apparently looked more like us. All five sprang from the truck and surrounded the car.

"Get out," the huskiest one snapped. "Who are you niggers and where are you going?"

I couldn't think of anything but the truth so I told them, "We're reporters down here to cover the murder trial. We took the wrong road and got lost."

"You niggers have no business around here," he sneered. "You're just stirring up trouble."

Directing us to keep our hands above our heads, they frisked both of us and then searched the car. For a second, I thought they would confiscate Dave's cameras, putting him out of business on this assignment. But then a greater fear gripped me in the gut. On one of our earlier trips to the Delta, Dave had carried a gun! I wasn't aware of it until we were packing to return to Chicago, when I spotted it lying on top of his open suitcase, and I erupted: "What the hell good is that going to do you down here? You'll get us both killed!" I told Dave never to bring a firearm on any of our assignments. Now, standing outside the car with my arms over my head, my intestines churned at the thought that he might not have heeded my warning. (As it turned out, he had not. In fact, he never stopped packing a gun when he went into the South, but he kept it in his luggage, and was prepared to use it if anyone came to get him in the middle of the night—a legacy, undoubtedly, of the kinds of stories we were covering.)

After what seemed like a lifetime, the "hunters" were satisfied with having scared the hell out of us, and having ended their search, ordered us to "get the hell out" of there. They were even charitable enough to give us directions to where we wanted to go. In the future, I was much more careful to avoid wrong turns.

The *Jet/Ebony* team members were not the only ones who were harassed. After telling the prosecution about the two potential witnesses reportedly being held in the Charleston jail, Jimmy Hicks was arrested on Sheriff Strider's orders for a minor traffic offense. (He was never sure exactly what, but it apparently carried a penalty of $300 or six months in jail!) He was released after the *New York Post*'s Murray Kempton and two local white reporters strongly advised the sheriff that this was not the kind of publicity the town needed right now.

On the day the State was to present its first witness, things began to happen. A Negro plantation worker, on the pretense of going to church, had made his way to Dr. Howard and told him he knew the whereabouts of several blacks who not only had seen Emmett being carried on a truck into a barn, but later heard the sounds of a beating and someone crying for mercy, coming from inside. Dr. Howard called a small group of black reporters together with Ruby Hurley and Medgar Evers of the NAACP to plot a course of action. Besides Dave, Clotye Murdock and me from the *Jet/ Ebony* team, the tight-knit group included Jimmy Hicks, Moses Newson, and Newson's boss, L. Alex Wilson, from the Memphis *Tri-State Defender*. If this turned out to be the evidence the State needed, it would be the hottest story of the trial. But there was a major problem: the vast wall of mistrust between the races. Several of us argued that any hasty action on our part could endanger lives. The potential witnesses should be taken into hiding for their own safety before their names were revealed. Others countered that time was of the essence and not making timely disclosure of this informa- tion would be an obstruction of justice. There was also the problem of whom to tell. Who would make sure the witnesses were protected and see that they got to the trial? We had grave doubts that we could make this hap- pen without help from some of our colleagues in the mainstream press. It was agreed, however, that the first order of business was to plan the evacua- tion of the potential witnesses. Next, we would call in the most reliable and sympathetic daily press reporters covering the trial. In return for getting to share in this headline story, the white reporters would be asked to make the first contact with law enforcement and the prosecution. The reporters would notify them of the new evidence, and as our part of the bargain, we would then produce the witnesses.

Our list of newsmen covering the trial whom we believed would be trustworthy included several topnotch reporters, but Dr. Howard took one look at it and rejected them all except one man. As I learned more about the South, I would come to understand why. Daily newsmen in Dixie often had an alliance with local police that choked off any attempts to change the status quo. I avoided contact with either. Newspapers in these areas were used more to immerse the readership in hatred and prejudice than to advance democracy. Often the white editor, inadvertently if not intention- ally, became a backer of the Ku Klux Klan and the White Citizens' Council. The only white reporter at the trial in whom Dr. Howard had any confidence was Clark Porteous, a Southerner whom he knew to be fair and square. We agreed that he should call Porteous.

Then came the first glitch. In his eagerness to meet with Porteous, Dr. Howard failed to make clear we wanted him to come alone. Not understand- ing that, Porteous brought along two *Jackson Daily News* reporters, James Featherston and W. C. Shoemaker. Then there was a further mix-up. Dr. Howard neglected to explain the ground rules to the reporters before he told them everything he knew about the "surprise witnesses." When he then told them the story was embargoed until after the witnesses, for their own safety, were brought in from the plantation, Featherston flat out refused and said he would run it the next day. Porteous intervened and Featherston finally agreed to hold the story on the condition that no other reporter would be tipped off. Everybody agreed. According to the plan, the whites would have the law enforcement officers at a rendezvous point in Mound Bayou at eight o'clock the next evening, when we would produce the witnesses.

The next morning, we could hardly believe it when our plan appeared to be working, and Judge Swango recessed the trial for the rest of the day to allow the State to bring in new witnesses.

When the time for our scheduled meeting rolled around at 8:00 p.m. our excitement went flat. The sheriffs of two counties showed up but not the witnesses. We discovered that "some white men" had visited the plantations in question in the morning and by the time our party (including the NAACP's Medgar Evers, Ruby Hurley, and reporter Moses Newson) reached there, the witnesses had vanished. Later, we learned that the visitors were law enforcers who somehow had been given advance information and had gone out on their own. Now we had new problems and only some twelve hours to locate the witnesses.

Sheriff George Smith of Leflore County, fair man that he was, promptly routed our pessimism. "These witnesses have a story to tell. We've got to find them if it takes all night. We'll stop court until we find them."

THE SEARCH IS ON

Mississippi's first major interracial manhunt was underway. Each sheriff agreed to take one black member of the group and go to a plantation home. All the sites we had identified would be visited by morning. The black escort would plead with the potential witnesses to testify. There would be no warrants issued. No one would be forced to come. We agreed that those who did would be brought to the State Enforcement Agent's office in Drew.

Three of us, Porteous, Featherston and I, followed Sheriff Smith in a seventy-mile-an-hour chase along dusty backwoods roads to get eighteen-year-old Willie Reed. This youth had actually seen Emmett on the truck and heard the beating. During the run, we ran into the next glitch. It was a dark night and the sheriff's car was too fast for us to keep up. We got lost. It's impossible to describe the thoughts that went through my head—we were three newsmen, at that moment in Mississippi a despised class if ever there was one, and worse than that, one of us was black. There was little or no conversation as we headed back to Drew, all three of us focused on every broad tree, every rise in the road, every twist and turn, praying (at least on my part) an ambush wasn't awaiting us. Finally, we made it back, and in about a half hour things began to pick up.

The first man who'd been rounded up refused to talk to anyone but Dr. Howard, who hadn't arrived at the office yet. It was decided that he would go home and wait for a call. An hour later, when a sheriff went after him he was missing. He didn't turn up again at his home until two days after the trial.

Throughout the night, the search continued. Each person brought in was asked to testify. All were frightened. Finally, Dr. Howard promised that each witness who agreed to testify would be given safe passage to Chicago. He, personally, along with NAACP workers Ruby Hurley, Medgar Evers, Amzie Moore, and Aaron Henry would see to that. This satisfied three witnesses, Willie Reed, Add Reed, Willie's seventy-four-year-old grandfather, and Amanda Bradley, 49, Willie's aunt.

When Judge Swango reconvened the trial the next morning, the new witnesses were in the courthouse. All of the reporters, black and white, settled in again to cover the trial. Newspaper headlines later screamed the news that new witnesses had seen Emmett taken into a barn, from which they then heard cries begging for mercy. None of the stories mentioned the all-night manhunt.

Of all the witnesses, Moses Wright's testimony was the most crucial to the prosecution. Without him there was no hard evidence that Emmett had been kidnapped. We were awed by the calm of this slight man. Interviewing him on his porch one evening before the trial, we would feel a chill as suspicious cars pulled toward his house and then moved slowly past. The retired minister sensed our nervousness and said softly, "Don't worry. It's alright here."

There was never any doubt that he would testify. What concerned us more was what the reaction might be, right there in the courtroom. It took a lot of guts for a black man, even in open court, to accuse white men of kidnapping and murder. Moses, in fact, had been warned that he'd better take his family and "get out of town before they all get killed." As incredible as it seemed, there was precedent for a lynching right in the middle of a trial. Some twenty years earlier, in another Mississippi courthouse, a white man pulled out a gun and started shooting when a black man accused of raping a white woman rose to testify in his own defense. There wasn't a single one of us at the Jim Crow table who didn't think it could happen again in Judge Swango's court. And every one of us was prepared to exit through that second story window if necessary.

Despite the tension some of us were feeling, when the trial resumed on Wednesday, a carnival atmosphere prevailed. Judge Swango, as usual, swigged from a bottle of Coke, as did most of the jurors, and some of the spectators. The judge had forbidden any photographs during testimony, but at other times, the cameramen roamed the courtroom taking pictures. One of them was a black photographer, Ernest Withers, shooting for the Memphis *Tri-State Defender*. Withers seemed perfectly at ease in the courtroom. Suddenly a white man jumped up and said, "Nigger, don't take my picture." Withers, so much more confident in this atmosphere than his Northern colleagues, shrugged, "Don't worry. I'm only taking important people today." I muttered, between nervous drags on a cigarette, "Man, you'll get us lynched down here."

Milam and his wife held their sons, Harvey, 2, and Bill, 5, on their laps when the boys weren't wandering about the courtroom, climbing on and off chairs. At one point, Bill waved a toy water pistol at Sheriff Strider, shouting, "Boom, boom, boom." Later, little Harvey amused himself by slipping a rope around his brother's neck and tugging at it. J. W. Milam smoked cigars and read newspapers during the proceedings. He seemed bored with it all.

Roy and Carolyn Bryant sat together while their two young sons romped playfully in the aisles with the Milam boys.

MOMENT OF TRUTH

Moses Wright, the prosecution's key witness, testified on Wednesday. As a packed courtroom watched, the sixty-four-year-old sharecropper was asked to identify the men who had come to his home in the middle of the night and kidnapped Emmett.

Standing straight as a flagpole, Wright raised an outstretched arm, pointing his finger directly ahead at J. W. Milam, as he testified, "There he is." Asked to identify the second man, he pointed to the other defendant, Roy Bryant, stating clearly, "And there is Mr. Bryant."

At this moment, disregarding the judge's prohibition against taking photographs during testimony, Ernest Withers raised his camera and took a picture of Moses Wright, a slight figure in yellow and brown suspenders over a white, long-sleeved shirt and thin black tie, standing and pointing an accusatory finger at Milam and Bryant. One of the wire services bought his role of film on the spot, and the iconic photograph was carried by newspapers around the country.

Uncle Mose also testified that there had been a third man who didn't come into his house, as well as a fourth man on the truck. He said he heard another person speaking from the truck's cab, with a voice higher than a man's, possibly a female, who identified Emmett.

When defense attorney C. Sidney Carlton started his cross-examination, he tried to pin down Wright on how he could identify anybody in the dark with the flashlight pointed at him. Wright reminded Carlton that Bryant had identified himself when he came banging on the door.

Carlton asked if the third man was white.

"I don't think so," Wright answered.

"He might have been a Negro?" the defense attorney pressed.

"He sure acted like a Negro. He stayed outside," Wright replied.

People laughed at this answer, and the judge banged his gavel to keep control of the courtroom. Moses Wright's testimony lasted about an hour.

Leflore County Sheriff George Smith was called next. The judge excused the jury while he listened to what the sheriff had to say. Smith said when he went to Roy Bryant's store at 2:00 p.m. on Sunday, August 28, Bryant admitted that he took Emmett from Moses Wright's home to his store. Bryant claimed that he turned Emmett loose when he learned from his wife that the boy wasn't the one who insulted her.

The defense lawyers made much out of the fact that Sheriff Smith and Bryant were friends and argued that the conversation between them was confidential. Incredibly, the Judge decided that Smith's testimony would be withheld from the jury.

The judge and the defense attorneys had an opportunity during a two-and-a-half hour lunch recess to learn what the testimony of "surprise" witnesses Willie Reed and Amanda Bradley would include, so that the judge could determine its relevance and admissibility and the defense could prepare their response to it. The interrogation was conducted in Swango's chambers with Willie standing about three feet from where Bryant and Milam were sitting. The teenager later described the experience as "intimidating," saying Milam not only gave him threatening looks, but also thrust his hand into his pocket "as if he had a gun."

Approved as a witness, Willie repeated his testimony before the jury. His account was powerful. He said that around 6:00 a.m. on Sunday he was on his way to buy meat for breakfast when he saw Emmett sitting in the back of a passing pick-up truck. Two other blacks and four white men were also in the truck, but he only recognized Emmett and J. W. Milam. The truck drove to a large shed on the Sunflower County plantation. Subsequently, he heard cries coming from inside. He ran to the home of his aunt, Amanda Bradley, and got her to come with him. The cries became wails and then a chant of "Mama, Lord have mercy! Lord have mercy!"

He said he saw J. W. Milam, with a gun in his holster, come out of the shed to get some water from the well. He knew Milam because he had seen him around the plantation before. Three other white men came out and joined Milam. The truck was backed out of the shed and three black men helped the others roll something wrapped in a tarpaulin into the back of the truck. Later, when the truck returned, he saw the black men washing something red out of the back of the truck. Next, they burned some clothing.

Amanda Bradley corroborated Willie's testimony, stating that she, too, saw J. W. Milam with a holstered pistol belted over his khaki pants.

While she had been closeted in the witness room, the feisty Amanda chatted with other blacks who were considered potential witnesses but for one reason or another were not called. She tried to get them over their fear of white retaliation, chiding one man who denied knowing about the crime, "Quit lying. You know you seen the truck."

On the third day of the trial, Sheriff Strider dispensed with his usual greeting as he approached our table in a fury, huffing and red faced. He got right to the point, asking where was that "nigger reporter Booker," the one that worked for "the little magazine called *Jet*."

Before I could breathe, or anyone else at the table could even blink, Jimmy Hicks shot back, "He left yesterday."

"If you ever see that nigger reporter, you tell him that I will take his head off his neck if we ever meet," Strider bellowed as he stormed away.

I never could thank Jimmy Hicks enough for that, and he knew it. His greatest satisfaction was telling the story time and again whenever we appeared on the same platform. I was happy to give him that. Somebody asked me once what I thought Strider would have done if he knew he had found me. I don't even want to think about it. Strider had apparently been shown a copy of *Jet* and found something I'd written less than flattering.

On Wednesday afternoon, the state called Robert Hodges, the youth who had discovered the body; Chester Miller, the black undertaker from Greenwood; and Leflore County Deputy John Ed Cothran. Miller described the condition of the body he came to pick up in an ambulance. He told about seeing a hole above the right ear, undoubtedly a bullet hole. He said part of Emmett's head had been crushed and a piece of the skull had fallen off into the boat.

The gin fan had been brought into court. It was a shocking reminder of what had happened. Miller said that several feet of barbed wire had bound the heavy fan to Emmett's neck.

"THAT WAS MY SON."

Mamie Till Bradley took the stand on Thursday morning and told how she had identified the body as that of her son. She described the scene at A. A. Rayner's Funeral Home in Chicago when she had examined Emmett's entire body, the legs, the torso, the face, mouth, teeth, ears. "I positively identified it. It was definitely my boy. Beyond a shadow of a doubt," she said.

The prosecutor showed her the photo of Emmett taken right after he had been pulled from the river. "That was my son," she said steadily, maintaining her composure. She was determined to do so. He brought out another picture, one taken the previous Christmas. Mamie said this, too, was Emmett. Next, she was shown the silver ring which was engraved "L. T." and the date "May 25, 1943." She said it was the ring she had given Emmett before he left Chicago to go to Mississippi. It belonged to his father, Louis Till, who had died in 1945.

Mamie was cross-examined by J. J. Breland, the oldest of the defense attorneys. His questions focused on whether she had insurance on Emmett and whether it provided for double indemnity. Then he wanted to know if she had worked for the NAACP. It was clear he was suggesting some kind of weird conspiracy, maybe even one in which Emmett himself was alive somewhere up North while it played out in Mississippi. The defense attorney knew the suspicions that were being bandied about in Sumner and he played them like a violin. He even asked her if she read the *Chicago Defender*, and was pursuing that when the judge stopped him and ordered the jury out while he asked Breland how far he intended to take this. Not satisfied with his answer, Swango brought questions about the newspaper to an end. With the jury back, the defense attorney shifted gears again, asking her if she was born in the South. Mamie told him that she was, and he asked her what she had told Emmett to prepare him for his trip to the South. She told him about the racial primer she had given Emmett, including telling him to humble himself if necessary. After an hour of this, Mamie was more dispirited than ever when she looked at the jury and the white spectators. She knew she wasn't connecting with them at all.

Willie Reed and Amanda Bradley gave their sworn accounts to the jury after Mamie testified. Basically, it was a repeat of what they had sworn in the judge's chambers. Then, the prosecution closed its case.

Jimmy Hicks was flabbergasted that the prosecutors made no mention of the two men he'd told them had reportedly participated in the kidnapping and murder, and were being held in the Charleston jail by Sheriff Strider. Gerald Chatham told Hicks that Strider had assured him that the men definitely were not in the jail. Did he send a neutral observer to the jail to check on the sheriff's story?

"No, I have to rely on Sheriff Strider to produce witnesses," Chatham said.

The defense moved for a directed verdict of acquittal, saying that the prosecution had failed to meet its burden of proof. The judge turned down this motion and said the case would be decided by the jury.

When the defense put Carolyn Bryant on the stand, Judge Swango ordered the jury cleared from the courtroom, expecting that her testimony would be inflammatory. She said a black man with "a Northern brogue" had come into the store on August 24 and gone over to the candy counter. He was buying bubble gun. When she held her hand out for money, she claimed that he grabbed her arm and spoke to her, asking, "How about a date, baby?"

She said she broke free and that he came around and grabbed her by the waist and spoke again. "What's the matter, baby, can't you take it? I've been with white women before."

She said he used foul language, so foul in fact, that she could not repeat it in court. She broke away from his grasp and ran to get a pistol from her sister-in-law's car. That's when she heard the wolf whistle. She demonstrated the whistle in court. The sound seemed to jolt the packed courtroom like a bolt of heat lightening.

After Special Prosecutor Smith argued that whatever happened on August 24 should not be connected to the August 28 kidnapping and murder of Emmett Till, the judge ruled that Mrs. Bryant's inflammatory testimony would be withheld from the jury.

The defense called six character witnesses who all agreed that the two defendants were "good ole boys" who wouldn't murder anybody.

When the physician, Dr. Luther "L. B." Otken, who had examined the body for the county, testified that he couldn't tell whether the corpse was that of a white man or a black man, the prosecutor scoffed, "We're wasting an awful lot of money in our schools educating people who can't tell a white man from a Negro. I don't want anybody filling prescriptions who can't tell black from white."

Otken conceded that his "expert opinion" had been formed a good distance away from the body on the riverbank because of the odor. But his testimony, as well as that of the Tutwiler funeral home director that the body had been in the water two weeks or more and was unidentifiable, bolstered the defense position that it was not Emmett Till.

STRIDER'S PERJURY

Finally, the defense called its most important witness, Sheriff Strider. He testified the body looked like it had been in the water between ten and fifteen days, while Emmett had been missing only three days. He said he couldn't tell whether this body was black or white, only that it was human. He said that he wouldn't have been able to recognize the body even if it had been one of his two sons.

Special Prosecutor Smith asked Strider if he had signed Emmett's death certificate. Strider perjured himself, swearing that he had not done so, even though he had indeed signed it on September 1. The Deputy State Registrar of Vital Statistics had certified the death certificate before the trial, on September 16. But since Smith did not have a copy of this document, Strider's testimony went unchallenged.

Even the *New York Times* gave this story of mistaken identity some credence. "There have been widespread reports that local law enforcement officers have developed doubts over the identification of the body," the newspaper reported on September 18.

Clotye Murdock, my *Ebony* colleague, was so upset by Strider's testimony, that she approached the judge as court was recessing. If Strider couldn't tell whether the body pulled from the river was black or white, how come he turned it over to a black funeral home? The judge agreed it was a good question, but he took no action.

By then, the stress of the trial was too much for Clotye. She was so distraught, she couldn't continue, even though it was almost over. With great regret, I saw that she was taken safely to Memphis, where she could catch a flight back to Chicago.

Neither of the defendants testified. They had nothing to gain from it and would have been subjected to cross-examination had they done so.

In his closing, District Attorney Gerald Chatham told the jurors they should not pay attention to the testimony of so-called "expert witnesses" who wouldn't have known Emmett under any circumstances. But they should take the word of his mother ". . . someone who loved him and cared for him. God's given witness to identify him." He called the murder "a cowardly act—a brutal, unnecessary killing of a human being."

The defense mounted a racist appeal. Defense attorney John Whitten told the jury that he had confidence "that every last Anglo-Saxon one of you has the courage to free these men" reminding the jury that several people who handled the dead body testified they thought it had been too badly decomposed to be identified. Another defense attorney, J. W. Kellum, told the jury that "your forefathers will turn over in their graves" if Milam and Bryant were convicted.

The jury was out just one hour and seven minutes before announcing that both defendants were "not guilty." Witnesses said they heard laughter inside the jury room during deliberations. One juror said they would have been back sooner if they had not taken time off for a soda pop break. The

THE STRANGE TRIAL | OF THE TILL KIDNAPERS

When an all-white, all-male Mississippi jury finally got around to deciding whether or not Roy Bryant and his half-brother J. W. Milam were guilty of murdering 14-year-old Chicago schoolboy Emmett Till, it took them only an hour and seven minutes to bring

an end to a trial that for five days had taken on all the appearances of a Sunday school picnic. The verdict of "not guilty" was merely a formal way of telling Bryant that he could go back to tending the affairs of his small town grocery in Money, Miss., and that Milam, whose cotton stood high on his plantation, could resume supervising its harvesting.

It had been that kind of a trial. From the beginning, Judge Curtis Swango, who was later to be commended for his fairness, perhaps unwittingly set the pattern for what would be acceptable courtroom conduct by uncap-

A white camera man is steadied on his chair-top perch by Milam during trial in humid, 90-degree-heat courtroom.

Five Sumner, Miss., lawyers—all the legal brains in town—defended Roy Bryant and John Milam in murder trial.

Beer and Coke in the courtroom; a congressman ordered to sit at a segregated press table; the sheriff threatening to take the head off "that nigger reporter Booker"; documented perjury; a midnight hunt for prosecution witnesses: these were just a few of the oddities that assaulted our senses during the five-day trial before an all-white jury took sixty-seven minutes to return a verdict of "not guilty," admitting that it wouldn't have taken so long had they not taken a soda break. (*Jet*, Oct. 5, 1955.)

jury foreman said the prosecution had failed to prove that the body fished from the river was Emmett.

As the crowd of bystanders and reporters surrounded them, Bryant and Milam were photographed kissing their wives and lighting up celebratory cigars. Their jubilance was only slightly tempered by the fact that they still faced kidnapping charges in Leflore County.

I was disappointed, but not surprised by the verdict. I convinced myself that some good might eventually come out of the travesty we had witnessed. At the very least, I thought, the trial had exposed many people around the world to Mississippi's racial injustice in its rawest form. Maybe the next time would be better.

Reaction to the verdict was swift. Mass protest rallies sprang up in major U.S. cities, while outraged editorials appeared in many newspapers, domestic as well as foreign. The NAACP sponsored huge mass meetings in Northern cities where Moses Wright described the terrible night when Emmett was kidnapped. The *Ohio Sentinel* (Columbus's black weekly) ran a front-page account of one such event under the headline "Thousands Hear Till

Murder Case Eyewitnesses," with a photo of some of the 4,000 people who packed that city's Shiloh Baptist Church to capacity to hear Wright, whose photo was captioned, "I have no fear. . . ." There was also one of me, accepting a donation to the NAACP from an assistant to Mayor M. E. Sensenbrenner, after my eyewitness account of the trial.

Mississippians were resentful of the angry accusations directed at them after the murder. One that really seemed to burn the moderates in the state was Roy Wilkins's charge that Mississippians had decided to maintain white supremacy by murdering children. A few weeks after the trial, their senator avenged his constituents. On October 15, the *Commercial Appeal* and the *Jackson Daily News* published articles reporting that Louis Till was executed by the U.S. Army in 1945 for raping two Italian women and killing a third. The information had been obtained and forwarded to the press by Senator James O. Eastland. He not only intended to embarrass newspapers that had called Louis Till "a war hero," but also to tarnish Emmett's youthful innocence by suggesting that the sins of the father were the sins of the son. Mamie was shocked that the Pentagon had turned over information to Eastland that it had steadfastly refused to release to the soldier's next of kin.

On November 9, an all-white grand jury refused to indict Milam and Bryant for kidnapping although both had admitted to a county sheriff that they had taken Emmett from Moses Wright's home at gunpoint.

Moses Wright and most of his family, as well as Willie Reed and Amanda Bradley, were spirited away safely to Chicago, where Willie suffered a nervous breakdown under the stress of all he'd been through.

In the Delta, racial violence continued unabated after the trial. On November 25, Gus Courts, the late Rev. George Lee's colleague, was shot twice while working in his Belzoni, Mississippi, grocery store. Courts had refused to halt his voter registration efforts after Rev. Lee's murder. His friends probably saved his life by avoiding the hospital in Belzoni and driving him thirty-five miles to Mound Bayou, where surgeons removed one bullet from his abdomen and another from his left arm. When asked if he thought Courts's voting rights activities were behind the attempted murder, Humphreys County Sheriff Ike Shelton said, "Hell no. Some nigger had it in for him, that's all." Although the FBI made a cursory investigation, no one was ever charged with the shooting.

Two months after the Till trial, another incident reinforced the notion that a white man could murder a black man in Tallahatchie County with impunity. The victim this time was Clinton Melton, who was shot dead in Glendora, four miles from the place where Emmett Till's body had been pulled out of the Tallahatchie River. According to witnesses, thirty-three-year-old Melton, the father of five children, was shot for reasons that made no sense at all, by a man who was the best friend of J. W. Milam. An all-white jury deliberated four and one-half hours in the same Sumner courthouse before acquitting the defendant.

When asked by a reporter for his opinion of the Till and Melton murder trials, one white Glendora resident said, "There's open season on the Negroes now. They've got no protection, and any peckerwood who wants can go out and shoot himself one."

Not long after the grand jury refused to indict Bryant and Milam for kidnapping, William Bradford Huie went to Sumner to do an article for *Look* magazine. A native Alabamian, Huie was known to have no qualms about paying criminals for their stories. He had a straightforward proposition for Bryant and/or Milam—a lump sum of $3,500. Since they couldn't be retried due to constitutional protection against double jeopardy, they seemed to have nothing to lose. To protect *Look* from a charge of checkbook journalism, the payment would be framed as consideration for an agreement not to sue for libel after the story's publication, or any movie based on the article.

"The Shocking Story of Approved Killing in Mississippi" was published in the January 24, 1956, issue of *Look*. At its core was Milam's assertion that, in essence, he had done the world a favor by killing a nigger who stubbornly refused to admit that he was inferior to his white kidnappers. Milam may have thought the interview would make him some kind of folk hero to white supremacists. Instead, it made both Bryant and Milam pariahs in their own communities, forcing them to leave the Delta to survive boycotts of their businesses by both blacks and whites.

Despite pleas from black Republicans and other prominent leaders, as well as angst-filled memos from beleaguered White House aide E. Frederic Morrow,[1] that someone high in the administration speak out on the violence in the South, the White House hunkered down in silence on the Till case, after the FBI claimed the Communist Party was behind all the "rabble rousing," including a massive letter writing campaign.[2] Then, after four months of ignoring the uproar, in January 1956, minority issues advisor Max Rabb, noting that the White House had received approximately 3,000 letters, wires, and cards on the matter, in addition to about 11,000 names and addresses on petitions, suggested that the administration might be "missing the boat" if it didn't take advantage of the opportunity presented by the president's upcoming State of the Union Message "to make a constructive reply on these." He wasn't sure, so he asked Eisenhower aide, Colonel Andrew Goodpaster, for his opinion.[3] The upshot was a couple of narrow and tepid sentences, buried near the end of the president's speech, taking credit for the "all but completed" elimination of discrimination and segregation in executive branch operations throughout the nation, but recognizing that there were still some persistent "allegations" that Negroes were being deprived of their right to vote in some localities and subjected to "unwarranted economic pressures." The Eisenhower administration had still "missed the boat."

One hundred days after Emmett Till's murder, Mrs. Rosa Parks refused to give up her seat on a public bus in Montgomery, Alabama. She later said she was thinking of Emmett Till as she sat steadfast in her seat. She was arrested, launching a citywide boycott, during which deputy sheriffs rounded up some ninety Negro citizens, including the Reverends Martin Luther King and Ralph Abernathy, and charged them with persuading Montgomery's 47,000 blacks to stop riding the city busses rather than take a back seat to whites. At a rally of 5,000 in a jammed Montgomery church, Dr. King set the tone for a movement in which he would play a pivotal role over the next decade, telling the spirited crowd that the tension was not between Negroes and whites, but "between justice and injustice." Many historians, journalists, and social scientists claim that this successful and peaceful boycott was the genesis of the modern civil rights movement. Others argue that it was the Till case. Still others, like me, trace the movement back to Dr. Howard's mammoth voter registration rally in Mound Bayou and the subsequent assassination of Rev. George W. Lee in Belzoni. Whatever the moment, the giant had awakened, and would not be held down.

POSTSCRIPT

Two years after Emmett's death, his mother married Gene Mobley. From the time of the trial until her death in 2003, at age eighty-one, Mrs. Mobley never gave up the hope that if the federal government intervened in the case, some measure of justice might be obtained.

Finally, in 2004, amid much fanfare, the U.S. Department of Justice agreed to reopen the case. An autopsy and genetic testing on Emmett's exhumed remains proved beyond a shadow of a doubt that the victim was Emmett Till. The cause of death was listed as a gunshot wound. And that was about it. Bryant and Milam were both dead. No accomplices were identified. Even if they had been living, federal civil rights statutes covering their actions had long since tolled. Egregious as it was, Strider's obstruction of justice had not violated federal civil rights laws at the time, and besides, he was dead, too. The federal government concluded that it had nothing to prosecute and quietly shut down the investigation.

7

"THE LITTLE MAGAZINE THAT COULD" COMES TO WASHINGTON

By the end of 1955, it was clear that a bureau in the nation's capital was a must if *Jet* were going to succeed as a news magazine. Much of the news germane to the civil rights movement was originating in Washington. The NAACP was pursuing cases in federal courts, including the highest court in the land; access to the American president was no longer through White House maids and valets—there was now a black assistant to the president, E. Frederic Morrow; and there were three black members of Congress—Detroit freshman Charles Diggs, Chicago's William Dawson, and New York's powerful and unpredictable Adam Clayton Powell, Jr., all of whom were pushing for civil rights across the nation and not just for pork in their own districts.

Jet, too, was growing and changing from primarily entertainment/sports/society tidbits and gossip, to a hard-hitting source of news about black progress on all fronts, providing eyewitness coverage of the spreading civil rights revolution in the South, as well as day-to-day strides in the North (although the cover still almost invariably featured a black beauty or someone from the entertainment world). In fact, so painstaking had the magazine become to include mention of every significant development in the struggle, that it came to be said over time, "If you didn't read it in *Jet*, it didn't happen." Managing editor Robert Johnson (no relation to the publisher) went even further, calling *Jet* the Negro "bible," reporting the gospel or "good news" as well as the bad, and providing a beacon (in convenient pocket-size) for the arduous trek to freedom.

Assigned by John H. Johnson to search for a suitable Washington bureau chief, I concluded after interviewing the candidates that I was the best person for the job, and easily convinced Mr. J. After the Nieman Fellowship, I'd lived in D.C. for two years and knew it pretty well. Returning in the role of bureau chief, with the backing of a publisher determined to make it a first-class endeavor, would enable me to pursue the stories I believed important to our readers. I would also have access to the White House, the Congress, the highest ranks of government, and the people outside government who had enough clout to be heard.

All this was a vast improvement over my 1951–53 stint in the capital; but Washington in 1956 was still one of the most segregated cities in the country, and even renting space for the first-class operation John H. Johnson wanted was a challenge. Our initial foothold was in the Negro "U Street" corridor, in the law offices of J. Leon Williams, a black attorney who handled criminal as well as civil cases in the D.C. Superior Court.

Johnson was discovering that the real estate market in the nation's capital was more segregated than in New York or Los Angeles, the other two metropolises where he was determined to establish first-class bureaus. In Washington, downtown was simply off limits to black businesses, even on its less impressive side streets, and we were told this in no uncertain terms. But Johnson was a man who refused to accept failure, and his persistence paid off with a tip that there might be an exception—a building owned by Standard Oil Company, a Rockefeller interest, at 266 Constitution Avenue NW, at the foot of Capitol Hill, that was willing to make JPC the first black-owned company with a downtown D.C. office.

The two-room suite we were able to lease wasn't large enough for the top-flight operation Johnson envisioned for his D.C. bureau, and as if that wasn't bad enough, no one in the building but the elevator operators talked to us. However, the location was great, and within months, utilizing a couple of borrowed conference rooms, we would be making the most of the building's bird's eye view of the Inaugural Parade, during which the publisher and his wife hosted our first open house, also inaugurating a JPC tradition.

I reported in Ticker Tape that the Johnsons welcomed an overflow 500 guests, but "overflow" had to be an understatement given the size of the suite. The item named a few of the VIPs who showed up, including FBI Inspector Deke DeLoach (Hoover had also been invited, but sent his regrets), Asst. Army Secretary George H. Roderick, White House aide Robert Gray, Senator Clifford Case (R-NJ), and ambassadors George Padmore of Liberia and Ibrahim Anis of the Sudan. How DeLoach happened to attend the reception is described in one of several interesting memos I found in my FBI file, after obtaining it recently under the Freedom of Information Act (FOIA). But more on that later.

After outgrowing the two-room suite on Constitution Avenue, we moved to the old Keith-Albee Building (originally the Riggs Building) at 15th and G Street NW, home of the historic Rhodes Tavern and the RKO Theater.

Again, getting a lease was not without hurdles, but this time, White House aide Max Rabb intervened on our behalf. Five years later, in 1964, talk of demolition plans led us again to look elsewhere. (As it turned out, there was more than a decade of wrangling between developers, the government, and preservationists before the building finally came down, except for some of its ornate facade, in 1978.)

We set our sights on a new building just a half-block from the White House, at 1750 Pennsylvania Avenue NW, and were initially turned away. Racial discrimination was certainly more subtle, but it was still a major factor in D.C. life. We secured the space only with the help of my friend Walter Trohan, Washington Bureau Chief of the *Chicago Tribune*. The *Trib* was our neighbor in the Keith-Albee Building, and since its staff was moving to the new, so-called "Communications Building," Trohan saw no reason why Johnson Publishing Company should not be able to lease space there, too. Trohan threatened not only to run a report in the *Tribune* about the agent's refusal to rent to a black publication, but also to urge colleagues in the National Press Club to boycott the building. As a result, JPC became the first, and for several months the only, tenant on the building's thirteenth floor. (Most D.C. buildings tall enough to have a thirteenth floor simply skipped it on the elevator pad, going directly from 12 to 14, presumably to satisfy superstitious tenants.) JPC not only got a large suite fronting the capital's "main street," but eventually had the company of stellar co-tenants such as *Newsweek*'s astute Eleanor Clift, the inimitable Art Buchwald, and political columnists Rowland Evans and Robert Novak, all of whom became our good friends as well as colleagues.

Once again overlooking the parade route, our suite would become the site of one of the inaugural's best private parties, as hundreds of guests were welcomed by Mr. and Mrs. Johnson to lavish refreshments and window views of the parade. The inaugural party ultimately became so popular that we moved it to the building's spacious main entrance lobby. (When the nation's first black president was inaugurated in 2009, the Secret Service, for security reasons, ordered that the building as well as others in close proximity to the White House remain closed on Inauguration Day, abruptly ending a fifty-year tradition at a most ironic moment.)

In addition to the Inauguration Day festivities, invitations to the annual Christmas party were as sought after as box seats at a baseball game, so much so that even these receptions eventually swelled beyond the bureau to the thirteenth floor elevator lobby. By 1977, the Yuletide party was even covered by *The Washington Post*. Mr. J. never failed to provide a generous budget for an elegant, hot and cold buffet, served by Washington's best black caterers, and a well-stocked bar.

The guests—black and white—at these events included major figures in the government, and thus major news sources and contacts, with the political make-up weighing in favor of whichever party was moving into, or remaining in, the White House. We never knew who might pop in. Senator John Warner showed up at one of the inaugural parties with his beautiful wife, Elizabeth Taylor, who graciously posed for pictures with the publisher and Mrs. J. When the senator was called back to Capitol Hill shortly after their arrival, the down-to-earth and very personable actress seemed genuinely disappointed as she was whisked away, objecting, "I didn't get my bourbon and branch." Other guests were quick to offer to look after his wife until he returned, but Warner declined, "No, no, she has to come with me."

Another unlikely guest at a Christmas party during the George H. W. Bush administration was the controversial—but personally very likable—Lee Atwater, the man behind the Bush campaign's infamous Willie Horton ads. Described by even his closest political colleagues as "ruthless," Atwater was known for dirty tricks and unscrupulous attacks on the character and fitness of candidates and their family members alike. Black Republicans, however, insisted that whatever his faults, Atwater, whose leisure pursuits as an R & B musician included playing guitar with B. B. King, was no racist, but that like so many others in the high-stakes game of politics, he was willing to use race as well as just about anything else to win. That defense did not satisfy Howard University students who protested in outrage when he was appointed a trustee of the historic black institution, and forced his resignation from the board. The political strategist would later undergo a crisis of conscience and religious conversion while battling an aggressive brain tumor that killed him at age 40 in 1991. In his last months, Atwater publicly apologized to the people his tactics had most injured, and acknowledged that he had learned something about the nature of love, brotherhood, and relationships that he had never understood before and probably never would have, if it weren't for his illness.

The Washington bureau also hosted seminars for groups of journalism students. The logistics for those were handled by my stalwart right-hand, our reporter/office manager, and eventually associate editor, E. Fannie Granton, a social worker in an earlier career and my first hire for the bureau. I met Fannie when I came to Washington on assignment. She worked at the Urban League, one of my regular stops, where she would make space available for me to work and use the phone. Fannie had some law school training as well as an uncanny ability both to see through phonies and to spot the rising stars. She was active in *The* Washington Press Club, organized by women when they were excluded from D.C.'s National Press Club, and had a devoted following of newswomen, government workers, and other professionals who

E. Fannie Granton (l), my first hire for JPC's Washington Bureau, managed the office like a mother hen, looking out for the rest of us, which by the mid-sixties included photographer Maurice Sorrell, reporter Ragni Lantz (for racial reasons my most controversial hire in fifty-one years as bureau chief), secretary Mary Whiteman, and reporter Bernard Garnett. (Courtesy of author.)

gathered for homemade holiday feasts at her condominium in the Columbia Heights section of Washington. A self-described "old maid," she lived with her father and two of her eleven siblings, a brother and sister, and knew everybody in Washington's "in" crowd. Better than that, the "insiders" told her things without her even asking, leading to her byline on a weekly column, "Washington Scene." Her steady hand on the helm enabled me to travel without worry, and even stay away for weeks as I did during the Little Rock school desegregation crisis in 1957.

In the 1960s, we added more reporters to the staff, including a young, blonde, Swedish journalist named Ragni Lantz who was as dedicated to the civil rights cause as anybody. I took hell from some quarters for hiring a white reporter, but I was not about to back down. I believed if blacks truly wanted integration and equal opportunity, we should practice what we preached.

The evening poker games around the office's sprawling conference table became not only a tradition, but something of a legend. The players and kibitzers over the decades included a diverse, multiracial, multicultural cast of political, fourth estate, civil service, foreign service, and civil rights figures. American Jewish Committee D.C. representative Brant Coopersmith, even better at chess than he was at poker, worked the delicate and sometimes broad gaps between the Jewish community and blacks, Christians, and Muslims. He had years of experience in civil rights from New York to

New Orleans, where in the early 1950s, he and a Catholic priest traveled like modern day circuit riders from churches to synagogues in the Deep South urging the congregations to take a stand on racial and social issues. In D.C., he hobnobbed with the Catholic hierarchy, while working closely with community leaders such as the Reverend John Steinbruck, pastor of Luther Place Memorial Church on Thomas Circle in the heart of what was then the red-light district, and founder of the block-long N Street ministry for the homeless that included a medical clinic, a temporary residence for displaced and abused women, and a thrift shop. One of the stories Steinbruck liked to tell about him was how Brant had volunteered himself, Steinbruck, and the Reverend Bob Pruitt of the Metropolitan African Methodist Episcopal Church (known as the "National Cathedral of African Methodism") as exchange hostages for those held by Hanafi Muslims at the District Building (city hall), the B'nai B'rith headquarters, and the Islamic Center in March, 1977. Members of the sect had killed one man, a young reporter, shot city official and civil rights veteran Marion Barry in the chest, and taken 150 hostages for almost two days. Steinbruck's punchline was that "Coop" had forgotten to ask his friends first before volunteering them! The offer was turned down anyway, and the siege finally ended with the release of the original hostages.

The U.S. Information Agency was a neighbor in our building, and its foreign press office was headed by Jim Pope, a veteran of more than twenty years with the agency. A native of Sharon, Pennsylvania with a master's degree from Boston University, and years of experience serving abroad, Jim was probably the most effective, respected, and valued emissary between Washington's black leaders and the growing number of African ambassadors.

When the Republicans took the White House in the early '70s, Nixon presidential aide and former Atlanta newspaperman Stan Scott joined the games. Like other blacks who served Republican presidents, Stan received few bouquets from the black press, but our office was one place he could let his hair down and feel at home. While Democratic aides had the support of the Congressional Black Caucus, a growing number of mayors and other local elected officials, as well as heavy sponsorship from the black press and millions of black voters, a black Republican survived pretty much by his own wits. When it came to the White House, blacks couldn't let four or more years go by standing on the outside, looking in. The period between Nixon's election in 1968 and Clinton's in 1992 showed how important it was to have effective insiders, when only one Democratic administration—Jimmy Carter's—interrupted the decades-long Republican hold on the White House.

While I believed it was important to support the black Republicans who were trying to keep equal opportunity on the agenda no matter who was in the White House, inevitably, a few came along who were beyond help.

One of them was a younger man whom I'd known for many years, and personally liked despite our differing perspectives on major issues affecting black Americans. Clarence Pendleton, brought up in Washington, D.C., was working with the Urban League in San Diego when President Reagan appointed him chairman of the U.S. Commission on Civil Rights, after he'd been recruited to the campaign by attorney Ed Meese. I have in my files a letter from "Penny," as we called him, attached to the text of a speech he'd made to the Akron Roundtable on November 15, 1984. In his note, he commented that it seemed as though our "difference of opinion" about where Black America was had "affected our friendship," and added that he understood. In fact, I still liked him, although I wondered whether he had flat out lost his mind.

When Penny switched parties and joined the Reagan administration, he became the point man for attacks on affirmative action, calling it a "bankrupt public policy." His Akron speech had made headlines around the country, although the first several pages read like a legal brief that would put even a luncheon audience to sleep. But after getting the constitutional references, founding fathers' pronouncements, and legal citations out of the way, Penny displayed his real value as a black man in that administration with comments like: "I say to America's Black leadership 'Open the plantation gates and let us out!' . . . We refuse to be led into another political Jonestown. . . . No more Kool-Aid. . . ." And for good measure, "I hear the call for freedom that the press will never report. . . . I even hear it from the guys at 9th and U Streets in Washington, D.C., with whom I used to hang out."

All of us around the poker table who knew Penny from his pre-Reagan days had a hilarious time suggesting the kinds of things he'd really be likely to hear from the guys at 9th and U Streets. Finally, his rhetoric became an embarrassment even to ultra conservatives in the administration when he affronted the women's movement by calling the theory of comparable worth (that is, equal pay for jobs of comparable worth) "probably the looniest idea since Looney Tunes." In concert with Reagan's other appointments to the civil rights commission and its staff, he managed to do the tiny agency irreparable harm, after its three historic decades of calling national attention to difficult issues and recommending legislative and administrative remedies. Although he had frequently criticized others for blaming problems on racism, he actually suggested that a cut in the agency's budget had "racial overtones." I wondered if he ever saw the irony in that.

One summer night in the mid-'70s, I went home around midnight pretty happy that I'd managed to win the last hand, and had a check for $25 tucked safely in my wallet. When I proudly presented the check to my wife with a bountiful, "Here, baby, this is for you!" she brought me back down to earth

An affable man, but because of his domestic policies not a favorite among the ten presidents I covered. (White House photo.)

by pointing out that the check was payable to one of the evening's other poker players. This was the kind of detail we didn't pay much attention to as we dealt the cards, sipped the scotch, and swapped the stories.

The Washington bureau was a haven for blacks who often were "firsts," or among the few, in a government agency, and relished the after-hours camaraderie at JPC. New appointees in the administration, as well as newly elected members of Congress, were often advised that JPC was a "must" stop when they came to D.C. We always made them feel welcome, regardless of political party or philosophical bent, whether liberal or conservative. Some of them came by to suggest a news item for Ticker Tape or plant the seed of a longer article. On one occasion, however, our guests were insisting that we drop what looked to us like a good story. That's when it got ugly.

THE "RAILROADERS"

It was early afternoon when my secretary buzzed me on the intercom, announcing that two men "from the railroad," whom I later could only describe as "goons," were in the reception area asking to see me. In a moment, two big, ugly, white guys in suits walked into my office and got right to the point. I had written something in *Jet* about a rumor that South Carolina segregationist senator Strom Thurmond had a black daughter whom he was supporting financially. (The rumor went even further to say that when she was a child, the girl was picked up at her home by a limousine and taken to school every morning.) The thugs told me in no uncertain terms that it would be very unwise for me or the magazine to pursue this story in any way whatsoever. When they finished, they seemed to look at me long and hard as I reached for the pack of cigarettes on my desk, tapped one from the wrapping, and hoping my hands wouldn't shake as I slipped it between my lips, lit it, and in the established custom of many newsmen of the day, drew in the smoke as if considering a response. In fact, at that moment, I was utterly speechless. If my visitors thought I was about to say something, they didn't seem to care. They obviously hadn't come to debate or discuss the issue, so before I had time to blow the smoke out between my dry lips (I never inhaled—honestly), they turned and left as abruptly as they'd appeared.

My secretary must have thought the visit very peculiar because within seconds she poked her head in the door—maybe to see if I was okay—and commented disapprovingly that "those men" had never removed their hats. It was all I needed to break the tension. I chuckled at how nice it would have been if the social faux pas had been their only transgression. I told her what had happened and we both agreed that I could probably use a stiff drink. We also knew I'd better warn Chicago, in case the publisher was about to be paid a similar visit. After I conferred with Bob Johnson, *Jet*'s managing editor, we agreed that the thugs were probably right—at least about it being unwise for us to pursue the rumors. The story was out there, and even without *Jet*'s help, it would continue to circulate as long as Thurmond lived. And sure enough, six months after his death at 100 in 2003, a seventy-eight-year-old retired teacher named Essie Mae Washington-Williams came forward and revealed that she'd been that little girl, and was indeed the illegitimate daughter of Strom Thurmond, who at twenty-two had bedded a sixteen-year-old maid in his parents' home. By then, it was sort of an interesting but ho-hum story, as everybody believed it was true all along. The news, it seemed, was that unlike so many hypocritical plantation men who had slipped into the slaves' quarters over the centuries, Thurmond at least had seen to it that his off-spring and her mother were taken care of financially.

LIFE AFTER *JET*

Over the half century when *Jet* operated a Washington bureau, the world of black Americans—and indeed the entire country—changed more profoundly than during any other period in American history. Coast to coast,

Jet reported it all, and with every passing decade of the movement, played such an intrinsic part in the struggle for freedom that in 1996, on its forty-fifth anniversary, veteran activist Dick Gregory said of John H. Johnson's little magazine:

> One day we are going to classify Black life—"Black life before *Jet* and Black life after *Jet*." I cannot imagine how miserable life must have been before, living on this planet if you were Black without *Jet*. *Jet* was the only publication covering us from the point of view of news. No one shocked the conscience of the nation and the world like *Jet*.

In 2006, civil rights activist Rev. Al Sharpton marked another anniversary with a similar observation:

> *Jet* has lasted fifty-five years because *Jet* became the single most important barometer of where Blacks were at any given time . . . *Jet* literally took us from the back of the bus to the front of Capitol Hill . . . We did it with a little magazine in our pockets that told us we were more than the large magazine of the newsstands would ever tell us we were.

John H. Johnson made it possible for me to venture out from our Washington bureau to any place in the country—or even the world—in pursuit of a story, while every week for fifty-two years my Ticker Tape USA column described what was going on behind the scenes in national politics, reported the smallest victories as well as opportunities, and served as a relentless recruiter, unabashedly telling our readers that this or that government figure was looking for a black aide, or that one of the nation's military academies was seeking black recruits.

From our perch on the top floor of 1750 Pennsylvania Avenue NW, our magazines had a front row seat as black Americans moved from being mere pawns in election campaigns to winning the presidency, in an amazing political drama that played out over half a century, and was memorialized in words and photographs between their glossy covers.

8

"A COMMUNIST UNDER EVERY BED"

In New York City in August 1956, a year after the Till kidnapping and murder, the Mound Bayou physician and voting rights activist who had spurred the middle of the night race through the backwoods to find prosecution witnesses solemnly told *Jet* that he had left the Mississippi Delta forever. With a $1,000 bounty placed on his head by white racists, forty-eight-year-old Dr. T. R. M. Howard said he felt he could "do more in the battle for Negro rights alive anywhere in the North than dead in a weed-grown grave in Dixie." Dr. Howard and his wife left behind a thriving medical clinic, a solid block of modern homes—described as probably the best housing for Negroes in the area—and hundreds of acres of rich farmland, ultimately sold, lot by lot, to Negro farmers. One 360-acre lot of cotton land, surrounded on all sides by white plantations, was sold to a white syndicate. He estimated his total losses at more than $100,000, but concluded that his own life and the safety of his family were worth the price.

Dr. Howard resettled on Chicago's South Side, accepted a post as medical director of a black-owned firm, and moved up to the presidency of the National (the Negro) Medical Association, where he proposed a broad educational campaign toward the integration of Negro doctors and patients into white hospitals. The most dramatic change, however, was in his political outlook. After twenty-five years as a Democrat, the Mississippi activist announced that he would support the Republican ticket that year and indefinitely into the future, explaining, "A vote for any Democratic candidate anywhere for any office is simply a vote for my former neighbor, Senator James Eastland," the diehard segregationist from Mississippi's Sunflower County. Reminded that Republican bedfellows would include the likes of Wisconsin Senator Joseph McCarthy, Dr. Howard acknowledged it was not a great choice, but he'd rather side with McCarthy "who thinks there's a Communist under every bed, than with Senator Eastland who thinks there should be a Negro dangling from every rope."

In 1958, Dr. Howard ran unsuccessfully against Democratic Congressman William Dawson for the latter's House seat, and although he never sought office again, by the time of his death in 1976 he was still a major figure in South Side Chicago politics and medical care, and remained an outspoken proponent of civil rights and equal opportunity for blacks. Even before he left the Delta, he had proven his fearlessness in confronting not only white supremacists, but also the nation's chief law enforcement officer.

Starting in late 1955, Dr. Howard provoked the anger of FBI Director J. Edgar Hoover by wondering publicly why the FBI, despite its almost legendary crime solving scorecard, could not solve the murders of so many Negroes in the South. Dr. Howard's criticism of the bureau followed unsuccessful pleas that the FBI take over the Till case and others involving racial violence against Negroes. The exchange made front-page news and included Hoover's angrily accusing Howard of making "false and irresponsible charges."

A few years later, Dr. Martin Luther King's similar criticism of the FBI would not only erupt into a public feud, but would escalate into Hoover's extraordinary effort to destroy the civil rights leader. The full extent of Hoover's campaign against King would not come to light until the late 1970s (when both were deceased), after congressional hearings on intelligence activities and the Freedom of Information Act (FOIA) opened miles of government files, including the FBI's, to public examination.

We knew very little in the mid-1950s about what the FBI, or more specifically J. Edgar Hoover himself, thought about the growing civil rights movement. The rights Negroes were seeking to exercise were constitutional rights, as the federal courts were confirming, and the FBI's repeated demurrer that it lacked jurisdiction in case after case of kidnap, murder, lynching, beating, and an unbelievable array of other crimes against Negroes, was provoking criticism and distrust of the bureau. *Jet* reported the criticism and in the interest of fairness repeatedly invited Hoover to respond. How that played out is documented in my own FBI file, which I requested under the FOI and Privacy Acts. The day before Thanksgiving 2009, I received it, and read not only about myself, but, to my amazement, my father.

According to the file, the FBI's interest in me began with a routine background check triggered by my application for federal employment in 1951, while waiting for my job at *The Washington Post*. The very first memo in the file was somewhat of a shock. Sometime in the late 1940s, someone had accused my Baptist minister father of being "pro-Communist!" As the FBI tells it:

> Bureau files contain a document headed "Portal to Portal Pay," dated January
> 23, 1947, at Youngstown, Ohio, the source of which is not indicated. In the
> document it is revealed [interesting that the writer used "revealed" instead of
> "alleged"] that one S. S. Booker, a Negro minister of the Third Baptist Church,
> Youngstown, Ohio, is pro-Communist. The source of this allegation is not
> revealed in the document, andno [sic] further information is set out concern-
> ing Booker other than the previous statement.[1]

The upshot of this information was that the Cleveland office would conduct a preliminary inquiry to determine "whether S. S. Booker is identical
with the applicant or a close relative" and "if identity is established, further
preliminary inquiry should be conducted to determine the reliability of the
above information."

The memo continued, "In view of the fact that the applicant has been
employed by newspapers in the past and he has been affiliated with the
Newspaper Guild, CIO, this case should be assigned to a mature and experienced agent, and discretion and good judgment should be exercised at all
times in conducting this investigation."

I guess I should be grateful for that, in light of how easy it was to ruin
someone's reputation and career in the days of the "Red Scare."

According to the file, the investigation continued and another memo to
FBI headquarters, dated November 6, 1951, concluded that Baptist minister
S. S. Booker was my father, and that the "reliability of the information" in the
original bureau memo "could not be ascertained." Furthermore, inasmuch as
"reliable and informed sources" had indicated that I was "anti-Communist,"
no further investigation was being conducted.

One of the FBI "sources" who had propelled me beyond the "non-Com-
munist," to the "anti-Communist" column, was a member of the Subversive Activities Squad of the Cleveland Police Department, who advised the
bureau (accurately) that I had written several "anti-Communist" articles for
the Cleveland *Call and Post*. The source went on to say that I was "interested
in such organizations as the National Association for the Advancement
of Colored People for the reason that [I] believed in civil rights," and that
the source believed that I would "fight for the rights of [my] race but never
to the extent of joining any organization subversive to the United States."
(The memo also mentioned that my father was a member of the NAACP,
which clearly was on Hoover's watch-closely list at the time, although he
had a friendly relationship with Walter White, its national secretary, and had
made public statements of support for the organization.) Another source,
like me a former officer of the Newspaper Guild, CIO, volunteered that I
had been outspoken in my desire "to better the colored race" but that I had

often spoken out against the tactics used by the Communists, and the source knew for a fact that the Communist Party had attempted to ruin my reputation and character because of my speaking against them.

A memorandum dated a day earlier from SAC, Baltimore, had also referenced my brief newspaper career in that city. The gist of this report was that I had written an article in the *Afro-American* about the shooting death of a Negro by a Baltimore police officer. According to a "Baltimore Security Informant," cited in the memo, I was soon contacted by a representative of American Youth for Democracy, which, according to the FBI, was a Communist-linked organization, who allegedly advised me, "We want to get him [the officer] fired and will bring pressure to accomplish this." My response, according to the informant, was that the *Afro-American* "would give the case suitable publicity." Nothing wrong with "suitable." Baltimore SAC had nothing further to report.

Although the inquiry found no evidence to substantiate the anonymous slander of my patriotic, Baptist father, the allegation and the fact that it was unsubstantiated were repeated in a later "synopsis" of a "summary" report on me. It's unclear whether this later report, dated May 27, 1957, was in response to a request dated the same day from J. Edgar Hoover to Messrs. Tolson, Boardman, Belmont, and Nichols:

> Honorable Bernard Shanley, Appointment Secretary to the President, called to advise that he attended a dinner Saturday night [May 25, 1957] given by the colored press. At this dinner there was an individual by the name of [name deleted] of Boston, Massachusetts, who made disparaging remarks about various individuals and later several friends of Shanley remarked to him that they believed [name deleted] to be a left-winger and indicated they thought he, [name deleted] should be checked. Mr. Shanley indicated that [name deleted] was affiliated with the Afro-American Newspaper. Mr. Shanley stated that if it is a fact that [name deleted] is a left-winger then he, Shanley, would also be suspicious of Simeon Booker, chairman of the above dinner. I told Mr. Shanley that I would be glad to check on these two individuals and would let him know the results.

Oddly, the memo closes:

> Very truly yours,
> John Edgar Hoover
> Director

Besides shuddering at the idea of a White House aide requesting an FBI background check on a newspaperman for making "disparaging remarks

about various individuals" at a press dinner, as well as a check on the dinner chairman for no apparent reason at all, I was curious about who the
dangerous "disparager" might have been. I was also curious as to whether
Hoover's odd closing to an internal staff memo might have been a signal to
the recipients that he knew the request was ludicrous. That latter answer I
still don't know. But I did learn the identity of the alleged "disparager" from
a long-saved souvenir, the silver-covered program from the Fourteenth
Annual Dinner of the Capital Press Club, of which I was president between
1956 and '57, and served as 1957 dinner chairman. The Club was founded
on February 2, 1944, years before the National Press Club admitted its first
black member, Louis Lautier, and even longer—twenty-seven years—before
it admitted women as members. The Capital Press Club was home to both.
Scanning the dinner program, I saw that the alleged perpetrator was William Worthy, Boston-born reporter for the *Afro-American* newspapers,
winner of the club's "Freedom of the Press Award," and, coincidentally, a
member of the Harvard Nieman Class of 1957 (the fourth minority journalist to win the Fellowship).

I have no recollection or record of Worthy's remarks at the dinner, but
whatever he had to say, one has to wonder where was Shanley, a Columbia University and Fordham Law graduate, when they covered the First
Amendment in either institution. The newspapers didn't focus on Worthy's
remarks, but rather on Mrs. Nixon's being awarded the club's "International Relations Award" in recognition of her grace and charm while traveling abroad with her husband. Besides the vice president and Mrs. Nixon,
who were the guests of honor, the dinner drew an audience of 500 people,
including African ambassadors and embassy staff, Senator Theodore Francis Greene (R-RI), oldest member of Congress and chairman of the Senate
Foreign Relations Committee, and Representatives James Roosevelt (D-CA)
and Frances P. Bolton (R-OH), who was the principal speaker. Elected to
Congress after the death of her husband, Congressman Chester C. Bolton of
Cleveland, she was considered one of the outstanding members of the Committee on Foreign Affairs, had served at different times as both chairman
and ranking member of the Subcommittee on the Near East and Africa, and
had excellent grounding in the problems of dependent countries.

I don't know what the FBI check revealed, or what Hoover told Shanley
about Worthy, but he was at the time a very courageous journalist who went
places the government didn't want reporters to go. In the 1950s, this included
mainland China. When he returned from that trip, the U.S. Department of
State confiscated his passport. Undaunted, he then went to Cuba to report
on Fidel Castro and the early days of the revolution, and was prosecuted
when he returned to the U.S. without a valid passport. (I was also one of

several black journalists who descended upon Havana in 1958 after Castro's forces rolled into the capital. Since travel by Americans to Cuba had not yet been prohibited—that was not until 1961—and the rest of us had valid passports, the worst problem we encountered was a mob that seemed about to overturn our taxi. They finally stopped rocking it and moved on when someone recognized the press passes we were frantically waving.)

Worthy's conviction was overturned by a federal court of appeals which found the statute under which he was prosecuted unconstitutional. In the 1980s and '90s, he taught journalism at both Boston and Howard universities, and until 2005 served as special assistant to the Dean of the School of Communications at Howard. Having lived a bold life as a journalist, and when he saw fit, a "disparager" of whomever and whatever he thought warranted disparaging, he undoubtedly nettled many bigger fish than Bernard Shanley.

Interestingly, a then relatively unknown young minister, the Reverend Martin Luther King, Jr., President of the Montgomery Improvement Association, which was currently leading the bus boycott in the Alabama capital, was also at the dinner, where he was named the club's "Man of the Year." The Capital Press Club was ahead of the wave in recognizing the rising star of the civil rights movement. Rev. King, if he said anything, apparently did not provoke any concern from Bernard Shanley.

According to a *New York Times* obituary in 1992, Shanley, in addition to being a top White House aide to President Eisenhower, was a prominent New Jersey lawyer and politician who twice ran unsuccessfully for the United States Senate, and remained active in politics until he resigned as a Republican national committeeman two weeks before his death at age eighty-eight. While in the White House, according to the *Times*, he was gatekeeper to the Oval Office, deciding who the president saw and for how long. He lived on a sixty-nine acre estate and raised sheep. Not a word about how he felt about freedom of the press.

It seems unlikely that the next memorandum in my file was written in response to Hoover's oddly signed request, because it is dated the same day—May 27, 1957—and the date stamp on the Hoover request indicates his memo was sent from the Director's Office at 5:26 p.m. It's possible, of course, that the Hoover memo only served to document an earlier oral request from the director, or that, because Hoover's request was prompted by a call from the White House, the priority assigned to a response caused it to be generated within hours on the same day. It also could have been a coincidence, and the information memo about me dated May 27, 1957, may have been initiated because I was about to travel to Africa with Vice President Nixon. In any case, the memo from "M. A. Jones" to "Mr. Nichols" serves to refresh my memory about how I became acquainted with then FBI Inspector Deke DeLoach, who later rose to the number three position in the bureau.

The "Synopsis" section of the memo mentioned that in September 1955, I was a speaker "at a mass meeting sponsored by the National Association for the Advancement of Colored People," adding later that the "case of Emmett Louis Till was discussed." Knowing now lots of things we didn't know in the 1950s about J. Edgar Hoover, it is clear that because of Communist efforts to infiltrate and influence minority groups, labor organizations, and other targets, anyone associated with even such a mainstream organization as the NAACP was considered suspect—a possible "left-winger," a Communist sympathizer or puppet, or even a Communist—until he or she did something to prove otherwise. And if the FBI reported, as in my case, that you were "extremely interested in civil rights," the rest of the sentence had better read, as it also did in my case, "but he was not believed to be Communist tinged."

While Hoover was suspicious of civil rights activists, blacks battered by threats and actual violence in the South had their own doubts about the director. Dr. T. R. M. Howard was not the only black activist asking publicly why the FBI couldn't— or wouldn't—do more to protect civil rights workers when local Southern law enforcement agencies were either complicit in or nonresponsive to the violence in Mississippi and elsewhere in the South.

The January 19, 1956, issue of *Jet* addressed the question of the day: "Why the FBI Can't Stop Mississippi Terror." Citing the recent murders of nine Negroes, including Emmett Till and another teenager, and the wave of fear gripping the backwoods cotton plantations of Mississippi, I reported that the FBI had found a jurisdictional basis to look into only three of the cases (Lee, Smith, and Courts), with no justice resulting from any of the investigations. In Mississippi specifically, FBI intervention was not enough to frighten "murder-bent" race rabble who knew that during the past twenty-five years, the FBI's investigations had not resulted in a single civil rights conviction in the state. Although FBI officials refused to discuss their operations in the state, observers argued that the agency was "stopped cold" in Mississippi for several reasons. First, its agents received little cooperation from local law enforcers, some of whom actually defied "the outside interference." Second, both Negro and white witnesses were afraid to talk because of fear of reprisals and the lack of adequate protection. It should be noted that the bureau didn't make it easy for anyone to chat with its agents, even if they wanted to. Since they no longer had an office in Mississippi, federal agents, always wearing dark, single-breasted suits, with a revolver bulging under the jacket, white dress shirts, dark, narrow neckties, and snap-brim hats would arrive from New Orleans or Memphis in government-issued black cars with black sidewall tires and Tennessee or Louisiana plates. It was never any secret when the FBI was in town, who they were, and who, if anybody, was talking to them. Third, the staffs of the U.S. attorneys (nominated by area congressmen), as well as the trial juries, were composed of whites, who did not appear interested in convicting their neighbors or kin. Therefore, although top FBI authorities denied it officially, some admitted privately and unofficially that the situation in Mississippi was "hopeless" unless and until the Federal government were to take stern measures to break the back of the "lawless white elements."

Congressman Charles Diggs had asked the FBI in early 1956 to open a Mississippi office in the aftermath of the violence in the Delta following the Mound Bayou rally.[2] Such an office had existed until 1946 when the bureau closed it, claiming insufficient caseload to justify its continuance. (There would not be another until just months before the presidential election in 1964, when President Johnson directed the bureau to open an office in Jackson, after the murders of civil rights workers Michael Schwerner, Andrew Goodman, and James Chaney.)

While "top FBI" officials had refused to discuss the situation in Mississippi on the record, I thought the director himself might be willing to comment, particularly in light of mounting criticism of the agency's track record in the state. According to my FBI file, after my *Jet* article, I offered Hoover the opportunity to do that:

> On January 30, 1956, Booker called at your [Mr. Nichols's] office and talked with Mr. Deloach. He discussed an article presenting the FBI's side of the racial controversy in the South. He desired an appointment with the Director in order to get the Director's views. He was advised of the Director's busy schedule, and, as an alternative, it was mutually agreed that he would forward a list of questions which we would answer. Booker forwarded such a list, and there were ten such questions listed having to do with racial conditions in the South. These questions were answered in detail, cleared with Mullen in the Department and forwarded to Booker under cover of a letter dated February 10, 1956. The March 15, 1956, issue of "Jet" magazine carried a feature article entitled "What the FBI is Doing in Dixie." This article was based on the answer to our questions submitted by Booker.[3]

The FBI answers focused on the bureau's limited jurisdiction, and the procedures pursuant to which it brought preliminary facts to the attention of the Civil Rights Section of the Justice Department, which would review them and order a full investigation if it appeared that a Federal law violation was involved. In addition to jurisdictional limitations, Hoover explained:

In some areas of the South, the FBI has found itself confronted with the problem of having to penetrate a "curtain of silence" in seeking the facts concerning
alleged Federal civil rights violations involving both Negroes and whites. There
are many persons who believe that civil rights matters are strictly the concern
of state authorities. These individuals feel that the Federal government is
intruding upon the sovereignty of the individual states . . . and fail to realize
that Congress, not the FBI, made the laws and so long as the laws remain in
force the FBI has a duty to investigate when directed.[4]

Declining to state whether he believed legislation was necessary to
help the FBI deal with racial violence, Hoover stated that the FBI was not
a "policy-making organization," and had a longstanding policy not to make
recommendations concerning legislation. He added, "[W]e feel that the FBI
is prepared to cope with any situation that represents a violation of Federal law within our jurisdiction." Asked whether Negro FBI Agents were
being used to solve racial crimes in the South, Hoover answered that "the
records of special agent personnel are not kept according to race, creed or
color." Hoover added that selection of an agent for a specific investigation
was predicated strictly upon the best available man, and that "Negro agents,
like all agents in the FBI, are assigned where they can render their most
effective service."

The article generated considerable interest, apparently, because according to the FBI memo, I wrote Hoover in June 1956, on behalf of the editors of
Ebony to ask if he would do a byline article for the magazine. "This request
was denied in view of the pressure of business."

I tried another approach, asking if the director would answer questions
off-the-record for members of the Capital Press Club, of which I was an
officer. Hoover again declined, citing his schedule, but also advising his men,
"We will not go in for panel discussions."[5]

Mr. and Mrs. Johnson invited both the FBI Director and Inspector
DeLoach to the January, 1957 Inauguration Day open house at JPC's Washington Bureau. The memo in my FBI file states that Hoover did not attend,
citing a "prior commitment," but DeLoach did, and Mr. Johnson made "com-
plimentary remarks to Mr. DeLoach concerning the FBI and the director."

And thus began a cordial, professional relationship with DeLoach, but a
relationship that at no time stopped *Jet* from publishing criticism of Hoover
or the bureau. In fact, in the November 14, 1957, issue of *Jet*, I commented in
Ticker Tape USA:

The growing number of violence cases directed against Negroes in the South
and the apparent laxity of police to take action is disturbing numerous leaders.

The administration has yet to successfully explain how FBI agents, who are used to track down—and often arrest—hunted men at gun-point, can only make investigations of civil rights cases.

Nor did JPC's contacts with the FBI make me feel any safer when I ventured into the Deep South. I told my wife that if I disappeared, she should tell DeLoach where I'd gone and maybe the G-men could at least find my body! For good measure, I always kept my own picture out of *Jet*, wore old clothes, and hoped that a Bible on the front seat of my car might disguise my identity as not just an outsider, but a journalist.

I shared this notion with DeLoach over lunch one day, and he chuckled, "Booker, they know who you are the minute you rent a car!" Of course, he was right, but I kept a low profile anyway.

DeLoach, in all those years, never asked me to compromise my journalistic integrity, "inform" on anyone, or share any information that I wouldn't publish in Ticker Tape. But he did tell me a couple of times if a trip I was planning would be exceptionally dangerous. (CORE Director Jim Farmer also had direct communications with DeLoach regarding dangerous situations he was about to confront. In his autobiography, Farmer describes one instance in which the FBI, if nothing more, apparently saved his life.[6]) While DeLoach would repeat the FBI mantra that it wasn't in the business of protecting people, he, like some other government officials we dealt with, could be very helpful in certain situations, including once helping us get a risky story. We were reporting on a lynching in Mississippi. A black convict had been taken from the jail by a mob the night before. I asked for a few minutes to interview the victim's cellmate while photographer David Jackson snapped some pictures, but the local authorities weren't about to let us in to see him. I called DeLoach and shortly afterward Dave and I were escorted into the jail. Dave got his pictures, while the witness and I had an extremely short conversation. Both of us were too scared to talk! On our way out of town, we heard the local radio blare: "Two frightened Negroes showed up at the county jail this morning." My God, I thought, that was some accurate reporting!

Any young reporter today who thinks it was inappropriate to maintain contacts in Hoover's FBI is simply clueless as to what it took to watch your back in the South of the 1950s and '60s. The conclusion that the bureau was "using" the black press belittles the intelligence of these pioneers and our own ability to "use" the bureau and any other means to get out a story that wasn't being covered in the white press.

The next memo in my file, and apparently the last one from the 1950s, documents DeLoach's response to a further invitation I extended, as president of the Capital Press Club, for Hoover to address the club on March 20, 1958. Getting brushed off again with excuses about the director's "other commitments" and "uncertain travel schedule," I was described as "persistent" for suggesting alternative dates of May 1 or 15. Still no deal, but the memo says I was assured that "the Director certainly had no hesitation whatsoever in appearing before any specific groups, however, he had found it necessary to decline many invitations that he personally would have liked."

The bureau offered an alternative—stories JPC might want to pursue about black agents. *Ebony* ran an article in September 1962, "The Negro in the FBI," which included many long quotes and observations by Hoover on the bureau's black agents, and on racial issues more generally. More than twenty years later, some critics of the FBI have called the piece propaganda. Whatever the FBI's purpose, that wasn't *Ebony's*. *Ebony* was about showing the superlative accomplishments of Negroes, particularly in rarified areas such as movie stardom, the bright lights of Broadway, and the palatial homes of self-made millionaires, and stellar sports figures. It was about projecting and preserving the dream of becoming affluent, of living like a movie star, of being recognized for superior performance. Or even becoming an FBI agent. The *Ebony* article did not challenge FBI recruitment practices or dispute Hoover's assertions. But it did show black men on the right side of badges and guns on the FBI firing range—and if that stirred some career aspirations on the part of any young black men, then it was all well and good. Just as it was all well and good if the photos of black agents upset the worldview of racist crackers.

Ebony generally didn't pick on anybody. It left that role to *Jet*. And in the December 10, 1964, issue, we pulled no punches in reporting on the decade-old war between Hoover and civil rights activists. On November 18, 1964, Hoover had held a briefing for a group of reporters from the Women's Press Club. In the course of "dispelling" certain "misconceptions" about the assignment of bureau personnel in civil rights cases—specifically, some assertions by the Reverend Martin Luther King, Jr.—Hoover gratuitously threw in his opinion that King was "the most notorious liar in the country." Undeterred by no fewer than three hastily scribbled notes from DeLoach suggesting he bracket the comment as off-the-record, Hoover told the women to "feel free" to print his remarks as given.[7]

Jet's coverage of that public eruption of hostilities between Hoover and King included a two-page spread in the December 10, 1964, issue, under the headline, "Fuss with Hoover Goes Way Back in Civil Rights History." Noting that Hoover not only refused to retract the "notorious liar" label he had pinned on Dr. King, the article described the "aging crime-buster" as trotting around the nation accusing unnamed targets of "carping, lying and exaggerating with the fiercest passion, spearheaded at times by Communists and moral degenerates," charging further that "they cry liberty when they really mean license." We noted that Hoover's vituperative oratory was nothing new, but a "shrill echo" from the past, and recounted in detail the angry exchange between Hoover and Dr. T. R. M. Howard almost a decade earlier, after Howard had challenged Hoover's suggestion that lynching had been halted and the KKK put out of business because of FBI action. The long history of Hoover's war with civil rights leaders included challenges from some who noted that while he criticized them, he failed to publicly condemn the murder of Negroes in Dixie. Nor were civil rights leaders alone on Hoover's list of the disfavored, which *Jet* noted included the U.S. Supreme Court, as well as the Warren Commission. (After reviewing *Jet* articles such as these, I'm amused by a latter-day historian's comment that I was on Hoover's "friends" list! There are two things of which I'm sure: it was a very short list and I wasn't on it.)

Had we known about it at the time, the *Jet* article might also have traced Hoover's reaction to any criticism from civil rights activists to a 1946–47 confrontation between the director and then NAACP lawyer Thurgood Marshall. Almost a decade before Dr. Howard, Marshall had criticized the bureau's failure to deal with hate crimes against blacks in the South and Hoover had erupted. The two men eventually shook hands, but only after Marshall's boss, Walter White, and Hoover's boss, Attorney General Tom Clark, as well as Hoover himself, apparently made clear to Marshall that only a fool would want the FBI as an enemy.[8] Thurgood Marshall was no fool.

My own FBI file contains two other memos in response to "name checks" requested by the White House in 1966 and 1971, respectively. Both repeated the same old information, but added two new items. The first was that a freelance writer I knew, Arthur M. ("Art") Brandel, who formerly worked for the *New York Times*, had registered with the Justice Department in 1965 as an agent for the government of Yugoslavia. According to the memo, in August 1963, "it was reported" that this acquaintance considered me "his best friend in the Washington area." And thus, we both wound up in each other's security files.

The second new piece of information was probably the best kind you could hope to have in your FBI file—the kind that shows you had integrity, professional ethics, and a backbone:

> In connection with another investigative matter, allegations were made that unknown individuals employed by the Federal Trade Commission furnished information to unauthorized persons, including Mr. Simeon Booker. These allegations were based on a story carried in the January, 1964 issue of "Jet"

magazine, relating to a then pending action of the Federal Trade Commission against a book publishing firm in New York City. At the instruction of the Department of Justice, Mr. Booker was subsequently contacted on February 26, 1965, at which time he declined to reveal the source of the information appearing in the January, 1964, article in "Jet" magazine, stating he felt to do so would violate his professional ethics and damage his reputation as a reporter.[9]

So all told, or at least based on all I learned from my FOIA request, I made out a lot better than my slandered father, who had never applied for a government job, never joined a union, never led a civil rights protest, and probably never met a Communist in his life.

THROUGH THE EYES OF HISTORY

Among the documents now housed at the Eisenhower Library is a short note from White House aide Max Rabb to Eisenhower press secretary Jim Hagerty that illustrates how sick was some of the behavior of official Washington, including the FBI, during the "Red Scare." On September 2, 1955, Mamie Till Bradley had sent a telegram to President Eisenhower pleading that he "personally see that justice is meted out to all persons involved in the beastly lynching" of her son in Mississippi. Although the case had aroused the entire country, and indeed the world, Eisenhower never responded. Today, among his administration's papers dealing with civil rights is a memo from Rabb to Hagerty dated October 23, one month after the Bryant/Milam acquittal, explaining that Mamie's telegram went unanswered not due to any oversight, but at "the direct suggestion" of the Department of Justice and Lou Nichols of the FBI.

Rabb, the president's advisor on minorities, explained, "While it cannot be said openly, the FBI had definite knowledge that Mrs. Bradley permitted herself to be the instrument of the Communist party, which seized upon the case as a cause célèbre and upon her as the means of making the race question a burning issue." Rabb went on, "while the facts in the case reflected discredit on those who perpetrated the crime," Lou Nichols had labeled Mrs. Bradley herself as a "phoney."[10]

Even today, all these years later, I can't find the words to describe how cold, myopic, and even delusional the thinking of these men must have been to draw the conclusions they did about the Till case, the "race question," and the depth of this mother's grief. They didn't know Mamie Till Bradley. None of them had ever met her. All they knew was that the Communist Party was demonstrating its sympathy for her, and with the cause of black Americans.

That was good enough for them to decide that the grieving mother did not deserve even a response, much less a word of condolence, from the president of the United States. And not that it was germane to the issue of whether the federal government should investigate whether this murdered black child's civil rights were violated, Rabb threw into the memo for good measure that the boy's father had been executed by the army in Italy on a sex charge. For these reasons, he concluded, it was felt "inadvisable to make a courteous reply." Mamie Till Bradley deserved better than that.

INFORMERS

After passage of the FOIA in the 1970s, there were other revelations about the FBI's tactics during the civil rights movement, including its use of paid informants, some of whom were involved in violence against blacks even while they were taking payouts from the bureau. One of the most curious revelations, however, has only recently come to light, apparently as a result of failure to redact information that the law permitted the FBI to withhold. It also has to do with someone who was at the Till trial.

The single most iconic photograph of that trial as well as of many other pivotal moments in the civil rights movement, was shot by a black photographer, Ernest Withers, for the Memphis *Tri-State Defender*. More than fifty years later, after Withers was deceased, a number of documents released by the FBI under the FOIA suggested that Withers had been a paid informant for the bureau during the latter days of the movement. Some people immediately called him a "Black Judas," while others, including one of the men closest at the time to Dr. Martin Luther King, Andrew Young (former congressman, Atlanta mayor, and U.S. Ambassador to the U.N.), have been less critical, observing that the nonviolent civil rights movement was at all times transparent, making it doubtful that a photographer, even one with broad access to the movement's leadership, would have had anything of value to sell the FBI. Whatever one concludes, Ernest Withers's photographs probably did more to advance the cause of civil rights than anything else in print, and that is his lasting legacy. As for anything else that's said about him, a dead man can't defend himself. Let him rest in peace.

9

IKE'S FIRST TERM

Dwight D. Eisenhower's eight years as president of the United States saw significant gains for America's Negro population, many of which were to his credit. But they were also years of horrific civil rights crimes that went unpunished, voting rights that were denied, and very difficult and dangerous challenges for blacks living in pockets of extremely reactionary thinking throughout the Deep South.

Early in his first term, the president demonstrated that he believed that public funds should not be used to discriminate against people on account of their race. He set about to complete the desegregation of the military, unfinished under Truman, and used the tools available to the White House, from legal strategies to privately exercised moral suasion, to desegregate the District of Columbia, from its public schools to its lunch counters. He even pressured the telephone company to hire blacks. He began appointing an unprecedented number of blacks to prominent positions in government, including the first black executive staff member in the White House, E. Frederic Morrow, and Chicago attorney J. Ernest Wilkins, whom Eisenhower appointed to several positions, including Assistant Secretary of Labor, making him the first black subcabinet member.

These and other actions initially convinced blacks that the president believed in fairness and had good intentions. I first covered some of Eisenhower's activities while I was reporting for *The Washington Post*. In a byline article on May 20, 1953, with the headline, "Ike Reaffirms Vow to End 'Second Class Citizenship,'" I reported on the president's remarks at the 10th anniversary luncheon of the United Negro College Fund at the National Press Club, attended by more than 400 guests, including Supreme Court justices and cabinet members. He gave a hint even then of the position he would repeat throughout his administration, that new laws would not bring about equality. He commended the Rockefeller family's contribution to the fund as doing something "within the framework of free enterprise" without "waiting for some kind of law" to get something done. Eisenhower would

Ike Reaffirms Vow to End
'Second-Class Citizenship'

By Simeon S. Booker
Post Reporter

President Eisenhower yesterday rearmed his campaign
promises against "second class

ties of leadership so evident, h
character and reputation in t
company so great that we h
to make special arrangemer
so that it was unnecessary f
him to pass completely t

At the United Negro College Fund's tenth anniversary luncheon in 1953,
President Eisenhower reaffirmed his campaign promise to end "second
class citizenship" but life for a black person in Washington, D.C., was still
"second class," even for me, the first black staff reporter at *The Washington
Post*. After two years, I left the paper and took a position with Johnson
Publishing in Chicago.

make it even clearer over the next eight years that he didn't believe in laws to
change how people acted.

Ike's presence at this event, plus his reiteration of his "no second class
citizenship" campaign pledge, impressed blacks, as did several of his early
actions and appointments. In his first year in office, he established a fifteen-
member Government Contracts Committee to prevent employers with government contracts from practicing race discrimination in hiring, and named
prominent Chicago attorney Wilkins vice chairman. In 1955, he signed an
executive order banning government hiring bias against Negroes, and order-
ing federal department heads to make periodic reports to the White House
on Negro hiring. *Jet* reported that blacks held fewer than fifty professional
jobs in all of Washington's federal departments and agencies at the time.
Agencies such as the Interstate Commerce Commission (ICC) and the Federal Communications Commission (FCC) refused even to consider Negroes
for any upgraded posts. The president also appointed a five-man Committee on Government Employment Policy to launch an immediate survey of
Negro employment in government and to recommend ways to increase
the "handful" of black professionals among its ranks. The committee was
chaired by Chicago minister-lawyer Archibald J. Carey, the first Negro to
head a White House committee, and Wilkins, who had since been appointed
Assistant Secretary of Labor.

But Eisenhower was also criticized for a number of omissions, such as
not taking steps to force builders who were getting federal aid to sell homes
to blacks, to whom less than half of one percent of new homes were available. This indifference to housing issues extended into his second term. In
late 1958, I reported in Ticker Tape that U.S. housing official Albert M. Cole
had just promised the nation's realtors that the administration had no desire

to use federal funds to "change local customs," while pledging more money for segregated housing.

Above all else, the president's silence on the 1954 Supreme Court ruling in *Brown v. Board of Education* was a sore point with blacks, who had persistently asked why he did not speak to the moral issue behind the Supreme Court's decision, use the influence of his office to urge compliance with the desegregation ruling, and make clear that as president he was prepared to enforce it. Nor were blacks alone in the perception that the White House was not fully supportive of the *Brown* decision. Earl Warren, Eisenhower's appointee as Chief Justice of the Supreme Court, wrote in his memoirs two decades later that the efforts of public officials and political candidates to thwart implementation of the court's decision were "aggravated by the fact that no word of support of the decision emanated from the White House," and moreover, that the president's "personal counsel," Bernard Shanley, "in an effort to allay Southern animosity against the administration," had even charged that the ruling had "set race relations in the South back a quarter of a century." Warren further included this blunt criticism of Ike's frequent mantra that new laws were not needed to protect civil rights: "The aphorism dear to the hearts of those who are insensitive to the rights of minority groups that discrimination cannot be eliminated by laws, but only by the hearts of people, also emanated from the White House."[1]

Eisenhower's arm's length relationship with civil rights leaders throughout his first term, during which he repeatedly refused their requests for a meeting, also suggested that he was overly sensitive to Southern white feelings. Some of his aides claimed he needn't bother to meet with black leaders because his record on race relations was good enough. Nobody bought it.

Civil rights was the hottest issue at the nominating conventions in August 1956. While Democrats assailed the president's nonexistent legislative record on civil rights, their own party came up with a weak civil rights plank that did little if anything to satisfy black demands. When the ballots were cast in November, Ike, despite black misgivings about his record, won almost 40 percent of the Negro vote. He didn't understand why he didn't win it all, or at least a big majority.

THE MOVEMENT CHOOSES AN IMAGE

As 1956 neared an end, the Montgomery bus boycott also ended, after the Supreme Court upheld a lower court ruling that segregation on the city's buses was unconstitutional. By some estimates, the boycott cost Montgomery's whites almost $1 million, and it gave the movement an enduring icon, the dignified seamstress Rosa Parks, whose arrest after refusing to relinquish her seat to a white person had touched off the protest. Mrs. Parks has been called "the mother of the civil rights movement" but many blacks believed that Mamie Till Bradley, when she insisted the casket of her mutilated and martyred son remain open for all the world to see, was really the flint that ignited the flames of protest in the breasts of the next generation. After being asked by the NAACP to speak at fundraising events, the organization turned on her, ostensibly because she asked for money to cover her expenses. She was on leave from a clerk's position with the U.S. Air Force in Chicago, and no longer had her government salary to cover her rent and other needs. Despite this, Roy Wilkins himself accused her of trying to capitalize on her only child's death.[2] However, FBI records that surfaced in later years reveal that the bureau probably played a part in Mamie's rejection for any role in the civil rights movement, by secretly and aggressively spreading their claim that the Communist Party was using her to "rabble rouse." It was a cruel blow to a woman who'd already suffered the cruelest of losses.

While the successful Montgomery bus boycott would inspire similar actions elsewhere, it was an isolated victory because it did not change the status quo anywhere else, even in the same state. The battle would have to be waged again and again in other cities. In Birmingham, for example, a black couple was jailed just weeks later for using a white waiting room in a train station. As another bus boycott in Tallahassee, Florida, dragged on, angry whites poured syrup into the gas tanks of anybody they considered a boycott sympathizer. As acts of violence against blacks proliferated throughout the Deep South, the Department of Justice professed a lack of jurisdiction in case after case. It was obvious, despite the president's dismissal of the need for new laws, that national civil rights legislation—the first in more than eighty years—was direly needed. At the end of his first term, Eisenhower finally agreed to submit a legislative proposal to Congress. In his January 1956 State of the Union Address, however, despite evidence that the black community was still seething in the aftermath of the Emmett Till murder and the travesty of that trial, Ike did not make a strong call for civil rights legislation. Instead, near the end of his long address, he merely recommended that Congress establish a bipartisan commission to thoroughly examine "persistent allegations" of voting rights violations. It was as if there'd been reports that cod were being overfished in the Atlantic, and someone should look into it. It would be a dismal four more years.

10

THE BATTLE OF LITTLE ROCK

On September 24, 1957, at about 6:00 p.m., 1,000 paratroopers of the 101st Airborne "Screaming Eagle" Division of the 327th Infantry Regiment began rolling into Little Rock, and dozens of reporters, followed by clusters of curious citizens, raced to watch them leap from trucks to their deployment at Central High School. When the first of the Negro troopers to dismount was brusquely ordered back on the truck, it attracted little notice. But when all the black soldiers in the convoy were ordered to remain on the trucks until they reached camp, they knew something else was unusual about this mission besides its domestic context. In one more bizarre concession to the radical, rowdy, and often violent segregationists of Little Rock, the pride of the integrated U.S. Army was being re-segregated for this mission. The apparent but unspoken rationale was to avoid further inflaming the passions of the mob. Nine months later, a local official gave the same reason for barring this reporter from attending the graduation of the first Negro student from the previously all-white Central High School.

Sixteen-year-old Ernest Green, wide-eyed with awe at the U.S. Army paratroopers that formed a protective phalanx around him and eight other Negro high school students as they entered the school the following day, predicted that one day, he'd "enlist in the 101st Airborne!"

As it turned out, Central High School's first black graduate went on to earn bachelor's and master's degrees from Michigan State University, become a successful investment counselor, and serve along the way as U.S. Assistant Secretary of Labor in the Carter administration. Nevertheless, decades after he uttered those words, Green acknowledged that he was forever indebted to the 101st Airborne for protecting the lives of black students as they courageously carved their names in history.

I was in Little Rock about a week before the effort to enroll nine black kids in the 2,000-student, white high school exploded into a civil rights battle viewed with horror and disgust around the world, thanks to mainstream media attention that even the most atrocious attacks on Southern blacks had never before attracted. One of my greatest satisfactions as a reporter has been living to see the brave young heroes of that battle achieve outstanding academic and professional success in an integrated society. I came to know them well in the days leading up to the greatest adventure of their lives, and in the painful months that followed, which for some turned into years. In addition to Ernest Green, the oldest of the nine and the only senior, the other students were Elizabeth Eckford, Jefferson Thomas, Terrence Roberts, Carlotta Walls, Minnijean Brown, Gloria Ray, Thelma Mothershed, and Melba Beals.

It was understandable that the soldiers of the 101st Airborne seemed like heroes to the nine teenagers. But the students knew there were other heroes in this story as well, and have repeatedly acknowledged their extremely brave parents, who, when told not to accompany the students to the school, had to rely on radio reports, some wildly inaccurate, for word of their well-being. Several lost the jobs they had held for years, solely because of their support for the integration effort. Just about all were threatened and ostracized in some way, and several ultimately had to move away. There was also the Reverend Dunbar Ogden, whom I considered one of the bravest, most conscientious, and dedicated men among the city's white clergy. There were a handful of other clergy who stepped up, but the unusual thing about the battle of Little Rock was the general lack of support of the black clergy, unlike their brothers of the cloth in Montgomery, Alabama, who had joined together in support of the ongoing bus boycott in that city. The black clergy in Little Rock did not want to rock the boat. And so leadership of the effort essentially rested on the shoulders of one woman, the indomitable Daisy Bates.

Any civil rights explosion in the South was a homecoming for the finest in the Negro press, who converged on the trouble spot knowing they could expect little help from the police. In Little Rock in September of 1957, their first stop—along with dozens of the 300 visiting newsmen from thirty-nine states and five other countries—would have been the brick ranch home of the civil rights activist and her husband, L. C. Bates, publisher of the *Arkansas State Press*. For some, the confident, well-informed co-editor of the paper may have been a surprise. No wild-eyed radical, Daisy Bates was a charming, attractive hostess who took the time to see that the visitors had cocktails or a piece of southern fried chicken as she gave interviews on the situation in Little Rock. I spent weeks there covering the unfolding drama, and never once saw a break in the cool, calm armor that surrounded Daisy by virtue of her extraordinary spirit.

I described the civil rights activist in *Jet* as being caught "like a cop" in a colossal traffic jam two weeks earlier, surrounded by a crush of newsmen, while absorbing and answering a withering crossfire of questions. She was, as usual, the center of controversy. Even so, with scores of reporters and commentators seeking exclusive stories, and white fanatics phoning almost every minute, she managed to talk to each parent and child about daily developments, meet with NAACP lawyers, and still iron her husband's shirts and fix meals. At day's end, near exhaustion from the month-long grind since school opened in September, she welcomed returning newsmen by name, and moved around cultivating the newcomers. Friend or foe, Little Rock Negroes, I wrote, regarded Daisy Bates as the "fightingest" woman in the state. Support for Daisy's efforts came from everyday folk, not the professional class, who criticized the NAACP as being too hard-hitting, and disparaged Daisy, the first woman to head the organization's Arkansas conference of branches, as a "one-woman show."[1] I had found similar attitudes throughout the Deep South in the 1950s, where most of the Negroes pushing for civil rights were lower-income people, except for a few independent leaders. Most professionals would have nothing to do with the crusade. When I covered a lynching in another city, a very prominent black family, which owned drug stores, shops, and a commercial building, had been asked by local activists to host my photographer and me in their home. They declined, saying that when it came to civil rights, "You can't win." One of the brothers, a doctor, went on, "Too many whites. Go along with them." There were many other professionals in the Black Belt who agreed with them. "Teach the lowly how to keep clean," one said, "and you'll do more in a year than in raising all of this hell in fifty years."

"We've been living well," a school principal told me. "We've had peace. Why start agitating?" Eventually the surge of sit-ins, African independence, and the emergence of impatient, often militant, black youth served to challenge these conservatives, and even remove some from positions of power within their communities.

The contented among the black middle class, including the majority of clergy who supported the segregated status quo, also bridled at the barbs regularly hurled at their complacency by Daisy and L. C. in the militant *Arkansas State Press.*

With a few college courses, but no degree on her resumé, Daisy carried the day with extraordinary determination and a strong will. She knew how to talk to power, and she had a fast tongue. White men undoubtedly felt more constrained engaging in repartee with the pretty, five foot three, 122-pound lady in a crisp, business-like dress and high heels than they would have in any exchange with a black man. Daisy knew the boundaries, but she could also be blunt and even testy. When the school board, for example, tried to select only "light Negroes" to integrate Central High, she declared, "We've got 215 kids. You can take the cream of the crop, or you can take them all." But they weren't going to do it based on skin tone.[2]

Standing rock solid behind Daisy, but neither desiring nor grabbing the spotlight, was rod-straight, stick-thin L. C. (for Lucius Christopher) Bates, twelve years her senior, and the fountain of her strength. Night after night, L. C. and a few volunteers stood guard outside their $30,000, nine-room "dream home" in an integrated Little Rock neighborhood. Through more than fifty attacks in two years, including four bombings, gunfire, and rocks hurled through the picture window, L. C. protected his home and his wife, while the Little Rock police insisted they couldn't spare a man to guard the embattled house. When the comfortable living room became too dangerous, the couple stopped using it, moving their strategy sessions and interviews to the back of the house or the basement. Much more difficult and heart-rending were the measures they took to protect the thirteen-year-old foster son whom they had raised. Early in the controversy, they spirited the boy away to an undisclosed location, where he remained for all the years the crisis dragged on. It was one thing to put their own lives on the line; they wouldn't do that to a young boy to whom they'd promised a decent life.

As the tension in Little Rock grew, and the segregationists threatened not only the Bateses and the nine students and their parents, but also anyone who supported them, the circulation of L. C.'s treasured newspaper dropped from a high of 20,000 to just 6,000. Its staff of nine declined to four. The pages also shrunk from full-size to tabloid after most advertisers stopped doing business with the weekly.

This wasn't the first time L. C.'s uncompromising journalism had threatened his newspaper's survival. The Bateses first caught the wrath of the downtown merchant class in 1941 (a year after they started the paper) by refusing to remain silent regarding the police killing of a Negro GI. Nine downtown stores withdrew ads when the paper instituted a drive against police brutality; one executive even predicted that the paper wouldn't last six months. But the Bateses turned their focus statewide, and pushed circulation by concentrating on churches and schools. After spending more than $10,000 to defend the paper's crusading policies in lawsuits, they found school integration the stumbling block to their personal security. In time, they would again lose most of their advertising.

Sitting with his gun by his side in an overstuffed easy chair in semi-darkness one night, alert to any sound outside the house, L. C. told me, "The only thing I hate about the whole business is that the Negro people are not responding to their own cause as I had hoped they would. It's not only here, it's a universal thing." He wasn't advocating violence—in fact, he'd never even shot to injure any of the vandals who attacked his home—but he just thought Negroes should stand up for their constitutional rights. Five feet eleven inches and about 150 sinewy pounds, L. C. looked older than his late fifties, and hardly able to fight anyone if it came to that. And yet he stood his ground and didn't run from the fight that would take everything he'd struggled years to build.

Born in Indianola, Mississippi (birthplace of the White Citizens' Councils), Bates had made a deal with his father, a farmer, to do all the plowing and pulling of corn provided he would not have to chop or pick cotton. Even as a boy, cotton picking and what it represented in the Mississippi social structure revolted Bates. Long before he went off to Wilberforce College and later became an advertising man in Memphis, his father gave him the philosophy that guided him from Indianola to Little Rock. "Never compromise a right," the old man always said. "Sacrifice a friend before you compromise a principle."

I asked L. C. if all the violence would ever make the couple leave and go North. His answer was so uncompromising, so steeled with quiet force, that I felt there was nothing more to say. He stared into the darkness and shaking his head ever so slightly, stated, "No one can drive us from Little Rock, no matter what they do. But on the day we realize what we set out to accomplish, and Negro children here have an unchallenged right to a decent education, then we'll leave Little Rock and the South, so that we can sleep nights." In the meantime, L. C. pursued his only hobby during the turmoil: a daily game of chess at a 9th Street barbershop. Some thought it was the quiet game that helped the newspaper publisher keep his calm amidst all the commotion.

Months later, after they had finally lost the newspaper, L. C. was not bitter. "I was at first," he told me. "But I talked with Rajmothan Gandhi, the son of the late Mahatma, and he explained that I should examine myself. Realize the scope of the contribution. Now I'm not angry or sorry. I believe it was the only decent course for us to take. I will always be struggling to improve conditions, wherever I am, wherever I go."

"WITH ALL DELIBERATE SPEED"

Almost a year after the 1954 *Brown* decision, a headline across a two-page spread in *Jet* had asked, "How Soon Will the South Abolish Jim Crow Schools?" The article reported that several border states had already begun to desegregate schools, but that in others, especially in the Deep South where the Negro population was a "formidable percentage," legislators were working overtime devising schemes to get around the desegregation ruling.

Georgia's governor, Herman Talmadge, had defiantly declared, "The races will not be mixed, come hell or high water," while Mississippi's governor, Hugh White, swore, "We will continue to have segregation in our schools, the Supreme Court notwithstanding." Some Southern Negro leaders even opined that the current separation of races would be okay if only the black schools were improved. After the Supreme Court decided *Brown* (and on the same day a separate case—*Bolling v. Sharpe*—that applied specifically to Washington, D.C. public schools), President Eisenhower ordered the district's schools to desegregate to serve as a model for the rest of the country. Some other major cities, such as Baltimore and St. Louis, also had begun to mix the races in public schools.

"In the final analysis," the article concluded, "the actual death date of the South's Jim Crow schools hinges on whether the Supreme Court sets a specific deadline and adds heavy penalties for failure to abide by its ruling. Failing this, desegregation will be a touch-and-go proposition of more lawsuits reaching down to county levels that could consume another quarter of a century."[3] The analysis was right on the mark.

The Supreme Court's refusal, two months later, to set a specific deadline for compliance with its desegregation order came as a devastating blow. Not only did it set the stage for years of litigation, it also inspired another loud chorus apart from those vowing "never." This second chorus frustrated Negro activists in another way, by insisting with apparently benign intentions that the timing was not "ripe," that whites were just not ready, and that blacks should be "patient." Leading this second choir was none other than President Eisenhower, who, although he never spoke publicly on the merits of the *Brown* decision, was widely regarded as believing that school desegregation should be a slow process, considering at every step the sensibilities of Southern whites whose greatest fear, he seemed to believe, was that their children, particularly their daughters, might marry Negroes.

Nevertheless, if anyone had predicted after the *Brown* decision in 1954 which school district would be the scene of the most violent reaction to even limited school desegregation, it is doubtful that Little Rock would have placed among the top five picks. Maybe not even the top ten. Given that blacks had attended the state's law school since 1948, and even the city's buses had integrated without incident, the state was considered "progressive" in terms of race relations, and its governor, Orval Faubus, did not seem as rabid a segregationist as many of his Southern counterparts. But in Arkansas, the gubernatorial election was biennial, and many observers felt it was the hot breath of a staunch segregationist opponent on his neck as he ran for re-election that inspired Faubus to take extreme steps to stop the very limited school integration that the Little Rock school board had been working on diligently and gingerly. Faubus was a politician who knew that school desegregation could become, if a candidate wanted to make it so, the hot button issue in a campaign. Instead of letting another candidate put him on the defensive, he pushed the button himself, and in the process not only figured out how to play it, but still win six more terms, incredibly with considerable black support. The fact that he destroyed Arkansas' reputation as a "progressive" state, and dealt a staggering blow to his country's image abroad, did not appear to faze him.

The Little Rock school board's plan initially was to involve just one school, Central High School, which, with about 2,000 white students, should have easily been able to absorb nine—the "cream of the crop"—of the approximately 200 black students who originally applied. But Faubus turned the tables on the board, the parents, the students—everyone—in a bizarre move that would astound the world. On the eve of school opening, Faubus called out the Arkansas National Guard and deployed them around the school. He then went on television and warned of impending violence at Central High School—without announcing that the guard's orders were not to protect the black students, but to prevent them from entering when they arrived in the morning.

In the confusion that followed, the parents of one of the nine, Elizabeth Eckford, who didn't have a telephone, did not receive directions given to the others to show up at a specific location to be escorted to the school by Daisy Bates. Instead, the fifteen-year-old arrived alone at the front entrance of the school (without her parents, since the school board had advised the parents of all the Negro students to stay away to avoid provoking trouble), where she was prohibited entry by bayonet-armed Arkansas National Guardsmen. A moment later, cameramen captured the ugly, contorted faces of a mob of white men and women shouting profane, threatening, racial epithets at this solitary, dignified, four-foot, ten-inch, 90-pound, black teenager. The image screamed the message of raw racial hatred around the world. And it was not just the silent scream of newspaper photos. This was the premiere entry into the world of racial violence of modern television news. And it would only get worse.

Faubus was defying the Supreme Court of the United States. The White House couldn't allow that to continue. Eisenhower was advised that it would be worthwhile to talk to the Arkansas governor about ending the constitutional crisis. Ten days into the standoff, while vacationing in Rhode Island, he invited Faubus to visit. They talked, and when Faubus left, the president thought they had reached agreement on the peaceful integration of Central High School. He was either mistaken, or Faubus double-crossed the president of the United States, just as he had turned the tables on the Little Rock school board and the Negro students. Upon returning home, Faubus issued a statement different from the one discussed with Eisenhower. Faubus was not budging.

After another week, during which the segregationist mob outside the school grew exponentially, reinforced by people from outside the school district and others who didn't even have kids in the school, a federal court issued a contempt citation against the governor for his continued use of the National Guard in defiance of court ordered desegregation.

On Sunday night, September 23, school board president Virgil Blossom called Daisy Bates and told her to take the black students to Central High to start classes in the morning. Governor Faubus had suddenly withdrawn the Arkansas National Guard. The students assured their parents that they still wanted to go, despite the danger. What no one fully realized was that Faubus had left Central High School to the mob.

The students were driven to Central High School in two automobiles. As they were slipped into the school by a side door, angry whites, spotting a group of black newsmen in front of the school set upon them, while police on duty refused to intervene. As I described the scene in *Jet*, I was one of the luckier ones. I was spat upon, but escaped injury only because I had remained in one of the automobiles that followed the students, and was later escorted out of the area by police. *Jet's* freelance photographer Earl Davy was beaten by the crowd, which also smashed his camera. *New York Amsterdam News* managing editor Jimmy Hicks was struck in the back and forced to run two blocks to escape the crowd. Alex Wilson, Memphis *Tri-State Defender* editor, was slugged to his knees, then pummeled with body blows by at least three whites. The mob also unleashed its fury on Baltimore *Afro-American* reporter Moses Newson. Meanwhile, carloads of white teenagers rolled through the streets adjacent to the school singing: "Two, four, six, eight. We don't want to integrate!"

In the midst of the confusion, someone shouted, "They've gotten in." Moments later, between thirty and fifty white students began filing out in groups of twos and threes as a detachment of state police, who had been standing by, roared up in squad cars to aid city police.

Inside the school, the black teens later reported, they were generally treated cordially.

"The teachers and students smiled at us," said Minnijean Brown. "Some of the girls offered to take us to lunch."

Even a white boy who had said, "Hey, black girl, you don't belong here," later apologized, Minnijean said.

School officials revealed the situation inside had been completely under control when police arrived at noon to withdraw the Negro students as ordered by the mayor. After the students left, however, crowds outside refused to believe a police announcement that they were gone. Only after they had sent an elderly woman into the school to investigate and report back, did the mob, which had grown steadily since morning, begin to thin out. Earlier, the local White Citizens' Council had called a meeting for the specific purpose of running out of town their No. 1 enemy: L. C. Bates. Later the Bateses received scores of anonymous phone calls. One caller said: "I hope you S.O.B.'s are satisfied with the trouble you've caused." Another threatened: "Get them black bastards out of school or we'll bomb your house and all the other kids." The couple, whose home had been under attack since spring (three crosses burned on the lawn), began a round-the-clock patrol.

My description of the violence outside Central High was accompanied in *Jet* by two pages of photos showing members of the mob kicking, shoving, and choke-holding L. Alex Wilson while the tall, dignified newspaperman, a former marine, reacted passively, holding on to his hat, his suit jacket still buttoned, before the crowd turned away, furious that the students had entered the school through the side door. The pictures were also carried by newspapers around the world. Later, Wilson explained why he didn't flee like the rest of us. He had done that once before when chased by the Klan, and the humiliation that haunted him after that episode made him determined he would never run again. Wilson didn't live enough years after Little Rock to see the fruits of his labor. His child, born just a month before the Little Rock crisis, would grow up in an evolving and more egalitarian society, but Wilson would not be there. He spared his wife, Imogene, the details of the chronic pain left by the attack. He tried to carry on his new duties as editor of the daily *Chicago Defender*, but soon began to experience uncontrollable shaking, much like Parkinson's Disease. He had surgery in 1959, after a doctor traced the pain and tremor to his head injury. But he was never the same. Wilson died in 1960 at age fifty-two. It wasn't until twenty years later that Imogene first saw the television footage of the beating her husband had sustained. He never wanted her to know how bad it really was. He was probably the toughest newsman I ever had the privilege of knowing, and I knew some of the best.

The mob violence in Little Rock was viewed with "undisguised disgust" by the world press, from Paris to Tokyo. *Jet* told its readers that the world was watching, seeing for the first time the atrocities against people of color, even children, in the "Land of the Free, Home of the Brave." In the major world powers, as well as the emerging Third World, popular opinion was on our side. For Washington, it was a major headache.

The mayor of Little Rock called for federal help after Faubus, facing contempt of court, withdrew the National Guard and left out-numbered police

ARKANSAS DEMOCRAT Today's News Today

EIGHTY-SIXTH YEAR—No. 257   LITTLE ROCK, MONDAY EVENING, SEPTEMBER 23, 1957   16 PAGES   PRICE 5c

Violence Explodes as 8 Negroes Enroll at CHS; Police Reserves Called

By ROBERT TROUTT
(Democrat Staff Writer)

Violence exploded at Central High School today as eight Negro students entered a side door while a diversionary group of Negroes appeared at the front.

Numerous fights broke out immediately and an appeal for state police brought 50 troopers racing to the scene to aid city patrolmen in battling the crowd.

Shortly after the Negro students slipped in and went to the principal's office, many white students began leaving the building.

One of the Negro adults was knocked down, beaten and kicked. Women screamed and men cursed and booed. A search the line of officers thrown around the high school ground.

Several fights broke out between Negro and white students in the corridors of Central High School after the Negroes entered, a student who left the school building said today.

The youth said he saw three Negroes with blood on their clothing. He said Negro students were chased through the hallways inside the building and that "several fights had broken out."

The situation was brought under control after arrival of state troopers.

Four men were declared an a change of inciting to riot.

They were booked as—

COULDN'T GET AWAY—This unidentified Negro man was unable to escape a crowd of irate segregationists at Little Rock Central High School today as violence broke out when Negro students entered the school. The white man riding the Negro's back is unidentified. (Democrat Photo by Counts.)

Faubus May Fly Back From Parley

By GEORGE DOUTHIT
(Democrat Staff Writer)

Governor Faubus told the Democrat from Sea Island, Ga. today that if integration troubles warranted it he would fly back to Little Rock.

He is attending the Southern Governors' Conference in...

Ike Mum On Local Situation

By JACK CLELLAND
(Democrat Washington Bureau.)

Washington — President Eisenhower and Attorney General Herbert Brownell held a conference today...

MannDenies He Sought Guard Help

Carl Jackson, 23, 1914 Louis; H. B. Brown, Benton, and Ram Richter, 1618 Rolds. The others quieted last as...

Mayor Says Little Rock Police Can Handle Situation

By RON BURNHAM
(Democrat Staff Writer.)

Mayor Mann today denied that...

'Here They Come'

RUNNING A GAUNTLET—This Negro man ran a gauntlet of anger at Central High School as violence broke out today when Negro students entered the other Men in the crowd slugged at the Negro as he ran and one unidentified hack hit set at him in the stomach. (Democrat Photo.)

Crowd's Yell Touches

The *Arkansas Democrat*'s Wilmer Counts photographed white toughs outside Little Rock's Central High School, attacking Memphis reporter L. Alex Wilson, whom the paper called an "unidentified man," while eight of the "Little Rock Nine" were escorted into the school through a side door. Although the paper ran Count's eyewitness account of the attack, a caption inaccurately reported that Wilson had been "slugged . . . as he ran." (Wilson never ran, and never fully recovered from the beating.) Other front-page stories reflected the pathetic lack of responsible leadership on the school desegregation issue, with President Eisenhower "mum" on it at his morning news conference, Gov. Faubus absent from the state, and the Little Rock mayor claiming that local police could handle the situation without help from the National Guard.

to deal with the crazed mob. Eisenhower finally responded. By nightfall, 1,000 riot-trained federal troops from the 101st Airborne Division deployed in Little Rock. It was an incredible sight. For the first time in weeks, we had a sense of hope, a feeling that maybe America wasn't going to let this end in a worse tragedy. World reaction not only was positive, but seemed to say, "It's about time." The *Toronto Star* summed it up: "President Eisenhower has at last had the courage to speak forcibly for law and human dignity. . . ."

Under the headline, "Negroes Ignore Mob Violence: Keep Busy with Day-to-Day Living," *Jet* reporter Francis H. Mitchell and I described the efforts of Little Rock's population to return to some semblance of normal life over the next week:

When 1,000 steel-helmeted 101st Airborne Division GIs rolled into Little Rock, Ark. under cover of night last week, white and Negro residents grimly awaited return of the racial harmony which had once brought the city fame and fortune. For a generation (following the 1925 lynching of a Negro whose body was dragged through downtown streets) leaders of both races had doped out peaceful integration of buses (most Negroes still sit in the rear), gingerly accepted mixing of races at Negro night clubs and other public places; quietly acquiesced to the enrollment of the first Negro students in former white city high schools. But in contrast to this calm planning, the booming state capital suddenly deteriorated into a virtual "mob rule town." And while local government officials nursed shattered plans to attract a billion dollars worth of industry in the next few years, an estimated 350 newsmen from all parts of the world saw the quick erupting climax of a 20-day build-up of tension explode like an atom blast over Little Rock.[4]

Most of Little Rock's 25,000 Negroes had only secondhand knowledge of the violence from media coverage as they went about their normal jobs—in jute and lumber mills, bauxite mines, professional and domestic work. But as rioting spread, and tension in the city soared, an already fatigued police force found an unwanted ally to stave off "occupation" by the mob: Little Rock Negroes. For many, remaining passive while white, teenage punks wreaked havoc in black communities was simply asking too much. A black porter told us, "The great thing about this struggle is that Negroes refused to run inside their homes and hide. They came out on the streets and fought." An estimated 150 persons, white and black, were booked on assault and disorderly conduct charges.

With the deployment of the federal troops came the restoration of order, and the big question in Little Rock was what would happen when the troops were withdrawn. Negroes had optimism about this that whites seemed not to share. Perhaps enlightened by decades of observation, the seventy-eight-year-old dean of Arkansas Negro surgeons, Dr. J. M. Robinson, a prominent Democratic leader, told us, "Things happen and pass quickly here. This will pass quickly too."

THE SCHOOL YEAR

After months filled with verbal and even physical attacks, during which one of the nine, Minnijean Brown, would be expelled for calling a taunter "white trash," Ernest Green, the oldest and calmest of the remaining students, became the target of a citywide hate drive. Racists called him a "25-cent nigger getting a $5 million diploma," a reference to the cost of the military deployment. Along with the others, he was threatened and bullied. Jefferson

Thomas was beaten and kicked two days in a row; honor student Carlotta Walls was called "half-breed," and a host of obscene names; and the window of a parent's car was smashed outside the school. In the last week of classes, race-baiting kids distributed "rump-kicking" cards that read in part:

PERMIT
GOOD ONLY UNTIL MAY 29, 1958
BEARER MAY KICK RUMPS OF EACH CHS
NEGRO ONCE PER DAY UNTIL ABOVE GRADUATION DATE.
LAST CHANCE, BOYS.

Daisy Bates pleaded for more protection for the students, saying they were "too terrified to study for exams." While police patrolled around the homes of the school superintendent and principal, they ignored the Bates home. The couple had to hire private security guards.

On graduation day, extra precautions were taken at the commencement to stave off a recurrence of the previous fall's mob violence. School board president Virgil Blossom even barred Negro press from all graduation services and refused to allow us to attend press conferences with white reporters. With logic that certainly escaped us, Blossom told photographer Ernest Withers, Sarah Black of the *New York Amsterdam News*, and me, "I know I'm wrong, but you've got to integrate one thing at a time." When a UPI reporter asked Blossom if it was true that the school board would not allow us to attend the ceremony, Blossom answered, "You didn't ask me that. You didn't see me tonight." He said to ask him the question again the next day.

Black newsmen in Little Rock were in a class by ourselves. Neither the Constitution nor reason was paid even lip service by local authorities. At the height of the crisis, I had arrived at a news conference sponsored by the school superintendent and was asked to leave on the grounds that I had not been invited, despite my press credentials. None of the other newsmen present or any of their editors protested my exclusion. At the end of what would have been the 1958–59 school year, had there been one, ex-superintendent Blossom would characterize himself in a *Saturday Evening Post* article as a "man-in-the-middle" during the nation's worst school integration crisis, which he said grew out of a lack of state and federal leadership and organized opposition from the outside. This was one point, at least, on which I agreed with him. Looking back, Blossom said that most Little Rock citizens had been prepared to obey the law, but anonymous phone calls had warned that an example would be made of him so no other Dixie school head would dare respect the Supreme Court's decision. The warning had been backed up by a bullet that hit his automobile while he was driving, newspaper ads denouncing him, and thousands of cards that were circulated, giving the holder permission "freely and energetically" to kick his rump.

When Ernest Green walked up to receive his diploma at the end of the 1957–58 school year, a 250-man force of police, armed guardsmen, and even some FBI agents were prepared for trouble in the school's auditorium. Instead of violence, there was applause.

After the ceremony, the handsome and affable teenager smiled when he told me, "It wasn't so bad," and then chuckled as he added, "but I'm glad it's over." He was referring not only to the tensions at the commencement ceremony, but to the entire past school year.

Encouraged to describe his experiences in his own words, the talented teen later wrote in *Jet*, under his own byline, that just before marching in cap and gown, he was told by a teacher that he would have to march alone in the double-file procession. However, just as the line reached the 4,000 parents and friends in the huge auditorium, a white classmate "shuffled up beside" him, and there was no gap in the 1958 class line. He revealed that throughout the past eight months of harassment and humiliation, such examples of friendship had served to inspire him. Within the school, he said, he had many friends and supporters, with only a small minority of bad apples causing the problems. This conclusion, he added, was borne out in the dozen or so inscriptions and autographs in his yearbook: "I have admired your courage this year, and I'm glad you made it through all right. . . .;" "I have found you a real nice fellow. . . .;" "You've stood the test and passed it. May you always have this much courage." And so on.

The hecklers and racists, he said, numbered about fifty to sixty in the student body of more than 2,000, but he also had four or five white friends who thought so much of him that they would telephone him at night to make sure he got the lessons, went out of their way to help him in school, spoke to him in the corridors, and were just "good Joes." Nevertheless, sometimes he couldn't help thinking of the days back at Horace Mann, the Negro high school where he'd been a popular, well-liked, honor student. At Central, the nine were barred from all extracurricular activities, except participation in chapel services.

One of the reasons it was all worth it, he wrote, was the superior equipment and quality of training at the formerly whites-only high school. Central's physics, biology, and science courses were "shoulder-high over our old school," something the nine at first found hard to believe. Like many others, they had been taught that facilities for Negroes really were "separate but equal." Nothing could have been further from the truth. Another thing, he said, that made it worth the risks they took was the example it set for other folks, as each of the nine showed "what this coming Negro kid is made of and what he can do under pressure." He added, "Sure, we got more than we bargained for, but we held out, and we tried to do it gracefully." Considering their youth, we thought they did it with remarkable grace, as well as stunning dignity and determination.

Ironically, although I was barred from attending the commencement ceremony, a man who was on his way to becoming a key figure in the civil rights movement was not. Witnessing the graduation with Ernest's parents was Dr. Martin Luther King, Jr., coordinator of the successful Montgomery, Alabama, bus boycott. Not yet the dominant figure he would soon become, Dr. King most likely was not recognized by anyone in the crowd, and certainly not by any potential troublemakers. UPI reported that about fifteen Negro spectators attended the graduation, but did not mention that he was one of them.

Outside the auditorium, a white boy was arrested for spitting on blacks as they filed out of the ceremony. Elsewhere around Little Rock, protesters distributed "Go Home, Ike" cards and urged celebration of a Liberation Day—the date of the departure of federal troops.

As the nine students ended the school year, the NAACP voted to award them as a group its prestigious Spingarn Medal in recognition of their heroism, but the teens' parents sent Roy Wilkins a letter saying, "The children will not accept the Spingarn Medal unless Mrs. Bates is included." According to inside sources, petty jealousies in the civil rights organization were at the root of her exclusion. Whatever the reason, the award committee was quickly polled and agreed to include the Arkansas NAACP president. The award was presented on July 11, 1958, during the NAACP's annual convention in Cleveland.

More than forty years later, President Bill Clinton presented the Congressional Medal of Honor to the Little Rock Nine in a special ceremony at the White House. Eighty-four years old, Daisy Bates had died a week earlier, on November 4, 1999, and her body was lying in state under the rotunda of the Little Rock capitol, the first person of color ever so honored. In presenting the medals, President Clinton said, "They have lived good lives and accomplished remarkable things. But we're giving them this award because they paid the price." Of his friend, Daisy Bates, he said, "She was an American hero."

FAUBUS PULLS ANOTHER SURPRISE

Normalcy did not quickly return to Little Rock when the '57–'58 school year ended. Faubus was not finished with his manipulation of the public school system to accomplish his political goals. Incredibly, before the '58–'59 school year was to begin, Faubus got the state legislature to pass a law allowing the governor to shut down schools and lease them to "private school" corporations as a way of preventing integration. He closed all of Little Rock's high schools, black and white. In a referendum in which few blacks were eligible to participate, the city's whites supported Faubus's action by a vote of 130,000 to 7,500. A pollster (Samuel Lubell) issued a report saying the majority of Faubus's backers did so "because he stood up for the South," but that they would accept integration.

The governor's political game had no concern for the toll this action would take on the educational needs of the city's children, regardless of race. In his game, children were no more than pawns.

The NAACP went back to court to challenge his action, and the Supreme Court scheduled an extraordinary summer session to hear the arguments in the case. After Ernest Green's graduation, two of the Little Rock Nine families found the pressure unbearable, and they were forced to move away. Minnijean Brown continued her education in New York. The remaining five took correspondence courses while waiting for Little Rock's schools to reopen. Jefferson Thomas, the only boy left from the original nine, spent his spare time as the neighborhood handyman, without charging for his work, but doing it, he said, just to keep busy and "keep from going crazy."

President Eisenhower admitted at a news conference that he thought integration should proceed at a "slower" pace, a comment that drew praise from Governor Faubus and criticism from the NAACP. Faubus crooned, "I am for him," while Roy Wilkins, addressing the 33rd annual convention of the National Bar Association in Chicago, countered:

> Integration has never started in seven states . . . [and] is on a token basis in three states. After four-and-one-half years it is estimated that the percentage of integration in Arkansas is four percent . . . Even if the present pace is maintained, one hundred years will be required. But the president thinks the present pace of integration should be slowed down. Would he give Arkansas 200 years, or only 150?

Appearing before the Supreme Court in September 1958, U.S. Solicitor General J. Lee Rankin and NAACP Special Counsel Thurgood Marshall argued that any delay in integration would be a concession to the pro-segregation "troublemakers" who had instigated the violence in Little Rock a year earlier. (Attorney General William P. Rogers and Solicitor General Rankin were credited with urging Eisenhower not to side with Little Rock's request for an integration "breather," resulting in the government's brief insisting that integration resume when school opened.)

In two dramatic appearances in the court's extraordinary Little Rock hearings, Marshall attacked as "unconstitutional and unfair" the requested two-and-one-half year "cooling-off period." The NAACP counsel argued that to grant the delay would be "bowing to violence," and water down constitutional rights "without a basis." He charged that the Little Rock School Board had not, to its best ability, moved against the agitators, and had no concrete integration program. Calmly, yet forcefully, Marshall attacked lower court testimony of a Central High School band teacher, who said his classes on the fifth floor were affected by the presence of Negro students on the first floor. Commented Thurgood, "Just how extreme can you get?"

Attorney Richard C. Butler, representing the Little Rock School Board, told the court that forced integration now would destroy the Little Rock school system as thoroughly "as if you planted a bomb under each school and lighted the fuses one by one." But Thurgood Marshall rejoined: "When a bank is robbed, you don't close the bank—you put the bank robbers in jail."

Butler also tried to minimize the effects of continued segregation on Negro children by referring to their rights as "intangible," leading Chief Justice Earl Warren to ask, "If you were denied life, liberty or property, would you call it 'intangible?'"

After he'd won his greatest (and twentieth) civil rights case before the United States Supreme Court, a *Jet* headline described the NAACP's fifty-year-old counsel as "humble" as he ambled, "grim and poker-faced," down the court's marble steps after the historic decision.[5] To photographers who tried to get him to smile and raise his hand in a V (for victory) sign, he refused, saying, "It's not dignified." He then implored jubilant well-wishers to refrain from demonstrating. About 1,000 spectators, many of them law students who'd arrived at 3:00 a.m., had come to the court daily to watch the battle of the legal giants, and particularly, the soft-drawling Thurgood, now unquestionably the country's greatest constitutional lawyer. The decision he'd just won would not only assure the continued integration of Little Rock's Central High School, but would guide the federal courts in other cases. Violence, or the threat of violence, had been defeated as an excuse to delay the integration of Dixie schools. But the Howard University-trained lawyer's demeanor demonstrated that he knew the fight was still just beginning.

Looking back over fifty years of *Jet* issues, I've been unable to find any other prominent person to whom we referred by his first name. By this time, Thurgood Marshall was already iconic in the black community. He was loved, respected, even revered. There was only one Thurgood as far as *Jet* was concerned.

STANDING UP FOR JUSTICE

In the wake of the Supreme Court order that Little Rock's schools integrate immediately, Justice Department attorneys mapped legal plans to deal with the closing of the schools by Faubus. Tension in Little Rock reached an all-time peak. Even Daisy Bates stepped up the defense of her already scarred home after hoodlums stoned the house three times in one evening. She picked up the gun her husband kept by his chair in the front room and fired over the head of a white man who stood poised to throw a rock at her picture window, ignoring the warning of a guard the Bateses had hired to protect their home. Like L. C., she had no intention of hurting anybody. Putting the gun back, she went into the bedroom and cried.

The campaign of violence had been stepped up not only against Daisy and L.C. Bates, but also against the Reverend Dunbar Ogden, the white clergyman who, at Daisy's request, had accompanied the black students on their first attempt to enter Central High in September 1957. President of the Interdenominational Interracial Ministerial Alliance, Rev. Dunbar told me he'd had to overcome his own fear the night Daisy had called him to ask that he and other clergymen walk to the entrance of the school with the children, since their parents had been told by the school board to stay away, so as not to incite the mob. With three other clergymen he had recruited for the task, and his son, David, who went along to protect his father, the group was shoved and jostled as they approached the National Guardsmen at the school, only to be turned back. From that point, despite threats to himself and his family, vandalism at his home, rejection by his congregation and the loss of his church, this son of Mississippi, a descendant of slave owners, stuck with the mission he accepted that night from Daisy Bates—or as he believed, from God—and never expressed any regret, even as he left Little Rock to start over in West Virginia. I called him a hero in *Jet*. He was one of the most decent men I've ever met.

Another object of the mob's wrath was Arkansas attorney Wiley Branton, who had steered the school case to the Supreme Court. Branton was a remarkable man, who also rose to the rank of hero in the Arkansas civil rights battles. Light skinned, with a soft, hill country drawl, he was one of the first Negro graduates of the University of Arkansas law school, and knew many of the judges and court staff personally. His folksy personality and down-home sense of humor helped him navigate smoothly through even the most redneck, backwoods courts, while his legal acumen made him a formidable foe for the best of the profession. He became a favorite speaker at dinners and conferences, where he would bring down the house with such stories as the time when he was chief counsel for the Negro students challenging the Little Rock school closing and the judge summoned him to his chambers, where, not realizing Branton was a Negro, commended him "as a white man for presenting the case of the Negroes." In his early thirties, he was one of only two Negro lawyers (the other was John Howard, also of Pine Bluff), who would handle NAACP cases in the state. As Little Rock entered what should have been the 1958 fall school term with all of its public schools closed, Branton told an NAACP meeting in Toledo, Ohio, "You don't always get what you want. We started out for desegregation in Little Rock public schools. Right now we have disintegration."

Like the Bateses, Branton lived in a racially mixed neighborhood. That was the damnedest thing about the whole Little Rock crisis. It was so unnecessary. The racial atmosphere at the time of the *Brown* decision was nothing like it was in the Deep South. People of both races lived in middle-class, laid-back neighborhoods, and greeted each other on the street. City parks had integrated without a fuss, as had the municipal buses. Except for the small minority of hoodlums—and that's what they were—whites were willing to accept school integration as the law of the land, although many did not like it.

I felt no extraordinary sense of danger going anywhere in Little Rock I wanted or needed to go, although I was careful to keep my lodging to myself. The instances in which I might inadvertently become part of the front-page story I was there to cover were isolated and usually obvious, so I was careful when confronting them. Because of my thick eyeglasses—without which I was helpless—I didn't step in front of a mob with a pencil and pad in my hands, because even a shove that separated me from those lenses would have put me out of commission. *Jet*'s freelance photographer, Earl Davy, who also worked for the *Arkansas State Press*, couldn't do his job without a camera, and took some bad body blows because of it. But since my first exposure to the Deep South's aversion to "outsiders," I had cultivated a tendency to "blend in." I could stand on the sidelines and pretend to be a passerby, while taking in the entire scene. I could also go to the Bates home, accept Daisy's offer of a cocktail, chat with her and L. C., and pretty much move about without the kind of constant tension a black reporter would experience in a backwater like Money, Mississippi.

The white moderates, who made the city livable for blacks, simply lacked any leadership—at either the local, state, or federal level. The rabble-rousers had Faubus, but the law-abiders had nobody. While Eisenhower's action in sending in the federal troops had put an end to the constitutional crisis, there was no moral leadership emanating from the White House on this issue. Thurgood Marshall summed up a lot of folks' feelings about it when he said that if Ike had handled the war in Europe this way, "we'd all be speaking German by now."

THE LEGACY

In June 1959, Arkansas' hastily enacted school-closing law was declared unconstitutional and the high schools reopened for the fall 1959 term. The five remaining Little Rock Nine students eventually graduated from formerly white-only high schools. But it was not until 1972—eighteen years after the *Brown* decision and fifteen years after the crisis at Central High— that all Little Rock public schools were finally integrated. It was the longest and most contentious civil rights battle in the history of the movement. It would leave the NAACP stretched to its limits with diminished coffers for other legal contests. Moreover, many young people were convinced that Thurgood Marshall's strategy of using the law to advance the cause of civil rights—rather than defying the law in headline grabbing, civil disobedience actions—was too costly and too slow.

Inspired by the Little Rock Nine, platoons of young people would step forward in the aftermath of the Little Rock School crisis. About the same age as Elizabeth Eckford, college students in the 1960s had witnessed the fifteen-year-old's bravery against an ugly mob of screaming whites, reported on TV, on the front pages of their local newspapers, and in *Jet*. And many of them, including recruits to a new organization that would come on the scene in the '60s—the Student Nonviolent Coordinating Committee (SNCC)—would also reveal that their zeal even as youngsters had been fueled by the brutally honest photograph in *Jet* magazine of Emmett Till's mutilated body in an open casket. They were ready to put their own bodies on the line. These young people did not have the patience of earlier generations of blacks. And even their parents had run out of that virtue when it came to winning freedom for their children in their own lifetimes.

In a few years, the civil rights organizations would differ publicly on strategies, and the action more often would be in the streets, and at lunch counters, as well as on voter registration lines, rather than in the courts. There would be marches, sit-ins, and more martyrs. From the rally at Mound Bayou through the battle of Little Rock, the movement was marching on.

11

EISENHOWER REDUX

I had no opportunity during Eisenhower's eight years in office to ask him even one question, much less get a full scale interview, but almost two years after he left office, he agreed to give me an hour at his farm in Gettysburg, Pennsylvania. I was writing *Black Man's America*, and, like lots of other people, I had a number of lingering questions about his civil rights record in the White House. When I arrived and was shown to his office, I found the former president congenial and relaxed, leaning back in the chair behind his desk as we talked. The only ground rule for the interview was that my article would contain no direct quotes.

Referring to the 1956 election, Eisenhower emphasized that he had been shocked at the number of Negroes voting "against" him despite his civil rights effort. He said he was puzzled after scanning the election returns from Negro areas, Harlem in particular. He couldn't understand it. He couldn't even believe it. He'd expected much more support from Negroes.

He acknowledged that Nixon had made a mistake by not seeking the Negro vote on a national scale in 1960, and specifically recalled that he mentioned to Nixon while in New York the matter of dropping by Harlem and explaining the GOP's record. After returning to headquarters that evening, Ike said he learned that Nixon had been too busy and had eliminated the Harlem stop, a decision the former President attributed to the back-breaking aspects of campaigning rather than willful neglect.

As far as his refusal during his first term as president to speak to Negro groups, Eisenhower said this was consistent with his policy of limiting engagements before separate racial, religious or nationality groups. As a former army commander, he believed all citizens were Americans and part of the whole, and that a president should appear before across-the-board groupings. Asked about the oft-heard criticism of his refusal to talk with Negro leaders at the White House, he said he wasn't aware there was such a feeling. He said this wasn't relayed to him by any of his advisors but that they knew about his feelings on dividing Americans and probably hesitated to ask him to break the policy.

I found it incredible that no one on Eisenhower's staff had brought to his attention the barbs the black press was hurling at him, particularly in his last term. In an interview after he left the White House, Fred Morrow had told me he wrote many memos of this nature to White House aides. Could they have neglected or even refused to share them with the boss? Upon giving that some thought, I concluded that Ike's professed ignorance of any black criticism of his administration could also have been an example of a tactic he often used at news conferences when he didn't want to address an issue: he'd simply state he wasn't aware of it.

I mentioned Eisenhower's appearance before a black publishers' summit, which had left a sour taste because he espoused "patience" in the civil rights arena. He still seemed puzzled about that, and said he couldn't see why this would offend them. He then suggested that perhaps he was misunderstood. He said that he wasn't telling Negroes to do nothing, but rather to keep pressing but not become so disillusioned they "quit" or become "fanatical." To me, that explanation was even worse. How could 18 million Americans "quit" their struggle for the rights guaranteed to all citizens by the Constitution? What would lead any responsible person to believe that black Americans who had fought for their country with honor and bravery in two world wars might become "fanatical" on the final leg of the road to equality? And how did Ike define "fanaticism"?

Besides desegregation of Washington, D.C., the Little Rock troop intervention, and appointment of Negroes to key U.S. posts, Eisenhower cited the passage of the first civil rights bill in more than eighty years as his biggest civil rights success. He described the legislative battle as a long and dreary road but one that ended with a law with some teeth in it to cope with voting problems. (This was an incredible observation as well, because if there was anything everybody else agreed upon about the law, it was that it had no teeth. All the enforcement provisions had been gutted from it.) Ultimately, the former president said, he saw voting as key to Negroes' "lifting themselves."

As to whether sending troops to Little Rock had caused an emotional crisis for him, he said no—he had no alternative in face of flagrant violation of a federal court order.

Regarding his protracted silence on the *Brown* school desegregation decision, he said he didn't think it proper or fitting for the chief executive to comment on a decision of the high court. As president, he continued, he was sworn to carry out Supreme Court decisions regardless of his personal opinion, which was not important. However, he believed the court's decision in the school case was absolute in constitutional and moral law, adding that as long as an individual was liable for payment of taxes, he should be given the right to benefit fully from the services of the government. Again, he seemed to link, and even limit, mandated desegregation to those areas supported by tax dollars.

Satisfied with the civil rights laws on the books and that his Justice Department was enforcing them, Eisenhower said he "didn't waste any time in getting more laws." In fact, he added, additional laws were unnecessary, and cited the elimination of segregation in the armed forces as an illustration of executive determination. His answer suggested that he wasn't aware that systemic discrimination still persisted in the military and that President Kennedy had named a committee to probe the problem. Eisenhower acted as if it had all been taken care of by executive order.

He went on to predict that segregation would disappear in America in ten years (the interview was in 1962), public schools would be open to all in every state, and factories and businesses would hire more qualified Negroes. There would also be housing for Negroes, who would be elected to high public offices in cities and states as well as appointed to key national government jobs. In sum, discrimination, the keystone of century-old controversy, would become a relic of the past. While rejecting the need for more legislation to achieve these goals, he took the position that "more education eventually will solve everything." He said that Negroes were "too focused on civil rights" and should focus instead on education. He also made a point of repeating the oft-quoted story about how he and the late NAACP Secretary Walter White had agreed that they didn't want their children to make interracial marriages. Since he made such a point of it, I felt compelled to tell him White's daughter had done just that. He showed no outward reaction at all. I don't know if he even believed me.

As I prepared to leave, Ike flashed his famous smile, extended his hand, and said he had a question for me. "Tell me," he said, "you've been here forty-five minutes and all you've asked are questions about civil rights. Is that all you're interested in?" I answered, "Well, Mr. President, you spoke out on other issues while you were president, but no one knew how you really felt about the major civil rights issues." He scratched his chin thoughtfully, as if pondering that, before bidding me a cheerful farewell. I still remember the perplexed look on his face.

Apparently Eisenhower still saw civil rights as a "special interest" question rather than one of the most important issues facing all of America in the 1950s and '60s. I continued to feel that he just didn't get it. I wondered if I'd had the skill of a Thurgood Marshall, could I have given the former president some new insight into the facts of life for educated blacks in

When I spoke with Eisenhower before *Black Man's America* was published in 1964, he was still perplexed by my apparent obsession with civil rights. (Photo by Maurice Sorrell.)

America—perhaps explaining how it felt that, with all my education, and my grandfather's and great grandfather's before him, racist voting practices and corrupt registrars would block me from voting in much of the Deep South. I couldn't even get a cup of coffee at a lunch counter in a five-and-dime store in those states. My kids would have to attend inferior schools. If it were known what I did for a living, I might not return home one night, and my body might never be found. Even in the North, we were still limited as to where we could live. What else would I be interested in but civil rights?

FOUR DISAPPOINTING YEARS

While Eisenhower's second term was woefully lackluster in the eyes of the black press, there were nevertheless a few events that, for better or worse, would not soon be forgotten. His second inauguration itself was noteworthy both for its unprecedented and very visual inclusion of blacks, as well as the absence of any official representation of the State of Mississippi. Gov. J. P. Coleman, a dyed-in-the-wool segregationist, refused to have his state represented in any of the inaugural functions to protest the president's civil rights policies. The snub produced the hottest gossip during the three-day inaugural program, but in no way dimmed the festive spirit of an estimated

5,000 Negroes from thirty-two states who attended what was described as the "most integrated" inaugural in the nation's history.

Some 500 invited guests joined Mr. and Mrs. Johnson and the bureau staff to watch the parade from our space overlooking Constitution Avenue at the foot of Capitol Hill. We saw the number of top government figures who accepted the invitation as a positive sign that JPC was coming into its own as a force to be reckoned with in the national press. At the Capitol, concert singer Marian Anderson made history as the first Negro artist to sing the National Anthem during the swearing-in ceremony. Afterward, White House aide E. Frederic Morrow, a black man riding in an open, white Cadillac as one of the parade marshals, fueled the optimism of blacks waving from the sidelines as the marching units moved briskly down Pennsylvania Avenue toward the White House. But one man's prominent role certainly was no reason to believe—or even to dream—that just over fifty years later, the most prominent black in the 2009 Inaugural Parade would be the president of the United States himself. That evening, an estimated 500 Negroes attended the four inaugural balls, an all-time record number of invited black guests.

Like most people, I regarded Eisenhower as a man of conviction. But the moral freshness he had brought to the nation's capital was tainted in his second term by what I considered some of the most insensitive bureaucrats he could find to bring into the administration. After his 1956 re-election, these officials repeatedly helped him slip into disfavor with blacks. Even his decisive action in sending units of the 101st Airborne Division into Little Rock came to be viewed as something he was obliged to do to defend a federal court order, rather than something for which he should be given any special credit. With Ike focused on other problems, both foreign and domestic, there was little news from Washington that inspired or uplifted the growing ranks of frustrated blacks. Even the small coterie of Negro appointees seemed disenchanted with Eisenhower. Many, furthermore, had little faith in his vice president, Richard Nixon. On too many occasions, he sounded like a well-rehearsed actor who played a role—sometimes not too well.

The only black professional staff member in the White House struggled to contain his frustration with some of the racial deadheads he had to contend with there. Fred Morrow succeeded at that most of the time, but he was the target of much black criticism for the administration's shortcomings, although, as administrative officer for special projects, he had no responsibility for civil rights issues. One of his lowest points, ironically, came in October 1957, just weeks after Eisenhower had sent federal troops into Little Rock. Morrow dreaded going to the office, where he was being bombarded with calls and letters from friends and strangers alike who were fed up with the president's moderate stand on civil rights. The lack of a strong, clear

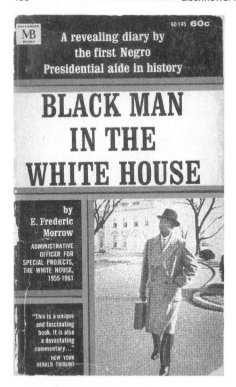

Eisenhower raised black hopes during his first administration, but by his second term, even those closest to him, including the first black White House aide, E. Frederick Morrow, were disillusioned. The former president was not pleased in 1963 when Morrow published his diary, recounting his White House years in stunning detail.

voice from the White House on civil rights issues was plaguing Morrow, too. Without such an expression of righteous indignation by the president, he believed it was hard for blacks to tell whose side the president was on—that of the 18 million Negroes fighting for their rights, or the unknown numbers of whites who would deny them.[1]

Morrow shared his pain with his diary and few others, but by then it was becoming more difficult to keep quiet. When he chose to raise an issue regarding race he would carefully craft a memo, usually addressed to his boss, Sherman Adams. Sometimes, he would also share his thoughts in discussions with senior White House staffers, but that could be risky, as he discovered on one occasion when he described his concerns to Max Rabb, the man charged with handling "minority problems," and someone he considered an ally. It was in the months following the 1955 acquittal of Emmett Till's murderers, and Morrow thought the increased incidents of civil rights-related violence and rising tensions in the Deep South and elsewhere justified White House action. Rabb couldn't have disagreed more, and as Morrow later described the exchange, almost took off his head for suggesting it. Rabb described feelings of "disgust" on the part of White House officials over what was perceived as a lack of Negro "gratitude" for the administration's actions in the civil rights arena. He also cited a feeling that Negroes were being too "aggressive" in their demands, insisting on measures that far exceeded what "reasonable" whites would "grant." Rabb had even used terms such as "surliness" in connection with blacks. The situation was such, he summed up, that he saw no political gain to be had from doing anything more for blacks, who'd lost the few white friends they had.[2] Morrow's account left me wondering how he could have continued working in the White House after hearing such an admission from the man who was arguably the most liberal professional on Eisenhower's staff. But Morrow felt Rabb's explosion was a frustrated reaction to political pressures, and nothing more should be read into it. He still credited Rabb as possibly the only member of the White House staff who ever showed deep personal concern about the plight of the Negro and other minorities in the country. That didn't say much for the rest of them.

Without naming names, Morrow told me that many others paid lip service to the administration's civil and human rights policies, but fell short when the time came to apply them. For him, personally, the insensitivity encountered in the White House was sometimes unbearable, especially when he felt his loyalty to the administration was pitted against his loyalty to his race. His biggest challenge was trying to explain the antipathy of young, intelligent Negroes toward Eisenhower's call for gradualism and patience. As obvious as it seemed to Morrow, Ike just didn't get it, and nothing Morrow said or did seemed to change that.

THE WHITE HOUSE AND THE BLACK PRESS

Coverage of Eisenhower's second term was a pathetic chore for a Negro reporter. I had stopped attending press conferences because he ignored the hands raised by blacks and said little on the topic of human relations. Press Secretary James Hagerty, in particular, seemed to consider the black press unimportant. I believed that much of the resentment Negroes were starting to express toward the administration during the second term could be traced to the image projected in the black press, and that Hagerty could and should be doing something about that, but wasn't.

In April 1957, Fred Morrow sent Hagerty a memo about the "swipes" the Negro press was taking at the president for refusing to recognize blacks at his weekly press conferences. Morrow said he hoped the president would "go out of his way" to recognize a black reporter at the next press conference. It didn't happen. Almost two months later, I reported in *Jet* that Alice Dunnigan of the Associated Negro Press (ANP), who was the first black newswoman to cover the White House, attributed the fact that she hadn't been recognized in a very long time to racism. But it was still more than a year after that before she got to ask Eisenhower a question at his news conference. The White House seemed as insensitive to this kind of criticism as Morrow was pained by it.

Eisenhower hadn't always been that way. He may have been reacting to the *Brown* decision handed down by the Supreme Court in the spring of 1954. Prior to that he had answered questions from Louis Lautier and Alice Dunnigan at a handful of press conferences, and even more from Ethel Payne, Washington correspondent for the *Chicago Defender*, and in 1954 still a newcomer to the White House press corps. But at a news conference in July she apparently caught Eisenhower off guard with a question regarding the Interstate Commerce Commission's opinion that it was time to end segregation in interstate travel. She asked the president if the administration would support such legislation. His reaction was fast and furious. The suddenly red-faced Commander in Chief angrily asked what made her think he would do anything for any special group, adding that he was president of "all the people," and was going to do what he thought right for "all the people."[3] All of a sudden, 18 million black Americans forced to ride in the back of buses or in separate rail cars were a special interest group instead of simply American citizens. His irritation at the question made the front page of Washington's afternoon daily, the *Evening Star*, under the headline, "President Annoyed By Query On Travel Race Ban Support."[4]

For many, the moment revealed the conflict in Eisenhower's own thinking on the issue of civil rights. In retrospect, some say he should be judged by what he did, such as the appointment of federal judges who were likely to support the *Brown* decision, rather than by what he said. His words, however, particularly when unscripted, often seemed to reflect an extraordinary deference to Southern fears of ever having to sit next to a Negro—other than, perhaps, your children's nanny.

After the incident, Ethel, my good friend over some four decades, told colleagues she'd been summoned to Hagerty's office and charged with violating some White House correspondents' rules because of pieces she'd freelanced to a labor political action committee publication. Hagerty threatened to revoke her White House credentials. She also learned the White House had asked the IRS to look into her taxes. When the NAACP intervened on her behalf, and the daily press even got involved, the White House backed off. But the president recognized her only once again in that entire year, and only once in 1955. Ethel's experience left the rest of us wondering whether it was better to be ignored. For me, it wasn't my choice. Eisenhower never recognized me.

Jet had another beef with Hagerty. The White House News Photographers Association, sanctioned by and operating under the benevolence of the White House press office, had never admitted a black photographer. *Jet* photographer Ellsworth Davis first applied for membership in 1958, sponsored by members George Tames of the *New York Times* and Paul Shutzer of *Life* magazine. His application was approved by the organization's board, but not by the membership, which included some diehard racists. I complained in a letter to Hagerty that the association's exclusion of Davis handicapped our bureau, since the WHNPA members decided photographic policies in the White House, and wearing the special lapel pin spared members from harassment by the Secret Service while carrying out assignments in the vicinity of the president. The association also held an annual photo competition of pictures of the president, which only members could enter, and that, too, was unfair to black photographers accredited to the White House. On top of that, the organization operated in a public building, used photographs of public officials for its exhibits, and unofficially influenced photographic assignments at the White House.

In his June 10, 1959, response to my letter, Hagerty expressed bewilderment at the points I had raised, responding that Davis's White House credentials were all he needed there. "Membership in any organization in Washington," he added, "is outside of my jurisdiction."

I wrote back to Hagerty the same day, expanding on my earlier arguments and adding that I had hoped that the feelings of a president who had removed color barriers for qualified reporters at the White House and opened opportunities to all regardless of race would rub off on the men working closest to him. Hagerty was unmoved.

In 1960, Ellsworth Davis again applied for WHNPA membership, this time sponsored by Douglas Chevalier of *The Washington Post* as well as George Tames of the *New York Times*. Again, the board approved his application, and again the same few members voted it down. The White House press secretary continued to turn a blind eye to the discrimination.

One year later, on April 12, 1961, I would raise the matter directly with the next president of the United States, and get a very different answer.

CALLING ON GOD TO MOVE MEN

During much of Eisenhower's second term, I didn't bother with the departmental or agency press conferences because compromise and retreat appeared to be the civil rights policy, leaving the black press with little to report that didn't include cause for Negro disillusionment with the administration. Given the prevailing atmosphere in Washington in 1957, it was no surprise when black leaders decided to appeal to a higher authority.

In May, A. Philip Randolph, president of the Brotherhood of Sleeping Car Porters, the NAACP's Roy Wilkins, and the Reverend Martin Luther King, Jr., rallied tens of thousands of Negroes to embark upon a "prayer pilgrimage" to Washington that at the time would be the largest mass civil rights demonstration in U.S. history. The leaders aimed to: 1) commemorate the third anniversary of the *Brown* decision; 2) demonstrate unity in demands for civil rights legislation; 3) protest terror and violence in the South, and 4) pay homage to Abraham Lincoln, on the steps of whose memorial the pilgrimage would end. But they also told me frankly in separate conversations in the weeks before the event, that they had additional hopes for the pilgrimage.

King was particularly perturbed that to date neither President Eisenhower nor Vice President Nixon had spoken out against white-on-black violence in the South, or in support of the *Brown* decision. Referring to the consistent lack of any discussion of human rights at White House press conferences, something of which I was well aware, he told me the leaders hoped the pilgrimage would be big enough to force reporters (the white press) to bring the matter up in the president's press conferences. Roy Wilkins acknowledged that he didn't expect the pilgrimage to bring immediate passage of civil rights legislation, but figured that with thousands of people involved, legislators couldn't ignore it. For A. Philip Randolph, the agenda was straightforward: "We have to demand our rights. I think some of us think they will come to us automatically. We are not going to get them by waiting." While aiming to avoid any appearance of militancy by emphasizing this was not a "march on Washington," the senior statesman nevertheless underscored with his tone the fighting spirit that was growing within the movement.

On the 17th of May, about 25,000 persons, mostly black, many from churches and the labor movement, arrived in Washington by train, plane, bus, and auto to participate in the "Prayer Pilgrimage for Freedom" at the Lincoln Memorial. The pilgrims included two entertainers who over the years would be deeply involved in the struggle, singer Harry Belafonte and actor Sidney Poitier, and their wives. I spotted several Communist leaders in the throng, but contrary to reports that they would try to capitalize on the event, they did no more than anyone else and were completely ignored. They included Eugene Dennis of New York, Benjamin Davis of the party's National Committee, and Roosevelt Ward of the *Daily Worker*. I also observed concert singer/actor/activist Paul Robeson, whose name had been linked with Communist activities, but to most people, his was just another face in the crowd.

The cheerful but serious "pilgrims" heard stirring, sermon-like speeches from Southern clergymen including William Holmes Borders of Atlanta, C. K. Steele of Tallahassee, and Birmingham's Fred Shuttlesworth, who had become a reliable news source for me and whose knowledge of his city would prove invaluable a few years later when I was stranded there with the first Freedom Riders. The throng responded, "Amen!" to the speakers' demands for civil rights. They also heard a typically fiery address by New York Congressman Adam Clayton Powell. Finally, a softer-voiced Rev. King, whose leadership of the Montgomery bus boycott had only recently propelled him to the threshold of national consciousness, took the microphone. Making his first major speech to a national audience outside of Alabama, the young minister would ensure his place among the civil rights leadership. His message was "to love and not hate." While elegant in its simplicity and spirit, it was but a hint of the earth-moving address he would make from those same steps some six years later, before a throng ten times the size of this one.

Like most events such as this, when three hours of speeches, prayers, and hymn-singing were over, no one was really quite sure what had been accomplished. The NAACP, already strapped for funds, was hoping it wouldn't be left holding the bill for uncovered expenses.

If nothing else, the pilgrimage and its tens of thousands of participants helped to focus political Washington on the fact that life in America was changing whether the South liked it or not. Heralding the change in the wake of the *Brown* decision were: the inevitable school desegregation showdown as the 1957–58 school year approached; the successful bus boycotts in Montgomery and elsewhere; the hot civil rights debates at the recent national nominating conventions; and the increasingly important Negro vote in Northern cities. At least some members of the Eisenhower administration believed the time had come for Congress to enact the first civil rights bill since the end of Reconstruction in 1876. Attorney General Herbert Brownell had drafted such a bill, and Ike supported it, although the president had said on many occasions that he didn't see the need for civil rights legislation, and that you couldn't force the kind of change of heart he believed was a necessary precursor to equal rights for Negroes. The administration had sent the bill to Congress in the months preceding the 1956 election, but the Dixiecrats made sure it didn't get anywhere. When the election was over, the administration revived the legislation, which had four major provisions, or "titles":

- The first title would set up a bipartisan federal commission on civil rights, which although lacking enforcement powers, could subpoena witnesses and make recommendations to the Congress and Executive Branch for remedial action;
- the second would replace the civil rights section in the criminal division of the Department of Justice with a separate civil rights division under a presidentially appointed assistant attorney general;

- the third—the real roundhouse punch in the bill—would give the Attorney General power to bring civil suits to address civil rights violations; and
- the fourth specifically provided new protections for voting rights.

While the bill had broad bipartisan support from Republicans and Northern and Western Democrats, the problem, as usual, was the Southern Democrats. With his eyes on the Democratic presidential nomination in 1960, for which he would need both Northern and Southern support, Senate Majority Leader Lyndon Baines Johnson ("LBJ") worked the magic that had earned him his reputation as "Master of the Senate," by gutting the bill of its most meaningful provisions so that the Southerners could be persuaded not to filibuster against it. He also added a provision requiring jury trials for contempt of court charges in noncriminal civil rights cases, in effect rendering worthless the government's power to bring such cases in the South.

The party's top Negroes pleaded with the president to keep the original bill intact. On July 12, White House aide Fred Morrow sent a memo to his boss, Sherman Adams, Ike's chief of staff. He felt compelled to weigh in on this legislation, although he knew that to do so, he'd have to walk on eggs. Disclaiming at the outset any presumptuousness on his part, he told Adams that Negroes were alarmed at reports that the administration was about to "soften" the provisions of the civil rights bill, and advised that they would rather have no legislation than a watered-down version. Any retreat on that, he added, would likely have serious political repercussions among black voters.

What Eisenhower did next was enough to confuse everybody. On July 16, the White House released a statement saying the president was demanding his full, four-point civil rights bill. However, at his press conference the next day, he seemed to waffle about Title III, the section the South wanted deleted, saying he didn't understand it, and suggesting that he wasn't even clear as to what it was intended to do.

The following day, another black Republican, the National Committee's Minorities Director, Val Washington, whom Morrow told me was his "only outside strength and aid" among blacks during those White House years, threw his political weight into the fray, and made sure his position was publicized. In an impassioned letter to the president, a copy of which he sent to me, Washington called what was going on an "unfortunate civil rights fiasco" and urged that Ike not let the bill be weakened. The black Republican Party official, as usual, did not mince words, pointing out that the president's civil rights bill was a "very moderate one," which did nothing more than call for protective measures guaranteeing all of the rights due any citizen under the Constitution and the Supreme Court decisions. So what, he asked, was there to compromise? He concluded, "I know you will not let us down."[5]

But Eisenhower did let them down. Despite such pleas, the bill was gutted, and a once cohesive Negro leadership was divided over whether to accept the weakened measure or call for a veto. For NAACP Executive Secretary Roy Wilkins, it was one of the most difficult decisions of his career, and he laid blame for it squarely on the administration. Not only had the president waffled on Title III at his news conference, but Vice President Nixon reportedly had suggested that Republicans were prepared to abandon the fight and let the bill die. While A. Philip Randolph and others concluded that no bill was better than a watered down one, and wired the president to veto the legislation, Wilkins ultimately was persuaded that even a weak bill was better than none after more than eighty years. He would be widely criticized for supporting a "half-a-loaf" bill, but found support from at least one great champion of civil rights, Democratic Senator Hubert H. Humphrey, who told him, in politics, "never turn your back on a crumb." Wilkins argued that despite its hollowness, the 1957 civil rights bill would lead to stronger legislation later, and that without it, blacks might be waiting "outside the bakery" for a much longer time.[6]

Congress passed the weakened legislation in August and Eisenhower signed it into law as the Civil Rights Act of 1957. It gave both Democrats and Republicans something to crow about. The Republicans could claim credit for it, such as it was; the Southern Democrats could say on the one hand they'd been big enough not to oppose it, and on the other (to their constituents), that it was meaningless anyway; and Senate Majority Leader Lyndon Johnson (looking for Northern support for his bid for the presidential nomination) could take credit for getting the first civil rights bill passed in the more than eighty years since Reconstruction. Rep. Adam Clayton Powell issued a press release all but calling it the best thing since apple pie. With an oblique reference to his recent indictment on income tax charges, he raved, "This [passage of the bill] completely vindicates my support of President Eisenhower regardless of what may happen to me."

Within months, the administration would be at work trying to absolve itself of any responsibility for the weakened bill. At a summit convened by black newspaper publishers, I was sitting near the stage, taking notes and, frankly, having a difficult time maintaining my focus on an otherwise unremarkable speech by Labor Secretary James P. Mitchell, when he said something that provoked a shout of "That's not the truth!" from the rear of the hall. The NAACP's veteran lobbyist, Clarence Mitchell, was on his feet, pointing indignantly toward the labor secretary, who had just claimed that professional civil rights organizations had deserted the Congressional fight for a strong civil rights bill. The indefatigable lobbyist, whose dedication over the years earned him the accolade "101st Senator," was not about to let the remark go uncontested. When Secretary Mitchell finished his speech, the NAACP bureau chief tried to get the platform for a rebuttal, but was turned back by conference officials, who appeared embarrassed by his outburst. The chairman of the conference was William O. Walker, the same publisher who turned his paper into a virtual Republican propaganda sheet before elections (and fired me when I organized a Newspaper Guild unit at the paper). He was not about to let anyone say anything negative about the Republican administration from the dais. However, he could not stop us from reporting Clarence Mitchell's outraged challenge to the labor secretary's version of events.

THE 101ST SENATOR

Clarence Mitchell was fearless when it came to dealing with the high and the mighty, as he proved time and again. In a Senate hallway one day, photographer Theodore Gaffney and I encountered him chatting with a rabidly segregationist Southern senator. Gaffney snapped a picture, the camera's light flashed, and the senator erupted, shouting, "Arrest that man!" This immediately brought two uniformed guards running toward us, slowed down only by the clusters of gawking and gabbing tourists clogging the Capitol corridor. In the few seconds that gave me, I slipped out a nearby door while Mitchell loudly objected to any interference with the photographer on First Amendment grounds. The guards persisted in escorting Gaffney away, while Mitchell angrily followed. Fully expecting that at a minimum, the guards would confiscate the film, the NAACP lawyer/lobbyist protested that their detention of the photographer was unlawful and outrageous.

A couple of hours later, Mitchell called me at the office and read me the riot act for not staying and supporting Gaffney. When he finally paused for a breath, I said, "Clarence, this was not a First Amendment situation." That only caused him to erupt again before I could explain. Finally, after running through all the reasons why it most definitely was a First Amendment issue, the civil rights expert paused again, and I said simply, "Clarence, Gaffney passed me the film, and as soon as I got back to the office I sent it to Chicago." Suddenly the "101st Senator" had renewed faith in the reporter from *Jet*.

THE BLACK SUMMIT

Even aside from the controversy over the labor secretary's remark, the black summit conference sponsored by the forty-member National

Newspaper Publishers Association in early 1958 was a public relations disaster for President Eisenhower. After refusing to meet with black leaders or address black groups throughout his first five years in office, Eisenhower had suddenly agreed to speak at this major black event, which included not only the black newspaper publishers, but more than 450 Negro church, fraternal, educational, and welfare organization leaders— perhaps the most distinguished assemblage of Negroes ever to discuss the course of race relations.

Fred Morrow, detailed briefly to White House speech writing,[7] helped draft the president's remarks, but for some reason, Ike at the last minute decided to junk the prepared text and ad lib. The result was pure Eisenhower. And for this audience, it was also all wrong. Seemingly oblivious to the rising frustrations of the nation's Negroes, he told his first black audience since the 1954 *Brown* desegregation decision to exercise "patience and forbearance" in their quest for equal rights. He added: "Laws themselves will never solve problems that have their root in the human heart and the human emotion. . . . we must depend on better and more profound education than simply on the letter of the law."[8]

Rigid courtesy at this level of black society made booing out of the question, but applause was skimpy. The assemblage remained polite while Eisenhower was on stage, and presented him with a citation for calling out the troops in Little Rock, whose own Daisy Bates gratefully shook hands with him. Afterwards, however, the speech would stir up a storm of criticism. NAACP chief counsel and civil rights mastermind Thurgood Marshall commented wryly, "I'm the world's greatest gradualist. I just think ninety-odd years is gradual enough." Another Marshall zinger made *Jet's* "Words of the Week:" "When somebody's choking me to death, that's no time to talk about patience."[9]

Kentucky Gov. A. B. (Happy) Chandler, baseball commissioner when the Brooklyn Dodgers signed Jackie Robinson, also assailed Eisenhower's remarks, pointing out: "Patience is a great virtue, but patience in the face of no action is not good."

NAACP Executive Secretary Roy Wilkins commented: "One can understand that he [Eisenhower] is not anxious that anyone kick up a fuss. If the men on the bench [the Supreme Court] told whites that thus and so was due them they would want it then and there."

Another jab came from New York mayoralty aide Anna Hedgeman, as the conference wound down, and word circulated that the president had ordered troops to South America to protect Vice President Nixon, whose limousine was stoned by hundreds of demonstrators in Venezuela: "We should send Ike a wire saying simply, 'Be Patient.'"

A WHITE HOUSE SUMMIT

At Fred Morrow's urging, on June 23, 1958, Eisenhower finally met at the White House with four black leaders, dubbed the "Big Four" by the press: the "Old Lion," International President of the Brotherhood of Sleeping Car Porters, A. Philip Randolph; rising star Rev. Martin Luther King, Jr., of the Southern Christian Leadership Conference (SCLC), riding the crest of the successful Montgomery bus boycott; NAACP Executive Secretary Roy Wilkins; and Urban League executive Lester Granger. Apparently, there'd been considerable discussion about whom to invite. Although he had bucked the Democratic Party and campaigned for Eisenhower in the 1956 election, Rep. Adam Clayton Powell was not invited to the meeting (possibly due to his recent indictment on tax evasion charges), but publicly took credit for it. White House insiders, including Fred Morrow, disputed that, telling me it was he who had petitioned, pushed, and argued the "desperate need" for such a meeting for months, until Ike finally agreed, which Morrow considered one of his greatest accomplishments in six years on the White House staff.

When he campaigned for Ike in 1952, Morrow had been told he would have a job in the White House, and quit his position as a writer at CBS in New York after the election in preparation for moving to Washington. But it would be two years before the administration fulfilled its promise. He never found out for sure who on the White House staff had blocked his appointment, although he had strong suspicions.

When Max Rabb left the White House, the "minority problems" portfolio was passed to Rocco Siciliano. Born in Salt Lake City, Utah, Siciliano, in his mid-thirties, was Eisenhower's youngest aide, and the first Italian-American to serve as a special assistant to a president. His expertise was in labor and federal personnel management. He knew very little about blacks.

Adam Powell had proposed that the White House invite Dorothy Height, the popular head of the National Council of Negro Women, and the president's failure to do so left some women's groups fuming. Although female civil rights activists were demonstrating as much courage and leadership as their male counterparts, they were not recognized or treated equally by the movement's male leaders, a fact that would stir repeated demands in the future for the inclusion of the eloquent and persistent Dr. Height in key meetings.

Just before the meeting, Siciliano had cautiously advised Ike that he shouldn't use the two words—"patience and tolerance," as Siciliano remembered them—that had prompted a negative reaction a few weeks earlier when the president addressed the Negro summit meeting. Eisenhower, according to the aide's account of the pre-meeting briefing, bridled at the suggestion, calling them "good English words." But the president heeded the

Sharing a laugh at my retirement party with a friend of many decades, NCNW president Dorothy Height. (Photo by Fred Watkins.)

advice. The aide described the meeting as a success, "even if success in this area is built on sand."[10]

The accounts given to *Jet*, however, indicated that what the aide saw as success was not necessarily the four leaders' evaluation of the meeting. The civil rights leaders came away feeling that Eisenhower didn't have a grasp of the race problem, particularly in the South, at one point having asked whether reports he'd received about racial conditions there were true. Roy Wilkins elaborated for him, describing how in one black college community in the South, even faculty members with master's degrees and doctorates were disqualified by local voter registrars. The president, Wilkins told me flat out, seemed unaware of what was going on in Dixie. Nevertheless, one of the group excused Ike's obtuseness on the subject, attributing it to errors "of the head, not of the heart," adding that "illness has kept him away from many vexing problems." (Eisenhower suffered a heart attack, and later a stroke, as well as other health problems while in the White House.) Another member of the group shrugged, "I suppose he got more out of the conference than we did. At least he got firsthand reports of conditions."

The four men had petitioned the president to take bold leadership action to advance the cause of civil rights, including further legislation to fill gaps in the recently enacted civil rights bill, and the convening of a White House conference on civil rights. According to Siciliano's account of the meeting, both the president and Attorney General William Rogers saw little merit in such a conference, and the president commented on the difficulty of getting civil rights legislation through the Senate.

The White House aide also reported that the president was extremely dismayed to hear that after five-and-a-half years of effort in this field, his visitors were saying that bitterness on the part of the Negro people was at its height. Eisenhower wondered aloud if further constructive action would only result in more bitterness. The civil rights leaders hastily assured him that the bitterness they described was not directed at the White House, but at communities where even slow progress seemed to have stopped.

In the end, the only immediate response the civil rights leaders heard to their proposals was a lecture from Attorney General Rogers that they should have opened their written statement with praise for the administration's civil rights record.

Several years after his White House experience, I asked Morrow about Ike and civil rights. According to the former aide, Eisenhower "could never fully come to grips with this all-important and vital domestic issue. He would moralize and philosophize about the problem, but as far as taking the one gigantic step that would have kept this issue from becoming the headache and great political football it became, he just could not seem to make himself act." Morrow surmised that perhaps Eisenhower's very background was his nemesis on the civil rights issue, as "he was born in Texas, raised in ("Bloody") Kansas, and many of his close friends were from the Deep South." Morrow concluded with certainty that "these factors influenced his decisions and made him vacillate in his determinations."

THE FINAL DAYS OF J. ERNEST WILKINS

Another saga that gave blacks pause about the Republican administration began to unfold at about the same time as the Negro summit, and, coincidentally, also involved Labor Secretary James P. Mitchell. Mitchell had suddenly removed J. Ernest Wilkins, the highest-ranking black in the administration, as head of the official U.S. delegation to the International Labor Organization (ILO) Conference in Geneva, Switzerland, and replaced him with thirty-two-year-old George Lodge, the son of U.N. representative Henry Cabot Lodge. Wilkins had headed the delegation for the past three years and was already packed for the trip. It was seen as a severe blow to his prestige, as the word circulated that Secretary Mitchell was trying to "get rid" of him.

I reported in Ticker Tape that Negroes felt burned by this, as there seemed no justification for it.[11] Wilkins, by all accounts, had done an admirable job in the highly visible subcabinet post. He had come to Washington in 1954 after a thirty-five-year legal career in Chicago, where he'd been president of the Cook County Bar Association. A Phi Beta Kappa graduate of the University of Illinois, he had worked his way through law school at the University of Chicago, after enlisting in the army and serving in France as a supply sergeant in the 809th Infantry Regiment in World War I. With no experience in international labor relations, he understood very well that his race was seen by the administration as an asset on the world stage, where the Soviet Union was consistently using America's racial problems to enhance its own influence in emerging Third World nations. Three quarters of the world's population was non-white, and Wilkins believed that his own racial background would "bear testimony that this government recognizes all groups in America."

Criticized by labor leaders for his lack of labor experience, Wilkins, according to department officials, quickly learned the ropes and within months was making a record in the job, receiving acclaim for his speeches, instituting exchange programs, and developing a labor presence in Africa. Said one, "When he made up his mind, he went all the way."

A teetotaling, non-smoking, non-cussing son of a Methodist minister, the soft-spoken Wilkins avoided Washington's party circuit, turned down social invitations by the score, and didn't serve alcohol at social gatherings in his own home. Described by some as "ultra conservative," the staunch Methodist churchman earned the sobriquet "the Puritan of Mahogany Row." At the same time, he won the respect of the rank and file at the department with his attention to key personnel issues, as well as his quiet demeanor and low-profile work ethic. He was responsible for the first Negro secretaries to accompany overseas delegations and the appointment of top race aides in his section. It was said that even while walking the halls, he noticed all-white sections and complained to personnel. Yet, his own secretary was white, and he made no effort to replace her.

Wilkins sought no attention from the press, although, as the first black subcabinet member, and the first Negro to attend a cabinet meeting with the president (in the absence of Secretary Mitchell), he was the administration's most celebrated Negro appointee. All of this made it all the more awkward for both men when Secretary Mitchell, after four years of apparent satisfaction with Wilkins's performance, suddenly started saying privately that he regretted appointing him in the first place, and was trying to ease him out.

Details of Mitchell's differences with Wilkins were never revealed, but appeared to be political rather than racial, although race always lurked in the shadows. One incident (as recounted by a labor leader) that might have ticked off Mitchell occurred during the ILO meeting in Switzerland in 1957 when a Russian delegate launched a spirited attack on the U.S. as a country spawning people like Mississippi Senator James Eastland. An American delegate urged Wilkins to object on grounds of irrelevance to the issue under discussion, but Wilkins reportedly retorted, "He's telling the truth, isn't he?" and refused to step in, leaving another delegate to do it.

In the fall of 1957, Secretary Mitchell, according to reliable sources, indicated to aides his displeasure with Wilkins as head of the eighty-person staff that handled relations with labor leaders in seventy-nine countries, and revealed that he had been responsible for Wilkins's appointment to the newly minted U.S. Commission on Civil Rights as a means of easing him out. If that was the plan, it didn't play out that way. Mitchell's removal of Wilkins the following May, just days before he was to lead the American delegation to the ILO in Geneva, was anything but subtle.

Three days after the delegation departed without him, Wilkins suffered a heart attack in his office. He was hospitalized and confined for almost three months during which his family feared first for his life, and then that the temporary blindness he suffered might be permanent. When he recovered sufficiently to return to work, he found the pressure mounting for his resignation, all of his former responsibilities delegated elsewhere, and his secretary reassigned.

His initial reaction to his removal as head of the delegation had been to draft a letter of resignation, but he'd suffered the heart attack before deciding whether to submit it. Now he was even angrier over his treatment upon returning to the department, and tore up the letter. Wilkins was determined that since the president had appointed him, the president should hear his case.

People who'd spent a lot more time in Washington than Wilkins were surprised by this stance, and opined that he didn't understand the rules of the game. One said Wilkins knew a lot about church politics, but was lost when "they hit him from behind" in national politics. Finally, in midsummer, Eisenhower agreed to meet with him, and Wilkins ducked into a side door at the White House for the face-to-face meeting with the man who had uprooted him from a successful thirty-five-year legal practice. The president was later described as firm in his position that Labor Secretary Mitchell had the right to appoint his own team. But he added that he would find another job of equal importance for Wilkins. No shrinking violet, Wilkins said he would think it over.

In mid-August, I reported in *Jet* that poor health might force Wilkins to resign and that George Lodge was being groomed to replace him. But someone in the White House decided to make his resignation certain by planting with nationally syndicated columnist Drew Pearson a version of events patently intended to humiliate Wilkins.

Pearson reported that Wilkins's meeting with the president was a "pathetic scene" during which the assistant secretary wept as he pleaded to keep his job. The imagery couldn't have been more demeaning, conjuring up the picture of a weeping slave begging his master not to sell him down the river. The story made convenient use of a byproduct of Wilkins's coronary and temporary blindness—the frequent welling of tears in his eyes.

A few days after daily papers all over the country had published Pearson's column, Eisenhower acknowledged during a routine news conference that he'd had a "congenial talk" with Wilkins, who was "considering resigning" because of his health, but the president denied that he was being forced out, as Pearson had reported. Wilkins, according to friends, finally realized he had lost the battle, and quietly began taking his personal things home from the department. But he did not officially resign for about three more months, when he was immediately replaced as expected by George Lodge. I noted in *Jet* that Secretary Mitchell never mentioned the outgoing assistant secretary at his successor's swearing-in ceremony. I also noted that Wilkins was the third, high-ranking Negro "dropped" by the administration. More than one top Republican confided that the whole affair was embarrassing, poorly handled, and without doubt, the "low-water mark" as far as Negroes in the party were concerned.

Publicly, Wilkins expressed no rancor over his reported "ouster," instead tackling head-on the challenges facing him and the other members of the civil rights commission as they prepared for their first hearing on allegations of voting rights violations in Montgomery, Alabama, where more than forty-five witnesses would be called to testify. No longer the reserved bureaucrat, he was now back in his element. His anticipation might also have been heightened by the dose of reality the investigative body faced in finding accommodations for the hearing. Instead of the choice hotels to which Wilkins was accustomed as a member of the U.S. delegation to the ILO in Geneva, the civil rights commissioners stayed at Maxwell Air Force Base after downtown Montgomery hotels refused rooms to the group because Wilkins was a Negro.

The hearing, like many more the commission would hold over the years, was riddled with drama as black witnesses, refusing to be intimidated by the crowd in the Federal courthouse, boldly recounted their experiences trying in vain to register to vote. White registrars balked at answering questions from the sharp Negro lawyer who had the audacity to question them, some taking refuge behind the Fifth Amendment protection against self-incrimination.

Some said the hearings were a turning point in Wilkins's life, transforming him from a quiet persuader to a powerful crusader for civil rights. At the close of 1958, I reported in *Jet* that Wilkins was being considered for another post, maybe a federal judgeship, although one Washington pol had told me he'd never get another government appointment after serving on the civil rights commission. Three weeks later, and just ten days after the second Montgomery, Alabama, hearing, such speculation became moot. J. Ernest Wilkins died alone in his Washington home, after apparently suffering another coronary in his sleep. He was interred in Chicago, while some in Washington hoped that with him would be buried all memory of J. Ernest Wilkins's last days in the Department of Labor.[12]

Fred Morrow had serious doubts about that, having seen Wilkins's departure from the subcabinet as another example of Negroes losing ground in Eisenhower's second administration. What Morrow found most disturbing was that even before Wilkins's resignation, his replacement had been chosen—and he was white. To Morrow, this was a major "bungling" that would hurt the Republican Party, because the Democrats were gaining tremendously among Negro voters. By spring of 1959, he would conclude that Republicans were failing to see the handwriting on the wall.

YOUTH—THE LEAST PATIENT OF ALL

Ebony's May 1960 issue reported in graphic detail on "The Revolt of Negro Youth" against the slow pace of desegregation. The text was white against a black background, and the photos were riveting: Howard University students kneeling in prayer in front of the U.S. Capitol; in Nashville, students singing hymns in the street before being arrested and charged with "conspiracy to obstruct trade and commerce"; in Richmond, a student from Virginia Union University, handsomely attired in business suit and tie, waving as he's escorted to a paddy wagon; thousands of Alabama State College students demonstrating at the state Capitol in Montgomery, undaunted by mass arrests and expulsions, and facing official threats to close the school; black and white Fisk University students sitting together at a segregated lunch counter; a fraternity man picketing in Fayette, North Carolina behind a sign, "Get in 'Step' With Time"; black Chattanooga high school students facing off with white toughs. In Houston, New Orleans, Greensboro, more protests, more sit-ins, more marches, and more arrests.

Underlying it all, the rising economic status of Negroes, the Supreme Court's decisions on school desegregation, African nationalism, the Montgomery bus boycott, and the agony that was Little Rock. Another important factor was the desegregation of the armed forces. After experiencing an integrated environment, young soldiers returning to homes in the South were far less likely to tolerate Jim Crow.

Now, here they were, in middle-class black America's most popular magazine. The children whose parents had sacrificed mightily to send them to college were being led to jail. Diane Nash, a twenty-one-year-old Fisk University junior, described being arrested and facing trial for the simple pursuit of freedom as a transformative experience. It was both a promise and a prophecy when she told *Ebony*, "This fight has not begun yet."[13] The biggest battles of the civil rights revolution were yet to come, and it would be black youths, rather than lawyers, leading the charge in the new decade.

12

BALTIMORE,
MY BALTIMORE

If one thing was clear as the Eisenhower administration waned, it was that blacks would get nowhere fast without increased voting strength, as the power of the ballot appeared to be the only force capable of moving the political machine. While in the South, registrars continued to use the most outrageous tactics to block Negro registration, in the North, the Negro vote returned solidly to the Democratic party in 1958's mid-term elections, rolling up majorities in Negro communities in Chicago, Los Angeles, Cleveland, Philadelphia, Baltimore, St. Louis, and San Francisco. As the presidential elections approached, Democrats and Republicans alike maneuvered for the growing black vote, and voter registration drives were infused with new enthusiasm, not only by political clubs, but also churches.

One city where that effort seemed to be doing particularly well was Baltimore, hometown of the NAACP's astute lobbyist Clarence Mitchell, who commuted to Washington five days a week on the train. The whole Mitchell family seemed to have politics and civil rights in their blood, including Mitchell's wife, Juanita Jackson Mitchell. A youth activist back in the '30s when her future husband was a reporter for the Baltimore *Afro-American*, Juanita had stood with her mother, civil rights pioneer Lillie Jackson, at the forefront of a "Buy Where You Can Work" campaign. The movement led to a boycott of the dozens of white-owned shops that operated with overwhelmingly white sales staffs in the black community.

In 1950, Clarence Mitchell's younger brother, Parren, successfully sued the then segregated University of Maryland for admission to its graduate school, and went on to become its first black graduate. Eloquent, soft-spoken, and scholarly, he was elected to Congress in 1970, becoming Maryland's first black representative and serving eight successive terms during which he championed civil rights and was one of the founders of the Congressional Black Caucus. (Another Baltimorean, Thurgood Marshall, had been

Fellow Baltimoreans Thurgood Marshall (center) and NAACP lobbyist Clarence Mitchell were proud of our hometown's enduring history of civil rights activism, dating back to the early days of the twentieth century. (Courtesy of author.)

denied admission to Maryland's law school in 1929, and matriculated instead at Howard University, which was about to turn out the battery of stellar civil rights lawyers who would defeat such racial policies in the courts over the next decades. As a student, Thurgood rode that segregated train back and forth between Howard and his home on Baltimore's Druid Hill Avenue.)

Another black powerhouse family in Baltimore in the '50s were the Murphys. I admired Carl Murphy for his fearless and uncompromising journalism. He was a hero in my eyes and the man I wanted to work for when I graduated from Virginia Union University. The newspaper had played a key role in the "Buy Where You Can Work" campaign, and in Carl Murphy's wise hands, remained a powerful voice for civil rights and Negro voting power in the ensuing years. Fearless and uncompromising, Murphy developed many top flight reporters who later moved into the ranks of daily journalism and beyond. Carl Rowan, who went on to become deputy assistant Secretary of State, U.S. Ambassador to Finland, and Director of the U.S. Information Agency in the Johnson administrations, worked there briefly before joining the *Minneapolis Tribune*. The *Afro-American* became a symbol of aggressive journalism, and during World War II, some prominent government officials reportedly sought to halt its publication because of its unending fight against discrimination.

Some historians say the modern civil rights movement actually began in Baltimore during the Depression, citing the fact that the "Buy Where You Can Work" movement between September 1933 and June 1934 had mobilized the city's blacks to direct action for the first time. That same year, several churches and the Fourth District Republican Club had started a voter registration drive with an urgency based on the prospect of losing Negro representation on the city council for the first time since Reconstruction, due to a 1932 redistricting that had diluted black voting strength. The *Afro-American* was at the forefront of this movement, as well, along with a peculiar, itinerant faith healer known as "Prophet Costonie," who drew crowds with his reputed healing powers, and sent them away with something far more useful—sound prescriptions for education and voter registration.

Decades before Baltimore's Depression-era freedom movement began, a group of black leaders had come together in 1906 for the betterment of life in its segregated Negro neighborhoods, and my own maternal grandfather wrote a small but significant sliver of that history.

In September 1906, a race riot in Atlanta, Georgia, sent shock waves across the country. Ignited by incendiary newspaper reports of alleged assaults by black males on white females, the riot resulted in scores of blacks killed or injured and horrific property damage in the colored community. Blacks everywhere wondered whether it could happen in their own communities and quietly took stock of the underlying conditions that fueled the riot, assessing whether those conditions were also present where they lived. One such assessment was made by Baltimore blacks, including James H. N. Waring, my grandfather, who looked at the state of the city's black neighborhoods, and while noting the absence of some of Atlanta's issues, still did not like what they saw. The differences, as Dr. Waring summed them up, were that unlike Atlanta, Baltimore had no "incendiary press to inflame the passions of the poor whites of the city, nor had she a class of hysterical women to take fright at the sudden appearance of a black face." And finally, Baltimore lacked "that loose attitude toward law and order that permits the disorderly elements of the population to disregard and defy" law enforcement authorities.[1]

Nevertheless, there were heavily populated colored sections of Baltimore that were "infested with saloons kept principally by whites of the lowest type . . . [and] dens of vice in too large numbers scattered throughout the city—all of which were exercising a demoralizing effect upon the colored youth and furnishing schools of crime for colored children." Some of the worst saloons and many houses of prostitution were within 300 feet of public schools, from which girls as young as thirteen or fourteen years of age were lured into lives of shame. Worse yet, these places appeared to enjoy a "quasi-police protection." When one mother, who had recently moved to Baltimore from the country, sought the help of a policeman in rescuing her twelve-year-old daughter from one of these dens, she was threatened with arrest for disorderly conduct. It was conditions such as these that had laid the foundation for the Atlanta riot, and thus prompted the apprehensions felt by many of Baltimore's "best colored citizens," according to a report written by my grandfather summarizing the "Work of the Colored Law and Order League."[2]

The League was the creation of a "little band of men," some of Baltimore's leading black professionals—a lawyer, a druggist, two physicians, several churchmen, and three educators, including my grandfather, who at the time was principal of the Colored High and Training School. Ultimately, the League grew to include "the best colored men of the city," who occupied its most prominent and influential positions, and were most often in the forefront of movements for civic betterment. But at the first meeting in October 1906, less than a month after the Atlanta riot, it was agreed that the original group would comprise a committee of just ten men to investigate and thoroughly document with reliable data the conditions in colored neighborhoods.

In addition to the saloons, gambling dens, and houses of prostitution degrading the colored neighborhoods, the report included sections of an earlier report by a nonprofit organization showing the lower Druid Hill Avenue district as the "tuberculosis centre" of both the city and the entire State of Maryland, and detailed the unsanitary living conditions in the neighborhood.

When the keepers of the saloons found out about the investigation, they threatened the members of the committee, including Dr. Waring, with everything from physical injury to economic ruin. They were successful in driving out some of the members, but not my grandfather, who stayed with it through publication of its now historic report. One thing the group quickly realized was that in order to contend with the powerful saloon interests, the committee would need active involvement of "the best white people" of the city. They appointed a subcommittee, which visited about a dozen of these movers and shakers, including a former president of Johns Hopkins University, a bank president, the president of the Chamber of Commerce, the diocesan head of the Episcopal Church, a leading lawyer, a retired capitalist, a foundation officer, a judge, the city's postmaster, and the U.S. Attorney, who became a legal advisor and advocate who "performed most helpful service for this committee."

The committee was encouraged by their hearty reception by all but one or two of the influential men, but the members were also struck by "the frequency with which certain questions entered into nearly all of these conferences, including the query as to "why the colored man will not work," intimating that some of the vice and immorality grew out of the black man's laziness and idleness in these neighborhoods. In response, the committee produced statistics from the U.S. Census Bureau, which showed, contrary to popular white belief, that a larger percentage of Maryland's colored men than whites were at work. The committee answered a handful of similar questions based either on stereotyping or ignorance of the conditions in the colored neighborhoods that impacted the lives of even the youngest school children.

At least one question, however, was based on fact. Asked why the colored jail population was so large, the committee acknowledged that, but also showed that in its twenty-five-year history, the Colored High School had furnished only one inmate for the penitentiary or jail. The League report showed in graphic detail that it was far cheaper to educate a Negro than to hang him.

Several of the whites actively interested in helping were ex-Confederates, and "the best Southern people" stood ready to lend a helping hand. With a supportive editorial from the *Baltimore Sun*, the League, represented by the U.S. Attorney, who was flanked by members of the clergy (both Negro and white), and the president of the school board, went before the Board of Liquor License. White property owners, concerned about declining home values in neighborhoods adjacent to the colored areas, had filed petitions in support of the League.

The Liquor Dealers' Association was also there, represented by "an array of some of the leading lawyers in the city," as well as individual saloon keepers with their own attorneys. Ordinary citizens of all hues vied for standing room at the hearing. Given the conflicting testimony, including a police witness who incredibly testified that a local black church gave the department more trouble than the saloons, the Board decided to do some investigating on its own. What it found was exactly what the League had claimed, and in the end, the Board revoked eleven liquor licenses, and denied approval of two others. In addition, authorities launched an investigation of the police department, which had clearly been derelict—and apparently corrupt—in its dealings with the white-owned saloons and bawdy houses in the black neighborhoods. Encouraged by this victory, the Colored Law and Order League continued its efforts for the betterment of living conditions in the black community.[3]

FAST FORWARD

When I returned to Baltimore on *Ebony* assignment in 1959, I found that blacks in the sixth largest U.S. city had made history again, achieving a "sudden, spectacular spurt" in voter registration, that had accelerated the pace of desegregation in education, employment and housing, with results unequaled anywhere in the country except Washington, D.C. Under the headline, "Baltimore New Negro Vote Capital," I reported how a massive NAACP voter registration drive, block-to-block, touching every neighborhood, had resulted in an unprecedented forty percent increase, bringing Negro voter registration to an all-time high of 104,000 in a two-year period.

In some fifty churches and meeting places, an estimated 2,000 workers were being schooled in voter registration, then doubling back into their neighborhoods to keep the issue alive. As a result, both major parties, aware of the growing power of the Negro ballot, were nominating black candidates for major state and local offices.

The Baltimore project was being copied in seven cities, including Atlanta and Houston, and was promoted by the *Afro-American* newspapers. At the helm of the project was a man until then unknown on the national scene, a soft-spoken former dean from Florida Normal and Industrial Memorial College, the Reverend John Tilley. After accepting a pastorate in Baltimore, Rev. Tilley had immediately begun neighborhood vote drives, a grassroots movement that caught the attention and endorsement of NAACP officials.

Perhaps motivating the quiet churchman's zeal was a grisly piece of his family history that had been passed down through four generations. Rev. Tilley's great-great-grandfather had been killed by white plantation owners in North Carolina after it was learned that he was one of the leaders of a slave insurrection. The ancestor's head had been impaled on a pole outside his blacksmith shop as a warning to others who might have harbored similar ideas. Instead of embittering them, the atrocity had fired in the blacksmith's descendants a passion for justice as white-hot as his anvil.

THE YEAR END

Ebony's annual retrospective (for years a regular feature of the January issue) observed that although black progress in 1959 could not be measured by any one spectacular event, there were "major steps forward" in almost every significant area of endeavor. In addition to political gains in Baltimore as a result of the massive registration and voting drive, the magazine cited token integration in Virginia, the reopening of schools in Little Rock, and wider opportunities for qualified blacks in federal and state government, as well as in private industry. But it was in two key areas—civil rights and education— that the greatest "measurable progress" had been made.

In the first area, the fledgling U.S. Commission on Civil Rights over the past year had conducted field studies in Louisiana, Mississippi, Tennessee, and Florida, as well as its inaugural hearing in Montgomery, Alabama, on voting rights complaints, resulting in legislative recommendations to the Congress for, among other things, a federal takeover of local voter registration if necessary, and a constitutional amendment outlawing literacy tests as a prerequisite to voting. While many of its recommendations were never adopted, many others eventually were, and the commission would be a strong and persistent voice against voting rights abuses, housing discrimination, and unequal education for blacks over the next two decades, until the Reagan administration turned it on its head in the 1980s. Reagan's right-wing appointees went to battle with the civil rights community, by, among other tactics, turning the commission's focus away from legitimate civil rights issues to such questions as whether people of East European descent were being discriminated against.

Ebony cited school desegregation as the second major area of Negro progress in 1959, although the details hardly gave rise to euphoria. The number of students (black and white) attending desegregated schools in the seventeen Southern and border states had increased by more than half a million over the previous year. The Little Rock schools had reopened under court order; and Virginia's leadership of massive Southern resistance had "collapsed." But the annual recap went on to note serious problems on the "debit" side, including Prince Edward County, Virginia, which closed its public school system rather than desegregate. *Ebony* reminded our readers that similar plans had already failed both in Little Rock and in Front Royal, Virginia, giving rise to hope that this one would fail as well due to a lack of private funds.

Underlying the painfully slow but unstoppable pace of school desegregation, *Ebony* gave credit to "firm court action and the aroused moderate citizenry." And aroused it was, by the Supreme Court's *Brown* decision and its progeny, by the series of 10,000-strong rallies in Mound Bayou, the successful Montgomery bus boycott, and the increasing number of "sit-ins" at lunch counters across the South. Aroused also by the stories and photographs in *Jet* and *Ebony* that reflected not only "the good life" of black artists, entertainers, and middle-class super-achievers, but at the same time, and in the same monthly and weekly issues, full exposure of race-based atrocities such as the Emmett Till murder, the mob violence outside Little Rock's

Central High School, and the arrests of growing numbers of students for protesting against segregation.

With black indignation rising across the nation, *Ebony* methodically summed up the last year of the decade in terms of measurable civil rights gains and losses, noting that not all gains in 1959 were forced by court order, and that fourteen Northern and Western states had recently passed two dozen laws addressing racial and religious discrimination, including fair housing and equal employment opportunity. The magazine's message, as always, reflected both progress and hope.

As 1959 came to a close, *Jet* reported that while the black vote was growing in importance to white candidates for the highest offices, it was also electing blacks in a number of Northern cities to state and local offices in record numbers. In Philadelphia, for example, twenty Negroes had gained office as the Democrats swept the balloting for city, county and state offices. One interesting result was Republican Harold Stassen's loss by a vote of two to one to incumbent Richardson Dilworth in the race for the mayoralty. The former Minnesota governor's campaign pledge was to prohibit the settling of any more Southern Negroes in Philly if elected. In the year's last *Jet* issue, a short paragraph reported that Rev. King, in Chicago to begin a nationwide fundraising drive for the Southern Christian Leadership Conference's campaign of desegregation "through nonviolent, Christian means," had warned that America must solve its desegregation problem within ten years or "it will be too late."

It was inevitable that the next decade would be hugely different from the last.

13

A TALE OF
TWO CAMPAIGNS

Ebony celebrated a milestone in the 1960 election year, publishing its fifteenth anniversary issue in November. The magazine had grown to an impressive 172 pages, printing more than 800,000 copies, read by about four million people around the world. It was shipped to some 30 countries, and could be found on newsstands in Paris, Addis Ababa, Lagos, Berlin, and Tokyo. Johnson Publishing Co. had well-outfitted bureaus in Beverly Hills, New York's Rockefeller Center, and downtown Washington, D.C. As for its editorial concept, the magazine noted that it, too, had evolved: "*Ebony* will try to mirror the happier side of Negro life—the positive, everyday achievements from Harlem to Hollywood. But when we talk about race as the No. 1 problem of America, we'll talk turkey." And it did, in its editorials, its year-end tallies of black gains and losses, its feature articles on the civil rights movement, and its stunning photographs by, among others, David Jackson, G. Marshall Wilson, Maurice Sorrell, Ernest Withers, and Moneta Sleet. Sleet would make history before the end of the decade as the first black person in journalism to win a Pulitzer Prize.[1]

In the closing weeks before the November presidential election, when reports from the field showed that Republicans were about to lose heavily in Negro precincts, GOP strategists came up with a last minute plan. Two days before the election, Secretary of Labor James P. Mitchell, campaigning heavily for the Republican ticket, unveiled a new report: "The Economic Situation of Negroes in the United States." The foreword of the study, signed by the secretary, included a hard-to-believe message, which received wide publicity in the press. Citing "steady improvement" in the social and economic status of Negroes, Mitchell claimed that in key measurable areas—including education, type of work, income, and housing, among others—the "historic differentials between whites and Negroes have narrowed." Backing up this claim were statistics carefully skewed to influence the reader to believe the "race gap" between white and Negro standards of living was slight after eight years of prosperity under the GOP.

Negroes didn't buy it, and the report had little if any impact on the vote in the fourteen states where it was important, possibly because up to that point, the party had shown little interest in winning the black vote. Several years earlier, an Eisenhower appointee, speaking in New Orleans about black gains in federal employment, had made the astonishing announcement that under the Republicans the rate of increase of Negroes in government employ there was 300 percent. Newspapers carried the story, with few reporters having checked to find that government employment of Negroes in the "Big Easy" had grown from two to six people.

Even in 1960, government exploitation of data on blacks in an effort to show progress and consequently win their support was not unusual or unique. Starting with Franklin D. Roosevelt during the New Deal, politicians learned how to use this information skillfully to attract votes in the North, and encourage Negro leaders to believe that racial problems were being solved, if very slowly. Following the same strategy, Eisenhower aides once estimated Negro income at about $20 million annually, setting off a boom in advertising in the black community as companies sought to tap into this reputed wealth. Unfortunately, much of the advertising was for products such as liquor and cigarettes.

In truth, the economic condition of the Negro on the whole was, in a word, miserable. A million Negroes were unemployed, many without skills or education or any reasonable prospects in an era of automation. Yearly wages for some Negro families in Southern states failed to reach $400 annually. Thousands were on relief, welfare, and unemployment compensation. National Urban League Executive Director Whitney Young also used 1960 figures to tell black audiences what they already suspected: that the masses of Negro citizens were actually farther removed, relatively speaking, from the mainstream of American life than they were twenty years earlier. Among the facts he cited: average family income of Negroes was 54 percent of the average white family's, after a steady decline from a high of 59 percent in 1952; nationally there were twice as many blacks unemployed than whites; blacks represented only 12 percent of those in professional, managerial and technical operations, as compared with 42 percent of whites. In housing, Negroes were more segregated than ever before. Less than three percent of the one million homes per year that had been built in the U.S. in the last ten years had been available to Negroes. In terms of education, black kids received three-and-one-half years less schooling—or more like double that if one considered the inferior segregated schools of the South or the slum schools of the urban North. Then there was life expectancy, for which all the negative influences combined to give the Negro about seven fewer years on this earth than his white counterpart.

Always looking for success stories to keep the dream alive, *Ebony* editors near the end of the decade searched the country for black millionaires. They couldn't find even twenty-five who could qualify in a financial examination.

THE NIXON CAMPAIGN

I started my coverage of the 1960 presidential campaign by following the Nixon camp around the country, but I soon asked to be reassigned. Nixon had been the Eisenhower administration's "Mr. Civil Rights." As chairman of the contract compliance committee, he had earned newspaper space, lots of publicity, and a good number of Negro friends. To his Washington meetings came black leaders from around the country, carefully selected to include Democrats who might change parties or votes. No opportunity was missed to snap a photo of a visitor with the vice president, and then rush it to both the guest and his hometown newspaper. In the 1956 campaign, Nixon was the GOP's civil rights workhorse. He shared credit for regaining some 22 percent of the Negro vote that year, boldly campaigning that the Eisenhower administration had "made the greatest advance" in Negro rights since the Emancipation Proclamation. He had even disclosed his NAACP membership at a press conference in Houston, Texas—quite an extraordinary act—and needled Democratic candidate Adlai Stevenson as "helpless and futile" in the race relations area.

It was Nixon who led the U.S. delegation to Ghana's independence celebration in 1957, and happily posed for news photos with African leaders as the delegation crossed the continent. It was on this trip that he was introduced to the Reverend Martin Luther King, Jr., also a member of the official delegation. King used the opportunity to ask the vice president to intervene with Eisenhower on behalf of Negro leaders with whom the president had repeatedly refused to meet. When we returned to the U.S., Nixon instead gave King an audience, sitting down with him, with Labor Secretary James P. Mitchell at his side, and answering a litany of questions from the civil rights activist. The black press announced the meeting on front pages—"Rev. King, Nixon to Meet June 13"—and afterwards, *Jet* ran a detailed report on the discussion, from which King, still relatively unknown on the national scene, gained some stature, while Nixon notched up his own image in the black community.

Despite his many contacts with American and African blacks during the Eisenhower administration, there was something about Nixon that blacks simply did not trust. Although he was probably in the company of Negroes more than any other member of the administration, Nixon never seemed really comfortable in that company. One incident that personally gave me pause occurred on a Sunday in mid-May 1957 at a reception he and Mrs. Nixon hosted for members of the press who had accompanied him to Africa. It was the couple's first social event in their new home in the exclusive Spring Valley section of Washington, an area that previously had restrictive covenants prohibiting sales to non-whites, but the clause reportedly had been removed from the Nixon deed. (This was almost twenty years before the federal government purchased the three-story Victorian home known as the "Admiral's House" on the grounds of the U.S. Naval Observatory as an official vice-presidential residence. Before that, vice presidents bought or rented their own homes in Washington or stayed in hotels.) Mrs. Nixon had been very excited about moving into the new house, and had shared her eagerness with staff and others who accompanied the couple on the African tour. When their guests arrived at the reception, the Nixons invited them to tour the house, which was built on three levels, with the living room, a large dining room, a smaller, more intimate dining nook, and the kitchen, about which Mrs. Nixon was particularly excited, on the first floor. She was also going to have household help for the first time because of her heavy engagement schedule.

When my wife and I arrived, the Nixons greeted us especially enthusiastically—almost a hero's welcome, it seemed to me. I was baffled by this because I wasn't outwardly a Nixon fan by any means, and my wife and I were both registered Democrats. After a maid took our coats, the Nixons personally showed us around the house, even leading us into the kitchen, where Mrs. Nixon was almost euphoric about the new, modern appliances. A moment later, when someone else joined the group, Mrs. Nixon presented us as Mr. and Mrs. Louis Lautier! Lautier was another black White House correspondent, but unlike me, a known Republican sympathizer. I corrected Mrs. Nixon and she apologized. I still thought that even for Lautier, this would have been an unusually warm reception. I had no idea why.

A year later, Ethel Payne and I decided to cohost a reunion of the African entourage, which had been a particularly congenial group. Ethel had just moved into a new apartment that she had yet to furnish, so I suggested we hold the party there, joking that without furniture, there'd be plenty of room to boogie. The invitees would include several members of Congress and foreign diplomats, as well as the thirty-five reporters and photographers who had accompanied the vice president to the Ghana independence celebration and the whirlwind tour of eight other nations. I also suggested that we invite the Vice President and Mrs. Nixon, although we agreed that they probably wouldn't come.

When the Nixons accepted, Ethel felt a bit unprepared. The party was suddenly a much bigger deal, and she would need more than just the few pieces of furniture she had, as well as a bunch of other things. Always a fast thinker, she cabbed down to the Hecht Company's flagship department store at 7th and G Street NW and told the manager her problem—which was not only the lack of furniture, dinnerware, etc., but no cash on hand to buy it all. Apparently as persuasive as she was resourceful, Ethel talked the retailer into sending a truckload of stuff and letting her pay for it on time. We also got expedited engraving on a leather pocket secretary personalized with Nixon's initials and the inscription, "Happy memories of our African Safari." For Mrs. Nixon, Ethel decided on a white orchid corsage as a gift. The party was a huge success. Our fellow journalists included Peter Lisagor, a 1948 Nieman Fellow who later was D.C. bureau chief of the *Chicago Daily News* for almost twenty years. A frequent panelist on Sunday's nationally televised interview shows, Pete was a genuinely good fellow and a great friend. Also among the guests was Howard K. Smith, who would be the only national TV reporter in Birmingham four years later when the Freedom Riders were beaten almost to death after Public Safety Commissioner "Bull" Connor turned the bus station over to the KKK; the AP's John Scali; David Reed of *U.S. News and World Report*; and Henry Burroughs, president of the White House News Photographers Association—which had yet to admit its first black member, a lingering source of contention between our *Jet* bureau and White House Press Secretary Jim Hagerty.

The Nixons arrived in high spirits, with the vice president commenting that there ought to be an annual reunion to keep alive the warmth and camaraderie developed by the people who made the trip. Instead of the quick pop-in we expected, the couple stayed about two hours, even bringing the hostess a souvenir bottle of bourbon that gave us all a chuckle, since we knew that Ike and the vice president were not particularly close. The label read:

The President's Choice
Richard M. Nixon

In 1959, the vice president interrupted his Florida vacation to greet visiting Guinea president Sekou Touré in North Carolina, the state having been chosen in part because Fred Morrow's brother, John, then serving as U.S. ambassador to Guinea, had been on the faculty of the University of North Carolina. Another reason was that other Dixie cities, such as Atlanta, didn't welcome Africans. They had no interest in photo ops such as North Carolina state troopers holding umbrellas over the heads of African women. Earlier in

Vice President and Mrs. Nixon attended a 1958 reunion I co-hosted with Ethel Payne of the *Chicago Defender* (to my right) for members of the press who accompanied the U.S. delegation to Ghana's independence celebration in 1957. (Photo by Maurice Sorrell.)

the year, Nixon had been the first member of the administration to speak of desegregation as a "moral issue," something black leaders had been trying to get Eisenhower to do without success.[2]

Still, blacks simply did not trust Nixon. One reason was his failure, in eight years in Washington, ever to hire a Negro for his Capitol office staff. As chairman of the government contracts compliance committee, Nixon had urged employers to hire Negroes, but had not done so himself. I had even put an item in Ticker Tape in 1958, noting that Nixon was scouting for a Negro aide, but nothing ever came of it. I had an opportunity to raise this with Nixon some months after he lost the 1960 election. I said I hoped he'd employ a Negro on his staff one day. At first smiling faintly, and then grinning as he seemed to remember something, he happily replied, "You don't have to worry anymore. I've got just the man. We hired a skycap from the San Francisco airport this morning." I was flabbergasted. "Hell, Mr. Vice President," I blurted, "I'm talking about your executive staff!" His face reddened as he realized his faux pas and quickly added, "Give me recommendations. I'd be interested. Don't forget." It was typical Nixon.

Negroes soon noticed, once the 1960 campaign got underway, that if Nixon had a message for the black community, he was neither articulating it, nor going where Negroes lived. After compiling what most would have agreed was an impressive civil rights record for a conservative Republican, Nixon virtually gave up the Negro vote by not campaigning vigorously in the big cities and ignoring current civil rights issues.

Even White House aide E. Frederic Morrow, who took a leave of absence to work in the Nixon campaign office, was taken aback by the shift in Nixon's persona. Morrow had been in the doghouse with his fellow Republicans early in 1960 when he quit an official delegation, headed by Ambassador Henry Cabot Lodge, to independence celebrations in West Africa after being told that the State Department was not allowing the four blacks in the group to take their wives on the ten-day trip, while most of the six whites could. Party officials were not pleased with the public way Morrow called out the department on the racial issue. The press coverage wouldn't help the Republican Party's prospects in the black community, but Morrow's stand was based on principle—the State Department was one of the most racist bureaucracies in the government—and he never intended to hurt the White House or the Republican ticket.[3] He liked Nixon, admired how the Vice President and Mrs. Nixon had handled themselves on their African trip (on which he accompanied them), and genuinely supported the ticket. But when he joined the Nixon entourage on the road, he was virtually ignored, never called into parlays or strategy meetings, never seen with the vice president, and given no support for outreach to black communities. The candidate's campaign aides weren't interested in Morrow's insights, advice, reactions—virtually anything he had to offer. Rather than waste his time, he asked to return to his duties at the White House.[4]

For me, covering Nixon's campaign quickly became a bore; it was also a challenge to come up with an angle of interest to *Jet* readers. Nixon's strategy was probably based on the theory that he wouldn't win more than the usual percentage of the Negro vote for a Republican ticket and shouldn't risk alienating the conservative, anti-Catholic vote in both the North and the South, where he had a chance to make some inroads. That was the vote he went after. After seeing Nixon play the role of administration "liberal," I was surprised to see the thoroughness of his campaign managers in ignoring Negro communities, even in swings through large cities, keeping Negro VIPs off the platform at rallies, and keeping civil rights out of the discourse.

One day I was near some of his top aides when they were discussing with wire service reporters running mate Henry Cabot Lodge's proposal that a Negro be named to the cabinet. After a moment, I realized they were concocting a Nixon reaction for the wire services that would neither back Lodge's proposal nor disenchant what the candidate thought was a large Negro following. Suddenly one of the aides realized I was within earshot and whispered, "Don't talk too loud, Booker can hear us." And I did hear them.

I found the episode emblematic of the campaign's whole antipathy toward Negroes and the black press.

A few months after Nixon's defeat, I asked for an *Ebony* interview with the former vice president. Incredibly, before agreeing, he telephoned my publisher and secured a guarantee that he could read the manuscript before publication because, although he told Mr. Johnson he wanted me to do the story, he didn't trust me. Ironically, by this time, the feeling was mutual. The last few months had provided substantive justification for Negro doubts about Nixon's sincerity. After witnessing the campaign firsthand, I was among the doubters. I didn't know what to expect from the interview in his 11th floor Los Angeles office. What I got was a glimpse of the Nixon of the future, a man who would spout his own version of the truth, of history, and even the president's constitutional powers, and expect people to buy it because he said it. Looking me right in the eye, and speaking as if with reasonable conviction, Nixon told me, "I could have become president. I needed only 5 percent more votes in the Negro areas. I could have gotten them if I had campaigned harder." I couldn't believe it, and wondered whether he believed it himself. Or whether anybody would.

It would be decades later, when many of the tape recordings Nixon had made in the Oval Office and elsewhere were finally released, that we would learn that Negro suspicions about Nixon's sincerity, not just about civil rights, but about the black race itself, were well-founded. In a conversation with aides John Ehrlichman and H. R. Haldeman on May 13, 1971, Nixon commented that he had "the greatest affection" for Negroes, but added, "I know they ain't gonna make it for 500 years." He allowed as how "you have outstanding Negroes" and "you have to help them. You've got to find the Booker T. Washingtons and the George Washington Carvers." Comparing Negroes with "Mexicans," he said the latter steal and are dishonest, but "they don't live like a bunch of dogs which the Negroes do live like."[5] A conversation two years later with secretary Rosemary Woods reveals that he held fast to his views. Nixon scoffed at Attorney General William Roger's prediction that, as Nixon recalled it, blacks were "'coming along, and that after all they are going to strengthen our country in the end because they are strong physically and some of them are smart.' So forth and so on." Nixon said his own view was "I think he's right if you're talking in terms of 500 years. I think it's wrong if you're talking in terms of fifty years. What has to happen is they have to be, frankly, inbred. . . . That's the only thing that's going to do it, Rose." Whatever he meant by "inbred" is anybody's guess.

Another bizarre observation emerged in a conversation with press secretary Ron Ziegler and chief of staff Bob Haldeman, in which Nixon commented that spies were most often Jews, and that "there are damn few Negro spies," to which Haldeman replied, "They're not smart enough to be spies. Not intellectual enough." Nixon agreed that "may be." He also observed that "very few of them (Negroes) become Communists," which he thought was "very lucky" without specifying for whom. Jews, however, according to Nixon, "are born spies . . . They're just in it up to their necks." To which Haldeman replied, "Well, they've got a basic . . . deviousness. . . ." Ziegler agreed.[6]

In a September 1972 telephone conversation with Henry Kissinger, Nixon opined that the U.S. needed a new Africa policy. The man who had toured Africa on the emergence of so many independent nations, now groused that "we shouldn't have forty-two ambassadors to these goddamned countries."[7]

So much for the intellects at play in the White House after Nixon finally became president in 1969. To our credit, the black vote never put him there.

THE KENNEDY CAMPAIGN

A *Jet* poll in August 1959 showed black Democratic voters split among presidential contenders Adlai Stevenson, John F. Kennedy, and Hubert H. Humphrey. As for the issues, there was no contest: civil rights was no. 1, with only a few readers citing the economy, jobs, or foreign affairs.[8]

John F. Kennedy was not my sentimental favorite prior to the 1960 Democratic convention. During the primaries, I had favored Minnesota Senator Hubert Humphrey, a liberal who had been a devout civil rights advocate for as long as I could remember. Hailing from a state with a relatively small Negro population, Senator Humphrey was nevertheless outspoken on the subject. When he entered the primaries, his campaigners had little money, and perhaps a minimum of political skill. The latter was made all too evident by one embarrassing gaffe right at the outset. In January 1960, when Humphrey announced his candidacy, his office failed to alert the black press, as it normally did for any civil rights statement, and not a single Negro showed up to hear the most liberal contender make his bid.[9] The candidate quickly apologized for the slight.[10] Massachusetts Senator Kennedy, meanwhile, had telegrammed invitations to each Negro press representative to hear him on the civil rights question.

My second choice for the Democratic nomination was Senator Stuart Symington, a man from a border state whom I respected for his record of pioneering in civil rights before it was fashionable. As an industrialist, he was one of the first to back fair employment policies, and as a government administrator, he hired Negroes in top slots. It wasn't the thing to do in those years, but Symington, when he was administrator of the Reconstruction Finance Corporation, even got into a row with the Department of State by insisting that one of his aides, George L. P. Weaver, a Negro, be sent to Bolivia to make a study of minerals.[11] Weaver later was appointed Assistant Secretary of Labor for International Affairs (the post held earlier by J. Ernest Wilkins) by President Kennedy.

The Kennedy machine that rolled through the convention, all but flattening those in its way, convinced me of the ineffectual role of the Negro at the kingmaking stage. After making pious and sometimes grandiose statements before the platform committees, black leaders retired to the stands to watch the fight. The few Negro delegates made little difference, even when some Negro labor unionists jumped to their feet on the convention floor, yelling loudly against Texas Senator Lyndon B. Johnson as the Democratic nominee for vice president. One hollered, "A sell-out!" while another unsuccessfully tried to start a "Down with Johnson" chant rolling across the delegations. Still others threatened to bolt, or to stay home during the campaign. They were whistling in the wind.

A day later, after a secret meeting with party heads, the Negroes were docile and cooperative. Those in labor were told to shut up or lose their jobs. Black politicos were threatened with loss of prestige and rank. The opposition melted like snow in the August sun. What followed in the next few weeks was a political blitz, backed up by money, promises of jobs, prestige and pictures in newspapers, that virtually covered the Negro community from coast to coast. It was estimated that more than a half million dollars—a lot more money in those days than today—was spent to insure the Negro vote. Black leaders on per diem salaries crisscrossed the country; celebrities from the entertainment world jetted in and out of cities; pamphlets, cards, letters and releases barraged every Negro of voting age. "It was the biggest vote hunt ever launched in a presidential campaign," according to one black insider.

In at least one instance, which happened to involve *Jet*, the campaign's enthusiasm prevailed over good judgment. For years, I had written my two-page column Ticker Tape USA, which had the simple design of a red border with the Capitol dome on the banner top. It was very popular for the tidbits of information reported nowhere else. Democratic promoters actually propositioned my publisher, seeking to "buy" the column for the campaign. When Mr. Johnson rebuffed them, they tried to buy space for a column that they wanted to be identical to mine in style, make-up, and typography. He again refused, but ultimately they placed a two-page ad in the magazine that looked an awful lot like my column (eleven pages earlier), including a red banner and similar layout.[12] Imitation may be the highest form of flattery, but I boiled to think that a political crew could be so lacking in ethics or judgment. Not to be outdone in the nation's top-selling black magazine,

Republicans placed a two-page ad in the same issue. Accusing Democrats of supporting civil rights in the North and white supremacy down South, the ad asked "Where Do Democrats <u>Really</u> Stand?" opposite an invitation—emblazoned with "White Supremacy" logos—in the *Montgomery Advertiser* to meet Senator Lyndon Johnson and Lady Bird Johnson at a campaign stop in the Alabama capital.

Traveling on a campaign as it crisscrosses the country, a reporter for the black press, particularly a weekly magazine, struggles to shape the story to fit the format of the publication. Kennedy's speeches were so literate and generalized, so lofty and principled, that no one could take offense. Few Negroes appeared on the Kennedy speaking circuit except in the big cities, and few Negroes held any campaign jobs outside of these discrete communities. Yet, in a matter of a few weeks, Kennedy transformed himself from a conservative to a man of sympathy in civil rights. Part of it was the simple step of making sure that a Negro newsman took his turn as a pool reporter on his private plane.

Some pundits credited Kennedy's telephone call to Coretta Scott King for sealing the deal on JFK's election. Rev. King had been arrested in Atlanta and jailed on a traffic violation. It was international news. Fred Morrow pleaded with the Nixon campaign to take some action—issue a statement, send a telegram to the mayor of Atlanta, anything. But he couldn't sell it. Nixon's aides thought it was "bad strategy." The candidate did nothing.

Jack Kennedy, meanwhile, made a supportive call to Mrs. King, while his brother Robert contacted the mayor of Atlanta and appealed for King's release. The incident was widely publicized throughout the black community, along with word that Nixon had refused to take any action. As a result, to thousands of black voters the image emerged of Nixon as hostile and insensitive, while JFK appeared friendly and sympathetic. When I asked Eisenhower about it a couple of years later, he said he hoped something like that would not have influenced the Negro vote. He still didn't understand the symbolic importance of JFK's gesture at that point in the civil rights movement.

I had firsthand experience with just how sensitive JFK could be on issues of race when the hotel in Paducah, Kentucky, where the campaign entourage was scheduled to stay overnight, refused me a room on racial grounds. Kennedy told everyone to get back on the three campaign planes, and we all returned to Washington. This was a very different response to race discrimination than one that occurred in an earlier Democratic presidential campaign. In 1952, Adlai Stevenson's campaign staff, learning that the New Orleans hotel where the candidate and his press entourage were booked would not allow Negroes, asked *New York Amsterdam News* reporter Jimmie

Hicks and two other black newsmen to stay in a dormitory at Dillard University, a nearby black campus. The two others happily went along with the plan, but Hicks insisted that he be treated just like the white press covering the campaign. When he got to the front desk and asked for his room key, he was "booted" by no less than the hotel's owner. Stevenson's press aide still tried to get him to go to Dillard for the night, but Hicks flew home instead, not even sure his paper, which was supporting Stevenson, wouldn't fire him. The story made headlines all over the country. The next day's apologies from Stevenson aides couldn't undo the damage they'd done to the campaign.[13]

Toward the end of the 1960 campaign, columnist Murray Kempton said to me, "The tragedy of a Kennedy victory will be that he has no Negroes close to him." On election night in Hyannis Port, Massachusetts, the truth of Kempton's observation was evident. A group of Kennedy supporters that I had described as the "black elites" of the campaign went to the armory to await the results, but were unable to gain admittance because they lacked credentials. Finally, a white aide from the campaign came to usher them in. The most expensive Negro vote-getting organization in history collapsed suddenly and completely. Its job was done. A few weeks later, the Negro politicians were lining up for jobs, but, except for some who were named to minor posts, most were ignored as JFK looked elsewhere to pick top-notch black candidates for key slots—starting out with Andrew Hatcher as associate press secretary. To many whites, this appointment probably represented nothing more than a political payoff, but to blacks, it was a major breakthrough. Hatcher became a symbol of success, comparable to Jackie Robinson when he broke into baseball's big league. When Hatcher appeared on television announcing one of JFK's news releases, his brown face was easily recognized, and it gave thousands new grounds for hope. The appointment was followed by others, including Harvard Ph.D. Robert C. Weaver in the important position of housing administrator.

14

A NEW DAY DAWNING

The day before JFK's inauguration, I received a telephone call informing me of my selection for the press pool accompanying the president-elect. For a Negro, this was as unprecedented as Kennedy's earlier rerouting of the campaign planes back to Washington after a Kentucky hotel refused me a room. And this was just the beginning.

Watching the inaugural parade as the marchers passed the White House reviewing stand, Kennedy noticed that there was no black cadet in the color guard of the United States Coast Guard Academy. When he asked why not, he was told the academy had no black cadets. He ordered a recruitment effort to address that.[1]

Kennedy also established new policies that assured the black press equal status at the White House. Unlike his predecessor, he routinely recognized us and took our questions. I also had an assigned seat at press conferences for the first time, in the second row, among the other accredited White House correspondents. Less than three months into the new administration, I had an opportunity I'd been looking forward to for four years, but never as much as in the months since being rebuffed by Eisenhower's press secretary when I objected to the White House News Photographers Association's refusal to admit our *Jet* photographer. The Kennedy news conference on April 12, 1961, in the Department of State auditorium was attended by more than 400 foreign and domestic journalists. For the first time in my years covering the White House, I was recognized when I sought to ask a question, and it made headlines.

"Mr. President," I began, "the White House News Photographers Association bars Negro members. Do you feel that a group attached to the White House should follow such a policy?" Kennedy replied emphatically, "No, I don't," adding, with some stammering, that he was sure once the matter was brought to their attention the association would admit every photographer accredited to the White House, and "that's the way I would certainly like to see it."[2]

My first question to President Kennedy was whether he thought it was all right for the White House News Photographers Association to bar Negros from membership. He said he didn't, and the discrimination quickly ended. (Courtesy of the author.)

JFK may have been personally unaware of the issue, but his press secretary, Pierre Salinger, had taken it up with the association's leadership the previous December, and was told they were going to review the matter. It would be several months before *Jet* photographer Ellsworth Davis could apply again, because the association's bylaws required a lapse of one year before a rejected applicant's next try. Davis had applied twice and been rejected, but the application of another black photographer, Maurice Sorrell of the *Afro-American* newspapers, was still pending. Sorrell's application had been approved by the association's executive board and would be voted on in several weeks at the next membership meeting, where, under the bylaws, a three-fourths affirmative vote would be required to approve it. It was at these membership meetings that black applications were rejected by a minority of the membership, led by the same outwardly racist members whose names are remembered even today by veterans of the association.

Even though he stammered, JFK's whole demeanor in answering my question was so different from Eisenhower's handling of any race question (at least the few he inadvertently fielded during news conferences) that it seemed a whole new era of enlightened thinking was permeating the White House—coming straight from the president. Salinger asked me for a copy of my correspondence a year earlier with his predecessor, Jim Hagerty, and I recounted how a small bloc of racists had repeatedly barred our *Jet* photographer's application, although it had been sponsored by *New York Times*, *Washington Post*, and *Life* magazine photographers, was approved by the association's executive board, and had the support of a majority of the approximately 150 members.

The Eisenhower administration had bought the group's argument that despite the privileges and advantages its members enjoyed while covering the White House, the organization was essentially a "social" club, which could exclude anybody it wished. Kennedy saw no merit in that argument. When the controversy hit the papers, the WHNPA tried to characterize it all as a "misunderstanding." But the association's clever way of allowing a few of its members to thwart black membership, without a specific policy doing so, was out in the open now. With that and the president's statement, Salinger had much more success in his discussions with the association. Very shortly afterward, Maurice Sorrell became the first black member of the organization, followed, after the mandatory waiting period, by Ellsworth Davis, who had moved on to *The Washington Post*, and was succeeded at *Jet* by Sorrell. There was no more pontificating about "patience" or "forbearance" emanating from the White House on issues of patent discrimination against blacks.

The incident provoked a challenge to another discriminatory practice as well, when a female reporter asked Salinger how the president felt about the White House Correspondents Association's policy barring its female members from the WHCA's annual banquet for the president. Salinger admitted he was unaware of this, but reiterated the administration's stand against discrimination in all forms, without commenting specifically on the stag dinner. Well known for her persistence, UPI White House correspondent Helen Thomas was not about to give up. She kept prodding until President Kennedy stated flatly that he would not attend the dinner unless the ban on women was dropped. The WHCA dinner in 1962 and forever after was open to all its members. Long-accepted customs were changing; racial and gender barriers were coming down.

BLACK EXPECTATIONS

In the weeks before the inauguration, my *Ebony* article on "What Negroes Can Expect from Kennedy" reported that supporters expected a bright new era of racial and social progress, but noted that "despite the facade of optimism, the new president is no tub-thumping liberal, not an active civil righter of the cloth of Minnesota's Sen. Hubert Humphrey or Illinois' Sen. Paul Douglas." Although he had polled a national 80 percent of the country's Negro vote, the highest since the days of FDR, Kennedy had few Negro personal friends, and wasn't the best discussant on the ways and means of civil rights. Besides, with a North-South combine responsible for his close victory, it was evident that he had to be considerate of Southern leaders—and faced a grueling negotiation to get his liberal legislation program through a hostile Congress.[3]

Nevertheless, we saw JFK as a president who could lead the nation through tough international and domestic controversies, including the increasingly more explosive Dixie race situation. I predicted more incidents and more strife, compelling the president to assert real leadership. Recalling that Kennedy had pointedly and forcefully emphasized in the campaign the responsibility of the chief executive to lead the nation on a "moral path," I reminded readers of JFK's greatest civil rights speech, delivered in Los Angeles early in the campaign. Even on his forays through the South, Kennedy had stressed civil rights issues. In a Columbia, South Carolina, speech, he accused Vice President Nixon of evading the issue, and promised advances in human relations if elected. Rep. Adam Clayton Powell, who had supported Eisenhower against Stevenson in 1956, and initially urged Negroes not to support the Massachusetts senator in the 1960 election because of his relationships with Southern senators, had stood on a platform during the campaign with Kennedy, Mrs. Eleanor Roosevelt, former Governor Averell Harriman, and New York Mayor Robert Wagner. Time and again before the election, JFK had taken pains to stress the greatness of a president in making a decision based on conscience rather than popularity.

But campaign talk was one thing, and getting anything done as president was another. Like waking up the morning after a drinking binge, and realizing everyone else actually remembers what you said the night before, the new president's advisors were now realizing that even the party platform plank calling for the end of segregation in federally assisted housing was actually impossible to do at this time without widespread repercussions. It was a vexing problem. In fact, the whole restlessness of the civil rights movement, particularly the youth demonstrations at the lunch counters in college towns across the South, took on a different meaning for the new administration now that it was time to work with Southern lawmakers on a legislative package. Kennedy was already finding Dixie congressmen rebelling at his liberal proposals. He couldn't afford to lose their support for his economic and other programs. The civil rights movement could get in his way. "Quiet as it is kept," I reported, "the new administration is fearful of the impact of more sit-in demonstrations and wants to find a solution to end them."

It was clear that the going would be tough, and there would have to be compromises made along the way. It was no surprise to blacks, therefore, when Kennedy backed off any civil rights legislation in order to get Southern legislators' support for economic and other proposals. But it was also clear that blacks expected a lot in return for delivering the election to the Democratic ticket. The GOP's defeat had resulted primarily from the loss of the Negro vote.

What JFK managed to do, even as the months turned into years and no civil rights legislation was sent to Congress, was keep the trust alive, in a way Eisenhower had failed to do. He did it, in large part, by the force of his words and his own powerful personality, emphasizing time and again that he had set a goal for himself, for which he expected to be held accountable. For Kennedy, the height of the bar, as he had told many audiences during the campaign, had been set by Abraham Lincoln, as he signed the Emancipation Proclamation:

> His hand did not tremble. He did not hesitate. He did not equivocate. For he was the president of the United States. It is in this spirit that we must go forth in the coming months and years.

Even though he would leave no new civil rights laws as his legacy, JFK nevertheless captured the heart of black America, becoming the best-loved chief executive in history. Applauded for appointing Negroes to high offices, Kennedy went even further, breaking down many racial barriers in informal ways. He probably hosted more blacks at White House events than had ever entered the mansion in all previous administrations combined. His appointment of top black leaders, including the NAACP's top lawyer, Thurgood Marshall, whom he named to the federal bench, for awhile had some blacks wondering if the new president was actually trying to stall the civil rights movement by a brain drain of its key resources. But his charm and the young first couple's unprecedented social schedule were disarming and mesmerizing. Following on the heels of a president who had angrily dismissed black Americans as a special interest group when they sought their constitutional rights, JFK's inclusion of blacks in what became a dazzling White House social scene was intoxicating for those caught up in the whirl of such events as the first couple's attendance at Nat King Cole's daughter's cotillion, or the presence of Sammy Davis, Jr., and his wife, Mai Britt, at a White House reception—probably the first interracial couple ever seen there, at a time when neighboring Virginia, just across the Potomac, not only still listed miscegenation as a crime, but prosecuted couples in interracial relationships.

These and other things so entwined with his personality enhanced JFK's standing in the black community, just as they established a new code of race relations for the administration. As many blacks saw it, "Lincoln freed us, FDR gave us jobs, and JFK gave us pride in ourselves."

15

THE FREEDOM RIDES

Driving the politics behind the nation's race revolution were the streams of Negroes moving from South to North, and from rural to urban communities, bringing with them the potential to build powerful voting blocs. In 1960, the census bureau reported more than fifteen cities with "exploding Negro populations," and experts pinpointed such centers as Atlanta, Detroit, and Philadelphia as places to watch—meaning to watch Negroes take over.

Yet there were federal laws on the books that Southern states were still ignoring, while continuing enforcement of their own Jim Crow codes. Black "patience" with this system had evaporated during the Eisenhower administration. Sit-ins at lunch counters had exploded all over the South, particularly in college towns. Bus boycotts modeled after the successful Montgomery bus boycott were breaking down the humiliating segregation of local transportation systems in city after city. The next target was interstate travel.

While most of the civil rights groups were concentrating on Southern voting rights drives, CORE's James Farmer, having developed expertise at promoting sit-ins, conceived a Freedom Ride from the nation's capital to New Orleans to test interstate bus transportation policies in the context of federal law prohibiting discrimination on such routes. The Congress of Racial Equality, known as CORE, had been founded in Chicago in 1942 by a group of students interested in the passive resistance tactics of Mahatma Gandhi. Its first sit-in was to get service for Negroes at Chicago's Jack Spratt Restaurant.

Each of CORE's projects was preceded by training, and the 1961 Freedom Ride followed this rubric. Farmer brought to Washington an integrated group of about fifteen volunteers, selected from a field of more than 300 throughout the country, for intensive training over three or four days. Plans called for blacks and whites to sit together and to use facilities interchangeably. Whites were to use Negro restrooms and stand at their lunch counters, while blacks were to use the main bus terminal facilities. CORE sent out press releases announcing the ride, describing it as the first major bus trip to challenge racial segregation since the Journey of Reconciliation, fourteen years earlier, which was also sponsored by CORE, following the first Supreme Court decision outlawing segregation in interstate travel. Riders at that time had been challenged by drivers and law enforcement as they tried to make bus desegregation a reality rather than merely a legal principle, but there had been no violence. Several had been arrested and served time (thirty-day sentences on North Carolina road gangs) on technical grounds while charges against the others were either dropped or successfully appealed. Fourteen years later, the buses and the terminals were still segregated.

CORE announced that the 1961 Freedom Ride would be different from the earlier "Journey" in several respects. First, it would penetrate into the Deep South; second, it would challenge not only segregated seating on the buses, but in eating facilities, waiting rooms, and rest areas in terminal facilities; and third, Riders who were arrested would remain in jail rather than accept release on bail or payment of fines. If all were arrested, CORE planned to move replacement teams in to continue the journey.

CORE stated that all it hoped to do was to demonstrate that a group could ride buses in the Deep South in a desegregated manner, and thus encourage others to do it. It should have been no big deal. Blacks rode on integrated buses all over the North and West, eating at the lunch counters, and using the restrooms without incident. There was no rational reason for it to be any different in the South. Yet everyone getting on the two buses in Washington, D.C., myself and photographer Theodore Gaffney included, knew it would be very different. Gaffney, a reed-thin, Washington-based freelancer, almost ten years younger than I, later admitted he didn't know what to expect, but wondered why a Johnson Publishing staff photographer wasn't going with me.

No mainstream (that is, white) press went along on the ride. I had called Farmer as soon as we heard about it, and told him *Jet* would cover it from start to finish. He was glad to hear it. Gaffney and I were the only newsmen boarding either of the two buses (one Trailways, the other Greyhound) on the morning of May 4. Moses Newson, reporting for the *Afro-American* newspapers, would join the ride later, in North Carolina. Newson took along a camera, intending to be his own photographer, although even carrying a camera—and more so using it—could get you killed on such assignments. It may have been his luckiest moment in Anniston, Alabama, later in the ride, when the smoke of the burning Greyhound bus was so thick he could barely breathe and the fear of what might happen when (and if) the Riders were able to get out of it was so great, that Newson forgot the camera under his seat. While he missed the picture of the burning bus, the choking passengers, and the mob watching the scene, his oversight may well have saved his life. When the camera was returned to him years later, he loaned it to a museum.

During an interview in April, I had mentioned to Attorney General Robert Kennedy that I was going on the ride, and his buoyant response— "I wish I could go with you!"—had surprised me. I wasn't quite sure if he understood the potential danger the Riders might encounter. The attorney general added that he planned to visit the South in the near future for a first-hand look at the Negro voting situation. He saw voting rights as one of the most important challenges facing the Justice Department, and an upswing in Negro voting a likely catalyst for improving race relations in Dixie. He also had announced a departmental policy of intervening quickly in school desegregation cases, and said that the Department of Justice would continue its campaign to end segregation at airports and rail and bus stations as well. Perhaps the most heartening of his statements was that there was now a new philosophy toward civil rights emanating from the Oval Office. He observed that the great problem in the past was that leadership in the sensitive area of civil rights did not come from the White House. Nor was there a follow-up from the Justice Department. This, he said, had now drastically changed. He cited the administration's action in the New Orleans school desegregation case as proof of the approach. He also told me he was shocked when he took office to find so few Negro lawyers in the department (there were only seven at the time), and had taken steps to improve that record, including contacting law schools and bar associations to aid in recruitment.[1]

Our *Jet* report on the start of the Freedom Ride ran in the same May issue as a piece on a change in the State Department's policy of steering dark-skinned foreign dignitaries away from Deep South states, especially trouble spots such as Montgomery and Little Rock.[2] It was five years since one of the most serious incidents had occurred in Alabama, while White House aide E. Frederick Morrow was serving as escort officer for Liberian President William V. S. Tubman, who was visiting the U.S. at President Eisenhower's invitation. In the middle of the night, the railroad car in which the visiting head of state was sleeping broke loose and went hurtling down the tracks. Investigators found that railroad workers at the train yard in Atlanta had failed to fasten the couplings properly. Tubman, understandably furious, threatened to cancel the rest of his visit.[3] The incident was kept out of the press, and the State Department made sure African VIPs henceforth were guided away from Dixie. Five years later, the department was conferring with Southern governors on a program to eliminate "risks of racial embarrassment." A few weeks later, State, as well as the Commerce Department, added teeth to the effort, warning sponsors of the International Trade Show scheduled for October 1961 in Charlotte, North Carolina, that the federal government

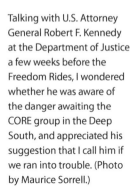

Talking with U.S. Attorney General Robert F. Kennedy at the Department of Justice a few weeks before the Freedom Rides, I wondered whether he was aware of the danger awaiting the CORE group in the Deep South, and appreciated his suggestion that I call him if we ran into trouble. (Photo by Maurice Sorrell.)

would not participate without a guarantee of nondiscrimination for visitors in hotels and restaurants. It was the first time the federal government had taken such a step to enforce a non-bias policy. But veteran—and even then revered—journalist Edward R. Murrow, who had taken the helm of the United States Information Agency, parent agency of the Voice of America (VOA), pointed out that the problem was not restricted to the South. Speaking out for the first time in his government post, Murrow asked, "Where do we house African diplomats in our nation's capital? Landlords will not rent to them; schools refuse their children; stores will not let them try on clothes; beaches bar their families."[4]

The Kennedy administration, struggling daily with the Cold War, was extremely sensitive to the bad press the U.S. was getting abroad on its racial problems. This resulted not only in quiet (and rejected) urgings to black leaders to "cool it," but VOA staffers later charged that Murrow capitulated to White House demands that the broadcasting agency's news reports of the violence against blacks be toned down in order to minimize criticism of the U.S. abroad. The news out of the Deep South was striking a starkly discordant note in the music of Camelot. But there was no way to tone it down. The dream, so long deferred, was about to explode in a youth movement that would not be denied. A torched bus in Anniston would help ignite it.

CORE had sent a letter to Robert Kennedy (as well as letters to the president, FBI Director J. Edgar Hoover, the chairman of the Interstate Commerce Commission, and the presidents of Trailways and Greyhound) announcing the Freedom Ride and describing its peaceful purpose. Farmer had received no response or reaction from any of them, which was as unsettling as the attorney general's "I wish I could go with you" comment when I mentioned that I would be covering the ride. I told Kennedy the Riders might need protection at some point, and he said to call him if trouble arose. Later on, he would say that he'd been blindsided by the Freedom Ride, a comment that may have reflected his anger at Hoover for not briefing him on the Klan's preparations to waylay the buses, information that the FBI's informers and field agents had passed along to headquarters.

One of the last things I did in the early morning hours before we left was to use the home phone number Deke DeLoach had given me, a gesture based not only on the good working relationship *Jet* had with both the FBI press office and DeLoach, but also the friendship Deke and I had developed over the past four or so years. I told him I would be traveling with the Riders as a journalist all along the route, and that I expected there would be trouble, especially in the Deep South, when the group, although well-trained for the past three days in peaceful, nonviolent protest, attempted to integrate restaurants and waiting rooms in the terminals and rest stops along the way. If he knew anything about what we were heading into, he didn't tell me, but just gave me the usual admonitions to be careful, and said he'd pass along my concerns. He did pass them along to field offices, but the FBI's follow-up memo reads as if this was the first they'd heard about the plans for peaceful protests, which was strange because CORE had already publicly announced them.

ON THE ROAD

The bus was fairly full when we left Washington, and despite the presence of a few local reporters in the terminal, the other passengers seemed unconcerned, and even disinterested in anything different or unusual about it. Although CORE's press releases had emphasized the peaceful intentions of the Riders, recent violence against students sitting-in at lunch counters across the South, and ongoing incidents of violence against blacks attempting to register to vote, plus the bold resurgence of Klan activity, suggested that violence awaited us anyway. Assistant Attorney General Burke Marshall, in charge of the Civil Rights division, was already in the South, and Justice aides had told us that the "bus testers" would be followed during the ride through Dixie because the administration feared that an outbreak of violence at a bus station could further harm U.S. prestige abroad. It would come out later that although J. Edgar Hoover had been tipped off about a deal between police and the Klan in Birmingham to allow ample time for an unimpeded thrashing of Freedom Riders, this was one of several pieces of critical information he hadn't shared with the attorney general.

The first test was just fifty-some miles away, at the rest stop in Fredericksburg, Virginia, where Jim Crow still reigned. Fredericksburg was a perfect opportunity to put the Riders' plan into action. Everyone knew what to do, since Farmer had gone over it repeatedly to make sure. One black Freedom Rider sat right up front in the whites-only section, while a black-white pair of Riders sat next to each other nearby. The others were scattered between the front and middle of the bus. They were free to discuss the purpose of the CORE project with other passengers. All were dressed professionally and instructed by Farmer to view themselves as role models in every aspect of their behavior. One member of the group on each bus was to serve as an observer, appearing uninvolved, and obeying the local conventions so as not to get arrested. Anyone who did get arrested was to refuse bond. Violence was to be accepted and not responded to in kind.

When the bus pulled into the terminal and the doors opened, the Riders disembarked with the other passengers and walked nonchalantly inside. We noticed immediately the first sign of the South's resistance to the fourteen-year-old Supreme Court decision banning racial segregation in interstate travel. The Fredericksburg bus terminal, just an hour's drive from the U.S. capital, was conspicuously outfitted with Jim Crow signs. Jim Peck, a white journalist who had been on CORE's "Journey of Reconciliation" more than a dozen years earlier, walked straight into the terminal and proceeded to the "colored" restroom, while a black college freshman, Charles Person, already a seasoned civil rights activist at just eighteen years of age, walked directly into the "Whites Only" men's room. The youngest of the Riders, Person had needed parental permission to participate in the ride. To me, he was a symbol both of what this demonstration was all about—the future of our black youth—and the generation that would bring about the overhaul of race relations in the United States or die trying. The fact that he sat in the front row of the bus said a lot about his determination. All over the South, students his age and even younger were pushing through to the front lines of what their elders started as a *peaceful* revolution, but which, as time wore on, the impatience of youth would find it difficult to sustain without fighting back. Charles Person, however, was fully onboard. The rest stop ended without incident.

(Fifty years later, Person and a handful of other veterans of the rides, including *Jet* photographer Theodore Gaffney and me, were honored guests at a commemoration of the event at Fredericksburg's University of Mary Washington. A stunning outdoor exhibit centered on a replica of the Greyhound bus, bathed in floodlights that stayed lit all through the night while

South of Richmond, bus terminals still displayed Jim Crow signs reminding the Freedom Riders that blacks and whites weren't supposed to be hanging out together. Always trying to keep the group's spirits up, Jim Farmer made retired professor Walter Bergman smile as he drew on his pipe. (Photo by Theodore Gaffney.)

a sound system played messages and songs from the original demonstration. Indoors, the students had amassed photos, signs and fixtures from segregated bus stations, and other historic memorabilia [much of it found on eBay], to enlighten a whole new generation to the courage of these pioneers. Protected inside a glass display case, a vintage copy of *Jet* was opened to one of my reports on the historic journey through the South. Charles Person, using a walker but still vibrant and bright-eyed, beamed his approval at the exhibit. At the conclusion of the evening, the university theatre's lights darkened for a preview screening of the first public television documentary on the Freedom Rides, based on historian Raymond Arsenault's outstanding book, *Freedom Riders.*[5] When the lights came on again, a thoroughly integrated audience of community members, faculty, staff, and students gave all concerned a standing ovation. It was quite a night.)

In Richmond, home of my alma mater, Virginia Union University, and the next rest stop, the Riders encountered no Jim Crow signs. But although the stinging directives had been removed from the walls and doors of the Greyhound bus terminal, blacks knew from experience which of the waiting rooms was for them. When two of the white Riders, deciding to do some "testing" in reverse, walked in and sat down in the historically "colored" waiting room, they confused black travelers, some of whom got up and left, uncertain what was going on.

THE LAW OF THE LAND

A recent Supreme Court case arising out of an arrest in the Richmond bus terminal should have settled the issue once and for all throughout the country as well as in the Virginia capital. It had been, after all, the latest in a string of Supreme Court cases finding discrimination in interstate commerce unlawful, including two cases dealing with bus travel. One of them was an interesting precursor to the incident that sparked the Montgomery bus boy-cott a decade later. In 1944, a spunky and courageous twenty-seven-year-old woman named Irene Morgan was seated next to another black woman with a baby in the rear of a crowded interstate bus in Middlesex County, Virginia. A white couple boarded, and the driver ordered the two women to relinquish their seats. Ms. Morgan refused, and the bus driver went to get the sheriff. When a deputy boarded the bus with a warrant and attempted to arrest her, Ms. Morgan, in the first of several moves that would guarantee her a place in history as well as in the local jail, tore up the warrant and tossed it out the bus window. When he then tried to drag her off the bus, she kicked him in the groin. With that deputy out of commission, another climbed aboard and also tussled with Ms. Morgan, who was about to fight him tooth and nail when she decided on nails only because he seemed so dirty, according to her obituary in 2007 in *The Washington Post*.

Charged with resisting arrest and violating Virginia's segregation law, Ms. Morgan refused to plead guilty to the latter charge and appealed her conviction. She was represented on appeal by a scholarly and brilliant black lawyer, one of the premier civil rights lawyers in the country, Spott-swood Robinson III, who would later become chief judge of the U.S. Court of Appeals for the District of Columbia. Rather than relying on the Four-teenth Amendment, Robinson made the novel argument that segregation laws impeded interstate commerce. The court disagreed and two other civil rights giants, Thurgood Marshall and William Hastie (later the first African-American judge on a federal appeals court), took the case to the Supreme Court, which ruled in 1946 that segregation in interstate travel was uncon-stitutional as an "undue burden on commerce."[6] Southern states ignored the decision, leading to CORE's "Journey of Reconciliation" in 1947 through Virginia and three other states to test what would happen. The answer was nothing good.

The Supreme Court, which had ruled in a 1941 railroad case[7] that the 1887 Interstate Commerce Act prohibited discrimination by common car-riers engaged in interstate commerce, took up a similar question in 1950,[8] again applying the 1887 act. But none of the Southern states was budging, and the federal government was doing nothing to enforce either the Act or the Constitution in most interstate travel. In 1958, Bruce Boynton, a black student from Washington's Howard University Law School, en route home to Alabama aboard Trailways, was arrested and charged with trespassing when he refused to move from the white to the colored section of a bus terminal restaurant. The student appealed his conviction on the grounds that the Virginia trespass statute violated his rights as an interstate traveler under both the Interstate Commerce Act and the Fourteenth Amendment of the Constitution. Thurgood Marshall argued Boynton's appeal before the Supreme Court in October 1960, winning the case.[9] Still, the South held fast, the Jim Crow signs (except in Richmond) stayed up, and the federal government did nothing about it.

MOVING SOUTH

For the Freedom Riders, the incidents finally started getting ugly in Charlotte, North Carolina, where CORE field secretary Joe Perkins was arrested for trying to get his shoes shined in a "whites only" shoeshine chair in the city's Union Station; then, black college student John Lewis was beaten to the ground by white thugs when he tried to enter a "whites only" restroom, and Al Bigelow, one of the white Riders, was attacked when he stepped between Lewis's prostrate body and the thugs. When Genevieve Hughes, a young, white Rider, was knocked to the floor, a policeman who'd been watching finally intervened.

Theodore Gaffney had only a couple of days' notice before joining me as *Jet*'s photographer on this trip. As a freelancer, he was happy to have the assignment, even though he wasn't sure what to expect. The only real preparation he'd made was to buy an additional camera, a new 35mm Nikon, a model he had never used before. Its usefulness was that it was smaller than the 4 x 5 Crown Graphic he usually carried, like most other professional photographers at the time. When he saw what was going down in North Carolina, he quickly decided to ship the 4 x 5 and its large carrying case to Chicago, where he'd retrieve it after the trip. It was not only cumbersome, but could easily get him beaten up or even killed. Although he wasn't in Little Rock during the violence outside Central High School, he was well aware of the assaults on Negro newsmen Alex Wilson, Moses Newson, Jimmy Hicks, and *Jet*'s freelance photographer, Earl Davy. Keeping only the smaller camera seemed a prudent precaution.

The Freedom Riders would encounter no problems in Georgia, where Atlanta's Mayor William B. Hartsfield that spring issued a warning in colorful language that included the observation that "Robert E. Lee wouldn't even spit on" the segregationist rabble-rousers he'd ordered the police to crack down on. He told *Look* magazine, "What happened in Little Rock won't happen here," promising that now that the state government had backed off its massive resistance policy, Atlanta's schools and lunch counters would desegregate without violence. Atlanta, he was confident, was leading the changing South. But Atlanta, in so many ways other than mere geography, was a long way from Birmingham.

The real deal was not to come until we hit Alabama, which, along with neighboring Mississippi, was more backward than all the other former Confederate states. Jim Peck had taken over as leader of the Trailways Bus group in Georgia when Jim Farmer unexpectedly had to leave to attend his father's funeral. Also onboard were Charles Person, Jerry Moore, one of several Morris College (Sumter, South Carolina) students, and Walter Bergman, 61, a white, retired college professor from Detroit, and his wife, Frances, 57, also a retired teacher, who was a designated observer. We crossed into Alabama on Mother's Day, May 14, 1961. We'd been riding more than a week, with rest stops, some overnights with CORE supporters, and dinner the evening before with Dr. Martin Luther King, Jr., in Atlanta. It was at dinner that Dr. King had taken me aside and told me straight out, "I've gotten word you won't reach Birmingham. They're going to waylay you." I joked that I'd be careful to stay behind Farmer, who was big and burly enough even for me to hide behind. Dr. King laughed good-naturedly, but the smile quickly faded. It was clear to me that he was concerned. A few hours later, Farmer got the call from home that his father had died, and he had to leave the ride. We boarded the bus that morning a little more apprehensive. The group's leader was no longer with us, and now I knew with some certainty that trouble lay ahead.

ALABAMA

As we rode through Alabama toward what was sure to be another depressing rest stop, I couldn't help but compare the towns we were bypassing with my own community in Prince George's County, just outside the nation's capital. "Braxton Village," as it was known, was an easy commute by car to JPC's downtown bureau.

The first homeowners in the community were Wilbur Braxton and his wife, Hilda. An auto mechanic by training, "Brack" as everybody called him, had been a chauffeur for the millionaire founders of the National Casket Company, a job in which he'd traveled throughout the country and Canada. When he settled in Suitland, Maryland, in the mid-forties, there were no decent housing developments open to blacks. He built their house on top of a hill, spearheaded the organization of the Dupont Heights Citizen Association, and worked to get paved roads, street lights, water, and sewage for what grew into the first decent development of its kind in the county. We lived just down the block from the Braxtons on Campbell Drive, named in honor of Hilda's family. Over the years he had remodeled their house to accommodate her wheelchair when a degenerative muscular disease left her unable to walk. Brack and Hilda were the unofficial mayor and first lady of Braxton

Village, and its heart and soul. Mrs. Braxton, with her soft voice and silver hair, was like everyone's grandma, and always had a kind word for anyone who stopped by. Brack was actively engaged in the community's voter registration drives, which brought him into contact with all the political types in the suburb. Congresswoman Gladys Noone Spellman, a straight-talking, former schoolteacher, was the first member of Congress to visit the community and hear its concerns, and was highly regarded as a pioneer for doing so. We had a Men's Club that constructed a playground and organized community picnics to let the kids know that the adults cared about them, and would help them stay out of trouble. We knew it "takes a village" and that's what we were about.

When Hilda died, a slight, young, white man with blond hair slipped alone into the small chapel as her funeral service began. In a few moments, with a nod from the preacher, he rose and walked to the lectern where without a single written note, he delivered a moving eulogy for a modest woman who'd never sought glory or power while she'd helped to grow a community of responsible citizens. As he left the chapel, Maryland Congressman Steny Hoyer, who would one day become one of the most powerful members of the House of Representatives as the Democrats' Majority Leader, embraced a tearful Wilbur Braxton.

Approaching Anniston, I put Maryland out of my mind. The tension was building the farther South we rode; reminiscing was the last thing one should do when every instinct had to be on the alert. When our Trailways bus pulled into the Anniston terminal, the sleepy Alabama town seemed peaceful, but oddly so. One white passenger mumbled to another that there would likely be a race riot when the locals spotted the two young black men sitting in the front seats. Charles Person, the Morehouse freshman, and Morris College sophomore Herbert Harris sat at attention, taking it all in. When the driver pulled into the terminal and opened the doors, Harris got out and looked around, but got back on the bus when he noticed that the terminal walls appeared to be lined with young toughs. One of the white Freedom Riders, Walter Bergman, also got off, and went into the terminal to buy some food. Mrs. Bergman followed and returned from the terminal with a newspaper, on which she'd scrawled, "It's touch and go," before handing it to me.

What looked like a gang of seven or eight white youths then boarded the bus. They looked like rough characters. Unkempt hair, collars open and short shirt sleeves rolled up in the style of the day to display their biceps, they exchanged crude comments, most unintelligible, as they boarded. Gaffney took their measure in a glance with his photographer's eye and wondered whether this was it. My own mouth was suddenly dry. Dr. King's warning the night before was running through my head. I thought, "This is it."

The bus driver started the motor, and one of the Freedom Riders called out that a passenger was missing. Bergman wasn't back yet. The driver stopped and got out, irritated, and tramped back into the station. A few moments later the professor ambled onto the bus with a bag of sandwiches, which he deftly distributed to members of the team without the rest of the passengers even noticing what was going on. It was a very smooth maneuver.

In a few minutes the driver returned, his face drawn and ashen. Standing facing the passengers, he announced that the Greyhound bus that left there a short time earlier was in flames, set afire by a mob. The passengers were being carried to the hospital by the carload. There was no information yet on injuries or deaths. Then he added bluntly, "A mob is waiting for our bus and will do the same thing to us unless we get these niggers off the front seats."

I was frozen in place, while concern for the Riders in that other bus, including my friend and colleague, Moses Newson, raced through my head. I wondered whether they were alive. The gruesome thought that they might have been trapped in the burning bus was too much to even consider. I struggled to bring my wits back to dealing with our own immediate situation.

"All right, let's move!" the driver ordered. He was talking to Person and Harris in their front seats. The rest of us sat as if suspended in time awaiting their reaction. There was none. They simply sat there, appearing calm, which we knew could not be true, and didn't budge.

The driver shrugged and sidled off the bus. He was not going to witness the explosion, but just let it happen. Suddenly the new passengers—the tough-looking white guys—took over. One of them snarled, "Niggers, get back. You ain't up north. You're in Alabama, and niggers ain't nothin' here." Without another word, one of them smashed his fist into Charles Person's head. A roundhouse right crashed into Harris's face. Within seconds, the toughs were raining blows on every Negro in the front section of the bus, while dragging Person and Harris from their seats. James Peck and Prof. Bergman ran forward in the aisle to object, but trained in nonviolence, did not fight back—not that it would have done any good in this mismatch—when they, too, were set upon by the toughs. A right hook lifted the slender Peck over two seats and into the aisle. One of the thugs battered Bergman into semi-consciousness, and then stomped on his chest as he lay in the aisle. His wife, Frances, screamed and begged them to stop. One of the hoodlums called her a "Nigger lover," but another cautioned, "Don't kill him."

I poked a small hole in the newspaper Frances Bergman had given me a few minutes earlier and pretended to read, watching the aftermath of the blood bath from my back seat through the gap in the front page, afraid that the toughs would beat potential witnesses senseless as well. When assignments like the Freedom Ride warranted such precautions, my photographer and I never stayed in close proximity. There were a number of reasons for this, the primary one being that photographers (black or white) were in a high-risk category all to themselves anytime the Klan was doing something illegal and didn't want to be photographed doing it. Some photographers took such risky shots, a reporter would have to be crazy to be standing next to them. Gaffney, for example, seated by a window a row or two in front of me, was much less circumspect than I—and incredibly brave. He actually raised the 35mm camera he'd bought specifically for this trip and, undetected—possibly by sheer luck—shot pictures of the assault, as blood, bread, and sandwich meat flew everywhere. In a matter of minutes, it was all over, obviously as carefully planned. The Freedom Riders were piled like pancakes in the aisle, between the white and Negro sections of the bus. The toughs sat on the armrests. A pistol protruded from the pocket of one. A Negro woman's plea to be let off the bus was answered, "Shut up, you black bitch."

When they'd finished their job, the driver returned and started the motor. A policeman boarded, grinned at the white thugs, and mumbled, "Don't worry about any lawsuits. I ain't seen a thing." Another white man, well-dressed, called up to the bus driver to change his route to avoid a "gang down the road." As we pulled out of the terminal, the driver confirmed that we were heading to Birmingham by an alternate route. I half expected him to be forced to turn onto a lonely road, where the bus would be burned, just like the other one. It took considerable effort to suppress the dark images bouncing around in my head. I had covered too many lynching stories; had seen too many hangings; had mourned over too many martyrs in the movement. I kept thinking that if I lived, I could be a valuable witness if I could keep my wits and remember faces and other details. Gaffney thought his photos might help with identification and prosecution of the toughs. (He would never be called upon to produce them.)

Suddenly, Bergman fell off the pile of victims in the aisle and tried to get to his feet, his face a mass of blood, cuts, and hair. "Aw, you goddam nigger lovers," bellowed one of the thugs, "get on back with the niggers."

I tried to retain an image of each of the thugs, so I could give a description to the FBI if I ever had the opportunity. I made a mental picture, framed it, and tried to store the image in my mind, but the details kept blurring until I realized that the only thing that was sticking was an image of hatred on a white face, and few other details, except that one of the punks seemed to have eyes that bulged out of his head. He was the one who kept taunting, "Just tell Bobby [the attorney general] and we'll do him in, too."

Jim Peck, who had spent hours telling me how he quit Harvard to join the cause, stumbled to his feet in the aisle and was slammed into a seat, his head hitting the window. He was bleeding profusely, but no one was allowed to go near him.

Although by now a veteran at covering civil rights assignments, I felt sick inside, weak, and powerless. My mind raced with images of other atrocities I'd covered. I knew I had to dispel the ghosts and concentrate on the here and now if I were going to make it. We were traveling on an interstate bus operated by one of the country's two major bus lines; we were in the United States of America, on a state highway, in the bright light of day, en route to a major American city; we were law abiding citizens; and we may as well have been rats trapped in a trash can.

Suddenly one of the thugs seemed bored, and started toward the back of the bus where Gaffney and I were sitting separately. I figured nothing could be worse than boredom provoking the hoodlums into violence against the innocent passengers in the Negro section of the bus. I remembered that I had a copy of the May 18, 1961, issue of *Jet* reporting "Integrated Group Starts Freedom Ride," in which the peaceful, nonviolent purpose of the ride, and its international implications were highlighted. If nothing else, I thought, the magazine might distract the gang for awhile and buy us some time until we reached Birmingham. I nonchalantly passed it to the bug-eyed fellow who seemed to be looking for entertainment. Apparently it worked, as they passed it around, laughing and jeering at various items they found funny, but no longer bothering the passengers.

BIRMINGHAM

A strange calm seemed to settle over the rows of seats as the bus rumbled into downtown Birmingham. The white toughs took seats in the front, no longer standing sentinel over the beaten Freedom Riders who had revived enough to sit straight and wipe blood from their faces. Outside, we could see groups of white men huddled on the street and spotted others clustered in the terminal as we rolled in.

The driver stopped the bus in its assigned space and opened the doors. Except for the hoodlums, there was no rush to get off—not by the white passengers in front or the Negroes (and the few so-called nigger lovers) in the back. Instead, the bus emptied slowly, the passengers filing out in an orderly procession. For the worst of the mauled Riders, there was little choice; they could barely move. I hesitated as long as possible, fiddling with my bag. Gaffney and I were almost the last to get off the bus. We were supposed to go from the terminal to a designated rendezvous point, the Birmingham home

Klansmen and young white toughs jumped *Birmingham Post-Herald* photographer Tom Langston moments after he captured their assault on Jim Peck in the Trailways bus terminal, where Public Safety Commissioner Eugene "Bull" Connor had promised the Klan fifteen minutes without police interference. Photo also shows FBI informant Gary Rowe (2nd right, with back to camera) participating in the beating.

of a veteran civil rights activist, the Reverend Fred Shuttlesworth, but I must have forgotten to tell my photographer that detail.

Even as my feet touched the ground, I became aware of the trouble ahead. The beaten and groggy Freedom Riders were slowly plodding into the terminal, heading straight for the white waiting room, like sheep heading to their own slaughter, as they took their final steps in defiance of Jim Crow. As I entered the terminal, I heard a wild roar. Ahead, I saw a mob set upon a white photographer who sank to his knees under a torrent of blows. A Negro man who had nothing to do with the Riders was attacked nevertheless as he proclaimed his innocence. A Negro woman, with no one else to call on, screamed, "Lord, help us!" Jerry Moore and Herman Harris had miraculously managed to slip away, but the mob quickly set upon Peck and Person, the white veteran civil rights activist and the young black college student, already badly beaten on the bus, who were now headed defiantly toward the white waiting room, side by side. Prof. Bergman looked futilely for a policeman, and then tried to help the pair, but was also set upon by the crazed mob, and wound up helpless on his hands and knees, covered in fresh blood on top of the caked residue from his earlier beating. His wife could not help him this time; he had insisted that she board a city bus to safety as soon as our Trailways bus pulled into the terminal.

I looked around for Gaffney and discovered we'd been separated in the melee. Seeing the mob, he'd headed for the "colored" waiting room. When he looked back, he saw white guys with bats and lead pipes running toward the "white" waiting room, but there was no sign of me. He wondered if I'd already been knocked to the ground or even killed, which he rightly figured might be his own fate if he came out of the waiting room.

Seeing Bergman on his knees surrounded by members of the mob, I knew there was no way for me to come to his aid except by getting help. Like Bergman, I, too, looked around for any sign of law enforcement, and seeing none, realized that the only hope was to get out of there as fast as possible. I had no idea where Gaffney was. I headed for the exit, and walking as fast as I could toward the street, passed groups of more young white men and boys racing crazily toward the terminal. Perhaps because they were so focused on getting to the center of the action, they hardly seemed to notice me, not even giving me a second look as they raced past. The mob was so blinded by their frenzy, we found out later that they even bashed one of their own Klansmen, whom they failed to recognize, as well as several innocent bystanders who had nothing to do with the Freedom Riders. Such was their determination to wreak as much damage as possible in the quarter-hour so generously allotted them for the attack by Birmingham public safety commissioner Eugene "Bull" Connor.

I spotted a solitary Negro cab driver cruising past the terminal and hailed him. After giving him the address, I slumped in the back seat and watched the scene as the driver maneuvered down the street. There wasn't a policeman in sight. I still didn't see Gaffney.

At Rev. Shuttlesworth's house, the clergyman alerted local Negroes (we referred to them as Rev. Shuttlesworth's "Birmingham deacons") to go down to the terminal to pick up the stranded Riders, some of whom were being chased all over downtown without police interference. Before heading back to the terminal, I made some calls, including one to the New York office of CORE to report what had happened, and another to my family, to tell them I was alright.

As if on cue (and in fact it was), the mob had left the terminal after its fifteen-minute rampage, and Gaffney thought it was safe enough to venture outside the "colored" waiting room. When two deacons encountered him, they asked, "Have you seen any Freedom Riders around here?" The shaken photographer replied that he didn't know if they were dead or scattered

Ahead of us by only one hour, the first group of Freedom Riders, accompanied by (Memphis) *Tri-State Defender* newsman Moses Newson, narrowly escaped from their firebombed Greyhound bus in Anniston, Alabama, when a mob backed away, fearful it might explode. (Birmingham, Ala. Public Library Archives, File #1076.1.87.)

around downtown, but he was glad to be taken along as the deacons headed out to look for the others, as he had no idea where we were staying in Birmingham.

Outside the terminal, I found Peck, bloodied and slumped on a wooden chair on the sidewalk. No doctor was available anywhere in Birmingham to treat him. Fearing further harm, he at first refused to be taken to a hospital, but finally relented when the bleeding just wouldn't stop. It took more than fifty stitches to close his head wounds.

Rev. Shuttlesworth asked me to help him get treatment for eighteen-year-old Charles Person, who had a deep gash in his head. With a Negro nurse, we went to the home or office of several Negro doctors, but each refused to treat him. Finally, the nurse stitched his wound.

Later, the Riders from the other bus, who'd been stranded at the Anniston hospital, trooped into Shuttlesworth's home. They looked like coal miners, covered in black soot, still trying to cough the toxic fumes out of their lungs. They had been rescued by a caravan of autos, all of them driven by the Birmingham deacons, many of them armed with guns, with instructions from Shuttlesworth not to stop for anything. The deacons had stepped up to take over the Riders' protection after state police had refused to help them get out of Anniston.

Finally, with everyone accounted for, we sat in Rev. Shuttlesworth's living room and tried to let the awful tension drain away, if only temporarily. For a few hours at least, it was over. But the worst violence most of us had ever witnessed in our lives was still more than just a vivid memory. The stench of smoke and soot and the horrible images of blood and swollen faces were right there in the room. Four of the white riders stayed at Shuttlesworth's home for the night after Negroes who had agreed to shelter them begged off out of fear. In the morning, there would be more to do than just pick up the pieces. The group had to decide what they wanted to do about the Freedom Ride.

"THEY NEED HELP"

There was no doubt in anyone's mind that the Klan had tried to kill the Riders on the firebombed Greyhound. There was also no doubt that the next attack could be worse, so incensed would the Klansmen be at the audacity of the integrated group's decision to continue the journey. From this point on, the Riders would be looked upon as challenging the Klan, and without protection, the small, brave band of nonviolent Freedom Riders would have little chance of making it to New Orleans alive. As soon as we hit the ground in Birmingham, I had recalled my conversation with Attorney General Robert Kennedy a few weeks earlier, in which he told me to call him if the Riders ran into trouble. If ever there was trouble, this had to be it. I called the Justice Department switchboard, and told them it was urgent that I get in touch with the attorney general. It was Sunday, but very soon John Siegenthaler, the special assistant and former *Nashville Tennessean* newspaperman (also a 1958–59 Nieman Fellow) who'd been with Kennedy during my April interview, called me back. He remembered my conversation with Kennedy, and my concerns—in fact, my prediction—that the Freedom Riders would encounter violence at some point in the journey. I knew Siegenthaler could be trusted to keep his promise to get my message to Robert Kennedy immediately. It seemed like only a few minutes passed before the aide called back with assurances that the Justice Department would protect the Freedom Riders, but needed time to work out the details. In the meantime, he suggested, we should try to diffuse the situation by keeping a lid on the most "sensational" aspects of the story. I couldn't believe my ears. I had seen reporters, including a Birmingham photographer, attacked in the terminal. I learned that CBS reporter Howard K. Smith had also happened to be on the scene, acting on a tip. I told Siegenthaler there was no way to put a lid on it. I emphasized that what the Freedom Riders wanted at this point— indeed, what they needed—was protection. Without it, all indications were that they'd be killed. (I might have said "we," because Gaffney and I were not about to leave the ride or abandon the story.)

The following morning, I was eating breakfast in Shuttlesworth's kitchen at 10:00 a.m. when I was called to the phone.

"The attorney general wants to speak to you." In a moment, Robert Kennedy came on the line.

"What are you doing down there?" he asked.

"I'm a reporter, remember?" I wasn't trying to be a smart aleck, and he ignored it anyway. I was tired. Nobody had gotten more than a few hours sleep.

"What's it look like?" he continued.

I quickly summed up the situation. With the Klan still watching the terminal—by now some of them in full regalia—we were trapped. "These people are in trouble," I warned. "They need help." I described the beatings, the serious head wounds and body injuries, the smoke-drunk Riders from the other bus, the lack of any police presence, the tension in the streets, the lack of adequate medical attention, and the uncertainty as to what might happen next.

When I gave the phone back to Fred Shuttlesworth, he listened to what he later described as words of encouragement from the attorney general. Kennedy was going to get police protection for the Riders. It was the first time during the modern civil rights movement that the leader of a Southern integration effort had the ear and undivided attention of the attorney general of the United States.

A few minutes after the call, the battered Freedom Riders took a vote. They wanted to continue on to Montgomery. We started preparing to leave. Meanwhile, from Washington, Kennedy tried unsuccessfully to get Governor Patterson to guarantee their safety. Informed of what seemed to be a stalemate, the Freedom Riders decided once again to put their lives on the line if necessary. Despite the certainty that the Klan was waiting, we all headed to the bus terminal, intending to board the three o'clock bus to Montgomery. The difference this time was that no law enforcement agency, from the city of Birmingham to the Department of Justice, could claim ignorance of our coming. Even without a formal agreement, it seemed doubtful to us that all of them would stand by and allow a repetition of the previous day's violence. And if they did, the whole world would be watching—unless the police allowed the Klan to take down the TV cameramen and bevy of reporters gathered there this time to record the encounter. The glare of the spotlight emboldened the weary Riders, just as they hoped it would dispel the bravado of the marauders. Some seemed confident that the group would be protected now that the president and attorney general were on the case. I think we all shared that optimism to some degree.

Sure enough, at least this phase of the plan was successful. The Freedom Riders, transported again in a caravan of cars by local blacks, arrived at the bus terminal and walked into the white waiting room while police held at bay a menacing crowd of males, a few as young as twelve or thirteen years old. The press was also in the station and eager to interview the battered Riders.

But the rest of the plan soon fizzled. Two bus drivers walked off the job rather than transport the group, which was no surprise after a report that Governor Patterson was disclaiming his ability to guarantee the bus protection along the route, almost 100 miles, from Birmingham to Montgomery. In Washington, Robert Kennedy was demanding that Greyhound find a driver. (This was when he made his famous comment that somebody had better get in contact with "Mr. Greyhound," which showed how ticked off and frustrated he was at the company's failure to get us on our way.) With nowhere else to go and no relief in sight, the Riders decided they had no choice but to head for the airport. Again, they felt confident that they'd be protected along the way. That feeling started to dissipate, however, when we saw the crowd, appearing to be easily as many as a thousand angry whites waiting for us there. State police had seen that we got to the airport, but a radio broadcast had alerted the entire Birmingham area that we were on the way. Suddenly the small phalanx of state policemen seemed very paltry compared with the size of the mob. We huddled together in the airport waiting room, smoking, reading, talking, trying to appear calm, as a few state police officers held back the crazy roughnecks, including dozens of robed Klansmen, some of whom had been at the bus terminal earlier.

Finally, we were about to board a plane when I saw Gaffney take a folder from a kiosk. Opening it, he wrote on what appeared to be a form, and then sealed it like an envelope.

"What are you doing?" I asked.

He replied as if it should be obvious: "Taking out insurance."

"You don't need that," I scoffed.

Gaffney, who had never been in an airplane before in his life and was somewhat apprehensive about it, was thinking that whatever happened in the air would have to be better than being beaten to death with a lead pipe. But in either case, he had a family to consider. He looked around and quietly reminded me that he'd had only a couple of days' notice before boarding the bus in D.C., and, unlike the CORE people, who'd had time to prepare themselves for nonviolent reaction to anything that might befall them, he was sure of one thing.

"If anybody comes at me, he's gonna have 'Nikon' imprinted backwards in his forehead!" He dropped the insurance packet in the mailbox before we boarded.

We were on the plane just long enough to believe we were finally getting out of our Birmingham hell, but we were mistaken again. Everybody was ordered off the plane and back into the terminal. There'd been a report of a bomb onboard. This time, it was my turn to head straight for the kiosk to fill out an insurance form. Like Gaffney, I also had a family to worry about. Getting out of Alabama was starting to become much more of an "if" than a "when" proposition. Again, we all huddled together, hoping the state police would maintain their positions. Another flight was cancelled because of weather over Mobile. Some of the Freedom Riders began to get panicky, one of them whispering, "This is a trap. We'll all be killed." Finally, at about 11:00 p.m., John Siegenthaler flew in on a commercial flight, and aided by four FBI agents and long-distance arm-twisting by the attorney general, got us flown out to New Orleans on Eastern Airlines. The sweat in our armpits wasn't just from the heat.

THE NEXT WAVE

The first Freedom Riders were going home to recover from what must have been the worst ordeal of their lives, for both the young and the old. Without question, it was the most frightening experience of my own career, and I'd had a few other bad moments in Mississippi in the '50s. But other Freedom Riders—ultimately more than 400!—would follow this brave band of peaceful warriors. A new group of young Turks, including future congressman John Lewis, who had departed from the first group of Riders for a job interview, announced they were picking up the trail and continuing the ride on to Montgomery and Jackson. When the governors of Alabama and Mississippi refused to protect them, the attorney general moved federal marshals in to avoid slaughter. Robert Kennedy urged the Riders to cancel their protest and wait out a "cooling off" period. At the same time, he acknowledged their right to proceed. Leaders of CORE, the NAACP, and the Urban League, Dixie ministers, and student groups combined for the first time in a united refusal to back off. The Kennedy administration didn't want bloodshed or another black eye in the overseas press, particularly with Soviet Premier Nikita Krushchev making the most of America's racial conflicts. But it was too late. Worldwide reaction to the onslaught against the Freedom Riders was loud and clear. Most cutting of all, perhaps, was Izvestia's labeling the violence as "wild, bestial mores in a country pretending to tell others how to live."

A *Jet* poll revealed that 96 percent of Negroes we surveyed believed the Freedom Rides should continue. Almost 74 percent responded that the nonviolence and passive resistance movement was the best way to win civil rights in the South. Far fewer, but still a majority (58.1 percent) believed Robert Kennedy "acted fast enough to protect the Freedom Riders," while more than 73 percent approved of the way he handled racial violence in Alabama. Readers were virtually united in urging President Kennedy to speak out forcefully for integration, and 89 percent said he should send troops into the South to stop race riots. Almost all (94.6 percent) said they had no faith in law enforcement by local officials in the South during racial disorders.[10]

Just months into his administration, despite his failure to urge the long-awaited passage of civil rights legislation, President Kennedy was still an overwhelming favorite of U.S Negroes—so popular that he could again win the black vote. His major appeal, however, according to *Jet* readers, stemmed from the administration's effort to enact a vast economic program—including minimum wage and health proposals. Other much admired actions were the equal opportunity drive in government and industry, and his appointment of Negroes to key federal posts, the most talked about being housing administrator Dr. Robert Weaver. Other pluses cited in *Jet*'s June 1961 survey were the Justice Department's role in voting rights, school integration, and interstate travel cases. For the first time in years, praise from blacks far exceeded their criticism of the chief executive.

After Birmingham, *Jet* associate editor Larry Still, a sharp and brave reporter on the Washington staff who in later years would head the journalism department in the Howard University School of Communications, took my place on the rides. Still joined the regrouped Freedom Riders as they pushed on from Alabama to Mississippi—and more bloodshed. There would be more beatings, and the near-fatal clubbing of Kennedy aide John Siegenthaler, followed by the outrageous incarceration of more than 300 courageous Riders, including John Lewis and James Farmer, in one of the country's most notorious prisons, Mississippi's State Penitentiary at Parchman Farm. Volunteering for the Freedom Rides had turned overnight from a sure likelihood of being mauled to an almost guaranteed ticket to Parchman for up to sixty days.

By now, the white press realized that the story of the Freedom Rides had "legs," and latched onto it. One double-decker Trailways Bus carried seventeen reporters (including Larry Still and two other black newsmen—George

Barnes of the *New York Amsterdam News* and Samuel Hoskins of the *Afro-American* newspapers), as well as a Mississippi National Guardsman. Sponsorship of the rides was also expanded from CORE to a new Freedom Ride Coordinating Committee. Called together by Dr. Martin Luther King's Southern Christian Leadership Conference, the organizers now included, in addition to CORE, SCLC executive director Rev. Wyatt T. Walker, twenty-two-year-old Ed King from the Student Nonviolent Coordinating Committee (SNCC), the indomitable Diane Nash, already a veteran of student protests and now secretary of the Nashville Christian Leadership Council, and the Reverend Ralph Abernathy, who succeeded Dr. King as head of the Montgomery Improvement Association. The NAACP contributed legal support in defense of the Riders who were arrested and jailed on bogus charges of disturbing the peace. But rather than pay fines, the Riders chose to fill Mississippi's prison cells to the point where it would tax the system that sought to oppress them.

While attention focused on interstate travel, the new leadership emphasized that the drive was being extended to "sit-ins, rest-ins, kneel-ins, shop-ins, move-ins and all 'ins' affecting first class citizenship." When told that the Freedom Rides were embarrassing President Kennedy, Rev. Abernathy, whose home had been bombed and church surrounded by a screaming mob, replied simply, "You must realize we have been embarrassed all our lives." As Clark College professor, Dr. C. Eric Lincoln, observed, "The passive Negro, who trusts that God and the NAACP will salvage his dignity while he concentrates on avoiding trouble, is becoming extinct."

As spring turned into summer and the Freedom Rides continued, *Jet* ran an editorial that poignantly reflected the Negro mood. A younger generation was calling the shots, interrupting their college educations to pursue justice before their academic degrees. These new voices would not be silenced. Predicting that the summer would bring "the most concerted effort in history to smash segregation not only in interstate travel, but in public facilities and accommodations as well," the editorial warned, "You haven't seen anything yet."

As the summer wore on and still the Rides continued, fueled by hundreds of black and white volunteers from all over the country and abroad, it was estimated that Mississippi had already spent $250,000 to keep the walls of segregation from tumbling down. With more than 300 demonstrators arrested as they arrived almost daily in Jackson, the state was spending $100,000 a month to house, feed, and clothe them, while losing millions in business and tourist trade because of the racial violence.[11]

Riveting, book-length accounts of the Freedom Rides have been written by others on those buses, including James Peck and U.S. Congressman John

Lewis, as well as by journalists and historians. Over the years, more details have emerged, particularly with the release of Justice Department and FBI files under the Freedom of Information Act. Television documentaries have captured news footage and personal interviews. It is a story that will never die and warrants retelling, if for no other reason (and there are many), as testament to the ultimate triumph of the human spirit over cruel oppression.

The day after his beating, Peck, his face and head bruised, swollen, stitched, and bandaged, smiled almost joyfully as he told newsmen he would do it again. But he made no secret of his disgust with the FBI when it came out that one of its paid informers had warned the bureau of a prearrangement between Birmingham's "Bull" Connor and the Klan to allow the mob fifteen minutes to beat the Riders, and that the informer also had participated in the beating. Peck sued the FBI for doing nothing to prevent the ambush. The FBI's defense, as usual, was that protecting people was not its mission, which was to investigate a crime after it occurred. The Bureau's position would have been more plausible, if history did not reveal something worse than ambivalence on FBI Director Hoover's part: a cold antipathy toward the civil rights movement, and a feeling that the Freedom Riders were troublemakers. Hoover's hostility was not fully understood at the time, and the storied crime stoppers of the bureau were still expected to be operating on the right side of the race equation.

The Freedom Rides and the ensuing months erased the aura of Kennedy infallibility as far as blacks were concerned. The vastly popular attorney general, for all the power of both his family and the department he headed, was now seen as just a human being—a white man caught in a web of racial passion and prejudice, suspected of having a great deal of political motivation behind some of his actions, but still a white man with a sense of fairness and decency. I heard him background many cases, from the violence in Albany, Georgia, to James Meredith's confrontation with "Ole Miss," and from voting rights issues to demonstrations. "Come up and see me," he'd say when I encountered him at a press conference or hearing. "For what?" I'd counter. "For you to tell me to have Negroes quit this or that?" He'd grin.

In a June 1961 broadcast on the Voice of America, the attorney general talked about the racial situation in the United States in the wake of the violence against the Freedom Riders, and stated confidently that a Negro could be elected president of the United States in thirty or forty years. He compared discrimination against blacks with the prejudice the Irish had faced in Boston forty or fifty years earlier, and opined that despite current problems, progress was being made. That, he said, was what was important.

I was in the press pool when the attorney general and his wife, Ethel, led the U.S. delegation to the Ivory Coast's independence celebration that summer. The Department of State had never been a bastion of equal opportunity for blacks, and so it was ironic to hear some department aides grumbling that the Freedom Rides would hurt U.S. prestige abroad, and especially in Africa. But Kennedy, peppered at a news conference with questions about civil rights, answered directly and candidly, and found that his reputation as a civil rights advocate had preceded him. Both publicly and privately, I found Africans praising him for his efforts to reduce discrimination.

These views were also shared by many whites. The February 1962 issue of *Ebony* reported the results of a survey of 500 Washington correspondents (almost all of them white) that produced some interesting results. Eighty-one percent gave the Kennedy administration an "excellent" or "good" grade in civil rights; 62 percent rated John F. Kennedy "high" as compared with other presidents on such issues; 92 percent said they regarded civil rights as a major national problem. The *Ebony* editors noted that one comment summed up the feeling of the overwhelming majority that JFK was not doing enough about it, but at the same time, that no president could, although he'd done more than any president since Coolidge. Also noteworthy was that while 29 percent said "not foreseeable or impossible to predict," 64 percent said it was possible that a Negro could be elected president or vice president in the next fifty years.

16

NO ORDINARY
FOOTBALL GAME

If Mother's Day, 1961, in Birmingham, Alabama, had unleashed a level of racial hatred I'd never witnessed before, Thanksgiving Day, 1962, in Washington, D.C., was a close runner-up. The difference was that in the latter instance, the people swinging the fists, and even some chains and other weapons, were black. They were my people. They were our youth. They also were out of control. I had never seen anything like it in my life. And it shocked me beyond description.

The Thanksgiving Day classic in D.C. at that time was the annual high school football championship game between the top Catholic league team, St. John's, and the public school champs, Eastern High School. The St. John's team, like the private high school, was predominantly white, while the Eastern team was all black, drawn from a school that despite desegregation, had only a handful of white students. It was a great day for a football game, and my two sons, Simeon, 11, and Jimmy, 9 (both of whom later played varsity football at St. John's), were equally excited. Along with another adult and five young friends, we joined 50,000 fans at the new municipal stadium near the banks of the Anacostia River in Southeast D.C.

Most of the fans, about 80 percent, were black, so the deafening roar that erupted when the Eastern team entered the field, versus the boos for St. John's, was not particularly surprising, although somewhat unsettling. When the Eastern team scored the first touchdown, the whole stadium seemed to shake, so thunderous was the cheering, stomping, and applause. The crowd was ecstatic. But just as suddenly, when St. John's pulled ahead in the second quarter with a 13–7 lead, the mood changed, as if a dark cloud had drifted over the stadium. Behind me, I could hear shouts of "Kill him" on tackle plays. My sons whispered to me that kids behind us were drinking alcohol.

At halftime, some of the white fans who left their seats for the bathrooms or concession stands were jostled, some even beaten, and others lost their seats to young blacks who decided to move down in the stands. Most of the incidents went unnoticed by all but a few bystanders in the immediate vicinity. Many people became apprehensive, however, about small, roving bands of rowdy black youths who seemed to be looking to make trouble. Still, when play resumed, most were thinking of little else than getting on with it. But the game was not going well for Eastern. The Ramblers fumbled the ball on the opening kick. St. John's Cadets recovered it and ran for the touchdown. The score was now 20-7. Then a fight started on the field. An Eastern player was ousted. I heard someone say, "Let's get out before the fighting starts."

But most people kept their seats, despite some eruptions here and there in the stands. St. John's kept the lead. The mood in the stands was turning worse than ugly. I told my younger son, oblivious to the danger, to quit waving his St. John's sign. Then the game ended and all hell broke loose. The scores of police ringing the field were not enough to keep hundreds of Eastern fans from swamping the field, sweeping in the direction of the St. John's stands, and grabbing anything with the Catholic school's name on it, while some pummeled anybody in their way. The fighting spread and spilled out into the streets. My friend and I tried to herd the seven kids to safety, along with hundreds of other parents trying to steer through the rage and pandemonium. My older son was pushed to the ground and trampled as a group of black kids chased a white boy. All around us, I saw fear, terror, and panic as happy family outings turned into an unbelievable nightmare. All I could think of was protecting the children we'd brought to the game. When it was over, all I could think was, how could this happen?

I couldn't sleep that night. Racing through my mind were the images of blacks chasing and beating whites—men, women, and children alike. I had never seen that in all the violent attacks I'd covered in the South. The face of hatred and blind fury had always been white. The next morning, the daily papers obscured what had happened at the game; even the police had reported only a fraction of the injuries that fans had sustained. I wondered whether I, as a reporter and an eyewitness, had an obligation to reveal what I had seen and experienced myself. But that would mean revealing the bitterest truth about the whole event: that it was not just a "boys-will-be-boys" outpouring of team spirit, as some were trying to portray it, but a race riot, black against white. What would that do for Southern arguments against school integration? What fodder would it provide to the racists in Congress who ruled the District of Columbia like a plantation? But on the other hand, what about the future? Didn't somebody have to address what really happened if we were to prevent it from happening again?

A jumble of conflicting arguments ran through my head. In hopes of sorting them out, I sat at the typewriter and drafted a letter detailing what I'd seen, describing to the best of my knowledge the chronology of events, and pinpointing what I thought were the immediate causes of the violence. Then I shoved the letter into a desk drawer and tried to move on. But friends kept calling. A black army officer got me on the phone and described how his son tried to help a neighbor's boy who had gone to the game with him. The young friend was beaten savagely, according to the colonel, "just because this kid is white," while his son was mauled for trying to help his friend. A Pentagon secretary told me how she came upon a white woman crying in the parking lot after the game. The woman's daughter was stretched across the back seat of their car, badly bruised and beaten. The daughter and her friend had been separated from the mother and slapped around by a gang of black youths.

People I didn't know also called throughout the day, urging me to write about what they saw or experienced. But there were others who wanted the whole affair to "blow over." I was advised by close friends that anybody who told the truth about what happened at D.C. Stadium would be called an "Uncle Tom," at best, or a traitor, at worst. I might even cause trouble for the Johnson Publishing Co. Certain elements would not understand what I was trying to do—lay bare the problem and get community action to address it. "This can harm you," I was warned. "You might be written off as a 'sell-out' to white folk." Another scoffed, "They've been beating us for years. It's time we gave them some of their own medicine."

Beneath all of this, my mind kept coming back to the innocence of my younger son, when hours after the game, as the family ate Thanksgiving dinner, he asked, "Dad, why did they beat up those St. John's people?" I could no more let that question go unanswered in my own mind than I could in his. I sent my letter off to all three Washington daily newspapers. Each of them published it on their editorial pages. Besides recounting what I saw that day, I urged that future games not be canceled, but pointed out what had not been done this time that needed to be done in the future. My letter specifically stated that the violence was not entirely racially motivated. There was a good dose of bad sportsmanship, too, as well as just plain rowdyism. A good number of blacks opposed the misconduct, and many were hurt trying to defend whites.

But school authorities as well as the police had badly misjudged the potential for violence. The school system, I wrote, had inadequately prepared for the game. There was little protection in place for the sports fans and their kids, and what little police manpower had been assigned to the stadium as a deterrent to violence was ineffective. Finally, I suggested that Negro leadership in Washington had a responsibility to tackle the problems of rowdyism and juvenile delinquency—not by issuing excuses or statements but by planned community-wide programs. Integration, I wrote, demands responsible citizens, and we must take the first step. It was probably that one statement that set off the biggest firestorm.

Calls jammed our phones at the Johnson Publishing Co. office, followed by an avalanche of letters, first from the Washington area and then from around the country as *Time* magazine and others picked up the story.[1] Most of the letters came from whites, commending me for pointing out the responsibility Negro leadership should assume—the part that most of the press seemed to emphasize in summarizing my letter. Reporters and wire services lifted from my letter the sections that blamed Negroes for the fighting, and dailies ran stories headlined, "Negro Blames Own Race For Violence." This one fact was deemed more important than any other, including the fact that in a city with a predominantly Negro population, not a single black served on any planning panel or session prior to a high school game in which a Negro team faced off against a white team.

The Negro response also was at first both disturbing and discouraging. I heard few words of support from either national or local leaders. Then hate mail started to arrive. One correspondent referred to me as a "white Negro bastard" and wished every evil on me and my family. I was compared to a "house nigger" who during slavery times carried every detail of a slave revolt to the master. Another man who telephoned was surprised that I would write a letter to a newspaper without getting NAACP permission. A vandal even slashed one of the tires on my car. Fortunately, that was the only act of violence. Then in the most hurtful jab of all, the editor of the Washington *Afro-American* labeled me an "Uncle Tom" and characterized my actions as typical of a Negro seeking political leadership. I considered it a particularly low blow coming from a fellow journalist, and one that demonstrated a deteriorated standard of ethics in the highly charged atmosphere of race relations.

Many blacks refused to accept the idea that the outbreak of violence had any roots in racial animus or hostility toward whites. "Just a boys-will-be-boys disturbance," one leader commented. Another pointed out that there were riots following games in other cities, and that none received as much newspaper coverage as the outbreak in D.C. Several blacks asked whether the attention had more to do with the school integration issue. For many others, the bottom line was, "Hell, Negroes have been on the receiving end of this kind of violence for years, so why the fuss when whites are attacked?"

The most positive result of the Thanksgiving Day riot was that the district's black leadership acted immediately, issuing a statement condemning

the "unsportsmanlike conduct and rowdyism," contending that it could neither be excused nor tolerated. The statement, however, was not well received
in the black community, showing that a gulf existed between the leaders and
the overall black population.

Despite the hostile reaction, the NAACP's local chapter president, Dr.
E. Franklin Jackson, and Urban League Secretary Sterling Tucker, agreed
to serve with me on a committee named by School Superintendent Carl F.
Hansen to investigate the stadium riot. Chaired by Dr. Shane MacCarthy, a
former White House aide in the Eisenhower administration, the committee's other members were a number of prominent whites, including a former
professional football star. An alumnus of D.C.'s George Washington University, where he starred on the varsity football team when still a sophomore,
businessman Alphonse "Tuffy" Leemans had been the New York Giants' no.
2 draft pick in the first ever college football draft, and was later inducted into
the National Football League Hall of Fame. More than all that, Leemans was
a particularly fitting choice for the committee since he had earned his nick-
name from all the scrapes he'd gotten into as a kid because of his given name.

Amid charges that the interracial panel would either whitewash the
violence or vilify blacks, we began our work behind closed doors. Early on
it became apparent that the holiday violence had wreaked a greater toll in
bodily and property damage than many Washingtonians imagined. The
police ultimately reported 554 cases, but actual casualties probably reached
a thousand because of the large number of unreported incidents. That the
majority of offenders were Negro and the victims white was a disquieting
factor that plagued several of our committee members. However, the discovery of laxities in many areas of school administration, including the athletic program, the selection of game sponsors and promoters, and the sale
of tickets, changed the initial feeling of some of the members that Negroes
were entirely responsible for what happened. As the hearings continued,
several members were surprised to learn that no Negro in any supervisory
position had anything to do with the sponsorship of the game, the planning,
or preparation for or handling of the crowds, although both the stadium fans
and Washington's public schools were over 80 percent black.

Another finding of the committee was that there were serious disciplin-
ary problems in some of the public schools, and a probe was begun in that
direction as well.

Following one of our biweekly hearings several days before Christmas,
Chairman MacCarthy called to tell me he was appointing me chairman of
the report-writing committee, adding that the report was needed within two
weeks. When I demurred that I couldn't do it, MacCarthy, a devout Catholic, countered, "You can—and the Lord bless you."

I figured that even with the Lord, I would have trouble writing the report, a feeling apparently shared by various segments of the public for other reasons. A white woman, for example, called our home and asked if I was a Negro. Getting the answer, she abruptly hung up. A Negro called and ranted, "Lousy fool."

I worked at home throughout the Yuletide, pouring over the testimony, the data, the figures, trying to detach myself from all outside influences as well as my memories of Little Rock, Birmingham, and other situations where my race in itself could easily have gotten me thrashed or even killed. Ever ready to come to my aid were fellow committee members Mrs. Henry Gratton Doyle, president of the D.C. School Board, and Sterling Tucker.

The report described deplorable conditions in black homes as well as in public schools. It addressed lawlessness; the need for more study of the "track system" that allowed a boy or girl to spend twelve years in school and still not be able to read or write, or even know a trade upon graduation; the lack of sufficient authority for teachers in the classrooms; and the crying need for fresh, imaginative programs to inspire every youngster, no matter what his skill level or intellectual ability.

Finally, we addressed the efforts of some who were attempting to misuse the stadium incident to advance their own social theories: ". . . there are some in Congress who believe the highlighting of our weaknesses is an admission that integration of public schools cannot work. School integration can work, but it requires the help of responsible leaders, parents, citizens and children." The committee's bottom line was a call to action to all relevant segments of the community to address the problems described in the report that fell within the purview of each.

When I finished and submitted the report to the full committee, I heard from one member who had apparently questioned the chairman's selection of me to write it. "Booker, I never would have thought a Negro could objectively handle such a sensitive subject."

I smiled and suggested, "Give us more opportunities. We'd fool you."

17

CAMELOT, THE FINAL ACT

As 1962 came to an end, *Ebony*'s editors cited as the "most spectacular break-through" of the year, the "successful, military-backed attack on diehard Mississippi's color line in higher education" that culminated in the admission of James H. Meredith to the University of Mississippi.[1] While the admission of one student might not seem a great achievement, it was a milestone in light of the "over-our-dead-bodies" resistance. Furthermore, it encouraged others to follow, both at Ole Miss and other all-white schools. The editorial noted that at the end of the year, there were more than 2,000 Negroes enrolled in formerly white colleges and universities in the South. Almost 300 public and private institutions of higher learning (including several formerly all-black schools) had dropped racial bars. At the lower education levels, desegregation continued at a snail's pace, or on a token basis, except in still-defiant Alabama, Mississippi, South Carolina, and some pockets in Virginia, where there was no movement to comply with court orders. I had reported in Ticker Tape USA that while the rants of the country's leading exponent of segregation, Senator James O. Eastland, against the integration of Ole Miss were adding fuel to the fires back home, the solon enrolled his own son, Wood, in the recently desegregated St. Stephen's School in Alexandria, Virginia. (Several other Dixie representatives had withdrawn their sons from the Episcopal church school the previous year, when the first Negro student enrolled.)[2]

In September 1962, the Kennedy administration had done everything it could to prevent what some would call "the last battle of the civil war" from erupting on the campus of Ole Miss when Meredith, after seven years in the military, attempted to enroll in the all-white institution. But neither political maneuvers nor reminders of the harmful image being projected overseas could move Mississippi Governor Ross Barnett, much less the racist mobs that appeared ready and willing to burn down a good part of the school rather than integrate it.

I sent *Jet* Washington bureau reporter Larry Still to Oxford, while I covered the crisis from D.C. For Still, the assignment was more than challenging. Mississippi highway patrolmen warned him and Memphis photographer Ernest Withers away from the Meredith caravan as it sped toward the campus, and when the two arrived at Ole Miss, director of development Hugh Clegg, one of Hoover's top men until his retirement in 1954 as assistant director of the FBI, barred them from covering Meredith's attempt to register. Clegg told Still it wasn't discrimination, but "with tensions as high as they are, any colored reporter might create a problem." Clegg added, "We feel it would be better if they [JPC] sent a reporter of another race." The two newsmen were turned around at the entrance to the campus by T. B. Birdsong, Mississippi commissioner of public safety.[3] It didn't stop them for a minute from doing their jobs. Still already had one exclusive interview with Meredith and would get another after he'd begun classes. Other parts of the story were unfolding outside the campus, and on the streets of Oxford.

In Washington, one of the first challenges to the civil rights gains of blacks was playing out at the White House. It was clear that as much as he wished to avoid it, President Kennedy, like Eisenhower before him, would finally have to send in the troops. God's "truth" may have been marching on, in the stirring words of the Civil War battle hymn, but it was doing so behind a multitude of bayonets. Descending on tiny Oxford and its state university would be an incredible 30,000 American soldiers. The first question the administration faced was whether any of these troops should be black, or whether these integrated units should suddenly appear all-white when they hit the "front lines," in a replay of the Eisenhower administration's makeover of the 101st Airborne in Little Rock. At a top-level, White House policy meeting, several administration aides argued that just as in Arkansas, five years earlier, the presence of Negroes would "inflame the mob," while two men, whom I identified in Ticker Tape as Deputy Press Secretary Andrew Hatcher and Democratic National Committee staffer Louis Martin, argued vehemently for maintaining an integrated force, the position that carried the day, at least initially. Negro GIs sent into Mississippi would be making their debut in a U.S. civil rights controversy: the Battle of Oxford.

Meredith, the soft-spoken son of a Kosciusko farmer, would later tell Still that all that had happened "was just about what I thought would happen. Nothing surprised me. It went just about how I figured it would go. I wanted to register and they wouldn't allow me."[4] But Meredith later acknowledged that he never imagined his arrival on the campus of the University of Mississippi would touch off a night of bloody rioting that would leave two dead, seventy-five injured (some seriously), and hundreds under arrest.

When it was over, the fires doused, and the tear gas blown away, I attended a ceremony at the Department of Justice, where Attorney General Robert Kennedy, and by telephone, President Kennedy, praised the bravery of the outnumbered U.S. marshals who had held the line protecting Meredith until the federal troops arrived to restore order. But the story the marshals told, while riveting, was only half of it. The fighting had been tough, continuous, and often hand-to-hand. The mob used stones, pipes, and firebombs before commandeering cars, fire trucks, and even a bulldozer that stalled directly in front of the Lyceum, the Greek-style administration building, where the lawmen were also under fire from snipers. After hours of this, they were not only fatiguing, but running out of tear gas. They needed help. The mob kept growing and coming at them, but the state police declined any assistance and eventually disappeared. Finally, after the marshals informed the White House of their desperate situation, military police units were activated, one heading into Mississippi by air, the other by land. Both took longer than anticipated. The airborne unit's helicopters could not land near the university because the campus was blanketed in gas fumes. Once on the ground, the troops had to fight their way through the campus crowds. The unit reported casualties even before it reached the marshals. The overland MP unit also met fierce resistance from hoodlums who threw stones, dropped railroad ties in the paths of the military trucks, smashed windows in the jeeps, and did whatever it took to slow its pace.[5]

Negro soldiers were among the engineers who established camp and drove the first trucks to the campus in a storm of stone throwing, and for the first two days, they participated in every phase of the operation. In the final stages of the nighttime riot, the mobs tried to smash everything in sight and managed to plunge most of the campus into darkness by shattering streetlights. At dawn, when the troops began to take over the city, Negro soldiers were primary targets of the mobs. Some got slugged. All weathered an incessant stream of taunts, such as "nigger, why don't you go back to New Jersey?"[6] Under extreme pressure and provocation, integrated MP teams held fire, thus preventing a massacre. U.S. Department of Justice aide Ed Guthman confirmed that Negro troops were picked out by the mobs for the "worst type of vilification," but took it all professionally, barely batting an eye.

Meredith walked solemnly to an American Colonial History class at 9:00 a.m. to shouts of "nigger, nigger" and "was it worth two deaths?" He was accompanied to class by three deputy marshals and Guthman. Around the city of Oxford, Still spotted mixed units of black and white troops, including one Negro staff sergeant heading a road block team at the entrance to Oxford, inspecting each car, raising the hood, opening the trunk, and checking under the seats. The inspection was carried out because snipers carrying .22 rifles still lurked in trees and bushes ready to pick off government officials.

Then suddenly history seemed to be repeating itself. Larry sent word back to the Washington bureau that the Negro GIs in the eight crack, integrated military units assigned to Oxford were pulled back from the front line because they were special targets of the mob during the first two days of murderous rioting. I called the Pentagon press office where Lt. Col Patrick Klein, Defense Department spokesman, confirmed Still's report, but maintained that the troops were not pulled by Washington, but at the discretion of their company commanders "as soon as they realized where they were." Although Klein insisted that no troops had complained about being taken from the "battle," members of the 101st (Screaming Eagle) Division, the 81st Airborne, the Second Infantry, and the 503rd, 516th, and 720th MP battalions bitterly told our *Jet* team, "We've been taken out of the battle we were prepared to fight." Many of the soldiers boldly demanded to be quoted in the magazine. S/Sgt. Howard Lomba of New Jersey declared: "We came here as integrated units with Negro officers and noncoms. . . . How can we face our companies now after being taken out of the fight? They wouldn't pull us back in wartime . . . we're professional soldiers and we're supposed to fight anywhere." Pvt. Jerry Jones added, "This is our fight more than it is anyone's and we wanted to be in the middle of it even though we were 'special targets.'"[7]

Some Negro noncoms were reluctant to be quoted, telling us they understood the reason they were pulled back, but adding that the way it was done "embarrassed and demoralized the troops." In a protest he said he was forwarding to military headquarters, Pvt. David Adams wrote, "In stunned disbelief and embarrassment, in resentment and resignation . . . we stood and watched the 'white troops' move off to the 'battle' while a collective voice in our collective souls screams out 'but, this is my fight, too, this is my issue; the wrong, the hurt was done to James Meredith, my forefathers, my children and myself.'"[8]

While admitting that the Negroes were pulled out and "given duties assigned to them by the company commanders," Klein and the 101st Airborne spokesman, Lt. Col. William Kochs, noted that the Negro and white troops, many from the South, stood side by side in the Dixie town and took everything hurled at them without losing their tempers or control. "They [the mob] threw soda bottles filled with acid, dropped 200 pound crates on our heads and broke every goddam window in our passing jeeps and trucks . . . it was a miracle that no soldiers were killed," Klein said.[9] The Defense Department spokesman estimated that about 11 percent of the 8,000–12,000 troops sent into the area were Negro.

As order was restored in the small university town, Negro troops again appeared at checkpoints and command posts, where they were placed early in the battle. Negro and white troops bivouacked in the area also were eating together in the small restaurants and stores, and on the historic "Ole Miss" campus mixed troops stood in line at snack bars in Hemingway Stadium, where Negroes had never been allowed to attend events.

Not one Mississippi elementary or high school had been integrated since the Supreme Court's *Brown* school desegregation decision nine years earlier, which made Meredith's bold and courageous stance at Ole Miss a lightening rod that sparked two different reactions among the state's black population, differing mostly by their age group. Negro youths told *Jet* they felt emboldened by Meredith, while many older blacks said they were fearful about the new burst of integration activity. One of the exceptions was the seventy-eight-year-old cotton picker who told Still, "Meredith is just like Moses to me. . . . He's delivering us from Mississippi."[10] When racists couldn't get to Meredith, they threatened and attacked other blacks, especially civil rights activists, whose homes and businesses they fire bombed, or shot up. Some blacks lost their jobs for supporting integration.

Before returning to Washington, Still visited Meredith's seventy-year-old father in his home at the end of a rural road. Mose ("Cap") Meredith said he'd had some trouble, including shots fired into his home, but that he didn't pay any attention to it. Even when told by a sheriff's deputy that his son could be killed, he had answered, "We all born to die." The elder Meredith and his wife, Roxie, received no protection, but lots of surveillance from local law enforcement. When Still left, three patrol cars surrounded his car and escorted it to the city limits. Said one sergeant, "We don't want no reporters around here. We already got enough troubles. Now you take that Highway 12 or go back to Natchez Trace parkway and git and don't come back no more."[11]

With Still back in the bureau, the staff sat at the conference table to talk about what had transpired in Mississippi, as well as in Washington, during and after the riot. Foremost on everyone's mind were the two deaths. Nobody had missed the disturbing fact that one of the fatalities of the riot was a fellow journalist—a Frenchman named Paul Guihard, who was on assignment for the London *Daily Sketch*, when he was discovered behind the Lyceum building with a gunshot wound to the back. The second victim was also a white man, jukebox repairman Ray Gunter, 23, whose only involvement in the chaos appeared to have been curiosity about what was happening. He was found with a bullet wound in the head, execution style. We also talked about the troops, many of them just eighteen years old, and how they had been children—eight to twelve years of age—during the first

Eisenhower administration, when the president of the United States led the chorus advising blacks to be "patient." Now they were old enough to wear the uniform of this country's military and to risk their lives for a nation where they were no better than second class citizens, unable to vote in some Southern states, unable to live where they chose, unable even to attend this mighty bastion of learning called the University of Mississippi where one man, himself a veteran, had dared to insist on being registered. And it wasn't just ignorant mobs who tried to keep him out and even to kill or maim anyone who got in their way—it was the governor of the state himself, Ross Barnett, who had put all the resources at his disposal into thwarting this black man's dream. Still and I both had children. We believed it would get better, but we knew that many more innocent people were likely to die in the struggle. It was a somber thought.

In early 1963, *Ebony* historian Lerone Bennett authored a sobering piece on "The Mood of the Negro" in America, replete with graphic photos of police beating, hosing, and using dogs to attack men, women and children in Birmingham.[12] In the North, the Negro was confined to the dismal conditions of the ghetto, with dilapidated schools, slum housing, and high unemployment, while statistically destined to die before his white counterparts. All of these conditions had led to unrest in both North and South, with demonstrations, sit-ins, freedom rides, voter registration drives, and even outbreaks of black violence, which, while relatively minor, usually wound up hurting other blacks more than whites, although the latter were probably left more frightened in the aftermath.

Citing the widening gap between blacks and white liberals, the rivalry among the civil rights organizations and the Black Muslim movement, the frustrations in the South, and the despair in the ghettoes of the North, Bennett predicted that Americans were headed for "a no-man's land of open and continuous protests," in the North as well as the South—"portents of a volcanic thrust that will not be denied."

For almost a decade, the slogan of the NAACP had been "Free by '63," the year that would mark the 100th anniversary of the Emancipation Proclamation. Bold and aggressive, the slogan had injected new life into tired and weary campaigners and supporters alike. But as that year drew near, freedom was not in sight, neither in the North nor the South, where in many areas, a Negro still couldn't walk in the front door of a hotel or restaurant, let alone sleep or eat there.

In December 1962, on the eve of the Centennial, the "Big Six," the traditional leaders of the civil rights movement, were finally afforded the "summit" meeting with President Kennedy that they'd been requesting for months. The NAACP's Roy Wilkins, Urban League executive Whitney Young, CORE's James Farmer, labor leader A. Philip Randolph, SCLC's

Martin Luther King, Jr., and Dorothy Height, President of the National Council of Negro Women (NCNW), were charmed as always by the interest and attention of the chief executive, who wound up spending almost three hours with them instead of the scheduled thirty minutes. But it was not racial issues in America that they had gathered to discuss. It was a subject that was much more of interest to the administration at the moment—aid for newly independent African nations, for which the White House hoped to gain black support. The civil rights leaders also had an interest in that discussion. There was growing kinship between the ambassadors from the new African nations and Negro leaders. Some of the envoys had volunteered for efforts at easing discrimination in housing and other areas. In return, the black American leadership was willing to support more aid for Africa. But the timing was poor, and the reaction, particularly of militant students on the front lines in Dixie civil rights struggles, made the Big Six look foolish.

When it was over, the group realized they had made a huge mistake. They'd met longer with the president of the United States than any other Negro group in history, but instead of demanding action on civil rights issues, as one of them angrily reflected afterwards, they'd been "asking for help for Africans, who've fought and won their freedom."

I spent several hours with the leaders' aides that evening, and even they were critical of their bosses. "How the hell can we tell these sit-in demonstrators we came to Washington, met the president and didn't demand help?"

Another objected, "We're not going about this right. We've got to stop asking the Kennedys for this and that. We've got to start demanding our rights."

A third gave voice to a gloomy outlook that seemed shared by all, "We're headed for a revolution; we're losing mass support."

In the 1950s, NAACP Executive Secretary Roy Wilkins had been regarded as the chief spokesman for blacks in America, and the civil rights movement's most skilled negotiator. But this meeting and its poor timing almost eliminated Wilkins from the power bloc. By 1962, it was clear that blacks did not view the NAACP as their greatest hope for breaking down the barriers to racial equality. Membership in what was once the flagship civil rights organization had declined by more than 15,000, not an insignificant figure for a group dependant on membership support for its existence. In a letter acknowledging my congratulations on reaching his thirtieth anniversary with the historic organization, Roy Wilkins sadly commented that the real tragedy was not that more people were not members of the NAACP, but that "more people have not heard of it and do not understand exactly what the NAACP does and how it does it." For years, the organization's battleground had been the courtroom, where it scored tremendous victories. But legal victories were costly, the courtroom battles prolonged and demanding. The organization's preference for orderly desegregation programs in cooperation with the administration and leading white citizenry simply wasn't paying off when it came to membership drives. Critics argued that the site of the battle should be shifted from the courtrooms and boardrooms to the streets.

The NAACP as well as the other traditional organizations were locked in a struggle to regain power from younger, more militant forces. As the largest and still strongest of the six organizations, the NAACP had the ability, if it chose to do so—and Wilkins did not—to unleash demonstrations nationally. Their other strong suit was their lobbying, led by veteran campaigner Clarence Mitchell of Baltimore. The NAACP was the only member of the civil rights "power house" able to launch an effective lobbying drive for a massive civil rights bill. The Urban League had no such national organization and was not geared up for a direct-action program. Whitney Young's strength was more evident as a mediator. The NCNW did good work, but more than anything else, Dorothy Height's inclusion in the Big Six was based on the fact that, unlike the other five, it was female-headed. CORE and the SCLC were simply too small.

In the face of negative reaction to the summit, the Big Six departed Washington a discouraged lot. Some felt the administration was wheeling and dealing with several of the group to break up any harmony of leadership. One of the leaders called what they had gotten from the president "the best snow job in history," adding, "We've lost two years because we admired him for [doing] what should have been done years ago."

Soon after their meeting at the White House, it was clear that the civil rights leadership was split into two camps. The group's elder, but still one of its toughest members, AFL-CIO Vice President Phil Randolph, went with the "go for broke" camp, teaming up with CORE's Farmer and the Reverend Martin Luther King, Jr. They made it clear they wanted no Kennedy favors. The other camp could be called the "moderates," although they would strenuously object to that label. Underlying the difference in their strategies was in large part the latter's belief that calls for all-out protests could erupt into a national bloodbath. That there was a split became apparent several weeks later, when the chief executive invited more than 1,000 Negro guests to the White House for an historic observance. Dr. King and A. Philip Randolph sent their regrets.

EMANCIPATION: 100 YEARS AND COUNTING

The Kennedy White House celebrated the Emancipation Proclamation centennial with the biggest White House reception in history on February 12,

1963. The crowd of more than 1,000 Negro VIPs was more than had ever attended any event in the executive mansion. *Ebony* ran a special anniversary issue replete with pages of photos of the celebrants mixing and mingling with the President and First Lady, top government officials, and a host of other notables from the judiciary, the Congress, and business.[13] Among them as well, Hollywood types such as Sammy Davis, Jr., and his Scandinavian wife Mai Britt, although some of the guests whispered their expectation that there would be no pictures of the couple at the affair out of concern for Dixie vote-getting two years hence. Planned as a strictly non-political affair, the precedent-setting reception honored Negroes from many walks of life who had made their mark on the American scene, including many "firsts" such as Edith Sampson, first female Negro judge in Illinois, and many others.

Turn the pages of that *Ebony* issue, after all the photos of beaming, well-dressed blacks enjoying the hospitality of the president of the United States, and there's another article that shows quite clearly the ongoing struggle that got them there. While the political elite were sipping fruit punch at the White House, some 430 miles to the south, my colleague, Hans Massaquoi, was covering "South Carolina's Moment of Truth." The new governor, Donald Russell, had set out to clean up his state's poor race relations image. Side by side with archive photos of the violent upheaval encouraged by Gov. George Wallace at the University of Alabama when Arthurine Lucy had tried to attend classes, and at "Ole Miss," when the demagoguery of Gov. Ross Barnett fanned the flames of racial hatred against James Meredith, the *Ebony* article pictured a solitary young black man arriving for classes at Clemson University in January 1963 without a police escort and without violence. The peaceful integration of South Carolina's most prestigious university followed a massive effort by the new governor that had included his hosting the first integrated inaugural reception at the State House.

South Carolina had been one of the five state defendants in the original *Brown* case, and was the last to comply with the Supreme Court decision. The state's efforts to thwart the court's mandate had been fast and desperate. The legislature had quickly repealed its compulsory school attendance law in order to allow the closing of any school the moment it was ordered to desegregate. Then, lest any school board be so enlightened as to consider compliance with a desegregation order, the legislature passed a law making racial segregation a prerequisite for a school's eligibility to receive state funds. For good measure, it threw in a punitive provision aimed at Negroes, providing that should any white school be closed to prevent its integration, South Carolina's State College for Negroes would automatically be boarded up as well. In the end, all these efforts fizzled.

Now, not only was the governor leading the way to acceptance of the change, but Clemson president Dr. Robert C. Edwards had also issued a stern warning that any Clemsonite caught demonstrating or disorderly would be expelled. And while some legislators reported that they were still receiving calls to close the historic university rather than bow to "ill-considered federal court decisions and ruthless and politically motivated federal executive action," as one member of the state's segregation committee put it, the lawmakers were responding with promises to continue the fight in the courts, rather than close down Clemson.

It was nine years since the Supreme Court ruling in *Brown*, and while the young black man arrived without police protection, it was not without fanfare as more than 160 reporters and news photographers were on hand to record what some called "the story of the year." Harvey Gantt, a twenty-year-old architecture student from Charleston, modestly told reporters it was not his objective "to integrate the school," but to get an education. For their part, some of the other students admitted wistfully that they'd rather it never happened, and one went so far as to suggest that "if y'all will let him alone now, he'll flunk out here." But the young man not only didn't "flunk out," he went on to a brilliant career in architecture as well as politics. After getting his BA degree two years later from Clemson, Gantt earned a master's degree at MIT in 1970, and later became the first black mayor of Charlotte, North Carolina, winning 52 percent of the black vote, and 36 percent of white ballots. He served two terms, and gave Senator Jesse Helms a run for his money in two unsuccessful tries for the segregationist's Senate seat. Gantt, who as a teenager had taken part in sit-ins to desegregate Charleston's lunch counters, was one of the shining stars of the "New South."

But other success stories such as Harvey Gantt's were still a long way in the future. The administration and much of the public were beginning to recognize that the civil rights movement in both the North and the South had taken on a sense of urgency. Invitations to the White House and high level appointments, much less rhetoric—even the noblest of any administration—were not going to dampen the fires threatening to leap into the streets from the breasts of young black Americans. Instead of an inspiring goal post, the passing of the centennial anniversary of the Emancipation Proclamation morphed into a cruel reminder of the lingering vestiges of black slavery. The struggle was taking too long. Blacks were sacrificing their scant liberties as well as their bodies before police barricades from Birmingham to Chicago, from New York to Los Angeles, in protests against Jim Crow and his more subtle Northern manifestations.

In the spring of 1963, Martin Luther King, Jr., Fred Shuttlesworth, and other activists were arrested and incarcerated in the Birmingham, Alabama, jail for violating a federal court injunction against further demonstrations in that city to undermine its systemic, rigidly enforced segregation. In addition to boycotts of businesses that discriminated against blacks, there'd been sit-ins and rallies calling for unity and perseverance in defiance of Jim Crow, but nothing drew national media attention more than Public Safety Com-missioner "Bull" Connor's allowing the police to sic attack dogs on peaceful demonstrators.

A number of clergymen criticized King for his actions in Birmingham, calling his presence "unwise and untimely," referring to him as an outsider, and, incredibly, blaming him for the violence that had occurred and for any that might follow. King spent some quality time in his cell responding to their criticism in a lengthy letter so filled with biblical, philosophical, and historical content, it is used today in college philosophy courses, and is often a centerpiece of other academic, theological, and sociological discussion. My own reaction to it was that it must have—and certainly should have—left the clergymen to whom it was addressed red-faced above their starched white collars. After debunking the "outside agitator" charge, he chastised the clergymen for deploring the demonstrations, but not the conditions that brought them on. He cited as among the "hard, brutal facts" of the case that there had been more unsolved bombings of Negroes' homes and churches in Birmingham, than in any other city.

Demonstrating that his scholarship reached far beyond the gospel of civil rights, King quoted St. Augustine, St. Thomas Aquinas, and even Socrates on the question of why it was right, indeed necessary, to disobey bad laws. The Supreme Court's *Brown* decision was the law of the land, too, and look who was disobeying it. In the end, he confessed grave disappoint-ment in white moderates who claimed to agree with the Negro's goals, but urged him to wait for a "more convenient season." Admitting to a lack of unanimity even among blacks on this issue, King acknowledged that he stood between two forces in the black community. On one side were those so long oppressed that they seemed completely drained of "somebodiness." (As Langston Hughes had put it in his poem more than a dozen years earlier, those whose dreams had dried up, "like a raisin in the sun.") On the other side was a force manifesting itself in bitterness and hatred (those whose dreams, Hughes would say, had "festered like a sore"). Best known among the latter, King reminded the clergymen, was Elijah Muhammad's Muslim movement, which had not only lost faith in America, but also had repudi-ated Christianity, while concluding that the white man was a devil.

Martin Luther King's letter from the Birmingham jail should have shamed the clergy whose charges it answered but it was way over the head of the likes of "Bull" Connor. The next outrage visited upon peaceful dem-onstrators, mainly young students, in Birmingham was the use of high-pres-sure fire hoses. That, too, brought media attention, national condemnation, and ultimately federal intervention on the part of the Kennedy administration. But still the violence and the bombing continued.

Finally, more than two years after he had taken office, President Kennedy, keenly aware of the surge of emotion in the black community, as well as the fear and near panic of many white Americans, told the nation he was sending a comprehensive civil rights bill to Congress. The bill would run the gamut from public accommodations and transportation to education, employment, and protection of voting rights. It was the Kennedy administration's boldest civil rights move to date, and by now black Americans were willing to accept nothing less. It was a move the "power house" could unite behind, and the rallying began to push it through the Congress. Sadly, however, the White House announcement was followed within days by yet another cause for mourning.

A MAN NAMED MEDGAR

I was in a funeral home in Clarksdale, Mississippi, one evening in the mid-1950s, talking quietly with the widow of a Negro school principal who'd been killed mysteriously outside the town. His body had been found floating in a pool of water.

"He's gone," she kept saying. "That's all I know. Somebody got him."

As we talked, we took little notice of a tall, young black man with an energetic stride who slipped in and stood silently next to the open casket. After a few moments, the young man turned, and recognizing me, came over and introduced himself to the woman as "Medgar Evers of the NAACP."

The woman erupted, grabbing my arm in a reflexive motion. "Lord, get him away! I don't want to talk to him. I don't want him here. Get him out of here!" She became hysterical, and kept screaming, "Get him out of here! They got my husband killed, and now they're going to get me killed."

Negroes were whispering that the principal had been murdered because whites thought he was a member of the NAACP. It would have been heresy for a Mississippi Negro educator to accept employment from whites and then betray them by becoming part of the civil rights movement. There'd been little investigation of his death by authorities, and little more was likely.

Evers was a new NAACP man in Mississippi. He had been assigned to investigate the case, but the woman's reaction unnerved him. I took him outside and far enough away from the funeral home so that the widow would calm down.

"Take it easy," I cautioned him. "It might be true." Evers was stunned by the woman's outburst, but it was quite possible that her husband had actually been working quietly with the civil rights organization.

From that unnerving baptism, Evers struggled to organize a civil rights front. He investigated every racial crime he heard about in Mississippi. Arrested several times on bogus grounds, he refused to quit. He was even cited for contempt of court, fined $100, and sentenced to 30 days in jail by the Forrest County Circuit Court for criticizing the burglary conviction of a black man. Mississippi justice was strange indeed, but the state's Supreme Court in 1961 overturned the conviction, confirming that under the First Amendment, the courts may be criticized like anybody else. Aggressive, uncompromising, and incredibly courageous, Evers was highly respected and admired, quickly topping the ranks as the outstanding Negro crusader in the state. He was one of the most unusual men I'd met in the South because if he feared anything, he never showed it. He was dogged in his determination to solve race crimes, and stayed on his cases long after the authorities, whether federal, state, or local, had given up. Talking to me, he was always optimistic, positive, and certain that he was making progress against white oppression. Blacks admired him, looked to him for advice, and in very short order, accepted him as a leader. That's what got him killed.

On June 12, 1963, returning home from a round of conferences, Evers was shot to death in front of his home as he emerged from his car. His body sprawled on the driveway, his young children stood frozen in horror in the doorway as he struggled to get up.

The murder of Medgar Evers angered blacks more than any other Mississippi crime. Instead of demoralizing the Negro population, as was obviously intended, the wanton murder solidified them. No longer asking, "How long, oh God?" they were itching for revenge, but not down the barrel of a gun. Evers had taught them all too well that their future lay in the ballot box.

Over the next year, however, violence against blacks, including ambushes of civil rights activists, would become so commonplace that Charles Evers, the slain activist's brother, told me he feared the day was coming when Mississippi Negroes would have to abandon nonviolence as a tactic and resort to force to gain their rights. Conceding that there were many good white people in Mississippi, Evers observed that there were "just as many nuts, who just don't understand the nonviolent approach" Negroes were following.

The first of three trials of Byron de la Beckwith for the murder of Medgar Evers ended in a hung jury, as would the second, both with all-white juries failing to render a verdict. It would be 1994, thirty years later, before his own bragging about the killing would finally result in de la Beckwith's conviction at the end of a third trial. He was serving a life term at Parchman when he died in 2001 at eighty years of age.

UNDER LINCOLN'S GAZE

In the midst of Washington's typically long, hot summer of 1963, hundreds of thousands of people, black and white, streamed into the nation's capital—the largest demonstration ever—to call for enactment of the pending civil rights legislation. This time, the fear and panic of the white population was misplaced. The event was distinguished by its order and peacefulness. "Dig this," one Harlem demonstrator told a white reporter. "Give us our daily bread—or we gonna take it." The dream had been too long deferred.

They came by bus, train, plane, automobile, bicycle, and even roller skates. One group walked 237 miles from Brooklyn. At least a quarter million human beings arrived in Washington, D.C., that day, lining the edges of the reflecting pool beneath the steps of the Lincoln Memorial, and stretching back to the Washington Monument. Many wore hats to ward off the bright summer sun, although the temperature mercifully never rose above the mid-eighties. Tens of thousands wore business attire, including dress shirts and neckties, and as many carried signs and banners, or wore large lapel buttons to convey what they wanted, indeed, what they were demanding—freedom, jobs, housing, desegregated schools, first class citizenship, the right to vote, equal access to all public accommodations, an end to police brutality—and that Congress pass the pending civil rights bill.

The mere anticipation of their numbers had worried official Washington enough to put nearby military installations at Fort Belvoir, Fort Meade, Fort Myer, and Quantico on alert with mobile and helicopter service ready to move troops where needed on minutes' notice. A Washington Senators baseball game was postponed a day to free up traffic officers. Local churches and parochial schools stood ready with food and cots to help anyone stranded. On the morning of the march, workers who didn't choose to follow the advice of City Commissioner Walter Tobriner, echoed by local newspapers, to stay home unless they planned to march were stunned by what they saw. Truck convoys of army troops and marines raced through the downtown area to designated positions, while D.C. police and National Guardsmen stood at every street corner. On Capitol Hill, police standing five feet apart formed a cordon around Congressional buildings. The government was secretly hysterical. The *Washington Daily News* described local feeling as something akin to when the Vandals were coming to sack Rome. Moguls of government, industry, and labor had urged that the march be called off, fearing chaos, violence, and heaven-knows-what. In response, march leaders intensified their planning and redoubled their efforts to ensure a peaceful march. To make sure that whites were not frightened away, they asked the youngest speaker, SNCC's John Lewis, to tone down his criticism of the administration just this one time.

Ebony and *Jet* teams of reporters and photographers from Chicago, Los Angeles, and New York joined us for the day, and when it was over, an *Ebony* cover photo by G. Marshall Wilson showed a sea of humanity of every hue standing in solidarity, shoulder to shoulder, behind the headline, "Biggest Protest March in History!" The picture conveyed the determination, the order, and the sobriety of the protest. The punctuation was emblematic of the reaction.[14]

The wild fears before the march turned out to be no more than nightmares, quickly dispelled by the reality of a dignified show of solidarity and hope. Police made only three arrests, reporting a rather unusual, peaceful day in the nation's capital, without even the usual morning or evening rush hours. Major league baseball pioneer Jackie Robinson, ignoring hysterical warnings to keep children away, marched with his son, pointing out to him the civil rights leaders. It was the power and grace of the black freedom movement at its best, as well as its most integrated, a portent of the future.

When it was over, of all the people who came, and of all who spoke to the throng, the voice and the image of one man would forever become its lasting symbol. The preacher who had shared his dream—of an America where black and white children could go to school together, and where all men and women were free—would be propelled to the forefront of the civil rights movement as never before, his words chiseled in the history of a still young nation's growing pains. Rev. Martin Luther King, Jr., neither conceived of the march nor strategized its execution, but in the end, it belonged to him. And everyone knew it who saw the tears of hope, of joy, of confidence in a better future, streaming down the faces of black and white men and women in that incredible mass of humanity when he laid out before them that incredible dream. Daisy Bates, chosen by the leadership at the last minute to speak, after the absence on the program of any prominent female civil rights figures threatened to become an issue, laughed when she told *Ebony* thirty years later what she found most memorable about the event.

"The thing I remember most was that Roy [Wilkins] scheduled me to speak after Mr. King. I couldn't understand why. . . . When they called me to speak, I went to the podium. They were applauding so wildly. No one could hear me, no one was listening to me. I couldn't even hear myself. I was supposed to tell the country to work with Mr. King. At the end of my two minutes, I realized that no one heard a word I had said.[15]

When Congress returned to Capitol Hill after Labor Day, the big question was whether JFK could win a vote on his civil rights bill. As to whether the March on Washington had had any effect, the consensus was that it had not, but that the growing unrest across the country, and white fears of a black upheaval, were making many Americans uneasy. There was an air of pessimism, however, as momentum built for one of the most far-reaching drives to enact legislation in the nation's history.

The administration's bill, while far-reaching, did not satisfy the NAACP, which wanted a permanent federal oversight committee on employment discrimination and other provisions enabling the attorney general to move immediately into Dixie racial crimes. The President's proposal lacked both, although it included other necessary provisions in the areas of voting rights, school desegregation, public accommodations, community relations, and federal projects. These disagreements were not marginal; a victory for the president's bill in its current form would not have satisfied many segments of the black community, including moderates who supported the president.

The GOP leadership, furthermore, was not endorsing the president's program, hedging particularly on the public accommodations provisions. In the Senate, Republican Everett Dirksen of Illinois had been elected in 1960 without black support, and couldn't care less about Negro votes in the future. He was considered lukewarm to civil rights, and while opposing the public accommodations provisions, was expected to wheel and deal on others. The chief opponents, however, were the Democrats' own senator from Georgia, Richard B. Russell, and Mississippi Senator James O. Eastland, chairman of the Senate Judiciary Committee. Both men were considered informed and farsighted in almost every area except civil rights, where they represented the worst Dixie elements. Against this backdrop, the civil rights leadership was mobilizing a massive campaign of letter writers and foot soldiers to sit in the galleries, visit the offices, and fill the mailboxes of legislators. But there wasn't much optimism.

BOMBINGHAM

In Alabama, meanwhile, back-to-school bells were ringing in some parts of the state, with a few blacks even attending previously all-white schools. But in other school districts, Governor George Wallace was continuing to defy federal court desegregation orders, amid growing white disenchantment with his anti-desegregation stance. Many whites had come to realize that the governor was merely postponing the inevitable at the expense of the education of white children every time he closed schools rather than allow them to admit blacks. In the U.S. Senate, Oregon Senator Wayne Morse decried Governor Wallace's actions as "a course of conduct which incites and encourages riots and the shedding of blood," angrily adding that the Alabama governor's hands already were "dripping with blood." Wallace was shameless, even telling reporters that "one good funeral" might slow down the efforts at desegregation.

The atmosphere of violence that prevailed in the state was nowhere more pronounced than in Birmingham. At one time the joke was that newspapers and magazines didn't sell well in Birmingham, because as soon as a Negro learned to read he left. But the boom brought on by the industries beneath the "Pittsburgh of the South's" belching smoke stacks led many more blacks over the years to stay and share in the growing economy. In a *Jet* interview in the late '50s, veteran Birmingham civil rights leader Rev. Fred Shuttlesworth had predicted that there would be no easy victories for civil rights forces there, citing not only the outright racism of its infamous public safety commissioner, Eugene "Bull" Connor, but the whole atmosphere that prevailed in the post-Civil War steel town. "This city," he cautioned, "has a heart as hard as the steel it manufactures, and black as the coal it mines."

Shuttlesworth's crusade as a civil rights leader had been launched in the mid-1950s when the state barred the NAACP because it wouldn't reveal its membership list, a fight the organization ultimately won in court. After he took over the civil rights leadership role, a bomb blast destroyed his parsonage and damaged his church. Bombs would become the weapon of choice for Birmingham's white supremacists. Blacks had good incomes in Birmingham—better than any other city in the Southeast, and even in the 1950s, 52 percent owned their own homes. But professionals moving into white neighborhoods did so at the risk of a bomb. As the campaign for passage of the Kennedy civil rights bill was gearing up in Washington in September 1963, Birmingham blacks were counting in double digits the number of unsolved bombings over the past several years, at least 18 in the surrounding county since 1957. The home of Arthur Shores, for example, an attorney who had desegregated the University of Alabama, was bombed in late summer for the second time in two weeks. He told me that crank callers revealed their belief that he was behind the federal court order to desegregate Birmingham's schools, although he had played no role in it at all. A policeman had told him, "Half of them [whites] don't know any other name but yours," an observation Shores said he could have understood fifteen years earlier, when he was the only Negro lawyer in the whole state. Shortly afterward, millionaire black businessman A. G. Gaston's home was firebombed a few days after he attended a White House dinner in Washington.

Then, on Sunday, September 15, there was an explosion that sent shock waves far beyond the city limits of Birmingham. In an abhorrently depraved act, white supremacists placed a bomb under the steps of Birmingham's Sixteenth Street Baptist Church. The blast killed four young girls attending Sunday school—Denise McNair, Cynthia Wesley, Carole Robertson, and Addie Mae Collins, aged eleven to fourteen. Twenty others were injured. It was one of the worst atrocities of the civil rights era, and demonstrated once again that racists were not above killing children. The Sixteenth Street Baptist Church had been a center of black life in Birmingham for more than half a century, and more recently had become a meeting place for the Reverend Martin Luther King, James Farmer, and other civil rights leaders engaged in months of demonstrations and a voting rights drive.

Within days, four suspects were under investigation—Bobby Frank Cherry, a demolitions expert, and three other white supremacists, Robert Chambliss, Thomas Blanton, and Herman Cash—but the wheels of justice ground to a halt when a local jury failed to convict Chambliss, the suspected ringleader, of murder, and FBI Director J. Edgar Hoover declined to pursue the case, citing the chances of a conviction as "remote." More than a decade-and-a-half later, after the discovery of FBI evidence that had not been turned over to local prosecutors, the case against Chambliss was reopened, and he was convicted of one count of murder in the death of Carol McNair. Blanton and Cherry were finally indicted in 2000, after the discovery of thousands of other documents and surveillance tapes that the FBI also had kept from the original prosecutors. Both men were convicted of murder. It was too late to prosecute Cash. He had died in 1994. The case against J. Edgar Hoover was left to the history books.

Outrage and despair at the murders of four Sunday school children would forever be entwined in the battle on Capitol Hill over the elements of a civil rights bill that could withstand every measure of opposition or indifference from any quarter in the U.S. Congress. Within weeks, black anger over the bill's being held captive in committee turned on the president's own brother, whom blacks accused of backing down on what some considered vital provisions. The headline on my *Jet* article declared, "RFK RETREATS ON RIGHTS BILL AS NEGROES SCREAM: 'SELLOUT!'"[16] The article charged that the attorney general, in a closed hearing of the House Judiciary Committee, had done exactly what the NAACP had predicted he would do: defang the civil rights bill. Kennedy had urged the committee to curtail the scope of the accommodations section, knock out protections for Negroes voting in state and local elections, and restrict a new Justice Department power to probe school desegregation cases. Responding to the administration's desperate attempt at compromise to get the stalled bill to the Senate floor by November 10 or risk ending the session empty-handed, NAACP lobbyist Clarence Mitchell claimed that by his count there were enough votes to ensure passage of a stronger bill. The weakened version the attorney general was offering would do nothing, Mitchell argued, for "Negroes who have been attacked with electric prods and driven out of their churches by tear gas." The article concluded that Robert Kennedy, considered the symbol of the New Frontier's civil rights image, and the most aggressive attorney general in history, had faltered at a crucial turn.

The following week, *Jet* gave Robert Kennedy the opportunity to answer his critics, and published his answers verbatim. On the issue of a strong versus a "weaker" civil rights bill, he argued that the debate should not be about the relative strength of the proposals but about their relative chances for passage. The administration bill, he claimed, had a much better chance of being enacted. Asked about various provisions left out of the latter bill, he argued that some people simply misunderstood provisions in either the bill or current law, or the Justice Department's current activities, or all three.[17]

In the next issue, Roy Wilkins responded, calling the civil rights bill as voted out of the House Judiciary Committee on October 23 "useful" but "not adequate" to meet the needs of the racial situation in 1963, and vowing to mount a vigorous campaign to strengthen it. Covering many of the same issues as were raised in *Jet*'s interview of the attorney general, the NAACP chief defended the administration in some instances and castigated it in others, particularly on the timing of its compromise proposal, advising, "We feel that alteration and compromise, even though the latter is the stuff of politics', should not be the procedure before the battle has been joined."[18] It was a polite way of saying that the administration was giving in too early, and its playing politics on the civil rights bill was not appreciated.

The last question we had posed to the attorney general concerned his reaction to the criticism—really, the thrashing—he was getting for the administration's compromise on the bill. His answer was vintage Kennedy: "When it comes to criticism, I think I have to agree with Lincoln that if the end brings me out all right, what is said against me won't amount to anything, but if the end brings me out wrong, ten angels swearing I was right won't make any difference."

Robert Kennedy encouraged a healthy relationship in which a black and a white could speak frankly and to the point, disagree and yet avoid emotionalism. I became angry at some of the positions he took from time to time, but then I would remember a visit to his home. To me it seemed that one way to test a family's values was to observe its children. If a black person found a white child backing off, feeling uncomfortable, or even blurting racial terms, it was probably due to the parents' influence or the child's lack of exposure to another race. During my visit, one of the Kennedy's young children asked a Negro couple to read a bedtime story. It was a telling and beautiful moment.

When Kennedy ran for the Senate from New York in 1964, I brought my elder son, Simmie, along on a campaign trip to Albany, New York. It was an eye-opening experience for a thirteen-year-old, and Kennedy couldn't have been kinder to the young teen. Blacks didn't agree with all the positions taken by him or the president, but were convinced by the actions they did take and their public statements, that these were men who felt terribly conflicted by what they knew was both morally and constitutionally right, and what they felt was not immediately possible without dire consequences for the administration, the party, and/or the nation as a whole.

In the end, the compromises, the politics, the debate, the whole battle on Capitol Hill would come to a sudden and shocking halt as three shots rang out from the Texas School Book Depository in Dallas, taking the life of the president of the United States, and leaving a nation in mourning. Within days, a new leader would take his position at the forefront of the legislative battle, and in this drastically changed atmosphere, would vow that there would be no compromise.

THE CURTAIN COMES DOWN

With the rest of the country and much of the world, I said goodbye to President Kennedy on November 25, 1963. I was honored to be one of twenty-five White House correspondents invited to cover the funeral in full morning attire at St. Matthew's Cathedral. I remember my reaction when I saw my name, no. 15, posted on the list on the White House press room bulletin board. My eyes brimmed with hot tears.

In the cathedral, I noticed how disparate was the assemblage of mourners, which included Alabama Governor George Wallace and Mississippi Governor Ross Barnett, two men who'd given the late president more than their fair share of heartburn during his tragically short administration. And there were many blacks in the pews as well, from the most prominent figures, such as Dr. Ralph Bunche, to two Negro women who worked for the late chief executive. Like many of them, I had trouble hiding my emotions. I had been one of eight pool reporters at JFK's inauguration, and twice had that role on his private plane during the campaign. I recalled how his press man, Pierre Salinger, had insisted that I have the same opportunities as any white journalist on the campaign trail, and how the candidate had turned back to Washington all of his staff and press planes when a Paducah hotel refused me a room. I thought how in every way possible this man had brought a new sense of dignity and equality to the blacks who covered the White House, both as journalists and photographers.

Now, as I looked from pew to pew, I saw in the faces of the meek and the mighty the same overwhelming sadness that must have etched the faces of the throngs that had watched Lincoln's last journey home. Many would later size up this administration's record on civil rights as mediocre or worse, but black Americans had found in this president's soul a connection rising not out of the man's personal experience, but out of an innate sense of decency, the ability to recognize wrong, even when he was powerless to correct it, and a desire to right that which was within his reach. Watching the world's great leaders sitting in the cathedral, often with heads bowed as though in prayer or somber reflection, these memories of my experiences covering John F. Kennedy, first as a candidate and then as president, flashed by in succession, uninvited but not unwelcome. He'd spoken on civil rights in every state during the 1960 campaign. He'd demonstrated leadership during the crises in Birmingham and Oxford. He didn't hesitate to use the White House to show what equal access for all Americans, regardless of race or color, was supposed to look like. Blacks have been criticized (as have other Americans) for being "too sentimental" about Kennedy. That's something the critics may never understand. Like millions of Americans, black and white, on that November day, I was as sad as I'd ever been in my entire life.

18

A SOUTHERN PRESIDENT

Two days after President Kennedy's assassination, Lyndon Johnson was on the telephone with civil rights leaders to secure their support for an all-out campaign to win passage of the late president's civil rights bill.[1] The first call was to National Urban League executive director Whitney Young. With the league's primary focus on jobs, Young had enjoyed frequent and cordial contact with the vice president in LBJ's role as chairman of the President's Committee on Equal Employment Opportunity. At forty-two, the former Dean of the Atlanta School of Social Work was an easy person for progressive-minded whites to do business with. The league was no pushover, however, when it came to the needs of America's black population. Just five months earlier, Young had issued a challenge to the administration on behalf of the organization's interracial board. Warning of a "tinderbox of racial unrest" on the verge of exploding in Northern cities, the Urban League was calling for a domestic "Marshall Plan" to close the economic, social and educational gaps between Negroes and others. Young had gone even further, criticizing both President Kennedy and his brother, Robert, for failing to advance civil rights, "reacting" instead of acting, and being more concerned about the embarrassment caused by demonstrations than about the root causes. He had even taunted JFK to "exhibit the kind of guts" the president had written about in his book, *Profiles in Courage*. Incidents in the South, the League warned, were mild in comparison with those on the verge of taking flame in the Northern ghettoes, where blacks, oppressed by joblessness, overcrowding, and more subtle discrimination, were reaching "the breaking point."

Young told Johnson he had been talking with the *New York Times* and had made the point that if they didn't already, he was going to see that Negroes had 100 percent confidence in LBJ—a tall order for an organization that itself, like the NAACP, was struggling to win the confidence of the Negro masses, and particularly of black youth. The president told Young he would call NAACP Executive Secretary Roy Wilkins next, but beyond that, he said, "I don't know who else to call." Young suggested CORE Director James Farmer, and gave him Farmer's number. LBJ asked about A. Philip Randolph, and Young agreed that he, too, should be called. Young then mentioned that he and Wilkins had not been invited to the Kennedy funeral, and LBJ agreed to check into it and get them in.

LBJ did call Roy Wilkins next, and also James Farmer and A. Philip Randolph, and separate meetings were set up with each of them, as well as with the SCLC's Rev. Martin Luther King, Jr., over the next two weeks.

For the first month after the Kennedy assassination, *Jet* was saturated with positive articles about LBJ, some of them quoting statements of support from these leaders, while others, many of them written by me, described LBJ's civil rights evolution in his three years as vice president. Then, in late December, I included mention of what appeared to be some awkward missteps in his race relations strategy, including an apparent attempt to manipulate the images emerging from the White House, failing to include key blacks in certain events, and including a black member of the Johnsons' domestic staff at an event where it seemed an odd choice at best.[2] These observations reflected some of the initial wariness many blacks had about a Southern president, but they were very minor at that. Nevertheless, the reaction in the Oval Office was volcanic.

It was about 10:00 p.m. on December 23, just a month after he'd taken the oath of office aboard Air Force One, and the chief executive was furious. He'd just read a press clipping from the little, weekly, black magazine called *Jet*, sent to him by Assistant Press Secretary Andy Hatcher, a black holdover from the Kennedy administration. Hatcher thought that on the whole, the article showed the administration was doing okay in the black press. But LBJ had zeroed in on the tidbits that seemed critical of him. He felt the article was both incorrect and unfair. He wanted something done about it.

He got Hatcher on the phone and told him he'd read the story by "Simon" Booker (apparently the president from the Bible Belt did not recognize my Biblical first name), and thought this fellow was "awful rough" on him. Of all the articles I had written since the late president's assassination, this was the only one that pointed out some apparent faux pas by the new president in the area of race relations. The other articles had been highly laudatory, including my entire Ticker Tape USA column in the first issue after the assassination, a column that for the first time ever was devoted to a single topic: a call for support for Lyndon Johnson, crediting him with quietly struggling to lift the aspirations and enhance the employment opportunities of thousands of Negroes in his role as chairman of the President's Committee on Equal Employment Opportunity.

Feelings of apprehension and uncertainty about the future of civil rights were rampant in black America in the wake of JFK's assassination. The new president had no positive civil rights image, and because of his past alliances with Dixiecrats and the positions he'd taken on civil rights legislation in the Senate, it would be an understatement to say that he was not widely admired among Negroes when he entered the Oval Office. But *Jet*'s coverage included cover to cover articles citing the support of Negro leaders, Johnson's pledge to meet with the "Big Five" of the civil rights movement in the very near future, his efforts in support of equal employment opportunity, and profiles of the top-ranking blacks closest to him. Even my byline article in the December 12 issue, "What Negroes Can Expect from President Lyndon Baines Johnson," was nothing but positive.

I had covered LBJ's activities as vice president, when *Jet* sometimes was the only news outlet that reported on his civil rights activities. He had never held a news conference for the black press, but we followed him anyway, especially when he'd spoken out in his role as chairman of the EEO committee on the need for increased hiring of Negroes. I had reported on his relentless drive for improvement of Negroes' working conditions. And in May 1963, when Johnson brought a black audience to its feet at a formal banquet of the Capital Press Club with an illuminating and stirring speech on race relations, we assured it proper coverage in *Jet*. It was just a few days after the Birmingham demonstrations that had landed Dr. Martin Luther King in jail, and racial feelings were running high in many American cities, including Washington, D.C., so much so that the press was speculating that the capital was "about to explode with racial violence." Yet, few Americans would ever learn of Johnson's remarks, or the fact that another guest of the black press club that evening was also a progressive Southerner, North Carolina Governor Terry Sanford. Neither wire service—the AP or UPI—bothered to cover the affair, and any mainstream press coverage was minimal. This was typical at the time for news coverage of blacks, who in many markets (though not all) were treated as separate from the core community, or worse, as an undesirable segment.

When Johnson suddenly became president, White House aides realized that his weakest flank was still in the area of civil rights. They were sensitive to that, and they may have made LBJ almost paranoid about it, because on this particular night, one month into his presidency, he went ballistic about trivial criticisms I'd mentioned in one article in *Jet*.

The offending article's headline was "President Johnson's Rights Stand Praised by Leaders," and it recounted his separate meetings between the end of November and the first week of December with NAACP Executive Secretary Roy Wilkins, followed by the Urban League's Whitney Young, then Martin

Luther King, Jr., representing the SCLC, James Farmer of CORE, and labor leader A. Philip Randolph. The article accurately noted that the White House had allowed news photographers to photograph Wilkins and Young with the president (in both instances sitting in earnest discussion within inches of the president), but had "closeted" the direct-action advocates, barring photographers from those meetings, even though the more militant members of the leadership group drew more press outside the meetings. The article stated that the White House never disclosed why the news photographers were not invited into the latter three meetings, but that an "intimate" had vaguely explained that some pictures could prove costly in Dixie areas the following fall when LBJ would be running for re-election. My guess all these years later is that the source of that observation was probably Andy Hatcher.

It's clear from LBJ's questioning of the assistant press secretary that the president had either forgotten about approving that photo-op strategy, or had never been privy to it, as he told Hatcher he thought he'd had his picture taken "with every damn one of them." Hatcher stammered and fumbled around, and as if he even remembered who had been photographed with LBJ and who had not three weeks earlier, he nevertheless agreed with the president, who ranted that at that very moment he was signing his White House photograph with Dr. King. As the conversation continued, LBJ misquoted the article and exaggerated that I had claimed he wouldn't pose with "a single one of the Negro leaders." The more he talked, the more he distorted the article, and the more furious he became, at one point asking if I worked for Rockefeller (a potential Republican opponent in the next election). He ran off a litany of things he'd done for Negroes in the past weeks, and even blurted that they should "thank" him. Apparently, I wasn't just wrong, I was ungrateful. Finally, he directed Hatcher to send me a letter demanding a retraction and to enclose copies of the pictures with each of the five leaders. Hatcher, still trying to placate him, assured the irate president that everyone who read my column knew that it was "inaccurate most of the time."[3]

In the end, I never got the photos because what I had written was true. Johnson may have had the White House photographer take a personal photograph to be autographed and sent to each leader, but he did not invite the White House news photographers into his meetings with King, Farmer, or Randolph. You can check every newspaper in the country. There were headlines reporting the meetings, but pictures of the president with the labor leader who called for the March on Washington? The minister who led the Montgomery bus boycott? The activist who organized the Freedom Rides? Nobody had them. But LBJ claimed he was sure they were taken because more than two weeks later, he was autographing a White House photo of himself with Martin Luther King, Jr.

LBJ was not at all satisfied by his conversation with Hatcher, and was not about to let the matter die. He got on the phone again—it was around 10:30 p.m.—and in succession called Roy Wilkins and Whitney Young. He tried to get King, too, but the operator couldn't locate him. After listening to Johnson's harangue, Wilkins and Young both tried to calm him down. Young actually chuckled that it was nothing to worry about.[4] In both instances, LBJ obscured what I had actually written and told them the article said that their pictures were not taken (although *Jet* had published both pictures with the article). He got their assurances that they would call my publisher and ask him to give the president a break. Wilkins seemed to think LBJ was in danger of having his second coronary over this, as the civil rights leader repeatedly urged him to take care of himself, adding, "We need you."[5]

LBJ may have continued to stew over this during the Christmas holidays, or it may have been another item in my column in late January that finally ticked him off enough to haul my publisher into the White House for a dressing down. *Jet*'s overall coverage of the new president remained highly positive, as was the feature article, "What Negroes Can Expect from Lyndon Johnson," by Lerone Bennett, in the January issue of *Ebony*. But the magazines would have lost all credibility among a large segment of the black population if we had never reported any criticism of the president. We had played it straight when reporting on President Kennedy, as well as his attorney general, just as we had done with Eisenhower. Thus, my column in that month's last weekly issue of *Jet* included mention of a jab from GOP National Chairman William Miller regarding the two party platforms LBJ ran on in 1960. Said Miller: "His vice-presidential platform favored sit-in demonstrations. His state platform called for 'enforcement of laws designed to protect private property' . . . from physical occupation. His national platform favored school desegregation. His state platform pledged to 'protect the decisions of the people of local school districts in the operation and control of their schools.'"[6]

I don't know whether LBJ had even seen that column. Whatever was still ticking him off, he directed Carl Rowan, the former U. S. ambassador to Finland, whom LBJ was about to name director of the U.S. Information Agency, to call my publisher to the White House. Apparently, the president did not share with Rowan the real reason for wanting to see John H. Johnson, because the two-page briefing memo Rowan prepared for the president definitely seems to anticipate a different kind of meeting than what actually went down. Rowan's "talking points' for LBJ suggested a thoughtful discussion of the poverty program, ending with a request for advice and an invitation to propose able Negroes to work on the program; a request for the publisher's views on civil rights problems likely to arise in ensuing months;

President Johnson called publisher John H. Johnson to the White House after complaining, "This Simon Booker feller is pretty rough on us." (LBJ Library; photo by Yoichi Okamoto.)

and finally, mention that the president had seen and appreciated the articles about him in the January *Ebony* and recent issues of *Jet* and *Negro Digest* (another JPC publication).[7]

Maybe Rowan hadn't read the same *Jet* articles that were irritating the hell out of LBJ, or maybe he just read them in the context of the magazine's overall favorable coverage of the new president. Whatever the case, the talking points never made it anywhere but a file cabinet. The meeting John H. Johnson walked into with the president was nothing like the one Rowan suggested.

The publisher loved to tell this story for years afterward, particularly relishing the laughs it got at any event at which I was honored or received an award, although the account of it in his own memoirs suggests it was anything but enjoyable at the time. He'd gotten the call on January 27, a few weeks after the president returned from the ranch, and perhaps, but probably not coincidentally, shortly after the January 30 issue of *Jet* would have hit the newsstands. Rowan told Mr. J. that the president wanted to see him, and the publisher agreed to fly to D.C. from Chicago the next day. He was shown into the Oval Office by Rowan at 5:30 p.m. for a meeting that, according to the president's daily diary, lasted only ten minutes, but which, by the account in John H. Johnson's memoir, seemed three times longer, such was the heated and bleepable language of the president's tirade.[8] When the publisher finally had an opportunity to speak, he apparently surprised LBJ by agreeing that some of the recent articles were unfair, adding (somewhat unfairly, in itself,

I thought) that "our people were Kennedy people who resented the fact that Kennedy was dead and that somebody was trying to take his place." But all Mr. J. assured him, by the publisher's account, was that he'd make sure the president got fair coverage in the future. Apparently satisfied, the president pulled out of his pocket a copy of the February 5th *Jet*, fresh off the press, suggested they pose together with it for a photo, and called in White House photographer Yoichi Okamoto to take it. LBJ wasn't going to let this meeting go un-memorialized.

For the next five years, Mr. J. was way up there on LBJ's best-black-friends list, invited to dinner at the White House so often, as he told friends, it was almost embarrassing. Furthermore, he would add, he usually sat next to the president. But Mr. J. always ended the story by assuring the audience that never, in my entire career with the magazines, had he ever had to publish a retraction of anything I wrote.

The whole incident convinced me of one thing. It wasn't that Lyndon was more thin-skinned than any other president, but like JFK before him (and much unlike Eisenhower), he understood the growing influence of the black press, particularly as it related to the burgeoning black vote. His tactics, however, were vastly different from his predecessor's. Early in his own campaign for the presidency (April 1958), Senator John F. Kennedy had invited the publisher and Mrs. John H. Johnson to dinner at Kennedy's Georgetown home. It was an informal supper with the young couple, with baby Caroline nearby, after which the senator revealed that the main reason he wanted to talk to Mr. J. was to grouse about how he was covered in *Jet*, specifically stories that mentioned that he didn't have a black secretary in his Washington office. Kennedy complained that it was unfair not to mention that he had a black secretary in his Boston office, and that Nixon didn't have a black secretary anywhere. Mr. J. agreed, and said he'd make sure the senator got fair coverage in *Jet* in the future. Then JFK asked the publisher what he would like in return—such as an ambassadorship or high government post when Kennedy became president. (According to Mr. J., the word "if" was not used, but "when.") Mr. J. said he didn't want anything like that, but could use some help with advertising. Less than a month later, Henry Ford II called the publisher and *Ebony* soon had its first ad from the automaker.[9]

Two powerful men with the same complaint. One offered dinner, the other summoned the publisher for a ten-minute dressing down. The outcome in both instances was essentially the same—each was assured of fair coverage. I think a review of the magazine's record shows that both got it, and both delivered a lot of welcome but unnecessary favors to the publisher in return.

The second insight one might glean from the incident is that LBJ could be every bit the coarse, overbearing bully every historian—and many of the people who ever worked for him—have said he was at times. Ironically, and more importantly to the black community, he was also about to move the cause of civil rights forward as no president had ever done.

THE CIVIL RIGHTS ACT OF 1964

Lyndon Johnson kept his word. He had vowed not to compromise unless there was no alternative, and he didn't back away from his commitment to drive through the Congress the strongest, most far-reaching civil rights legislation possible. After seventy-five days of Southern filibustering and months of debate on proposed amendments, the bill on the president's desk on July 2, 1964, prohibited discrimination in public accommodations, banned employment discrimination, authorized the attorney general to file suit to compel desegregation of public schools, parks, libraries, and swimming pools, tightened loose ends in existing laws to protect Negro voting rights in federal elections, and much more. Moreover, it had teeth, allowing federal agencies to withhold funds from programs that discriminated on racial grounds, a weapon that if used effectively could make a huge difference in a poor state such as Mississippi. It also extended the authorization of that annoying thorn in the butt of Southern voting registrars and school administrators, among others, the U.S. Commission on Civil Rights, while giving the agency new powers to collect and disseminate information.

LBJ was keenly aware, however, that enforcement of the law he was about to sign would not come easy, particularly in the Deep South. He had an important telephone conversation with J. Edgar Hoover on this subject just hours before signing the bill.[10] The president and the FBI director had been in frequent communication over the past several days regarding the search for three civil rights workers missing near Philadelphia, Mississippi. Michael Schwerner, 24, and Andrew Goodman, 20, both white, and James Chaney, black and twenty-two-years-old, were working for the Mississippi Summer Project, a massive ten-week effort sponsored by a coalition of organizations (COFO) in an effort to improve educational opportunities and political power of Negroes in the poorest, most backward state in the nation, when they disappeared.

Hoover acknowledged during the phone call that the bureau, which was in the process of opening an office in Jackson, had no Negro agents in Mississippi, a fact that *Jet* and others had been unable for years to get Hoover to confirm, although the truth of it was never doubted. The issue came up in relation to a prospective landlord's reluctance to rent space to an "integrated agency," which Hoover said he expected to be "thrashed out" in an imminent conference call. Regarding the search for the missing civil rights workers, LBJ was being urged to send 5,000 troops into the Delta, which both men agreed would be a mistake. Johnson directed Hoover to find a way to send in 50 to 100 additional FBI agents instead, so that the president could respond that he had sufficient resources there already. Johnson also told Hoover he wanted him to construct an intelligence system around the KKK that was "better than you have on Communists," so that "they can't open their mouths without you knowing it."

"That outfit [the Klan] will be flogging people and violating this statute [the Civil Rights Act] that goes into effect tonight," Johnson predicted, and he wanted them stopped in every state where they were operating. Hoover agreed, as heartily as if it had been his own idea. Just as he had once sought a Communist under every bed, he was now being directed by the president to ferret out the Klan from every dark corner of Dixie.

Earlier in the day, LBJ called Roy Wilkins, who by then had become a frequent sounding board for the president on civil rights issues, to ask whether he should postpone signing the Act until after the Fourth of July to avoid kicking off "a wave of trouble," in the South during the usual rounds of holiday drinking and firecrackers. Wilkins advised him that not to sign the bill as planned might look as if he wanted to delay. The president added that another reason to sign it as planned was that Republicans would be leaving that night for their nominating convention, and should be represented at the signing ceremony. Wilkins agreed that would be a gracious gesture.[11]

At 6:45 p.m., from the East Room of the White House, with a host of onlookers seated and lining the walls—Cabinet and agency officials, members of Congress, civil rights leaders—LBJ addressed the nation on television and radio before lifting the first of seventy-two pens he would use to sign the bill into law. His remarks called upon the patriotism and morality of every American to bring about voluntary compliance with the law's provisions. It was a somber, but hopeful, speech, strategically invoking many of the words of the founding fathers regarding equality, inalienable rights, and the blessings of liberty. He told his countrymen, as perhaps only a Southerner could, that he understood how it came to be that some Americans were denied these rights for no other reason than the color of their skin. But, he declared, "it cannot continue."

After months of hard work, the president left the White House that night for a long-awaited Fourth of July holiday at his Texas ranch.

A WOMAN OF GOOD CHARACTER

When LBJ became president, he directed the White House Office of Personnel to send him secretarial candidates who were young, smart, and pretty, as well as able to work at night and on weekends. That fact is well-documented. It's been alleged, however, without any evidence, that of "six beautiful secretaries" hired, he slept with five, a number that seems more related to selling a book while avoiding a libel suit than any factual knowledge. Pathetically, the only woman identified by name in that allegation was also a woman the author must have known could not sue him for his slander. Geraldine Whittington, the first black secretary to a president of the United States, was already deceased.

In his phone call to Andy Hatcher in the late evening of December 23, 1963, LBJ confided that he was about to throw some color into his staff.[12] He had spotted an attractive Negro secretary already working in the White House, and being keenly aware that his predecessor as well as other top elected officials had been criticized (by me, for one) for not having a black on their personal staffs, he was about to preempt that particular criticism. He asked Hatcher what he thought about it, inquiring specifically about the young woman's good character and whether she was respected. Hatcher vouched for that, as well as for her ability, and agreed this would be a good selection. LBJ added that he was going to hire a "Mexican," too, although he couldn't recall the man's name, and told Hatcher to make sure "all the minority groups" knew that the first man he'd hired was an Italian, Jack Valenti. The president apparently had an expansive view of affirmative action.

Johnson had already called Geraldine ("Gerri" to her friends) Whittington at home just before ten o'clock, opening the conversation by asking her where she was, followed by what was she doing. Although he told her he was the president calling, the inanity of his first two questions made her wonder aloud if someone was playing a prank. No, LBJ assured her, calling her "honey," he wanted to talk about work, so could she come to the White House right away. The weather was bad and she wasn't sure she'd be able to get a cab, so he said he'd send a car for her.[13] She arrived at the Oval Office about an hour later. Although he had recorded their phone conversation on his secret taping system, he apparently did not record her office interview, which took only a few minutes. The next morning, according to the President's Daily Diary, Gerri Whittington began a high profile assignment as one of the president's personal secretaries, the first black woman in that role, boarding Air Force One for Christmas holidays with the first family and other guests and staff at the LBJ Ranch.[14]

A couple of days before Christmas 1963, Gerri Whittington became the first African-American secretary to a U.S. president. On New Year's Eve, President Johnson turned heads when he attended a party with friends and staff at Austin's segregated Forty Acres Club with his attractive, black secretary on his arm. (LBJ Library; photo by Kevin Smith.)

Gerri's mother confided to friends that she was not happy about suddenly losing her only daughter for the holidays, even if this was a big promotion and exciting opportunity for the thirty-two-year-old, tan-skinned beauty. Gerri, the only daughter of Dorothy and Henry Whittington, lived with her mother, to whom, according to friends and colleagues alike, she was devoted, and often took her to social functions, of which there would be plenty over the holidays, including events at their church. The sudden departure for Texas left the older woman unsettled and her holiday plans up in the air. Her daughter was a hard worker, that was certain, ever since leaving Virginia State College in Petersburg in 1950 to work for the federal government. Born in West River, Maryland, and educated in Anne Arundel County schools, Gerri was as accomplished and gracious as she was lovely, factors that had made her a standout in her job at the U.S. Agency for International Development, and led to a detail at the White House in 1961 to work for Ralph Dungan, a JFK aide.

As head-turning as that must have been, her new assignment as one of LBJ's personal secretaries would be like none other. Even its impromptu launch, as extraordinary as it must have seemed, was only a hint of the whirlwind that was to come. At 8:30 p.m. on Christmas Eve at the LBJ Ranch, Gerri was seated at dinner with the president and Mrs. Johnson, daughter Lynda Bird, Cousin Oreole, Aunt Jessie, sister Lucia Johnson Alexander, her husband Birge, their daughter Becky, White House photographer Yoichi Okamoto, and two of the president's other personal secretaries, Yolanda Boozer and Marie Fehmer. After dinner, she joined members of the group for a walk with LBJ and his elder daughter to the home of ranch foreman Dale Malechek.[15] LBJ loved to walk around the ranch in the evening, often strolling down to Cousin Oreole's house after dinner.

Other young women might have been blown away by the sudden exposure to the intimate family life of the most powerful man in the world. But Gerri Whittington was no ordinary woman. After more than a decade of government service, she was poised, composed, charming, and, outwardly at least, completely at ease. Another of the young secretaries, Marie Fehmer, many decades later recalled her as "elegant . . . trustworthy . . . and a principled lady."

On Christmas Day at the ranch, White House photographer Yoichi Okamoto took pictures of the president with each of the staff members. Later in the evening they were joined by Tennessee Governor Buford Ellington, as the President and First Lady distributed gifts from under the tree, followed by supper at 10:15. The next days also served up a heady itinerary of activities and meals with the family and VIP visitors, sometimes followed by after-dinner work, with Jack Valenti and Bill Moyers joining the president and his secretaries.

On New Year's Eve, Lady Bird stayed at the ranch with other guests, while LBJ took off by helicopter for Austin with a small group that included his longtime lawyer and family friend Don Thomas, General C. V. Clifton, LBJ's military aide, and three executive secretaries, Gerri, Marie Fehmer, and Vicki McCammon. Their destination was a party at the Forty Acres Club, the private—and segregated—faculty club of the University of Texas. Segregated, that is, until that evening, when the president and his party entered—he with the beautiful, tan-skinned woman on his arm. Gerri later revealed that she had no idea she was integrating the club. LBJ didn't mention it until they were flying back in the chopper. Some of the people in the club, however, obviously knew it. She recalled that one little lady said to her, "Are you the photographer's [Okamoto's] wife?" When Gerri answered that she was one of President Johnson's secretaries, the woman still seemed perplexed and asked if she was "foreign."

"No," Gerri replied, "I'm a Negro." Other than that conversation, she didn't think anyone acted strange about her presence in the club, which she believed LBJ had set out deliberately to integrate that evening.

As much as he wanted to make sure everyone knew it, LBJ had decided not to issue a press release announcing that he had appointed the first Negro secretary to a U.S. president. Instead, he thought it much more clever to arrange for her to appear in mid-January on *What's My Line?*—the popular network television show in which contestants tried to stump the celebrity panel. As usual, *Jet*'s Washington Bureau wasn't about to let LBJ manipulate the news. *Jet* broke the story in the first week of January with a full-page profile and thumbnail photo of the elegant and serene Negro woman.[16] (Gerri had no interest in appearing on a *Jet* cover, despite several opportunities. She was much too reserved for that.) The *Jet* story didn't detract in the least from the success of the television guessing game, as the white press never picked it up.

LBJ went home to his ranch, aptly known as the "Texas White House," as often as he could during his presidency. But the trips in early 1964 were short and few, partly due to the administration's all-out drive for passage of the civil rights bill, as well as LBJ's election campaign. After New Year's Day, 1964, he was able to spend only three other weekends there, including Easter and Memorial Day, before signing the landmark legislation on July 2. According to the presidential diary, Gerri was one of the secretaries along on two of those visits. She told her friends she loved these trips, and the President's Daily Diary suggests why. The secretaries not only joined the president and Lady Bird at mealtime, but on boating trips, high-speed rides in the open convertible, helicopter jaunts to other ranches, and deer hunting, while in the evening they handled whatever workload there was. Gerri even went to church with President and Mrs. Johnson on that first Christmas at the ranch, and Lady Bird took her to Austin to get their hair done.

Gerri's last trip to the Texas White House would be on the weekend of July 4, 1964. Lyndon was always casual and relaxed at the ranch, which, much more than the real White House, he considered his own space, where he could do as he pleased. According to his aides in earlier years, this included nocturnal wanderings with a flashlight into staff bedrooms. What happened behind those doors is known only to the staff members whose rooms he entered, but it was certain that others would know he was there. There was little likelihood that the president of the United States could wander about in the night—even in his own home—without someone hearing him and drawing his or her own conclusion. Regardless of his motive, this kind of behavior would be highly offensive to someone like Gerri, who valued her reputation as much as anything in life. This was something Lyndon apparently didn't understand. From all accounts, he sometimes was oblivious to (or dismissive of) how his actions might appear to others. Historian Doris Kearns Goodwin's account of the "curious ritual" that developed while she was working with him on his memoirs after he'd left the White House is a good example. About 5:30 in the morning, after she was up and dressed, LBJ would come to her room in his robe and pajamas and climb into her bed, while she sat in a chair by the window. To Goodwin, in her mid-twenties at the time, the behavior was not of an aging Lothario, but of a "cold and frightened child."[17] Only someone who was intensely interested in understanding the former president would probably have agreed.

LBJ's apparently impromptu decision to integrate the Forty Acres Club with his beautiful Negro secretary on his arm instead of a male aide, such as Carl Rowan, at his side, was another instance in which the tall Texan demonstrated that he could care less what anyone thought. When it came to racial or any other hang-ups, his unspoken message to others was to get over it. So he probably gave it little thought before he showed up at Gerri's room one night after everyone had retired. Gerri thought she handled it quite well. Without waiting to learn why he was there, she told LBJ she wasn't feeling well, and although it was nothing serious, just her time of the month, she had to get to sleep. With that, she nixed the possibility of anything from chitchat to—well, Lyndon did have a reputation, although with Gerri he'd always acted appropriately. He left, and that's the way it was. Mulling it over later, she thought perhaps he just wanted to talk. But this was not the right time or place. She realized, however, that her calm and quiet brush-off did not assure that it wouldn't happen again, and she wanted to make sure that it didn't. When the president and his entourage returned to Washington after the holiday weekend, Gerri avoided the president while she thought it over. She told me she had considered resigning, but hoped it wouldn't come to that. She really wanted to return to the Department of State, and perhaps have an opportunity to travel abroad, which she had never done. At the end of the week, when she finally came face to face with the president in the secretaries' office, he commented (with some exaggeration and maybe a little sarcasm), "Did you decide to come to work—haven't seen you over here in a week or so?" The secretary keeping the president's diary that day noted the comment, as well as some good-natured banter with the other secretaries. Gerri felt she may have made her point by her absence. In any case, the president seemed ready to move on.

Gerri was one of the many people close to LBJ who saw both the good and the not-so-good in his character, the generosity as well as the pettiness, the temper as well as the good nature. As Roy Wilkins put it, you might love LBJ for what he stood for and what he did, but when you left him, you still checked to make sure you had your wallet. But she also had the highest regard for the first lady, who treated her with the utmost kindness and respect. It was Lady Bird who discovered that Gerri couldn't swim, after inviting her to join the president and first lady at the White House pool one summer evening. It was one of the legacies of segregation. When public pools in many areas, not just the South, were forced to integrate, they simply shut down, and it was predominantly the black kids who didn't learn to swim.

However she managed it, it appears that she never went back to the ranch again, and a year later, in August 1965, after the president talked to Protocol Chief Lloyd Hand about a position for her, Gerri happily transferred back to the Department of State, where she worked first for Hand, and then his successor, Ambassador James Symington. When the president appointed black economist Andrew Brimmer to the Board of Governors of the Federal Reserve in 1966, she helped Brimmer with his transition to the Fed. She visited the president in the Oval Office at midday on two occasions after that, once in 1967 at his invitation after seeing her at a reception, and again when she asked for a few minutes to talk about her career in September 1968, as he prepared to leave the White House. LBJ respected her, and she appreciated that, as well as his advice and encouragement. After the Republicans won the White House, she returned for a few months in the early days of the Nixon administration as secretary to Presidential Special Assistant Robert J. ("Bob") Brown, the second black Republican presidential aide in history. Brown told me he didn't know anyone who had worked in the White House before, except Fred Morrow, whose job more than eight years earlier had been very different. She was the ideal person, therefore, to teach him the inner workings of the mansion, and although she had come into the spotlight in a Democratic administration, she was regarded as a consummate professional by Republicans and Democrats alike.

In 1970, at thirty-eight and the height of her career, the unthinkable happened. Gerri suffered a massive and debilitating stroke, a cerebral thrombosis, the effects of which would handicap her for the rest of her life. The right side of her beautiful face was left paralyzed; the brown eyes that still sparkled when she smiled no longer seemed synchronized, the right eyelid drooping. Her once dazzling smile was now drawn down at one corner. Her right hand hung limp at her side, and her right leg was partially paralyzed. On top of all that, her once clear and confident speech was now halting and difficult. Her twenty-year government career came to a sudden, wrenching halt. No one would ever know how much the stress of long work hours contributed to the stroke. Considering how much she seemed to enjoy the life she was leading, it may have been very little.

A year after suffering the stroke, Gerri was making progress relearning to speak, and to walk with the help of a leg brace and cane, but her long hospitalization and medical bills had depleted the resources of the former GS-12 government employee, and she still faced months and perhaps years of physical therapy. White House aide Bob Brown helped to organize a fundraiser in the Capitol that drew more than 300 of her friends, admirers, former bosses, and colleagues (at $17.50 a ticket) to toast her courage and help with those expenses. During the evening, Brown read a supportive letter from President Nixon, and Ambassador James Symington recalled what an asset Gerri's detailed knowledge of the State Department had been to him when he served as protocol chief. *The Washington Post* ran a Style section feature article on the event, with a photo of Federal Reserve Governor Andrew Brimmer making Gerri laugh as he greeted her, gently lifting her left hand in his. White House Assistant General Counsel Clifford Alexander, the Urban League's Sterling Tucker, black businessman Chester Carter, publicist Ofield Dukes—a healthy sampling of the capital's who's who list, black and white, Republican and Democrat—paid tribute to a gallant lady and urged her onward.

Gerri lived twenty-three years after suffering the stroke, managing after intensive physical therapy to carry on an almost normal life, although never fully recovering. Most remarkable, perhaps, was that she remained forever upbeat, and would tell friends, "The only time I know I'm disabled is when I see myself in the mirror."

Gerri died in 1993, on the same day as Supreme Court Associate Justice Thurgood Marshall.

19

"ALL THE WAY WITH LBJ"

Lyndon Baines Johnson began his Great Society doing something no American president had ever done before: he danced with a Negro woman at his Inaugural Ball. He didn't give a damn if every newspaper in the country ran the photograph. Lynette Taylor was the wife of fellow Texan Hobart Taylor, co-chairman of the Inaugural Committee, and vice chairman of the President's Committee on Equal Employment Opportunity, one of two Negroes with offices in the White House.

Snow blanketed the nation's capital during the three-day inaugural celebration, but neither that nor the cold weather dampened the high spirits of the black revelers who came to D.C. to honor the man who had championed their cause by pushing the Civil Rights Act of 1964 through the Congress, and to urge him to finish the job of securing equal rights for all Americans.

Jet's Washington Bureau, having recently relocated to the top floor of the new "Communications Building" at 1750 Pennsylvania Avenue NW, opened in time for John H. Johnson to host a guest list of nearly 1,000 federal officials, business people, and civil rights leaders for viewing of the Inaugural Parade, while the magazine's staff covered every phase of the festivities.

Thanks to a well-integrated Inaugural Committee, blacks were represented in respectable numbers at every event during the celebration, from early morning prayer services to late-night ballroom dancing, and that was the way the president wanted it. LBJ started the day by inviting Negro leaders to join him in services at Washington's National Christian Church. A few hours later, Leontyne Price sang "America the Beautiful" at the swearing-in, after which Roy Wilkins, Whitney Young, Marian Anderson, Ralph Bunche, attorney Floyd McKissick, chairman of CORE, and Mrs. James Farmer, representing her husband, CORE's director, were among the 100 guests viewing the parade from the presidential box. James Farmer was engaged at the moment in civil rights work in the South, as were Dr. Martin Luther King, Jr., and James Forman, Executive Director of SNCC, whom the president had also invited to his inauguration. King, in fact, was leading a voter registration drive in Selma, Alabama, where 200 Negroes had already been arrested, a "massacre" was on the horizon, and one of the most dramatic events of the civil rights movement was about to explode, giving LBJ all the support he would need for his next legislative battle—passage of the Voting Rights Act of 1965. Against this backdrop, LBJ used his strongest civil rights language ever, calling anyone who discriminated against blacks a traitor. "When any citizen denies his fellow citizens saying, 'His color is not mine or his beliefs are strange and different,' in that moment he betrays America, though his forebears created the nation."

Johnson had won the 1964 presidential election handily, defeating conservative Republican Senator Barry Goldwater with over 61 percent of the popular vote, and 94 percent of the black vote. Black voters in Virginia, Tennessee, and Florida, three states that had voted Republican in the last three presidential elections, helped swing those states to the Democrats. With black support in New York, Robert Kennedy won a U.S. Senate seat. Detroit sent another black man, John Conyers, to the U.S. House of Representatives. In fact, more blacks won political office in 1964 than in any year since Reconstruction. The victories ranged from local school boards to state legislatures and courts, and crisscrossed the nation from East to West. But black registration still represented only a small fraction—and in some diehard areas of the South, no fraction at all—of the eligible black population.

LBJ had signed the Civil Rights Act on July 2, 1964, after weeks of filibuster, an unprecedented cloture vote in the Senate, and final House passage by a 289–126 vote. In some areas of the South, hotels and restaurants finally started serving Negroes. "White" and "colored" signs began to come down from water fountains and restrooms, and some progressive white leaders began the steps necessary to lead their communities forward in transition from the myth of "separate but equal" to equal rights and equal access, regardless of race. But there were plenty of diehard areas as well where no federal law by itself would make an iota of difference in the way the system operated. Alabama was one of them.

With Negroes outnumbering whites by more than 4-to-1, Lowndes County, between and to the south of Montgomery and Selma, looked like a good place to scout out support for a black voter registration drive, since all the eligible whites, according to a report of the U.S. Commission on Civil Rights, were registered to vote, but no blacks. The SCLC sent David Bey and the Reverends Andrew Young, James Bevel, and Bernard Lafayette to visit local black preachers who told them there was already a voter registration movement. Since the late 1950s, local black leaders Amelia Boynton and attorney J. L. Chestnut, among others, had been attempting to get Negroes registered to vote, and were joined in the effort by representatives of SNCC in the early 1960s. Confronted with arrests, beatings, even killings, they struggled on. Now they would welcome SCLC support. The news sent the quartet back to Selma happily singing freedom songs.[1]

Thus began Dr. King's "freedom drive" in Alabama. The reaction of whites was panic, followed by a reign of terror unleashed by the local police. In Selma alone, thousands of Negroes were arrested and taken to jail just for marching to the courthouse to attempt to register to vote. News photographs began to appear in the nation's major dailies. One of them was of Mrs. Boynton, grabbed by the collar of her dress and shoved a half-block to a police car by the notorious Sheriff Jim Clark. Another showed Mrs. Annie Lee Cooper being wrestled to the ground by three sheriff's deputies. A middle-aged woman, Mrs. Cooper had lived up North, where she had also voted, all her adult life, but returned to Selma to care for her ninety-eight-year-old mother. Mrs. Cooper was in line at the courthouse with all the other Negro would-be registrants, as ordered by Sheriff Clark, when she was shoved by the racist lawman. She reacted by slugging him, whereupon three deputies wrestled her to the ground. Clark, who had a legendary temper, stood over her with his nightstick, hesitating just long enough for Mrs. Cooper to practically dare him to hit her. No number of eyewitnesses or press cameras could ever persuade the burly, hot-tempered cop to check his fury. He brought the club down on her head. Even the bad press that others worried reflected so badly on Selma didn't bother him. Afterward, Sheriff Clark explained point-blank why he refused to call her by a customary courtesy title when describing the incident: "She's a nigger woman," he sneered, "and she hasn't got a Miss or a Mrs. in front of her name."[2] His larger objective was to make sure that name, whatever it was, never appeared on a voter registration list in Dallas County, Alabama.

Meanwhile, some thirty miles away in Marion, nearly 1,000 students boycotting school were among those arrested in demonstrations protesting "whites only" public accommodations, while other Negroes went to the courthouse to register to vote. Unlike the "slower than molasses dripping from a barrel" approach taken by registrars in Selma, Marion moved rapidly to process applications at a rate that saw eighty-five persons pass through the "A" line (for people who'd been unsuccessful in earlier attempts to register) and sixty-five in the "B" line (first-time applicants) in half-a-day. In contrast, one applicant in Selma might have needed as long as an hour for the complicated voter registration test. At that rate, Dr. King predicted "it would take at least 103 years to register the 14,873 Negroes" in Dallas County, if nothing changed.[3]

Dr. King and other SCLC leaders led the marches protesting voting restrictions that kept the majority Negro population almost nonexistent at the polls, and in the process, he and 3,000 other men, women and children went to jail in Selma and Marion.

A delegation of more than a dozen members of Congress descended upon Selma in a show of support, with the intention of seeing King in the city jail where he'd spent five days, but they were turned away. He was released in time to meet with them on the outside. The legislators were preparing to introduce voting rights legislation.

In Washington, LBJ called for a show of national support for the Negro voting rights drive in Alabama, calling on all Americans "to be indignant when one American is denied the right to vote," adding, "I intend to see that the right is secured for all our citizens."[4]

The eyes of the nation were watching what was happening in Alabama. The news media were descending upon the black Alabama counties as never before. But state and local officials, from the governor on down, seemed totally disinterested in public opinion outside the state, although newsmen were starting to become the first ones clubbed to the ground to put them out of commission before the marchers got their licks. But if the authorities were stubborn, they were matched toe to toe in that regard by the demonstrators. Neither the beatings nor the arrests turned them around. In fact, violence on the part of local law enforcement was what the media were waiting for, and what the movement needed to galvanize public support.

SCLC's leaders had a long record of arrests, as did SNCC's John Lewis, who also had a reputation for surviving "head knockings." He would suffer another concussion while leading demonstrations in Selma. But something about this particular place at this specific time made it seem a lot hotter, a lot more dangerous, and somehow innately different from any the movement had encountered before. At one point, Dr. King was attacked in a hotel lobby by a white thug who suddenly started bashing him. Then the rumors started that he'd been targeted for assassination. There were all kinds of rumors. Some said the police were told specifically to get King if they had the opportunity. Others said thugs would be brought in from outside to do the job. King brushed the reports aside. He knew he wasn't the only one in harm's way in this steaming cauldron. Before long, hundreds would be beaten either by thugs or law enforcement as they peacefully paraded. It was a responsibility he accepted but did not relish. Some people might be killed. They might be old, very young, disabled. It didn't matter to these lawmen or to the mobs they both inspired and conspired with to end the marches. Day by day, we could see the weight of these decisions in King's eyes. He refused a formal bodyguard for himself, but allowed his brother, the Reverend A. D. King, to shield him during the Selma campaign. His lieutenants believed that to lose Martin Luther King would be too great a blow to the Alabama freedom movement, and would only encourage the white supremacists to kill even more innocent people.

The movement was facing down a system so corrupt that it could no longer be tolerated. Those who got to the Selma courthouse were assigned numbers and told to report when called. The voter registration test included 300 questions, taking an average of one hour per person. With whites in the line as well (and not required to take the test), few blacks got into the court-house in any given day. It took six weeks to six months to learn if you had passed. The process was humiliating, but nobody except the blacks excluded from the polls seemed to care about it.

Meanwhile, in nearby Marion, in Perry County, a scene unfolded like no other the movement had seen in recent years. Five hundred people, men and women, young and old, had gathered at Zion United Methodist Church on the evening of February 18 for a march that had been announced in advance as a peaceful, hymn-singing show of support for a young civil rights worker held in the Perry County Jail, about a half-block away. Among the marchers was twenty-six-year-old Jimmie Lee Jackson, a church deacon who had tried without success to register to vote every year since his twenty-first birthday. His mother, Viola Jackson, and his eighty-two-year-old grandfather, Cager Lee, were also with the marchers. As soon as they left the church, the group was intercepted by an array of city police, state troopers, and sheriff's deputies. The law officers later claimed they were anticipating an attempted jail-break. Suddenly the streetlights went off—some say shot out by police. In the darkness, the helmeted officers set upon the marchers with batons, gun butts, sticks—many never knew what or who hit them.

It was all so sudden, so unanticipated, and so chaotic on the darkened city street. Jimmie Lee and his mother ran into Mack's Cafe behind the church, hoping to find cover. But they were pursued as if felons by Alabama state troopers. Cager had already been felled in the onslaught. He later told *Jet*: "I was behind the church when white men with helmets came running through and knocked me down. When we got out in the light, they said, 'God damn, this is old Cager; don't hit him anymore.' So I think they must have been local people. My head was bleeding so I went to the cafe to tell Jimmie. He was taking me to the doctor when they [Lee didn't know whether deputies or troopers] forced us back inside. Then they rushed in and told us to get out. I was outside when Jimmie came running out, half-bent. A group of four or five whites with helmets chased and beat him as he ran. Folks lined up on the sidewalk hit him. One man broke a nightstick. I didn't know then that he was shot."[5]

A state trooper had shot Jimmie twice at close range in the abdomen when the young man tried to protect his mother from more blows. He died at Good Samaritan Hospital in Selma on February 26, 1965. The movement's leaders were dismayed when no words of condolence came from the Johnson White House, but local blacks and the civil rights activists who'd joined them vowed, as did Cager Lee, that his grandson would not have died in vain. It was time to make a statement—not with words, but with actions—about the denial of voting rights to blacks in Alabama. It was time to go right to the top. After considering several options, SCLC decided to lead a peaceful march on a four-day trek to the state capital in Montgomery. When they arrived, they planned to deliver a petition to Gov. George Wallace for better voting conditions and an end to police brutality against Negroes who tried to register to vote. Bloody Sunday was in the offing.

On Sunday, March 7, 1965, close to 600 men, women and children (including about seventy whites) gathered at Brown AME Church in Selma for "the moment of confrontation." A violent reaction on the part of local authorities—and the Klan—was fully expected. In fact, some kind of "trap" was anticipated, but exactly what it would be was uncertain. Reporter Larry Still and photographer Maurice Sorrell went down from our Washington Bureau. Still, who'd followed me in covering the Freedom Rides and on other assignments in the former Confederacy, was by then accustomed to dealing with its harsh realities for blacks, but Sorrell hated going into the Deep South and had avoided it like the plague. It turned his stomach to see black people having to bow and scrape, shuffle and apologize for any perceived indifference to white supremacy, just to stay alive. He was quiet and modest, but he was also feisty. Maybe a few inches over five feet at best, he'd learned to use his elbows and shoulders effectively to hold his ground against bigger photographers jockeying for position in photo shoots. He didn't take any guff. The same attributes that made him successful in a gaggle of white photographers could also get him killed in the South. He preferred not to take the risk. But something was happening in Selma, and Sorrell was the first *Ebony/Jet* photographer on the scene.

Civil rights workers roamed the alleys, poked into garbage cans, and scanned the rooftops for bombs, sniper positions— anything out of the ordinary. No sleepy Sunday morning, the town of Selma was now headquarters for the final campaign. The parking lot of Brown's AME Church had made room for buses from Marion, carrying several hundred demonstrators from that town who wanted to protest the killing of Jimmie Lee Brown as well as Perry County's outrageous voter registration record. But they would soon learn that the Alabama campaign's leader would not be accompanying them on this march. Dr. King had obligations in Atlanta, one of which was to preach to his congregation at Sunday service. It seemed like a poor reason to miss a march he had organized, and it was speculated that there was another reason for him to stay away. The word was that King might as well have had a target painted between his eyes. The assassins this time, according to one report, would be Klansmen brought in from Chicago, who would then be whisked out of town before anyone could apprehend or pursue them. The FBI was said to be checking it out, but by then everybody knew the bureau did not prevent crimes; it only investigated them. That was Hoover's mantra.

According to his aides, Dr. King still wanted to lead the march, and had told them to postpone it until Monday. But when march coordinator Rev. Andrew Young arrived back in Selma from Atlanta, he found that preparations had gone too far. Hundreds of police were already massed at one end of the Edmund Pettus Bridge over the Alabama River to stop the marchers. Young called King in Atlanta and convinced him that, with hundreds of protesters ready to move out and police waiting for them, SCLC would lose credibility if it postponed the march now. King, according to Young, reluctantly agreed, and the bloodiest demonstration of the movement, with perhaps the greatest impact on the American conscience, stepped off without its leader. Instead, SCLC's Rev. Hosea Williams and SNCC's John Lewis walked at the front of the double line of some 600 marchers.

Although disappointed that King wasn't there, most of the protesters were more concerned about getting the march underway regardless of who was at the front. Most of them didn't even expect to get very far—and certainly not all the way to Montgomery, although a few had backpacks and toothbrushes with them, just in case. Most of the marchers, however, men and women from all walks of life, many of them residents of Selma's George Washington Carver Homes, a black housing project, were still dressed in their Sunday-go-to-church clothes. Some of the women were even in heels. Their kids, too, were in their "Sunday best." For many of the marchers, what they were embarking on was as much spiritual as civic, as much a prayer as a protest, a sacrifice the extent of which they did not yet know. The Selma marchers on this Sunday were ready, they believed, for whatever was to come; they just didn't know what it would be.

As the marchers started across the Edmund Pettus Bridge over the river some 100 feet below, they couldn't see the staggering array of force awaiting them at the other end until they reached the apex of the bridge's arc. There, on the other side, state troopers in riot gear, complete with gas masks, were massed like a wall. As if that wouldn't be enough to handle a peaceful march, Sheriff Jim Clark had called out a posse of white males whom he had "deputized." The eager volunteers were standing by on horseback.

The marchers, walking two by two over the bridge, didn't have a chance—no chance to kneel in prayer before turning around, no chance to talk rationally with the officer in command, no chance to do anything—before the order was given and the troopers advanced on them, shoving them back, knocking them to the ground, beating them over their heads and backs with nightsticks. Then came the tear gas, shot directly into the clusters of retreating, terrified marchers, while more troopers charged in on horseback, knocking them down, and galloping over their bodies.

There would be hundreds of eyewitnesses to the atrocity, but no oral history would be needed to describe this event. It was the television age, and the SCLC had made sure that the media were there and ready for whatever happened. Despite vicious attacks on reporters and cameramen, mostly by mobs of white bystanders who struck after the police began their onslaught against the marchers, a nationwide television audience on a Sunday night saw it all in a context that could neither have been planned nor predicted. One of the major TV networks interrupted its primetime broadcast of the movie *Judgment at Nuremberg* with horrific footage from Selma: the unarmed, neatly dressed men, women and children, screaming, falling, running, and still being beaten, gassed and chased relentlessly by armed men in gas masks, many on horseback, trampling downed marchers. Some of the injured lying on the ground looked as if they were dead. Among them, her body limp, her eyes closed, was Amelia Boynton, the Selma activist whose only crime was wanting to vote. Others were beaten by the armed horsemen all the way back to Brown AME Church, nearly a mile away. It was a scene like no other ever experienced in America. In the end, the comparatively tiny march in a small town—no match by any measure for the huge, quarter-million rally (also called a "march") at the Lincoln Memorial in Washington, D.C., less than two years earlier—wouldn't have warranted even brief mention on the Sunday night network news, but for the insane reaction of the state troopers, supposedly following orders from Governor Wallace to stop the march, and one burly, redneck sheriff who'd already demonstrated that he harbored more racial hatred than good sense. In the end, the march packed a public relations wallop like none other thus far, and the biggest blow on that Bloody Sunday fell on the head of Jim Crow.

Dr. King seized the moment by sending out a call for people of conscience and goodwill all across the country to join the protesters in Selma for another attempt to march to Montgomery on Tuesday. Even as he headed back to Selma, more press and more protesters began arriving. Leaving Washington Monday morning, I joined Larry Still and Maurice Sorrell on the scene and found myself running into hundreds of demonstrators, many of them clergy, who had also arrived, eager to take up the march. I heard from them over and over again a word former President Eisenhower had been reluctant to use for eight long years of his two administrations. It now seemed to slip from the lips of every other protester, particularly the clergy: the rights being denied Alabama Negroes weren't simply a constitutional question; this was a moral issue. They were there in Selma to put their lives on the line if necessary to bear witness to that. To the shock and sorrow of many as events unfolded, that would be exactly what they were doing.[6]

The protesters were ready and impatient to set out toward Montgomery, regardless of whatever action local law enforcement might take against them, and as members of the press, we were just as eager for the next march to begin. At SCLC's request, the NAACP Legal Defense Fund went to federal court in Montgomery for an injunction against police interference with a second march, but to everyone's dismay, the court ordered a hearing on the matter before it would act. Judge Frank Johnson ordered that the march not proceed until the court had ruled, which was expected to take a couple of weeks. While Dr. King was confident that Judge Johnson, an astute jurist who had sided with civil rights protesters before on constitutional issues, would do so again, he knew it was best to wait. He did not want to be found "in contempt" of this court, but he had to do something on Tuesday to satisfy the impatient marchers, now arriving in droves, as well as to keep national attention on Selma, a town most Americans had never heard of before Bloody Sunday. As it turned out, only Dr. King and his aides knew what he had decided to do when he led the line of about 2,000 protesters, including several hundred members of the clergy, across the Edmund Pettus Bridge almost to the point where the troopers were waiting to beat them back again. There, he suddenly stopped and knelt in prayer before turning the line of confused marchers around and back into Selma. If most of the protesters were surprised by his action, it was because there had been no announcement of the plan in advance, perhaps because Dr. King himself wasn't sure how this strategy would play out. As a result, in addition to confusion, there was some bitterness on the part of more militant protesters who'd prepared themselves for the worst. In contrast to Bloody Sunday, some of them called this "Turnaround Tuesday."

Later that evening, Maurice Sorrell and I, along with Jimmy Hicks of the *New York Amsterdam News* and Mary Stratford from the *Afro-American*, joined a group of more than twenty ministers in one of Selma's popular black eateries, Walker's Cafe. It was the kind of place where you were sure to get real Southern cooking, and all the "soul food" you might crave while listening to a jukebox that could take you from Blues Alley to Blueberry Hill. That night, Sam Cooke's "Change is Comin'" played over and over in the background while fellowship and laughter filled the air amid clinking dinnerware in the packed dining room. In case anyone still didn't get it, jars of pigs feet and thick sausage lining the counter let visitors know this place was the real thing. The cafe didn't have many whites among its clientele, but the visiting clergymen had come to Selma to take a stand, and they lost no time doing it. Besides, Walker's was about as good a place as any to get the lowdown on what was going on.

Among the clergymen eating and chatting with us was Boston Unitarian minister Rev. James Reeb, a scholarly and convivial man who laughed heartily with the rest of us when one of the group teased, "Imagine a Harvard theologian eating 'soul food!'"[7] Later that night, we were stunned when we learned that Rev. Reeb and two other ministers who had left the cafe with him were attacked by white thugs after making a wrong turn into a seedy white neighborhood less than a block away. SCLC aides had gotten them to a first-aid center where a doctor advised that Rev. Reeb's condition was serious and he needed to be taken to a hospital. For a number of reasons, the decision was to take him to the University Hospital in Birmingham, ninety miles away. He was carried to one of the movement's ambulances, and sped away. But once on the highway, a tire blew out and the vehicle was marooned. The blood clot pressing against the young minister's brain was growing larger. State police stopped to see what was going on, but refused to help, declining even to call for assistance. Finally, someone got word to SCLC and after another half hour, a second ambulance arrived on the scene.

When Rev. Reeb was finally examined at the Birmingham hospital, the clot was the size of a baseball. Doctors operated immediately, but offered little hope that they could save his life. In the end, they couldn't. He died two days later, March 11. The clergy who were descending upon Selma now had another reason to be there.

Across the country, demonstrators had started taking to the streets to protest the police brutality in Selma and to demand federal protection for Alabama blacks seeking to register to vote. In Michigan, the governor himself (George Romney) joined Detroit Mayor Jerome Cavanaugh in a march down the city's main street. With that kind of brass at the forefront, the police made no effort to interfere, despite a conservative city council member having blocked issuance of a parade permit. In Chicago, thousands of young militants blocked the busy intersection of Madison and State Streets, stalling rush-hour traffic and refusing to move until police hauled them away. Thousands of others were in the streets of Los Angeles; Boston; Hartford; New York City; Beloit, Wisconsin; Springfield, Ohio; and other cities. In Washington, D.C., protesters added a novel twist. A small, interracial group of youths broke off from a White House tour and staged a sit-in for nine hours while some 400 protesters picketed outside the mansion, demanding immediate aid for Alabama civil rights demonstrators, and urging the admin-istration to introduce voting rights legislation. Less than two months into his new term, Johnson seemed startled by the events in Alabama. A political cartoon by Bill Mauldin said it all, depicting the president in combat gear in a foxhole in Vietnam, looking over his shoulder with wide-eyed surprise as Alabama exploded behind him. The war in Southeast Asia was going poorly, just as the one at home was reaching crisis stage. Another Pulitzer Prize–winning cartoonist, Herblock, depicted the cravenness of the Bloody Sunday attack with a gloating state trooper rinsing blood off his night stick, while boasting, "I got one of 'em just as she almost made it back to the church."

LBJ rushed his race-relations expert, former Florida Governor LeRoy Collins, now U.S. Community Relations Service Director, to Selma as an arbiter. The president also directed J. Edgar Hoover to move additional FBI agents into the area, and the attorney general to dispatch Justice Depart-ment staff into Alabama. At the White House, he called in civil rights and religious leaders, as well as key members of Congress to confer on the ele-ments of a new voting rights law, and a strategy for getting it through the usual opposition. But he hesitated to send in federal troops.

No U.S. president had ever reacted swiftly and firmly to explosions of violence against Dixie blacks. Since 1957, Negroes twice had been left to fend for themselves while presidents negotiated with racist governors. Despite demonstrations all over the country—including a sit-in at the White House—in the wake of the outrageous violence inflicted on Selma blacks by Alabama state and local authorities, five days passed while LBJ, among other things, tried to reason with Gov. Wallace, before finally showing federal power in Alabama. During those five days, the White House was deluged with the heaviest barrage of verbal protests ever lobbed by white leaders in a civil rights matter. Finally, to his credit, LBJ moved more boldly than any previous president to strike at the roots of the discontent: voting inequities.

In an address that will endure for all time as a milestone in the prog-ress of the civil rights movement, LBJ on March 15 urged a joint session of Congress to pass a stringent voting rights law without delay. It had been one of his goals since the '64 campaign to do so. In fact, he'd hoped it would be the keystone of his presidency's civil rights legacy. His aides had been working quietly on such a bill, but he had felt that it could not pass so soon after enactment of the Civil Rights Act of 1964. Now, he was of a different mind. The huge presence of clergy in Selma and the insane clubbing death of Rev. James Reeb were two of the factors that finally brought White House deliberations to an end. Another was the intensity of the protests around the country, echoed daily right outside the executive mansion, where the strains of "We Shall Overcome" being sung over and over beyond the front gates got to the point where daughter Luci had to switch bedrooms to study or even sleep. All of this appeared to evidence broader support for voting rights legislation than had ever existed before Bloody Sunday.

"The real hero of this struggle," LBJ told the Congress, "is the American Negro. His actions and protests—his courage to risk safety and even life—have awakened the conscience of the nation. . . . Their cause must be our cause too. It is not just Negroes but all of us, who must overcome the crippling legacy of bigotry . . . And we shall overcome." I wasn't in the room when Rev. King heard LBJ invoke the very theme of the civil rights movement, but those who were said he wiped away a tear when he heard it.

MARCHING TO MONTGOMERY

LBJ followed up his tough talk with an even tougher show of federal power. When the marchers set off again from Selma with a federal court order enjoining the state government from interfering with the demonstration, they also had—in front, alongside, behind them, and overhead—thousands of federal troops, augmented by the federalized Alabama National Guard, and (although of dubious help) hundreds of state troopers. Military helicopters swept low over the patches of swamp and forests the marchers would have to pass on the fifty-four-mile trek to the state capital, while a demolition team worked both sides of the highway for signs of explosives. GIs with bayonet-tipped rifles stood patrol for miles, while FBI and U.S. Department of Justice agents moved quietly through the shantytowns along U.S. Highway 80, looking for signs of trouble. Behind the scenes, truckloads of federal troops were on call for immediate action, while two truckloads of soldiers and radio-equipped jeeps followed. Every piece of equipment used by the marchers required military guard as it was moved from one campsite to the next.

Rev. King had seized the moment, and it was his. His call for more marchers, more protesters, and more clergy after Bloody Sunday was answered from around the country. Those that had arrived within hours of the broadcast of the Bloody Sunday onslaught had since been augmented by thousands more—ministers, priests, rabbis, nuns, civil rights workers, students, laborers, teachers, business people, housewives—from coast to coast and the American heartland. They came by bus, plane, rented or borrowed cars, and trucks. Airlines in key cities called in extra staff and scheduled additional flights to handle the traffic to Selma. Two chartered planes filled with religious leaders flew in from St. Louis, sponsored by the local Conference on Race and Religion. They brought backpacks and sleeping bags. By the time the marchers set off again, two weeks after Bloody Sunday, they numbered at least 10,000, and had turned the streets around the town's black housing project into what looked like a battlefield encampment with the most diverse assemblage of people ever seen in Alabama, and certainly in this small farming and cattle-grazing center. It was not only a conglomeration of all races and walks of life, but of all ages and even disabilities, including a blind man from Atlanta, and an amputee from Michigan who with some help made the entire march on one leg and a crutch. A California couple pushed a stroller carrying their fifteen-month-old toddler; two men played chess on a small board they passed between them. A nun would return to the march day after day, undertaking the entire distance in her heavy, ankle-length habit, through incredible weather changes—subzero nightly cold, torrid midday sun, drenching humidity, and near the end, torrential rain.

Wherever they were able to do so (and the state police seemed to give them ample opportunities), race-baiting clusters, mostly of young men, taunted the marchers. A car with "Coonsville, USA" painted on the doors cruised along the highway for days while its driver chatted amiably with state troopers. Graffiti on other cars called Dr. King a Communist or advertised "cheap ammo here" and "open season on niggers." They blasted "Bye Bye Blackbird" from loudspeakers attached to boom boxes. A small plane buzzed the line, a day after another had swooped low to drop hate literature, but both were chased away by army aircraft. The worst taunts seemed to be aimed at the whites in the march, not even sparing the nuns and other clergy.

Several white Northerners told me they had never known how bad the situation was in Alabama for blacks or the depth of hatred many whites seemed to harbor. "God," one of them blurted, "I never thought the South was like this. I absolutely believed we were making progress and the passage of the Civil Rights bill last year was all we needed." That comment was echoed by the many others I talked with as they walked, ignoring the jeers from rednecks standing on top of their cars to get a better view. These marchers' innocence reminded me of my first trip to the Delta just a decade earlier, and the book of horrors to which it opened my own eyes.

After the first night on the road, the biggest complaint, except among the native Alabamians, was the bitter cold, which most of the Northerners had not expected. Local blacks, as march coordinator Rev. Andrew Young explained, were used to life in drafty cabins with leaky roofs and holes in the floorboards.

Thousands of marchers had returned to Selma at the end of the first day, some of them ferried back by volunteers, many intending to rejoin the march the next day or at the final rally in Montgomery. But those marching on still numbered in the thousands on the second day, and camped along the road in three large tents, where they sang around fires in huge steel barrels and listened to rousing freedom speeches. The first campsite was on the land of a black farmer, David Hall. The father of eight children, his livestock consisted of a small herd of cows, a few hundred chickens, and four guinea hens. He was the first to defy threats from whites and encouraged other farmers along the way to offer campsites as well.[8]

Then came the most dramatic transformation in the march. For public safety purposes, federal Judge Frank Johnson's court order limited the number of marchers to 300 on the stretch of Highway 80 that narrowed into two lanes through snake-infested swampland. At this point, the marchers split into two groups, dubbed "the chosen few"—mostly Alabama sharecroppers and townspeople—and the "blessed souls," the outsiders and supporters who would handle the housekeeping chores that would keep the people's army moving on schedule. Many of the latter were white, and included television and movie actors and other "celebrities," university professors, ministers, and priests. They did the hard work, setting up the tents, cleaning latrines, clearing fields, running a shuttle service, and passing out food. I wrote in *Jet* that Michigan housewives operated the shuttle service. We didn't learn until after the march had ended that it would be the most dangerous mission of all.

That night in the downsized campsite, I roamed through the marchers, looking for anyone from Lowndes County, the very county we were marching through. There was no one. Not one local Negro dared accompany the march through his own rural county.

There were sharecroppers there from other counties in Alabama's "Black Belt"—men such as Perry County farmer Jim Brown, father of twelve children, two of whom marched with him. Looking older than his fifty-six years, his eyes glowing like coals in the firelight, Brown told me, "This is the greatest thing since I been born."

One of the few Washington officials I recognized on the march was former JFK White House aide Harris Wofford. Now an official with the Peace Corps, he showed what he was made of, making the entire march, eating the camp food, and sleeping on the ground at night.

On the last night of the march, a host of entertainers arrived at the campsite. Tony Bennett, Joan Baez, Odetta, Sammy Davis, Nina Simone, Billy Eckstine, conductor Leonard Bernstein, actresses Shelley Winters and Ina Balin, Nipsey Russell, writer James Baldwin, prize fighter Floyd Patterson—and where else would Dick Gregory and Harry Belafonte be on that night other than among these marchers! They came to raise the spirits of the chosen few who had stayed with the march through the swamplands of Lowndes County and now faced another night of bitter cold followed by bone-chilling rain. An estimated 30,000 people had returned to join the marchers on the eve of the final, triumphant trek to the capitol. They erected an impromptu stage on top of casket bases lent by a local mortician. It was an incredible sight.

I never covered entertainment, so I paid little attention to the show, which was pulled together on the spot. I was more interested in the reaction of the crowd. It was a thrill for the Alabamians who but for this demonstration of support, would likely never see anything like it in their lives. To the black marchers, it was also flesh-and-blood evidence that powerful people with loud voices beyond this, at times seemingly godforsaken, state were not going to let them down.

The next morning, Dr. Ralph Bunche, the United Nations undersecretary, like Dr. King a Nobel Peace Prize winner, who for years whites had considered the most impressive Negro in America, was at the minister's side, as they led a people's army into the state capital. Out of the swamps of hate and despair, the line of marchers stretched three miles long as it entered Montgomery. Suddenly shouts, cheers, and singing erupted from some 500 well-wishers who had waited hours at the city limits. I saw many faces with tears running down their cheeks. From the windows of motels, chambermaids waved and cried with joy as the marchers waved back.

Supporters had arrived in Montgomery from all fifty states, swelling the number massed before the capitol building to some 50,000. Some said the day belonged to Dr. King. Others thought it a fitting funeral for Jim Crow. Our team of photographers had no problem finding Confederate flags in the background of their shots. One flew under the Alabama state flag right over the Capitol dome. What they couldn't find was the Stars and Stripes. As a band proudly played "The Star Spangled Banner," the nation's flag was nowhere to be seen. (Gov. Wallace later objected that it did indeed fly in the capital, and in a very special place—although not visible from in front of the seat of government.) The Confederacy had fallen a hundred years earlier, but Alabama was still Alabama.

At the conclusion of the march, and Dr. King's rousing address to the crowds, the only question was, where was Gov. Wallace? He had said he would receive the marchers' petition, but in the end, politics and cowardice won out, and like the nation's flag, he went unseen.

As the thousands of demonstrators dispersed, our *Ebony/Jet* team raced to get our material back to Chicago. We were already on our way when we heard the tragic news of Viola Liuzzo's murder. The Michigan mother of five children had been shot ferrying a black civil rights worker back to Selma from Montgomery. In the car from which the shots were fired were members of the Ku Klux Klan, including a paid FBI informant. The jubilation of the largest, most successful march for civil rights in the nation's history was forever dimmed by the addition of its third martyr, as Mrs. Liuzzo joined Jimmie Lee Jackson and Rev. James Reeb among those who had already given their lives to right a terrible wrong.

In Chicago, John H. Johnson made a critical decision. Since it was the end of March, *Ebony* was in the middle of production of the May issue, and most of the copy had already been run. But the story of the Selma to Montgomery march, he decided, was too important to wait another month for the June issue. Sparing no expense, he pulled back the cover and everything else necessary to clear the way for a special issue on the march, including the longest story ever in the magazine, which I was privileged to write. We worked around the clock to prepare text and caption more than 100 photos selected from among the thousands taken by the magazine's outstanding photographers. Among them is one rare photo I had totally forgotten about. The caption identifies Dr. King holding the last strategy meeting before the march, with Hosea Williams taking notes, as the Reverends Ralph Abernathy, James Bevel, and C. T. Vivian listen intently. And there in the background is this reporter. For my own safety, as a rule, we almost never included my picture in any of the magazines, and I'm not identified in this one. I was there because Dr. King trusted me to tell the truth. The real importance of the photograph, however, is that it reflects the weight of the moment in the eyes of Dr. King. Two people had already died to bring voting rights to black Alabamans. He acknowledged that others might be lost as well before this mammoth undertaking succeeded. But he was determined that it would succeed. Whatever happened, our team was there to make sure the world knew the truth about the Selma to Montgomery march.

When the magazine hit the newsstands in April, *Ebony* told the dramatic story in all its pain as well as its glory. *Jet* had already run extensive coverage of the march in its April 8 issue. It was one of the few times a serious news picture supplanted a smiling beauty on the magazine's cover. One of my articles singled out for debunking "Nine Lies" about the march, the racist propaganda that included accusations of rampant sex in the camps (the tents, in fact, were organized by gender), paltry numbers of actual marchers, and whatever slime and slander could be thrown in the mix. We were there to do what the black press had done for generations: to let the world see the truth about black life in America.

A REASON TO ACT

Over the next four months, using the magic that had made him a legend in the Senate, working, bullying, threatening the members, particularly the

Southerners, as only he knew how, LBJ played the hand Dr. King delivered to him, drawn from the deck of the Alabama Freedom Campaign, and came away with legislation that over the next several decades would change the complexion of almost every elected body in America, as well as the presidency of the United States. He signed the Voting Rights Act of 1965 on August 6, 1965, just thirteen months and four days after signing the most far reaching civil rights act in the history of the country. The 1965 act would provide the enforcement tools for the Fifteenth Amendment to the Constitution. The law declared that no person shall be denied the right to vote on account of race or color, outlawed literacy tests as a barrier to voting, and provided enforcement mechanisms in areas where there had been a history of racial discrimination.

Five days later, Watts, the black ghetto outside Los Angeles, erupted in violence. It wouldn't be the last to do so. Some fires simply smolder too long to be put out by the stroke of a pen. In his book, *To Be Equal*, published just months earlier, National Urban League Director Whitney Young had asked, "If all barriers to the Negro's entrance into the American mainstream were miraculously removed tomorrow, would he achieve full equality in our lifetime?" In response, he argued that after 300 years of deprivation, the answer had to be "No!" There was a "discrimination lag" so crippling to the Negro that only a special national effort would equalize his chances of competing with whites. Young called it a "domestic Marshall Plan"—not preferential treatment but a dedicated special effort. Three years later, the Kerner Commission Report would find that all the barriers to the Negro's entrance into the American mainstream had not been miraculously removed, and that white racism was the cause of urban riots.

20

FIGHTING ON

The flames burned in riot-torn Watts for five days, occupying 100 fire brigades and almost 14,000 National Guardsmen, called up to supplement police amid widespread violence and looting. The incident that ignited the rioting was a traffic stop, in which a white California Highway Patrolman had stopped a black driver whom he suspected of being intoxicated. Onlookers gathered, the crowd became hostile, then violent, and in minutes the scene exploded into a disastrous nightmare. *Jet* and *Ebony* reporters on the scene over the ensuing week likened it to a war zone in some distant country. Ironically, that's exactly where I was, having just landed in Vietnam for a firsthand look at how black soldiers were faring.

It was my first of two trips to the Southeast Asian warfront over the next nine months. When I arrived there, upwards of 800 black military and civilian personnel were in the country in strategic roles, often in serious trouble spots. I set out to learn who they were, where they hailed from, what they were doing, and how they were being treated in the military. My first attempt almost turned out to be my last, as suggested by the headline, *"Jet's* Booker Narrowly Escaped Vietcong Sniper."[1] I was visiting marine outposts with two other reporters, Hank Miller of the *Deseret News* (Salt Lake City) and Jim Mullin of the Los Angeles *Herald-Examiner*, in a jeep driven by Marine Sgt. Benny Marrufo of Deming, New Mexico. We had just left a battalion stationed in a mountainous area eight miles west of Danang, and were riding along a dirt road en route to visiting another group of marines when we ran into a rifle and mortar clash between Vietnamese troops and Vietcong raiders up ahead. Suddenly spotting a Vietnamese soldier cross the road and fire his gun less than 200 yards ahead, Sgt. Marrufo ordered us to duck into the rice paddies parallel to the road while he stood lookout. The whole episode lasted twenty minutes, during which we three newsmen crouched low in the swampy muck. I wondered if the rest of my stay at the warfront would include more of the same, and then brushed the thought aside, concluding correctly that it would probably get worse.

The "hooks" or story lines I was seeking for *Jet* articles were blacks who were in some way "unusual" either by virtue of their assignments, accomplishments, heroism, or other distinction. The marine press officers I encountered on this first trip were not at all "hip" to what that meant in the context of the civil rights movement back home. The blacks they produced in response to my request were invariably outstanding mess sergeants! An army, as has been said, may travel on its belly, but such stories were not about to inspire anybody in Harlem to enlist in the marines.

Another anomaly I reported was that the air force currently had no black helicopter pilots in-country—not a single one—while the army had six. The air force lamely tried to explain the disparity by claiming a lack of interest among younger black men, while subtly implying the lack of ability or ambition. I found scores of black airmen handling ground operations in multiple roles, and one, Danang base crew chief Sgt. Alfred Jackson of Satellite Beach, Florida, an eleven-year veteran keeping the bombers in shape, told me, "Nothing makes me happier than to see a brown face in a plane around here."[2]

I suggested in Ticker Tape that the NAACP and other national organizations visit Vietnam, noting that thousands more Negro troops would soon be at the warfront, and it was still early enough to work with military commanders who thus far had managed to keep racial problems to a minimum.

The Vietcong propaganda machine was well aware of the problems black GIs faced back home, and made the most of it, taking two approaches. On one side, they unleashed attacks on the treatment of Negroes in the U.S., while on the other, they published leaflets charging that "Negro troops are inferior, won't fight, and have no sustaining power." I was told that when attacking troop convoys, the VC would shoot at whites, and not blacks, seeking to drive a psychological wedge between the troops. Apparently, a conference about it was held at a high level, and one remedy suggested was that whites blacken their faces in combat. Whether that was true or not, it seemed that the black soldiers were bearing the brunt of psychological warfare. According to those I interviewed, their main strength in this man's army was to demonstrate that they were the best comrades any soldier, black or white, could have.

At My Tho in the fertile central delta, U.S. forces were housed in a former Catholic institution of some sort, heavily guarded and always under threat of VC attack. The men and officers, regardless of color, slept in large dormitories, in bunks almost touching one another. Looking around at the integrated facility, an officer commented, "This is what we're fighting for, what they'll take back home—and we've got men here from the Deep South." Heroic actions of black soldiers helped cement the relationship. There were

I needed more than a cigarette to calm my nerves after a wild chopper ride from My Tho to Can Tho in the Delta, with Vietcong sniping from below, and our crew firing back. (Photo by Ted Williams.)

so many examples to write about: a black helicopter pilot from Wichita, who had dropped his chopper into the midst of a gunfight to evacuate wounded Americans near Danang (he was later toasted in an officers' club); a twenty-one-year-old from Birmingham, who had volunteered for his sixth mission in a single day as a helicopter gunner; a black aerial observer from Inman, South Carolina, who located a coastal target and signaled navy ships to strike; a former Howard University swim team member, now a captain working with Vietnamese troops in the mountains, learning to speak the language, while surviving on a diet of fermented fish and rice.

One officer with the First Logistical Command sized up the new Negro GI, "This is our new class of military. We've got trained people, qualified, efficient, and progressive. The officers and men are not from the old school of bending and bowing. They don't think or act like the old-time Negro soldiers. [Some of those "old-time Negro soldiers" would have taken strong exception to that!] They're on the make on their own. They're the first products of integration and it's working." A black civilian who served as public safety director for South Vietnam's National Police organization told me that although there was still some social segregation between black and white troops in Saigon, it was nothing like in World War II, or even Korea, where certain units were still segregated.

One captain I met who served as advisor on administration and logistics to South Vietnamese troops in the Delta's Phong Dinh province predicted vast gains for blacks in the army, including "a general or two in the years ahead." He was right on the mark. Among those who would make it to the top would be Colin Powell, who would go on to serve as National Security Advisor in the Reagan administration, Chairman of the Joint Chiefs of Staff in Bush One, and after his military service, as Secretary of State in Bush Two. A larger than life air force fighter pilot was on a similar trajectory. Asked time and again in his star-studded career how he managed to fit his 230 lb., six-foot, four-inch frame into the aircraft's cockpit, future four-star general Daniel "Chappie" James would answer, "I don't fit in; I just strap it on."

I returned to Vietnam with photographer Ted Williams in the spring of 1966, when American troop presence had escalated sharply. We stayed eight weeks this time, flying on helicopter missions and venturing far into the mountains to follow American soldiers working with Montagnard tribesmen, about the best Vietnamese fighters in the entire theatre of operations. Everywhere we went, the GIs asked if we'd brought any copies of *Jet*, and we often did. It wasn't just the pretty pinups in bathing suits that graced every issue that they were interested in either. The black soldiers wanted to know how the freedom movement was going back home—the unvarnished version. That picture was still not very pretty. It would be another year— 1967—before two major cities would become the first to elect black mayors (Carl Stokes in Cleveland, and Richard Hatcher in Gary, Indiana) and blacks would start to see concrete results from the 1965 Voting Rights Act (as well as the political and economic effects of white flight to the suburbs). But Ted and I were impressed that morale among the black troops still remained remarkably high. As one soldier shrugged, "I've been fighting Charley [nickname for the Vietcong] over here, so I guess I'll go back home and fight Charley back home."

Being introduced to Gen. Westmoreland by Maj. General Frederick Weyand on one of my two trips to interview black troops in the Vietnam War. (U.S. Army photo.)

We did *Ebony* articles on the "The Angels of Saigon,"[3] black nurses trying to mend the physical and psychological wounds of the young soldiers; and "The Black Tiger of Mang Buk," a Morgan State University ROTC grad working with the Montagnards in a forward post in the mountains. Some of it was gruesome.[4]

I had a particular interest in doing a story on the 101st Airborne, "Birdmen with Black Rifles," because of the circumstances under which I had first encountered this impressive force. In the quiet of a September night in 1957, paratroopers of the 101st Airborne Division from Fort Campbell, Kentucky, had rolled into Little Rock to enforce the federal court order for the integration of Central High School. The next morning, we watched the soldiers—their bayonets in position—keep crowds of angry whites back as nine Negro students entered the school. Conspicuously absent at the time were the division's black troopers. They were "prudently" kept in the rear of the action, because it was feared that their presence might further inflame white bigots. But in Vietnam in 1966, it was a different story. Negro paratroopers, who comprised more than a third of the 101st's crack 1st Brigade in Vietnam, were on the frontlines, among the gut fighters of the jungle war, and were considered one of the best fighting forces in that country.[5]

The fact that black soldiers were seeing more than their fair share of action at the front was not being reported by the mainstream press when I went to Vietnam in 1965. (Photo by Ted Williams.)

There was also a disproportionately high percentage of blacks in the 101st Airborne and other frontline units, in sharp contrast to World War II, when civil rights organizations demanded that Negroes be integrated into combat rolls, instead of being assigned to Jim Crow housekeeping units in the rear. In Vietnam, there was now concern over whether too many Negroes were being "slaughtered" on suicide missions in forward lines. So many black soldiers were stationed in frontline areas, wisecracking GIs referred to these sectors as "Brotherville" or "Soulville." "Many times," one staff sergeant told me, "half of our casualties are Negroes." This wasn't given much publicity back home because few reporters journeyed to outlying areas to report day-to-day jungle action. Top brass was also concerned that too much emphasis on the extensive utilization of Negroes in combat might irritate black populations back home. As a result, few black GIs were getting credit due them for heroic feats and sacrifices.

Another fact Ted Williams and I encountered was the glaring lack of Negro officers, particularly frontline commanders. One of the most decorated units in Vietnam at the time was the 101st's Five O Deuce (502) Battalion, which was 50 percent Negro, and whose Recondo squad was 90 percent black. Ted and I found no Negro officers in any of its frontline components, and we were looking hard for them.[6]

Sorting through my brittle, yellow files and long-forgotten photos to put this book together, we found a letter I'd airmailed to the office in June 1966, with a three-by-four-inch black-and-white snapshot of me shaking hands with General Westmoreland. After cleaning up the typos I made on the portable Olivetti I carried with me, it reads like this:

Dear Bureau—crats,

A day past the midway point and we're still pushing through this 100-plus temperature, the monsoon season, the 10:30 curfew, an occasional bombing, artillery fire at night at the front, and mosquitoes enough to make sure you take malaria tablets every Monday and salt tablets every day.

I'll return to Washington with mildew, rash and a yen to fish.

We've spent the last five days with the 25th Division in Cou Chi, way out front, and ran into a D.C. physician, Capt. Williams, a battalion physician. Then we flew to Bien Hoa to do a story on the 173rd Airborne but while en route got call to hold everything and be picked up by helicopter and return to Saigon. Gen. Westmoreland flew us on private plane to Big Red One. Imagine sitting next to a four star general and attending briefings sitting beside him at the camp. . . .

Next week we fly with the Air Force and sail with the Navy. Then back to the 173rd and First Air Cav infantry units. They're the roughest. . . .

We flew seven times yesterday by plane and helicopter, got fired on once, saw an air strike, and had only one meal. . . .

Vietnam is no place for the sentimental. It's metal and death. . . .

I've had some narrow episodes and every time I've gotten past, I sigh, catch a drink, and push on. The other evening, we rode a convoy to Cou Chi, the headquarters of the 25th Division. The night before, the convoy was attacked and an attack was expected this time. I lost five pounds riding down that road in a 50-truck convoy with tanks, machine gunners and troops ready for a hard hitting fire fight. Then after getting the hell scared out of me, I couldn't sleep that night because of continual artillery fire, so loud that it rocked tents. . . .

I love all of you—except Sorrell [our bureau photographer Maurice Sorrell who'd taken a pass on this trip]. I admire him. . . . Send the *Jets* air mail. Book

The flight I took aboard General Westmoreland's helicopter was not uneventful. As I sat beside him, doing an interview as we headed north, he seemed unconcerned as a "ping . . . ping . . . ping" sounded against the fuselage. I nodded just as nonchalantly when he commented, "They're firing at us." Later I thought it odd that, flying over the Mekong Delta in a chopper under fire from the Vietcong, I felt safer than I had four years earlier, in a Trailways bus in Alabama.

Even while enemy fire pinged the fuselage, I felt safer in Gen. Westmoreland's helicopter in 1965 than I did on a Trailways bus in Alabama in '61. (U.S. Army photo.)

Sharing a story with Stokely Carmichael (right) and *Jet* reporter Bernard Garnett. (Photo by Maurice Sorrell.)

While black soldiers and civilians in Vietnam were carrying on the fight with hopes and dreams of returning to a better life, maybe even a "post-racial" society, if anyone dared dream that, back home blacks with as divergent viewpoints on how to achieve black aspirations of freedom and equality as Stokely Carmichael and Dr. Martin Luther King would soon be in agreement that the war in South Asia was not just a mistake, but morally wrong. By spring of 1967, the peace movement had a formidable following. Dr. King, as well as Senator Robert Kennedy, came out forcefully against the war, adding high-octane fuel to the movement.

In March 1968, with the war going worse than ever, and Americans in every corner of the country fed up with it, Lyndon Johnson made a monumental decision. Complaining that it wasn't his war but one that he'd inherited, he sought assurance from his trusted Negro servant—White House butler Preston Bruce—while they were riding alone in the mansion's elevator, that he had done a good job as president. Martin Luther King had said that he wasn't, and LBJ wanted to know what Bruce thought. Then he confided something he apparently at that moment had told only a few people, maybe only Lady Bird and their daughters. He whispered to Bruce that he was not going to run for re-election. And then, in typical LBJ style, he gave the man a look that left no doubt what would happen if Bruce told anybody, adding that if he heard it anywhere, he'd know where it came from, and he'd "better not hear it." Bruce may have wished he'd never been told in the first place![7]

In the spring of 1968, I had started a sequel to my 1963 book on race relations, *Black Man's America*, intending to update the status of the movement, noting such milestones as the Civil Rights Act of 1964 and the Voting Rights Act of 1965, as well as the tensions among various civil rights groups, the decline in NAACP membership, the evolution of the black power movement, and the tragic shooting death of three young men in February, on the campus of South Carolina State College, an incident that came to be known as the Orangeburg Massacre. What added to the pain of that senseless killing was that *Jet*, like most other publications, initially had run an untrue version of the shooting as reported by AP.[8] (The exceptions were the *Los Angeles Times*, the *Charlotte Observer*, and NBC. Two outstanding white Southern journalists, Jack Nelson and Jack Bass [both Nieman Fellows], wrote the articles for the two newspapers, and later coauthored a factual account of both the event and the ensuing cover-up.)[9] The wire service had reported that there was a "gun battle between law enforcement officers and students of South Carolina and Claflin colleges," after four straight nights of violence, triggered by a bowling alley owner's refusal to admit Negroes. The AP report said a State Highway Patrolman had been struck in the head by a bullet. The story also reported that three students had been killed. That fact was true. Most of the rest of the AP story was not, including the report of a "gun battle," because the students had been unarmed, and no shots had been fired by anybody but the police. Also untrue was the claim that a policeman had been shot; in fact, he had been hit in the head by a banister tossed from the crowd of students, who were demonstrating on their own campus. By the time the magazine hit the newsstands, JPC knew it had made a mistake in publishing the AP account. I sent *Jet* D.C. bureau reporter Bernard Garnett down to South Carolina to get the real story for the next week's issue. His report described how the police had rained "murderous gunfire" on the unarmed students, shooting many in the back as they fled for the protection of the dorms, and others as they lay wounded on the ground. Garnett's report also questioned the editorials in white South Carolina newspapers that blamed "black power activists" for fomenting the trouble, in large part because SNCC's Cleveland Sellers, who was also wounded by police gunfire, was on the campus at the time.[10] The AP never issued a correction of its earlier, inaccurate account. The Department of Justice, which Orangeburg blacks had urged repeatedly to take court action against the bowling alley owner under the Civil Rights Act of 1964, finally did so, and the owner integrated his establishment after being told by the court that it was not exempt from the law.

Great strides had been made in the civil rights struggle through legislation and court battles, but incidents such as this evidenced the level of tension still seething on both sides of racial issues—particularly where young people were concerned—across the country. I intended to use my new book to revisit my predictions from the early years of the decade, and assess the current status and likely future of the freedom movement. I felt pretty confident that I could turn out a manuscript in a matter of months, when suddenly it seemed as though the world had been turned upside down. Dr. Martin Luther King was shot down by an assassin's bullet in Memphis, where he'd come to lead a nonviolent march for better working conditions for the city's sanitation workers. Within hours, tens of thousands of black Americans felt as though the sniper's bullet had ripped through their own hearts in ways only those who'd shared the dream could understand. I put away my book notes and abandoned the project entirely, no longer confident that it was even possible either to assess the current state of black America or to predict the future.

I had covered Dr. King and the SCLC for the thirteen years of his crusade for justice and equality for black Americans. The shock of his assassination wasn't because we'd never expected it. Far from it. Dr. King's aides had long ago taken steps to protect him, always over his objections that what was meant to be would be. Even though King refused to employ bodyguards, Andrew Young and the other top SCLC aides would devise methods of throwing off a potential assassin, such as positioning other similarly dark-suited men on his flanks during the Selma-Montgomery march, or having his brother, Rev. A. D. King, walk ahead of him. What seemed to weigh more heavily on Dr. King's mind during that particular march was the danger to others besides himself, after the deaths of Jimmie Lee Jackson and Rev.

James Reeb. But Dr. King had also had some close calls in the past, including violent assaults in New York, and most recently, in a hotel lobby during the voting rights drive in Alabama. Still, what sometimes seems inevitable, can also appear inconceivable. The thirteen years of King's presence on the national stage suddenly seemed like an action film, run at double speed, and ending too quickly, with no time to savor each important highlight.

I remembered the first time he spoke at the National Press Club in 1962. I was only the second black reporter in the club, and unlike the first, Louie Lautier, I was determined to be active in every phase of it, and not just a name on the membership roster. I joined the Speakers Committee, which played a crucial role in the club, because it selected the newsmakers who would address its high-drawing weekly luncheons in the thirteenth-floor ballroom. When I proposed that the club invite Dr. King to speak, he was thirty-three-years-old, and while he had become well-known in civil rights circles, he was still a year from making the "I Have a Dream" speech on the steps of the Lincoln Memorial that would place him front and center on the national stage; still a year from being named *Time* magazine's "Man of the Year"; and still two years from becoming at thirty-five the youngest recipient of the Nobel Peace Prize. He had never addressed a large audience of the national press corps. But he had already twice replaced the usual starlets and celebrities on the weekly covers of *Jet*. FBI Director J. Edgar Hoover had already targeted the young black minister as a troublemaker and likely Communist pawn, and had put rumors out on the street to defame him to members of the white press, among others. But to black America, he was an up-and-coming leader, and I believed that whites should get to know him. My proposal shook up the committee, and when it voted to invite King, the chairman resigned.

Between that press club lunch in 1962 and his assassination on April 4, 1968, Dr. King would answer journalists' questions about his philosophy, activities, and the state of America's racial problem during five appearances on NBC's *Meet the Press*. On Sunday morning, August 13, 1967, his last MTP appearance before his death, I was the reporter who asked him this question:

"Dr. King, do you believe that the American race problem can be solved?"

"Yes, I do. I refuse to give up. I refuse to despair. I refuse to allow myself to fall into the dark chambers of pessimism because I believe in any social revolution, the one thing that keeps it going is hope. When hope dies, sometimes the revolution degenerates into some kind of nihilistic philosophy that says you must engage in disruption for disruption's sake. I refuse to believe that. However difficult it is, I believe that the forces of goodwill, white and black, in this country can work together, and we have the resources to do it. At present we don't have the will. But certainly the Negroes and the decent, committed whites—maybe in a minority right now, but they're there—must work together for this nation, and at the same time, articulate by direct action that our demands can no longer be eluded by government or congress or all the forces in power."

When Dr. King was gunned down, there were blacks all around the country who did fall into those "dark chambers of pessimism," as well as those who believed that they must engage in disruption for disruption's sake. Black anger, frustration, and despair erupted in the streets. From our top floor offices at 1750 Pennsylvania Avenue, we could see the smoke rising into a red nighttime sky from fires just north of the White House in the black U Street corridor where *Jet* had opened its first D.C. bureau in 1955, when no downtown properties would rent to us. Out on the street, you could smell the rancid fumes from buildings engulfed by flames. Thousands of panic-stricken government workers had fled the city, creating one of the worst traffic jams the capital had ever experienced. Calling for federal troops, D.C.'s first black, elected mayor, Walter Washington, appealed for "peace and calm," but his plea was lost in a wave of firebombs, widespread looting, and reckless rampaging, mainly in black sections of the city.

Our *Jet* reporters set out on foot for the riot areas, after taxi drivers—very few of which were anywhere to be found—refused to go anywhere near the fires. Rioters at first made no distinction between black businesses and those owned by non-blacks, until signs reading "Soul Brother" suddenly appeared in windows and on autos in hopes of protecting a property from the madness. I knew there was one establishment that shouldn't need such a sign, it was so much a part of the black community. I also knew I could find a momentary sanctuary there, out of the turmoil of the streets. Restaurateur Billy Simpson stayed in his widely known watering place—The Ebony Table—for three nights while the riots raged. Dubbed "where the elite meet," it was exactly that, as well as where they ate, drank, argued politics and policy, and planned strategies for advancing causes ranging from African independence to home rule for D.C. Occupying a two-story building at 3815 Georgia Avenue NW, Billy Simpson's House of Seafood and Steaks opened in 1956 with a distinctive Tudor frontage of half-timber and stucco framing simulated leaded glass, diamond-paned windows that let it be known to all passersby that this was an establishment of note. It was the interior, however, that provided the most appropriate stage for the dialogues that occurred there between the courses and the rounds of drinks. Rising from a pine-paneled, first-floor dining room, a narrow, carpeted stairway led to another world, where the course of history was debated and plotted. Stepping into the "Gold Coast" lounge, one could have been entering an exclusive club in Accra, Ghana. A smoky mirror running the length of the wall behind the elaborately carved bar reflected an African mahogany-paneled room, over which hung, parallel to the ceiling, an enormous, carved map of the African continent, dotted with lights displaying the capitals of newly independent countries. Opposite the bar, a large banquette hugged a round table in one corner of the lounge, shaded by a huge umbrella-like canopy, reminiscent of a tribal chief's court. This was The Ebony Table, the scene of the nightly "uptown forum," where members of Congress—mostly members of the Black Caucus, but also some like-minded whites—would thrash out the issues of the day with Billy and a random handful of notables, including federal and city officials, and members of the press. *Washington Post* columnist Bill Raspberry was a regular at the table, and probably took away from it a number of ideas for his columns.

On this particular night, Billy was holding court as usual, but there was none of the normal conviviality. Everyone looked worried. No one had come to stay—just to make sure he was okay, and catch their breath before moving on to do their job or protect their own property. One thing was understood. What was happening in the streets was nothing less than an explosion of long pent-up rage, obviously fueled in part by opportunism, but laced with deep-rooted rage nevertheless. The rampage seemed random and either misdirected or undirected. Billy Simpson's House of Seafood and Steaks and the Gold Coast lounge were among the well-known black establishments that were not likely to be on the haphazard radar screens of the roving bands of burners and looters, but looking at Billy's worried face that night, it was obvious even he wasn't sure that if the rioting spread up Georgia Avenue, The Ebony Table would be spared in the madness.

Back out on the street, I headed south toward U Street and the worst concentration of smoke and flames, where I sensed an intensity and fury among the rioters and looters that I believed had eluded not only the white establishment, but the black middle class as well. One young black who'd been running with a group of eight or ten others, picking up and throwing anything that wasn't pinned down, slowed down to breathe and noticed me in a doorway. "You shouldn't be out here!" he yelled. I told him I knew that, but I was from *Jet* and I needed to see for myself what was going on. He seemed to be about nineteen, and possibly even a college student. I could see that he didn't want to be separated from the pack and would likely move on quickly, so I blurted something to get a reaction, like, "I don't think this is what Dr. King would have wanted." I had pushed his button. He paused and told me emphatically, with the same passion I'd heard from the most radical militants I'd ever encountered, "Martin Luther King wasn't our leader but he was black," he almost spat. "If white people can't tolerate him when he tries to help the poor, they certainly can't tolerate us. We don't believe in conciliation and negotiation. You can scrap the NAACP and the Urban League. Keep their leaders talking on radio about how great King is—dead." With that he trotted away, toward the group he'd dropped behind, which now included a dozen or so kids in their early teens, who were carrying merchandise out of the stores where the older guys had just knocked out the windows. I shook my head. This was worse than most of us had ever imagined.

Later, a middle-aged black man standing behind police lines watching the mayhem had a different reaction to my suggestion that the violence desecrated the memory of Dr. King: "The best tribute we can pay him is to say that all this wouldn't have occurred if he was still alive and not gunned down by a sniper's bullet. Many whites now will see—they can't help but see—what he was struggling for." Another onlooker, a black woman, agreed: "Someone will begin now to listen to the poor people. These are disenchanted youngsters, and they're the new guerrilla warriors of the ghettos."

Singer James Brown was one of many popular young entertainers who took to the airwaves to urge the brothers and sisters to "cool it." Appearing on television in Washington, Brown told a poignant story of how as a boy he'd shined shoes on the steps of a radio station in Augusta, Georgia, for a few cents a shine, never even working up to a dime. The story reminded me of a short poem, "The Shoeshine Boy," I'd written in my own youth. I could easily see a young James Brown buffing those shoes on the radio station steps. Then he added, "Today I own that station." Pausing a moment for emphasis, he pointed an index finger toward his head before continuing, "That's 'black power.'"

"Quit terrorizing and organize," he urged the cats in the street. "Ownership" was what it was all about.

Blacks rioted in some 110 cities, leaving a death toll of thirty-five, with more than 2,500 injured. Seventy-five thousand National Guardsmen and federal troops were deployed and curfews imposed in urban pockets thick with smoke and flames. In Chicago, ten persons, all Negro, were reported dead from riot-connected fire, shooting, and looting in the two days following King's assassination. About 1,000 others were injured. Half the city's firemen and equipment were called Friday night to fight some of the 125 major fires that made hundreds of people homeless in Negro ghettos. A policeman was shot during a sniper attack on a police station in a Negro area. In Detroit, two eighteen-year-old Negro youths were shot to death by police near looting scenes—one by a policeman whose gun reportedly fired while he searched the youth. Three others were wounded by police, and two police officers were shot. In Tallahassee, Philadelphia, Baltimore, and even tiny Frederick, Maryland, black anger flowed through the streets, taking its toll on everything in its path like lava flowing from an awakened volcano.

Offering condolences to Mrs. Martin Luther King, Jr., after her husband's funeral in Atlanta. (Photo by Maurice Sorrell.)

In one major city, however, there was no such reaction. In Indianapolis, blacks first learned of the tragedy from Senator Robert F. Kennedy, who'd come there for a street-corner campaign rally. The police advised him to cancel his appearance, because it was in a black neighborhood they considered too dangerous, but he insisted on going. When he arrived, he discovered that the crowd had not heard the tragic news, and he took the stage to tell them. His voice brittle, his face drawn in the sorrow of the moment, framed by the personal and national tragedy of his own brother's assassination just five years earlier, he put before them the choice between hatred, revenge, violence, and all the things Dr. King stood for—love, compassion, and an effort to understand. He asked them to pray for the King family, and for our nation. Finally, he proposed that he and they alike dedicate themselves to taming the savageness of man and "make gentle the life of this world."

Two months later, on June 5, 1968, Robert Kennedy was killed by another assassin's bullet during a celebration of his victory in the California presidential primary.

In a special issue of *Jet*,[11] bound in solemn black, we reported from cover to cover the many different ways in which Bobby Kennedy, with his extraordinary wife, Ethel, at his side, had not only built bridges between the races, but had won the affection of black Americans while doing so. Ticker Tape USA was expanded to three pages, in which I paid my own respects to a man

Jet's special issue on the assassination of Senator Robert F. Kennedy.

I had come to love. I recalled that one day several weeks after his brother's assassination, I received a call telling me to come over to the attorney general's office in the Department of Justice. Entering the dark paneled room, I found Robert Kennedy at his desk, his head in his hands. When he looked up, I could see that he'd been crying. His eyes were red and moist.

"Come on, now," I told him lightly. "You're Irish. You're supposed to be tough. I'm Negro and you think you can push me around."

My ribbing made him laugh. "Booker," he said, smiling, "you always know how to knock somebody off balance."

In almost twenty years in the nation's capital, I had known no public figure as warm and friendly as Robert Kennedy. As a reporter in competition with white press from all segments of the media, I had found few of the capital's VIPs even considerate of the black press, few willing to accept me as a working journalist, much less invite me to confidential briefings or dinners at their homes, as they did favored members of the mainstream press. Robert Kennedy was the exception. He was the first Cabinet member ever to invite me to briefings, to his home at Hickory Hill in McLean, Virginia, for a swim, or to join his entourage on plane trips out of town that he thought would make good copy for *Ebony* or *Jet*.

When I first met Bobby, I was the only black reporter on the Kennedy campaign trail. After almost two months on the road, I arrived in Hyannis Port on election night to find that my hotel was almost five miles down the road. Citing my seniority among the press there, I raised hell, and thanks to Kennedy and Press Secretary Andrew Hatcher, got better quarters. Kennedy said he "understood the point" of my beef, and on inauguration day, I was the first Negro ever selected to be one of eight reporters riding down Pennsylvania Avenue behind an incoming president. I wouldn't say that I succumbed to the Kennedy charm, and the record shows I didn't. But I did appreciate it, and I used my access to crusade for more opportunities for blacks. I also used it to save the lives of a dozen or so Freedom Riders stranded in Birmingham in May 1962 when my telephoned description to the attorney general of what had happened to the two buses when we crossed into Alabama was probably the best reporting of my life!

Political columnist Jules Witcover later wrote a book entitled *The Year the Dream Died: Revisiting 1968 in America.* Undoubtedly there were many people, disciples of either Camelot or the Great Society, or both, who felt that way. For blacks to believe so would have been a devastating option. As Dr. King said, "When hope dies, sometimes the revolution degenerates." For black America, two great men were gone, but the dream lived on. It had to. And both men would have wanted it that way.

21

A FAMILIAR FACE

At seven-foot-two, NBA star Wilt Chamberlain towered above the heads of the thousands of mourners outside Atlanta's Ebenezer Baptist Church for the funeral of Dr. Martin Luther King, Jr. Even at a distance, I spotted him inching his way toward the entrance, but didn't notice until he was almost there that following behind him was a much smaller, slim white man whose face I recognized instantly. At the door, the security guard saw only the hoop star, and yelled, "Back up folks and let Brother Wilt in," opening the way for Chamberlain but momentarily blocking the path of his white companion, Richard Milhous Nixon.

Almost a year later, on January 20, 1969, Nixon was sworn in as thirty-seventh president of the United States, having won the election without support of a majority of white and black voters. (He had only a plurality of the popular vote, with third party candidate George Wallace taking more than 13 percent of the ballots from him and Democratic candidate, Vice President Hubert Humphrey.) As for blacks, less than one in ten backed the GOP nominee. I wrote in *Ebony* that outside of the familiar breed of segregationists and white supremacists, few men in American public life had incurred the wrath of blacks as Nixon had, which largely explained their cool reaction to the former vice president as he'd made his way into the church through a crowd that warmly welcomed other VIPs such as Governor Nelson Rockefeller, Senators Robert Kennedy and Eugene McCarthy, and Vice President Humphrey.[1]

Blacks were not about to forgive or forget how Nixon had coldly ignored their communities in his unsuccessful presidential bid in 1960 against a man who started out as an underdog, Senator John F. Kennedy. In that election, the black vote was the difference between victory and defeat. In 1968, blacks' ninety-percent anti-Nixon vote didn't matter.

As incoming president, Nixon faced his biggest challenge in winning the confidence of the country's 25 million blacks. In his speeches, he mentioned a goal of "reconciliation of the races," but the real issue was whether Nixon could achieve his own reconciliation with blacks. I didn't see that as

Vice President Hubert Humphrey was the black favorite in 1968, but it wasn't enough to save him from the backlash against Johnson's Vietnam policy. (Courtesy of author.)

an impossible thing to do. While there was definitely something uncomfortable about his social interactions with blacks during the Eisenhower administration, he had also compiled a pretty good official record. In addition to that, he was on good terms with many prominent Negroes, both leaders and followers, and had helped to bring down segregation barriers in the nation's capital. There was no question, however, that his "liberalism" had snapped sharply in 1960 when he sought the presidency, and "wrote off" the black vote to get it.

Opening his campaign in 1968, Nixon went out of his way to woo black support but found little interest, with most black Republicans urging New York's Nelson Rockefeller to enter the race. At the nominating convention in Miami Beach, Nixon turned to South Carolina Senator Strom Thurmond for advice, and wound up with Maryland governor Spiro Agnew, like Nixon, a liberal-turned-conservative, as his running mate. This time, however, he did not run a lily-white campaign, hiring black Republicans to begin a self-help dialogue in black communities. But since all those in campaign strategy positions were white, he had to start from scratch once in office to fulfill a campaign pledge to name blacks to key positions in government. There were so few black Republicans, a Nixon aide cracked, "we've got more available jobs than we've got blacks to fill them."

An encounter with President and Mrs. George H. W. Bush. (Courtesy of author.)

One of Nixon's first black hires was businessman Robert J. ("Bob") Brown, of High Point, North Carolina, a former Democrat, whom he appointed to the White House staff as a special assistant to the president. Brown was founder and CEO of B&C Associates, the oldest black-owned and operated management consulting, market research, and public relations firm in the country. Another appointee was renegade Republican Arthur Fletcher, son of a buffalo (black cavalry) soldier and a Comanche woman. Fletcher was a giant of a man who made a lasting mark as assistant secretary of labor with his revised Philadelphia Plan, which established minority employment standards for contractors doing business with the federal government. He went on to serve in the Ford, Reagan, and George H. W. Bush administrations. In the latter, he struggled long and hard as Chairman of the U.S. Commission on Civil Rights to restore the credibility of that beleaguered agency after the Reaganites all but destroyed it.

Constance Berry Newman, a savvy young lawyer born in Chicago, but reared in Tuskegee, Alabama, rose through the ranks of the civil service before her appointment in 1971 as Director of VISTA (Volunteers in Service to America). Established seven years earlier as one of LBJ's war on poverty programs, the agency had a rocky start and had been without a permanent director for the last three years. Newman set about to make sure the volunteers were not only properly trained, but also understood they were to serve as resources for poor communities, rather than dictate their priorities.[2] It was at VISTA that Newman earned her lasting reputation for hard work (sixteen-hour days except on Sundays, when she put in only six), and laser sharp administrative skills that would take her to top-ranking positions in later administrations, including Director of the Office of Personnel Management (OPM, the federal government's personnel manager) in Bush One, Assistant Secretary of State for Africa in Bush Two, and a number of other posts including a seat on the Financial Control Board for the District of Columbia, and Undersecretary of the Smithsonian Institution.

Newman and Fletcher were moderate (sometimes called "Rockefeller") Republicans who believed it political folly for blacks to throw all their support to one party, where they would be taken for granted, while being regarded as irrelevant by the other. I believed in this strategy so strongly that some people jokingly accused me of being a Republican, even while they knew I was a registered Democrat. Talented black politicos proved over the last half-century that the Democrats did not have exclusive dibs on them. The Republicans among them, however, often took a beating for their independence from the pack, getting whacked from the left by Democrats and from the right by conservative Republicans who considered them "too liberal." They took the heat, and kept a black presence in the administration no matter which party was in power. Despite what was perceived as an anti-black shift to the political right with Nixon's election, a talented group of black Republicans managed to make a difference, as one of them told me, because the president was preoccupied with other things, including foreign relations, particularly with China, and let them do their "own thing."

Still, it wasn't easy with strange cats like Haldeman and Erlichman in the White House, and black appointees had a tough time wielding influence or effecting positive change. Twenty-three blacks, we later learned, were among a list of 200 Americans on a White House list of political enemies, including twelve of the then sixteen members of the Congressional Black Caucus, as well as activist/comedians Dick Gregory and Bill Cosby, SCLC President Ralph David Abernathy, and columnist Carl Rowan. The White House harassed them with IRS tax audits, and dispatched Vice President Spiro T. Agnew, who, until his resignation, ironically after a plea of "no contest" to tax evasion charges, made attacks on "irresponsible" black leaders a theme of his public appearances.

Bob Brown had signed on as special assistant to the new president more than a month before the inauguration. He liked Nixon, who assured him he'd have a direct line to the Oval Office, and also attend Cabinet meetings. I asked Brown about his years in the White House (exactly four years and two months), and what he thought about the criticism that Nixon didn't focus on civil rights. His answer was that the administration's top priorities in the race arena were the promotion of black capitalism and support for historically black colleges. "We need your help," he recalled Nixon saying. "Anything you can do in these areas, you have my full support." He was then somewhat surprised when Nixon added, "You know I went through this in the Eisenhower years. What Eisenhower did with Fred Morrow was very cruel. He had a staff position but no responsibility—like a black man sitting by the door. Fred was a very smart guy and should have had responsibility. That will not happen to you."[3]

Brown specialized in producing minority enterprise gains, and he managed to rack up a formidable record, even while the administration was dismantling the anti-poverty program, and other White House aides were getting caught up in the Watergate scandal. Among his accomplishments was a new commission on black enterprise, comprised of top industrialists. A specific area of concern was the paucity of government contracts going to black firms.

"So we changed the rules!" Brown recalled.

"I had people monitoring the situation at every major agency with big contracts, and they would let me know if the agency was doing what we asked them to do. If not, we called them over to the White House. Suddenly the big government contractors wanted me fired. They sent word to Nixon that they wanted to meet with him, and when Nixon was told what they wanted to meet with him about, he said, 'You'll have to meet with Bob about that.'"

Another issue in Bob Brown's portfolio was the difficulty historically black colleges were having getting a share of the government's work-study grants because of the matching requirement. The schools had to raise sufficient funds to match the government grant.

"We changed that rule, too!" he recalled. The matching criterion was waived for all schools of higher education with enrollment that was 50 percent or more from poor families, as defined in the regulations.

But the ugliest fact of life that confronted the White House on the racial front were the problems in the military—all over the world, and particularly in Vietnam, where the war dragged on until 1975.

"I started reading the complaints," Brown told me, "and it made me sick. We set up the first training facility in race relations for officers and NCOs at Pensacola. We also set up a commission with three whites and two blacks to go around the world talking with soldiers, and we found things we could correct."

At one point, NAACP chief Roy Wilkins called Nixon about complaints from Keesler Air Force Base in Biloxi, Mississippi, that establishments outside the base that were 100 percent supported by the military were segregated. When White House Chief of Staff H. R. Haldeman turned the matter over to Bob Brown, he called Deputy Assistant Secretary of Defense Howard Bennett, a black former judge from Minnesota, to arrange for a plane, telling Bennett, "We're going down to Mississippi, and we might spend the night." A short while later, he met Bennett at Andrews Air Force Base outside of D.C., and the two flew to Keesler.

"We met with the general, who said flat out, 'We have no race problems here.'" When Brown said he'd like to take a look around, the general put the colonel who was base commander in charge, and they left the base in a couple of cars, including a military police escort.

"As we were going out the gate," Brown recalled, "I saw all these juke joints around, and all the airmen going in them were white. I said, 'Stop the car.' The colonel said, 'What?' and I repeated, 'Stop the car!'"

"When Judge Bennett and I, the only blacks, walked into the first establishment, followed by the colonel and others in the entourage, a white woman immediately walked up to me and said, 'We don't serve colored in here. I don't own the place, and I don't make the rules, but we don't serve colored.'"

Brown remembered saying something "very polite, like 'Sorry, Ma'am,'" before turning and walking out. Heading straight for the car, he turned to the colonel and said, "I want to see the general, and get my plane ready. We're going back to Washington."

They went back to the general and Brown told him, "General, you have to get this problem solved in twenty-four hours. Otherwise, people in Washington will want to know about it." The next day—the very next day!—as Brown recounted the incident, "an order was issued directing that anyone caught going into a segregated establishment would be court-martialed. And you know what those places did? They integrated!"

The military's race problems extended far beyond Keesler Air Force Base. According to the official summary of a survey released in 1970, army investigators found that "all indications" pointed toward "an increase in racial tension on bases throughout the world," with tensions described as more serious overseas. On bases in Europe, one in eight soldiers was black while one of every four non-judicial punishments (minor penalties fixed without trial) was imposed on blacks. The number of black junior officers had been decreasing, while the number of black noncommissioned officers had increased. The report called for commanders to address these problems, rather than taking "the ostrich-like approach to racial fear, hostility, and misunderstanding." What Bob Brown and others found time after time were instances involving a failure of leadership. That's not to say that all black soldiers were perfect and white soldiers were not, or that all young men who went into the military were respectful of authority and ready to take orders. Until it ended in 1973, many were there because of the draft, and even afterward, others often enlisted simply because they couldn't find a job and were tired of hanging around the streets. Some young blacks were caught up in notions of "black power" with its special salutes and insider handshakes, while some whites forgot to leave their Confederate flag—and all the baggage that went with it—at home.

By the time the Pentagon had mounted an all-out offensive against discrimination in the ranks in the European field, blacks were fed up with being singled out for punishment, including bad conduct discharges, the Confederate flags flying in camp, even cross burnings, and rampant use of the "n" word. My colleague Hans Massaquoi reported in *Ebony* that they were about "to take this mother apart" when a fifty-six-year-old, two-star black general, Frederic E. Davison, the army's first black division commander, took charge of the 8th Infantry ("Pathfinder") Division, which was 22 percent black, and made it his top priority to end the racial polarization that had threatened its disintegration as a combat-ready force. Nearing the end of his two-year tour before heading back for his next assignment as Commander of the Military District of Washington, D.C., Davison said he'd had to "kick out" several battalion commanders who were dragging their butts before they realized he meant business.[4] That was the kind of leadership the military needed, and had been sorely lacking.

ON THE AIR!

During the second week of March 1971, a contact at the Department of State called me with sad news. He'd just seen an unclassified cable from the U.S. Embassy in Lagos, Nigeria, reporting that National Urban League Director Whitney M. Young, forty-nine-years-old, had died suddenly while swimming at Lighthouse Beach, about twenty-five minutes from Lagos. Young was a member of the U.S. delegation to the African-American Dialogue, a conference sponsored by the African-American Institute to strengthen the relationship between Africans and Americans of African descent. He and a few others in the delegation, including former Attorney General and Mrs. Ramsey Clark had taken a break from the conference to swim at the ocean beach. I immediately called Chicago, where *Jet* was about to go to print. After a rush of activity searching through photo files and changing the layout, we got the civil rights leader's death into the weekly magazine in a matter of hours.

After filing my *Jet* copy, I banged out a two-minute tribute to Young as my next scheduled Westinghouse radio commentary. In those days, I was on the air three days a week on Westinghouse ("Group W") stations across the country—the first black commentator on a syndicated, mainstream network of radio stations. It was an opportunity to reach audiences I'd never reached before in the black press. I used it to broaden the scope of my subject matter to all sorts of human rights issues from the failure of the federal trusteeship on Native American reservations to anything under the sun that cried out for exposure, discussion, or remedial action. I raised hell for about eight years and enjoyed every minute of it, including the "fan" mail, some of it praising me to the heavens and some suggesting I drop dead immediately if not sooner. My commentaries got so much attention that CBS soon signed *Chicago Defender* reporter Ethel Payne to do commentaries for the CBS radio network.

What I didn't know when I left the Westinghouse recording studio on K Street in Washington after doing my commentary on Young was that State Department officials were having difficulty reaching his widow, Margaret, at their Westchester, New York, home. Until they did, the department was not making a public announcement of his death. So when my eulogy aired, one Westinghouse station immediately got calls complaining that what I was saying wasn't true—that Young wasn't dead. The station pulled the commentary and called Sid Davis, Group W's Washington bureau chief, to find out what was going on. For someone accustomed to weekly magazine reporting, it was an odd experience. Commentators usually didn't break the news; they commented on it. Here I had a "scoop" and I didn't even know it. When Sid called me to ask for confirmation, my first thought was chilling. What if my source had been wrong? The embarrassment might cause Westinghouse to cancel my contract. I called the State Department press office and asked for confirmation, but because Margaret Young still had not been contacted, State would not confirm the story. I was never more concerned about a story I'd written in my entire career, and for what seemed like an eternity (but was probably a few hours), I sweated it out. Finally, I got an unexpected call from the Pentagon. On the line was Brigadier General Daniel "Chappie" James, at the time the Air Force's highest ranking black officer, and an old friend. He sounded as though he were crying. He'd just learned of Young's tragic death through official channels. I breathed a heartfelt sigh of relief.

"Booker, he's my hero," he choked. "He's my kind of guy because he gets in there and proves what a black cat can do—with his head instead of a brick." Chappie could probably write a list as long as both of his massive arms of the people who might not be where they were in their careers if it weren't for the work of the Urban League, whose focus was jobs, jobs, jobs. While other civil rights organizations hammered away at school desegregation, voting rights, and public accommodations—all of which were important—the Urban League had its own niche—and it was economics—the economics of having a job, and after that a better job, until a black man or woman reached his or her fullest potential.

The next day, at Chappie's invitation, *Jet* photographer Maurice Sorrell, Ethel Payne, and I boarded an air force plane under his command for the 6,000 mile flight to Lagos to bring Young's body home. Already aboard were Young's sister, Arnita Boswell of Chicago, presidential assistants Donald Rumsfeld and Robert J. Brown, State Department officials Barbara Watson and W. Beverly Carter, and Urban League officials Sterling Tucker, Dan Davis, and Charles Hamilton. In the cockpit were three Southern white pilots and a black navigator. To Whitney Young it would have been a planeload of examples of the kind of equality for which he had struggled.

We covered the memorial service in the Cathedral Church of Christ in Lagos, at which the Reverend Jesse Jackson, then director of SCLC's Operation Breadbasket, revealed that President Nixon had offered Young a seat in the Cabinet, which Young had turned down, after sadly concluding that "the brothers" just would not have understood. Then we went on to New York where Mrs. Young met the plane at JFK International Airport. The funeral was at the Riverside Church in New York, where more than 20,000 people stood in line to pay their last respects, followed by Young's burial in the still segregated Greenwood Cemetery in Lexington, Kentucky, symbol of a task as yet unfinished. The services were attended by the high and the mighty, from President Nixon, who delivered a eulogy, through the Cabinet, the Congress, state houses, city halls, the civil rights organizations, and corporate boardrooms.

Back in New York, several of Harlem's street-corner pundits complained that the funeral should have been held in Harlem rather than in the Riverside Church. To me the answer to that was this: the tributes that followed Whitney Young's death emphasized that perhaps it doesn't matter where a man lived or where he died, but how he lived. Whitney Young did not live in Harlem; he did not die there. But as his funeral cortege moved through the ghetto streets, Harlem turned out to say goodbye. Perhaps it was because more than a few Harlem residents knew that every time Whitney Young had knocked on a corporate door he'd carried the hope of Harlem and other black communities in his breast pocket. And when he had brought home the bacon, he had brought it home, really, to the people of Harlem. That's what I believed, and that's what I wrote.

SPOOKS IN THE MAIL, BUGS IN THE PHONE

In the spring of 1974, I had a delightful conversation with Associate Supreme Court Justice William O. Douglas at a book party celebrating publication of his autobiography, *Go East, Young Man: The Early Years*. We talked about some of the blacks mentioned in his book, one of whom was Paul Robeson, the famous black actor and singer. Until reading Douglas's book, I wasn't aware that he had been a friend and Columbia Law School classmate of Robeson, who was then seventy-seven-years-old and in poor health. In the 1920s and '30s, Robeson was probably the best-known black man in America. The former All-American football player at Rutgers went on to become a Broadway star, acclaimed for dramatic performances in roles ranging from Eugene O'Neill's Emperor Jones to Shakespeare's Othello. His deep bass electrified audiences when he played Crown in Gershwin's *Porgy and Bess*, and when he sang "Ol' Man River" in Jerome Kern's *Show Boat*. His concert appearances sold out around the world, and he was especially popular in Europe where he lived much of the time. He was an outspoken advocate for civil rights, and after visits to the Soviet Union, became involved with many social causes supported by Communists. After winning the International Stalin Peace Prize in 1952, he was hounded relentlessly by Senator Joseph McCarthy, becoming probably the most vilified, persecuted black in America for the rest of the decade, as the Cold War escalated and the Red Scare menaced all walks of American life. In 1956 the government denied him a passport—thus preventing him from performing abroad—for refusing to sign an affidavit saying whether he was or had ever been a Communist.

On May 7, Justice Douglas sent me a short letter on Supreme Court stationery, mentioning our meeting a few days earlier at his book party, and asking me to tell him more about Robeson and his family. The letter was addressed to me at Johnson Publishing Company headquarters in Chicago, instead of our Washington bureau. The strange part was that the letter didn't reach me until October 16, more than five months later, and it had been opened. If the envelope had been opened in our Chicago office, company procedure would have been to put it in a company envelope and send it to me, not to cross out the Chicago address, write our Washington Bureau address on the original envelope, and add "Please Forward," as somebody had done to this letter. The envelope was also stamped "NOT USIA." Why it would have been delivered to the government's overseas information agency was another question. Although USIA had offices at 1750 Pennsylvania Avenue NW, so did a number of news organizations and journalists, including *Newsweek*, the *Boston Globe*, columnists Rowland Evans and Robert Novak, and Art Buchwald, as well as the Johnson Publishing Company, which was specified under my name in the address.

I wrote to Justice Douglas about the strange handling and delay of his letter, and the next day, he wrote back, "The story you tell really does not amaze me although it makes me rather sad." He went on to relate how mail he'd sent to his Supreme Court office from the state of Washington in September 1973 finally reached its destination almost a year later, in August 1974. Moreover, he wrote, a memorandum he'd sent in June via airmail to the Supreme Court in the Nixon tapes case was not delivered for "nearly a month." He added, "So how many read it I do not know." Douglas was referring to the case in which the Supreme Court, on July 24, 1974, voted 8–0 to deny President Nixon's claim of executive privilege, ruling that he had to turn over White House tape recordings subpoenaed for the Watergate cover-up trial.

All of this occurred more than a year before a Senate committee, chaired by Senator Frank Church of Idaho, issued the results of an investigation that revealed that the CIA and FBI routinely had opened the mail of numerous persons, including some government officials, and that Dr. Martin Luther King, Jr., was not the only civil rights figure the bureau had harassed as part of its many programs, including "Cointelpro" and "Black Rag" in a nationwide drive to root out anybody Hoover considered "rabble-rousers, agitators, key activists, and black extremists." At one time, more than 10,000 blacks in leadership roles were listed on a security index and targeted for postal mail openings, wiretaps, Internal Revenue Service audits, and acts of sabotage affecting job applications and other aspects of their lives. The Senate investigating committee reported that more than 7,000 blacks had been recruited to "provide information" on civil rights activists in their communities while many government departments and agencies cooperated in the massive effort to quell the so-called "black revolution."

After reading the committee findings, there was hardly a reporter with access to the highest echelons of government—or for that matter, anybody who associated with black leaders—who didn't suspect that his or her telephone was tapped. It simply became the norm to assume it was and proceed accordingly.

President Ford chatting with Carol and me at a White House reception for visiting Pakistani Prime Minister Zulfikar Ali Bhutto. (White House photo.)

UNHINGED

By Nixon's second term, blacks were becoming more and more concerned that minorities and the poor would lose much of the ground gained in the Kennedy and Johnson administrations. Advocates for the disadvantaged were pretty much swimming upstream, as Nixon preached "self-help" to all but the rich. The U.S. Commission on Civil Rights, which had become a watchdog on federal agencies, charged that most were deficient in their enforcement of civil rights laws, and issued a report that blamed their poor performance on a lack of "presidential leadership." The Congressional Black Caucus blasted Nixon's proposed domestic budget cuts, especially in manpower, medical and housing programs as "repressive and inhumane."

While black Republicans in the Nixon administration were trying to address minority concerns in the midst of the president's preoccupation with things foreign, as well as political, others in and around the White House were doing their own thing, too, which in some cases included burglarizing Democratic National Committee headquarters in the Watergate complex in the early morning hours of June 17, 1972, in an effort to place wiretaps. For others, their "own thing" would be a botched cover-up of the bungled burglary. There were no blacks involved in either bungle. Ironically, presidential chief of staff, H.R. "Bob" Haldeman, who in a relaxed moment with Nixon in the Oval Office had opined that blacks weren't "smart enough" and lacked "the intellect" to be spies, was one of the president's men who would go to prison for his role in the political spying fiasco. Also ironic was the fact that the security guard who discovered the burglary-in-progress was a young black man, with only eight years of formal education, but smart enough to do his job.

Jet photographer Maurice Sorrell and I lost no time getting over to the Watergate, a half-dozen or so blocks from our bureau, to interview Georgia-born Frank Wills. He was a quiet, unassuming young man, who at first didn't realize (and to be fair, who did?) the enormity of what he had discovered. He showed us around, stopping at the door to the stairwell leading to the DNC suite. He had noticed a strip of tape preventing the door from locking, and after removing it, found another in its place when he returned. The original door was gone now, seized as evidence, and another hung in its place. Lying on the floor next to the doorjamb were the hinges the FBI had left behind. We took some photos of Wills picking them up and examining them.[5]

"You might as well take these," he said. "They're just going to get thrown away." For the past thirty-plus years, those two pieces of hardware to me have symbolized the Nixon administration—a presidency unhinged.

22

THE END OF
THE BEGINNING

In journalism, as in many professions, if you're around long enough and do a reasonably good job, you're likely to gather a few awards to hang on your walls. From a professional standpoint, the recognition of one's peers is an unparalleled tribute. That's how I felt when the National Press Club honored me with its prestigious Fourth Estate Award for "a distinguished career in journalism" in 1982. I was the club's tenth honoree, following to the podium such giants of the journalism world as Walter Cronkite, Scotty Reston, Vermont Royster, and Herbert Block. I was also the first black recipient. The award was presented at a dinner in the temporary dining room set up to accommodate club functions while its main ballroom was under renovation. *Los Angeles Times* Washington bureau chief Jack Nelson, a 1962 Nieman Fellow, and a colleague for whom I had the highest regard, led off a rollicking program that was as much a roast as a tribute. My publisher, John H. Johnson, topped off the evening with an account of his fearsome meeting with President Lyndon Baines Johnson at the White House in 1964 when the subject was "what the hell is wrong with 'Simon' Booker that he's not writing about all the good things I've done for Negroes!" Mr. J. had the audience howling with laughter, and then, as always, he added seriously, "I never had to publish a retraction of anything Booker has ever written."

THE CONGRESSIONAL BLACK CAUCUS

In September 2010, I felt like an ant at a much larger gathering, as the Congressional Black Caucus Foundation celebrated its annual conference and banquet, at which it would honor me with its Mickey Leland Award, named in remembrance of the forty-four-year-old Texas congressman who founded and chaired the House Select Committee on Hunger. Leland was

295

With National Press Club president Vivian Vahlberg and dinner chairman Joseph Slevin after receiving the club's Fourth Estate Award in 1982. (Courtesy of author.)

killed in a plane crash in Ethiopia in 1989 while on a humanitarian mission to a refugee camp.

When I set about preparing some brief acceptance remarks, I realized that I had no idea how many members were now in the Congressional Black Caucus. When I looked it up, I was astounded to find there were more than forty. Moreover, I didn't know half of them personally.

At the outset of my career in the early 1940s, there was only one black member of Congress: William Dawson of Chicago, boss of the city's teeming South Side, and at one time probably the most powerful black politician ever developed in America. Born in Georgia, he moved to Illinois in 1912 to study at Northwestern University Law School and in 1943, won election to Congress, where he served thirteen terms, until his death in 1970. In the Truman era, Dawson was powerful enough to be considered almost an ex-officio member of the cabinet, a race relations advisor who handpicked blacks for high posts and helped set policy affecting Negroes. As vice-chairman of the Democratic Party, he ran the national political show for minorities, who feared him more than any other lawmaker in Washington.

Outwardly conservative on social issues, he was firm and sometimes heart-
less if it appeared a person or group was attempting to embarrass the party,
even on civil rights. Considered "safe" by the white power structure, he once
told civil rights leaders to "go to hell" when they urged him to support a
particular move. But even while he avoided publicly supporting any type
of militancy, he wasn't above putting others up to doing what needed to be
done, as when he sent proxies before the convention platform committee to
denounce tentative proposals as "weak."

His seniority landed him the chairmanship of the House Government
Operations Committee, with oversight over billions in annual U.S. expen-
ditures, but by the early 1960s, he had lost much of his national clout. In
1962, dissatisfaction with his control over the South Side became apparent
when Dawson's machine tried to keep a white man from representing the
heavily black Hyde Park District. Although the Dawson-backed candidate,
attorney Chauncey Eskridge, claimed support of Dr. Martin Luther King,
Jr., and Kennedy White House aides, Negroes voted seven-to-one for the
white man, citing a stronger human rights record than the entire Dawson
machine.

Despite his conservative positions on many issues, Dawson was a stri-
dent opponent of the poll tax that kept so many blacks disenfranchised. This
was probably why he was the featured speaker at the first voting rights rally
in Mound Bayou, Mississippi, three years before a *Jet* assignment took me
there in 1955 for the third and largest such gathering.

In 1945, Dawson was joined in the House by a man with a completely
different personality, the flamboyant Adam Clayton Powell, Jr., from New
York's Harlem. Powell earned the title "Mr. Civil Rights" when it was unpopular even to whisper about integration. Powell yelled it. Barging into politics,
the son of a pioneering Negro clergyman had no difficulty lining up support
from the church membership, leading to his election as a New York City
councilman and then the first black congressman from the East Coast. For a
long time, Powell was the voice of black aspirations and Negroes rewarded
him by overlooking his often scandalous personal life. Any criticism of the
lawmaker in his Harlem district was virtually forbidden—whether in the
Negro press, from civic leaders, or even the man in the street. His popularity precluded any serious examination of his claimed attainments for "my
beloved Harlem," which twenty years later was still a tenement slum easily described as the most blighted neighborhood in America. Moreover, its
percentage of voters was one of the lowest among northern Congressional
districts.

In the early '60s, when I was writing *Black Man's America*, I asked a
constituent, "What has Adam done for Harlem?" His answer typified the

"attitude" Powell's "stickin' it to Whitey" had cultivated in the district. "What the hell have *you* done?" the man retorted before turning away, leaving me to wonder how smart it was to criticize Powell on his own turf. But outside of Harlem, his problems started to mount, with probes into Congressional payroll and travel abuses. Even his positions on civil rights issues seemed to become confused, as when he attacked the NAACP for being "white-controlled," and most civil righters sighed, "Where has Adam been in the last few years? We've integrated." Another "off the track" position was his 1965 call for the replacement of black housing expert Dr. Robert Weaver as U.S. housing agency administrator by a former Alabama congressman, Albert Rains. I echoed the reaction of the leadership when I urged Ticker Tape readers to write Powell and tell him to "get in tune with the civil rights movement." His other problems were also reeling out of control.

In 1960 Powell had called a constituent a "bag woman" in a televised interview. A lawsuit ensued and spiraled out of all proportion over eight years, reaching a point where he couldn't return to New York for fear of arrest for contempt of court. By the late '60s, he'd retreated to Bimini in the Bahamas where he spent his days deep sea fishing, ending every after-noon playing dominoes, and drinking scotch and milk in a one-room dive called the End of the World Bar. Before sunset, he'd walk down the one (at its widest)-by-seven mile island's only street, accompanied by a gaggle of local men almost skipping with delight to be in the company of "the king," to the dock where his handsome young Bahamian captain, twenty-five-year-old Patrick Brown, son of the owner of the local hotel/restaurant/fishing center, would motor *Adam's Fancy* across the inlet to the house on South Bimini where his former Congressional receptionist—1959 Miss Ohio, *Ebony* Fash-ion Fair runway model, and *Jet's* October 1960 cover girl—Corinne Huff, awaited him.

Occasionally the daily Bimini routine was interrupted by something unusual, such as when he preached a Sunday morning sermon to a group of vacationing Seventh Day Adventist students, making the front pages state-side, but getting the students in a heap of trouble with church elders. His daily routine also was interrupted from time to time by press conferences for reporters, photographers, and TV cameramen who flew in for a few hours from Miami, a short flight away, after some development in his case, or by visitors from Washington or New York, some of whom urged him to clear up the defamation suit so he could return to his district. Stokely Carmichael was among those who made the pilgrimage. But by 1967, the infrequent visi-tors more often would be political hacks, has-beens, and hangers-on from Harlem who came to curry favor or get something from him.

Photographer Maurice Sorrell and I endured weeks of sunshine and good fishing for an *Ebony* article on Adam Clayton Powell's self-exile on Bimini. On this Sunday, he was dressed to deliver a sermon to a group of visiting Seventh Day Adventist students, a service that landed them in hot water with church officials back home. (Courtesy of author.)

I was on Bimini to do an *Ebony* article in March 1967 when, coincidentally, the New York Supreme Court reduced damages against Powell in the slander case by $100,000, leading some to suggest he should settle the case and come home. By this time, however, the bigger story was how Powell was handling his expulsion by the Congress, which he was appealing to the U.S. Supreme Court. The newsmen observed that he seemed "undaunted" by his ouster, and I can verify that Powell put on a good show, most of which was reported the next day in the *New York Post* and other metropolitan dailies.

After four hours trolling the Atlantic without catching a fish, Powell, dressed as usual like a wealthy, trophy-seeking sportsman in white shirt and Bermuda shorts, his eyes hidden behind black-rimmed sunglasses, had powered *Adam's Fancy* into port himself, where the first arrivals, including an Associated Press team, awaited him. Adam was ready. They followed him to his usual table to the left of the door—the only source of light—in the End of the World Bar. At first, Powell seemed to relish the attention, joining the locals in gospel songs, smoking a cigar, and drinking his scotch and milk, all the while playing dominoes. The press loved it, and Powell didn't mind either, when "Tanyiki," a well-endowed exotic fire dancer, braless in an orange tank top and short shorts, stepped inside the bar to invite everybody to her performance that night at the island's tourist hotel. The flashbulbs popped as she leaned seductively over Powell's shoulder, flashing a wide, neon smile for the cameras while toying playfully with his ever-present sunglasses. Tom Johnson, a black reporter from the *New York Times*, was delighted to learn there might be something to do on the island that night besides drink, and left with the dancer to try to arrange a post-performance rendezvous at the hotel. The rest of the press stayed in the bar, where as the hour wore on, the scotch and flashbulbs soon took their toll on Powell. I could see that his mood was souring, although the newcomers probably didn't see it coming. The next minute, he ordered the photographers out of the bar. The AP reporter stayed behind, but later wished he hadn't. First, Powell ordered him to put his notebook away. Then the dominoes partner joined in the fun and told the newsman he'd have to buy Powell a bottle of scotch and some milk if he wished to remain in the bar. I watched the reporter pay $5 for the scotch and $1 for the milk. I could only shake my head a minute later, when Powell ordered the guy out of the bar anyway, and all the locals laughed as if they'd just been party to an old trick.

Powell's sudden mood swing was not unusual. One supporter who had flown in to see him groused that one minute he'd be relaxed and charming, and the next he was "cutting your guts out." It was getting more difficult to get anybody to go down there in a show of support, except what this New Yorker called "dissidents and third-partyites." Powell didn't act this way toward Tom Johnson, or my photographer, Maurice Sorrell, or me, but we knew when to leave him alone. He also decided to rely on me for the time I was there to keep other newsmen and strangers away from him during his afternoons in the bar. The man who never seemed to care about his public image suddenly didn't want any more bad press. I didn't relish the role, but it allowed me the access I needed to do my *Ebony* story (while also getting in some enjoyable fishing time). Perhaps to show his appreciation, or maybe because he wanted the company, Powell took us back to his house on South Bimini one night for dinner, which gave me an even more intimate look at how he was really faring in "paradise." It wasn't good.

Despite all his bravado—he invariably replied, "Why go back to Washington when you can enjoy a place like this?" to newsmen who asked the obvious question—the ordeal was taking its toll on Powell. Beneath his trim physique and great tan, behind the sunglasses that he rarely doffed, he wasn't doing well at all, and his avoidance of strangers on the island started to border on paranoia. While "Huffy," as he called her, sometimes went fishing

Charlie Rangel's campaign to oust Adam Clayton Powell from his House seat representing Harlem was effective at the ballot box in large part due to Powell's record of absenteeism. (Courtesy of author.)

with him, ducking down in the boat to avoid tourist cameras, she usually hid out at home while he fished alone, followed by the daily dominoes and the drinks at the End of the World. He was getting bored with life on the island. We could see that his cover girl was also growing discontent, but for other reasons. The young model made no secret of the fact that something about the island appealed to her, and she didn't want to return to Washington. As it turned out, she never did.

Eventually, Powell won the special election to fill his own House seat, and the Supreme Court ruled that his ouster by the Congress had been unconstitutional. He still spent much of his time on Bimini, but not with Miss Ohio. In 1969, the twenty-eight-year-old married Powell's twenty-five-year-old Bahamian fishing boat captain.

Two years later, in Harlem's Democratic primary election, Powell's sorry record of absenteeism was a major reason for his defeat by Charlie Rangel, who pummeled him with it.

A freshman when I met him in Mound Bayou in 1955, Detroit Representative Charles Diggs came to Congress with a passion for civil rights. A congenial man with a good sense of humor, Charlie Diggs was a favorite of our D.C. staff during his twelve successive terms in Congress. He was a regular at our parties as well as at our other favorite nighttime haunt, the upstairs Gold Coast lounge at Billy Simpson's Ebony Table on Georgia Avenue. The young congressman had been best man at Billy and Edith Simpson's wedding in 1957, a year after they opened the popular eatery and watering hole. But Charlie Diggs also liked to frequent other places not quite as healthy for him—the horse racing tracks in suburban Maryland where he indulged a passion for gambling, to the point where it seemed to be an addiction. He ran into financial problems, at one point having to mortgage his household furniture. In 1978, he was charged with taking kickbacks from longtime members of his congressional staff after raising their salaries. Although he insisted he had done nothing wrong by accepting money from loyal staffers who were aware of his problems, he was convicted of mail fraud and filing false payroll forms. Censured by the House in 1979, he resigned a year later, before serving out part of a three-year prison sentence.

The lawmaker's friends and supporters never abandoned him, staying with him through the disgrace, after which he returned to his original profession as a mortician, and opened a funeral business in Prince George's County, Maryland.

I walked among the hundreds of mourners who gathered for Diggs's funeral after he suffered a heart attack in 1998, listening as one after another remembered him as one of the century's hardest working, most effective members of the House of Representatives—and above all, one of the most committed to the cause of civil rights. Former House colleague, Cleveland Representative Louis Stokes, recalled in his eulogy that "long before many of us came to Congress, Charlie Diggs was a legend to us." Atlanta's Andrew Young praised his former congressional colleague as one who "bore the cross not expected of a congressman" by extending support and a voice to the Emmett Till case, even traveling to Mississippi to attend the trial; by joining Dr. King in Selma, Alabama, in support of the civil rights movement; by being a strong advocate for Africa and the ending of apartheid in South Africa, even before it became a popular cause; and by getting home rule passed as chairman of the House District Committee. To black Americans, Diggs's legacy was enormous, although sadly, some may only remember him as a man whose one weakness led to a tragic mistake for which he paid a high price.

Robert Nix was elected to Congress from a predominantly black section of Philadelphia in 1958. A painstaking lawyer but a lackluster lawmaker, he rarely spoke on the House floor or led any civil rights move. He was joined in the Congress in 1963 by a fifth black lawmaker, Augustus Hawkins, who had served for twenty-eight years in the California legislature where he authored or sponsored progressive bills ranging from fair employment practices to workers' compensation for domestics. So light skinned that most people outside his California district wouldn't have known he was African-American,

I tagged Detroit's John Conyers as a rising star when I followed his first Congressional campaign for an *Ebony* article in 1964. (Photo by Maurice Sorrell.)

he liked to tell the story about his first weeks in Sacramento, when a fellow legislator turned to him and said, "There's a new nigger in here." Hawkins smiled and retorted, "Yeah, I know. I am he." He served in Congress until 1991, and stayed in Washington for the rest of his life, living with his wife, Elsie, in a townhouse on Capitol Hill, just down the street from Carol and me. Making daily treks to the grocery store, a good hike away, well into his nineties, he demonstrated the same energy he'd brought to Congress forty years earlier. He told us he loved the exercise. When he died in 2007 at 100 years of age, he was the oldest living person to have served in Congress.

John Conyers, the son of a UAW international representative, was a referee with Detroit's Workers Compensation Board when he decided to run for Congress. The thirty-five-year-old's strengths in organization and political technique helped him amass one of the largest volunteer organizations in the Motor City's history, leading to his seat in the House in 1965. I covered his campaign from start to finish, and followed his outstanding career as a legislator, still going strong long after I retired in 2007.

The number of blacks elected to Congress doubled from five in the 90th Congress (1967–69) to ten in the 91st, followed by three more in the next. Parren Mitchell became the first black elected to Congress from Baltimore. Cleveland sent Louis Stokes to Washington, and Missourians elected William Clay, while the first black female, the delightfully irrepressible Shirley

New York's Shirley Chisholm became the first black Congresswoman in 1969 and made a bid for the Democratic presidential nomination in 1972. (Courtesy of author.)

After more than a decade in Congress, Californian Ron Dellums, sharing a moment here with Fannie Granton and me, was ready for a showdown with President Reagan on U.S. policy toward South Africa's apartheid government. (Courtesy of author.)

Chisholm, arrived from Brooklyn, New York, and later would be the first African-American to make a serious bid for the Democratic presidential nomination.

Tall, strikingly handsome Ron Dellums came to Congress from Oakland, California, in 1971 with his vivacious wife, Roscoe. Like most of the black members at the time, Dellums was a champion of civil rights for the oppressed blacks of South Africa as well as at home. When he bucked administration policy by pushing forward his Comprehensive Anti-Apartheid Act of 1986, President Reagan vetoed the bill, and Congress, for the first time in the twentieth century, overrode a presidential policy veto.

Ralph Metcalfe, handpicked by Chicago's William Dawson to succeed him, was joined by another black from the Windy City, George Collins. (Collins died in a plane crash days after starting his second term. He was succeeded by his widow, Cardiss, who proved her mettle by serving twenty-four years after winning the special election for her late husband's seat.) Walter Fauntroy joined the ranks in 1971 as the nonvoting delegate from the District of Columbia (still today the most undemocratic corner of America, despite nominal home rule). Together, the thirteen comprised the newly formed Congressional Black Caucus, destined to become a powerful and growing voice for black Americans across the country.

As Washington bureau chief for Johnson Publishing, I was on the mailing list of every caucus member, and they were on my Rolodex. They were so few at first that we got to know them all very well, and could count on them not only for news, but also support for various causes in the black community, from turkey dinners for poor families during the holidays to appearances at seminars for black student groups visiting the D.C. bureau.

A ROSTER OF "FIRSTS"

As I watched the CBC grow, black influence at 1600 Pennsylvania Avenue changed dramatically, too. Louis Martin, Deputy Chairman of the Democratic Party in the 1960s, and regarded as "the godfather of black politics," told me he'd spent more days in the White House during the Kennedy and Johnson administrations than he did at party headquarters. When he accepted the party post, he vowed to make his prime objective putting a black in the Cabinet and on the U.S. Supreme Court. He achieved both goals with President Johnson's appointment of Robert C. Weaver to the top housing post, and Thurgood Marshall to the high court.

Martin returned to the White House as a special assistant to President Jimmy Carter (whom some consider the first truly "Southern" president

Louis Martin, the Democratic National Committee Vice Chairman, was regarded as "the godfather of black politics" in the 1960s. (Courtesy of author.)

of the century, rather than Texan Lyndon Johnson; but to blacks, LBJ was "Southern" enough), and was proud of Carter's record of appointing more black judges than all other previous presidents combined. He also appointed the first black female cabinet member, Patricia Roberts Harris, Secretary of Housing and Urban Development. Three years later Carter named her Secretary of Health, Education, and Welfare, and shortly after that, Secretary of the new Department of Education. Educator, lawyer, and diplomat, Secretary Harris already had a long string of "firsts" on her resumé, including first black woman to hold diplomatic rank when President Johnson named her ambassador to Luxembourg in 1965.

President Bill Clinton had more black special assistants—seven—on his White House staff than any other president, and they were stellar. Elected to his first of two successive terms in 1992, he was so popular among blacks, he was affectionately called "the first Black President" until he had to relinquish the title to the "real McCoy."

Starting in the '60s, we witnessed a new era in politics on a statewide level as well. Among the first blacks elected to state office in 1962, Republican Edward Brooke went from two terms as attorney general of the

At a White House Christmas party, our son Teddy met President and Mrs. Clinton, as well as a number of the outstanding black aides he appointed, more than in any previous administration. (White House photo.)

Commonwealth of Massachusetts to two more as a United States senator, the first African-American elected to that body by popular vote. In Richmond, Douglas Wilder entered the Virginia State House in 1990 as the first black elected governor of one of the fifty States.

As the number of black elected officials nationwide rose into the thousands, another stunning fact emerged—a majority were in the eleven states of the old Confederacy. And of the hundreds of black mayors elected, most of them in the South, several did so by winning crucial white support, as in the election of Dutch Morial in New Orleans (1978), Richard Arrington in Birmingham (1979), and Andrew Young in Atlanta (1981). Tears ran down Young's cheeks at his swearing-in, when the choir sang: "Nobody told me that the way would be easy, but I don't believe He brought me this far to leave me . . ." The new mayor, who was beside Dr. King at every major step of the freedom movement, could tell you the way hadn't been easy.

Now, here I was on September 18, 2010, looking at a lineup of black Members of Congress and able to identify barely half of them by name. Sitting with me at the honorees' table was a man anyone in the movement would recognize instantly, because he always seemed to be there when the leaders needed him. I wondered how many of the new faces Harry Belafonte recognized.

President and Mrs. Obama with the 2010 CBCF honorees (l-r) Harry Belafonte, me, Judith Jamison, and the Honorable Sheila Y. Oliver, first black female Speaker of the New Jersey Assembly. (Courtesy of author.)

I recalled the first gala of the newly formed Congressional Black Caucus in September of 1971. Twenty-six hundred people showed their support by attending the $100 a plate dinner. On this night in 2010, caucus supporters in the Washington Convention Center filled a ballroom as large, it seemed, as a football field, at $700 a plate, or $30,000 for one of the less expensive tables.

The highlight of the evening was the appearance of President and Mrs. Obama. Backstage for a photograph with the awardees, the first lady, dazzling in a bright red chiffon gown, graciously kissed me on the cheek, followed by a warm handshake and "Thank you for your contributions" from the chief executive.

The president's address that night was rousing and strong, not unlike his campaign appearances. When it was over, and the Obamas had departed, many in the audience immediately started to roam around. For them, the program was over. They'd seen and heard the president and now they were ready for networking and socializing. The lifetime achievement awards were just background noise to their table-hopping conversations. Waiting backstage to be called to the podium after a brief video introduction, I caught enough of Harry Belafonte's remarks to note that we were singing in the same choir, although he with a better voice than I.

Accepting the Congressional Black Caucus Foundation Phoenix Award in 2010: "There is much left to be done. It won't be easy. It never has been." (Courtesy of author.)

What we told the audience that night was that the job is not yet done. As I put it, what we have witnessed was not the end of the Freedom Movement. It was merely, as Thurgood Marshall told *Ebony* when he was appointed U.S. solicitor general, "the end of the beginning." Even as late as 1992, speaking as an associate justice of the United States Supreme Court before an audience in Philadelphia, Marshall cautioned that "the battle for racial and economic justice is not yet won; indeed, it has barely begun." No longer in the courts, nor on the streets where it smoldered and sometimes erupted, the battle, he advised, had now moved to the legislative arena, where government at all levels must be pressured "to fund vital social programs—for job training, affordable housing, child care, decent education, health care—programs necessary for the attainment of true liberty."

When a recession and vulnerable economic climate plagues much of the world, anyone hearing that is tempted to smirk, "Good luck!" Two decades since Marshall described the challenge, black Americans are still on the bottom rung of the economic ladder, farther from the whites at the top, in fact, than in the last dozen years, according to a 2011 Pew Research Institute report.

Like the generations that rose up from the silt of the Southern bayous and the desolate slums of Northern cities to claim their civil rights, it's up to a new generation to continue the fight for true equality, when the psychological and physical scars of slavery and discrimination are finally erased. Today, we are almost fifty years beyond the passage of the major civil rights legislation that finally buried Jim Crow 100 years after the Civil War, but we are still dealing with the ugly legacy of discrimination that affected black lives even beyond the eleven states of the former Confederacy. Yes, a black man was elected president of the United States in 2008, but there are still disproportionately more blacks than whites among the unemployed; more blacks in jail than in college; more blacks in the prison population than our percentage of the overall population; more teenage pregnancies that are fueling the poverty cycle; more blacks living in substandard housing than any other racial or ethnic group.

The election of a black president was a remarkable achievement for this country, occurring less than fifty years after passage of the Voting Rights Act of 1965, but it was not an ending—and certainly not a "Hollywood ending." At most, it was the end of an early chapter in the history of a still young nation. Looking back over Ticker Tape in the months before I retired, I have to chuckle at one item on July 10, 2006, that was as foresighted as any in the fifty-three years I wrote the column:

> Proving to be spectacular on the campaign trail for others, popular U.S. Sen. Barack Obama of Illinois, currently America's only Black senator, may soon be asked to switch his role to an active candidate. He's drawing the crowds and filling the coffers, but hasn't mentioned any intentions. No Black currently on the trail has been so warmly received without his name being considered for a spot on the ballot . . .

My generation, and several behind me, have long since passed the baton, or as JFK put it, "the torch," to a new generation, and they to another. It's now up to yet another to work toward a truly "post-racial" society, and if you think it's going to be easy, I would suggest you consider the past. It's never been easy.

Acknowledgments

Carol and I have benefited from the support and encouragement of many friends and family members during this daunting venture to turn more than sixty years of reporting into a meaningful and lasting retrospective. It was an effort I could not have undertaken without my wife's research and writing skills, honed over thirty-plus years as a lawyer in the civil rights and public policy arena, as well as her unflagging support. We are indebted to our neighbor, Neal Gregory, a former newsman and hawk-eyed editor, who encouraged us to write this book, and introduced us to former investigative reporter/TV producer Charlie Thompson, who started us off with his research into my long-forgotten coverage of the murders in the Mississippi Delta in the 1950s. We would not have written this book had it not been for Charlie. Neal, an alumnus of Ole Miss who as a young reporter covered the turbulent admission of James Meredith to the university in 1962, provided hours of astute editorial guidance, and also introduced us to W. Ralph Eubanks, himself the author of two books about growing up in Mississippi during the Freedom Movement. Ralph introduced us to agent Martha Kaplan, and together they helped our book find its publisher.

Carol's brother, Gerard McCabe, library consultant and editor, also provided expert editorial and publishing guidance all along the way, as well as strong encouragement. My cousin Lynn French shared with me some of the family history her late mother, Carolyn French, had so thoughtfully collected over the years. My former JPC Washington Bureau reporter and longtime friend Carolyn Dubose (author of the only biography of Congressman Charles Diggs) helped us fill in memory gaps, and offered the insightful tip that it might be useful to request my FBI file under the Freedom of Information/Privacy Acts. Corinna Zarek an attorney in the Office of Government Information Services, National Archives and Records Administration (NARA), helped us immeasurably in obtaining those materials when we ran into roadblocks.

Allen Fisher, archivist at NARA, was very helpful in locating Johnson Administration documents and recordings from the Lyndon Baines Johnson Presidential Library in Austin and the Miller Center for Public Policy. Christopher Banks, also of NARA, generously assisted us in obtaining photographs from the Library.

Al Lenhart, Youngstown YMCA Historian and archivist, sent us cherished mementos of my father's tenure there as Secretary of the Negro branch on West Federal St.

We also thank Vicky Wilson, archival specialist for Johnson Publishing Co., for fact-checking assistance.

Several friends read the manuscript and gave us insightful comments as it matured, and we are grateful to them all. My stalwart secretaries over the decades, especially Pat Washington, Mary Whitehead, Vanessa Fox, and ultimately Barbara Best must be thanked for helping me preserve many treasures in my files, including letters, clippings, documents, and photographs that contributed greatly to our recollection of the events and conversations memorialized in this book.

Finally, we acknowledge the generous time and support of University Press of Mississippi director Leila Salisbury, who brought this project to fruition, and associate editor Valerie Jones and the other members of an astute and thoughtful staff who helped guide us through the publishing process.

We take full responsibility for any errors in the text, which we'll blame on age anyway.

Notes

CHAPTER 1

1. See, e.g., Douglas Brinkley, *The Wilderness Warrior: Theodore Roosevelt and the Crusade for America* (New York: HarperCollins, 2009), pp. 404–6, and 431–32.

2. Simeon Booker, Ticker Tape USA, *Jet*, June 16, 1955, p. 9.

3. Aaron Henry's autobiography gives vivid, firsthand accounts of the bombings and other attacks he and his family endured because of his civil rights activities. Aaron Henry and Constance Curry, *Aaron Henry: The Fire Ever Burning* (Jackson: University Press of Mississippi, 2000), pp. 141–44.

4. See Ralph Eubanks, *Ever Is a Long Time: A Journey into Mississippi's Dark Past* (New York: Basic Books, 2003).

5. *Jet*, Apr. 21, 1955.

CHAPTER 4

1. Rosenwald's friendship and collaboration with Booker T. Washington is described in a well-researched and fascinating book by Stephanie Deutsch, *You Need a Schoolhouse* (Evanston: Northwestern University Press, 2011).

2. Letter from Camp Devins, MA, http://www.org/amerianexperience/features/primary-resources/influenza-letter.

CHAPTER 5

1. Shortly before her death, Mamie Till-Mobley wrote a very moving memoir of her life before and after Emmett's murder, *Death of Innocence* (New York: Random House, 2003), with my former *Ebony* colleague Christopher Benson, whom she trusted to help her tell her story.

2. Simeon Wright and Herb Boyd, *Simeon's Story: An Eyewitness Account of the Kidnapping of Emmett Till* (Chicago: Lawrence Hill Books, 2010), p. 50.

3. Ibid. at p. 51.

CHAPTER 6

1. Memorandum for the Record from E. Frederick Morrow, Nov. 22, 1955. http://www.eisenhower.archives.gov/research/online_documents/civil_rights_emmett_till_case/1955_11_22_MDR_re_Till.pdf.

2. Memorandum from Max Rabb to James Hagerty, Oct. 23, 1956. http://www.eisenhower.archives.gov/research/online_documents/civil_rights_emmett_till_case.html.

3. Memorandum from Max Rabb to Colonel Goodpastor, Jan. 6, 1956. http://www.eisenhower.archives.gov/research/online_documents/civil_rights_emmett_till_case.html.

CHAPTER 8

1. Memorandum, SAC [Special Agent-in-Charge] Cleveland to Director, FBI, Oct. 22, 1951.

2. *Jet*, Feb. 9, 1956.

3. Memorandum from Milton Jones to Louis Nichols re: "Simeon S. Booker, Jr.," May 27, 1957, p. 3.

4. *Jet*, Mar. 15, 1956, p. 10–13.

5. May 27, 1957, memorandum, *supra*, p. 3.

6. Farmer described the lynching he was headed for in Plaquemine, Louisiana, when the FBI intervened—albeit not at all to the extent they might or should have. *James Farmer: An Autobiography of the Civil Rights Movement* (Fort Worth: Texas Christian University Press, 1998), p. 253.

7. Cartha D. DeLoach, *Hoover's FBI: The Inside Story by Hoover's Trusted Lieutenant* (Washington, D.C.: Regnery Publishing, 1995), pp. 203–205.

8. Juan Williams, *Thurgood Marshall; American Revolutionary* (New York: Random House, 1998), pp. 158–62.

9. Letter from [name illegible or deleted] to Marvin Watson, Special Assistant to the President, Aug. 5, 1966.

10. These documents are available at the Eisenhower Presidential Library and Museum website at: http://www.eisenhower.archives.gov/research/online_documents/civil_rights_emmett_till_case.html.

CHAPTER 9

1. Earl Warren, *The Memoirs of Chief Justice Earl Warren* (New York: Doubleday, 1977), p. 289.

2. Till-Mobley and Benson, *Death of Innocence*, p. 207.

CHAPTER 10

1. "Daisy Bates: Arkansas Fighter," *Jet*, Oct. 17, 1957, pp. 6–9.

2. Ibid.

3. *Jet*, Mar. 3, 1955.

4. *Jet*, Oct. 10, 1957, p. 6.

5. *Jet*, Sept. 25, 1958, p. 6.

CHAPTER 11

1. E. Frederic Morrow, *Black Man in the White House* (New York: Macfadden Books, 1963), p. 130.

2. This is Morrow's diary entry for Feb. 28, 1956. Morrow, p. 33.

3. President Eisenhower news conference Jul. 7, 1954. http://www.presidency.ucsb .edu/ws/index.php.

4. *Evening Star*, Jul. 7, 1954, p. 1.

5. Letter to President Dwight D. Eisenhower from Val Washington, Director of Minorities, Republican National Committee, Jul. 15, 1957.

6. Roy Wilkins, *Standing Fast: The Autobiography of Roy Wilkins* (New York: Da Capo Press, 1994), p. 246.

7. *Jet*, Nov. 28, 1957, p. 4.

8. "Negro Leaders Irked as Ike Asks 'Patience' at 'Summit,'" *Jet*, May 29, 1958, pp. 8–10.

9. *Jet*, May 29, 1958, p. 31.

10. Memorandum for the Files, "Meeting of Negro Leaders with the President—June 23, 1958; Rocco Siciliano, Jun. 24, 1958; http://www.eisenhower.archives.gov/research/ online_documents/civil_rights.

11. *Jet*, July 10, 1958, p. 14.

12. Simeon Booker, "The Last Days of J. Ernest Wilkins," *Ebony*, Mar. 1959, pp. 141–146.

13. *Ebony*, May 1960, p. 42.

CHAPTER 12

1. James H. N. Waring, *Work of the Colored Law and Order League: Baltimore, Md., 1908*. See *The Capital and the Bay: Narratives of Washington and the Chesapeake Bay Region*, ca. 1600–1925; http://memory.loc.gov/ammem/index.html.

2. Ibid.

3. Ibid.

CHAPTER 13

1. Although magazine journalism was ineligible for the prize, Sleet's photograph of the widowed Coretta Scott King and her youngest child, Bernice, at Dr. King's funeral qualified for the Pulitzer in 1969 because it was picked up by newspapers around the world via the Associated Press (AP) wire.

2. "Words of the Week," *Jet*, Jun. 4, 1959, p. 30; Eisenhower was close behind, however, calling segregation "morally wrong" when it interfered with a person's equality of opportunity in "the economic and political fields." He made the comment a few days after Dr. King, who had called on Ike every six months since 1956 to make such a statement, had decried the president's failure to do so as "tragic." "Ike Calls Segregation 'Morally Wrong' For 1st Time," *Jet*, Jul. 23, 1959, p. 7.

3. "E. Frederic Morrow Leaves Mission to Africa," *Jet*, Jan. 14, 1960, pp. 3–4.

4. Morrow, *Black Man in the White House*, p. 213.

5. http://whitehousetapes.net/clip/ richard-nixon-john-erlichman-hr-haldeman-nixon-race.

6. Jul. 5, 1971. http://whitehousetapes.net/clip/nixon-jews-are-born-spies.

7. These tapes are among hundreds of hours of Nixon's recorded conversations made public beginning in 1996 under a settlement agreement between the National Archives and the Nixon estate, which had sued to keep them secret. Among the first tapes released was one of Nixon and aides discussing underwriting a presidential bid by an independent black candidate such as Jesse Jackson—who was too young at the time to run anyway—in order to siphon votes away from the Democratic candidate. *Jet*, Jan. 16, 1996, p. 8.

8. Simeon Booker, "The Candidates Negroes Prefer for President: Nixon, Stevenson, Humphrey Score Heavily in National Poll," *Jet*, Aug. 20, 1959, pp. 14–18.

9. Simeon Booker, Ticker Tape USA, *Jet*, Jan. 21, 1960.

10. Ibid., Jan. 28, 1960.

11. Simeon Booker, "Tough Man for a Tough Job," *Ebony*, Nov. 1961, pp. 55–62, at p. 57. In 1951, Symington refused to withdraw senior aide Weaver from a mission to determine cost factors in producing tin in Bolivia when the U.S. Department of State balked on the grounds that Bolivians would not accept a Negro envoy. State proved to be wrong, and Weaver successfully completed the mission with a show of appreciation from the Bolivian government.

12. "CAMPAIGN TRAIL" (advertisement), *Jet*, Nov. 10, 1960, pp. 22–23, and Booker, Ticker Tape USA, ibid., at pp. 10–11.

13. Jimmy Hicks recounted the episode in vivid detail several years later in his column, "Another Angle. . . ." James L. Hicks, "Bravo, Baylor!," *New York Amsterdam News*, Jan. 24, 1959, p. 9.

CHAPTER 14

1. A few weeks later, while welcoming visiting Ghanaian President Kwame Nkrumah to Washington, Kennedy also noticed the absence of any Negroes in the Presidential Honor Guard, and asked his aides to look into it. It turned out the unique military group, which stands guard at important VIP occasions and patrols historic installations, had few black enlisted men, and no black officers. The president made his dissatisfaction with this known to the brass at Fort Myer, Virginia, the home of the unit. *Jet*, Mar. 23, 1961, p. 3.

2. President John F. Kennedy News Conference (9), Apr. 12, 1961. http://www .jfklibrary.org/Research/Ready-Reference/Press-Conferences/News-Conference-9.aspx.

3. *Ebony*, Jan. 1961, pp. 33–38.

CHAPTER 15

1. Simeon Booker, "How Attorney General Kennedy Plans to Aid Dixie Negroes: Will Take Personal Trips to Inspect Plight of Voters," *Jet*, Apr. 20, 1961, pp. 12–15.

2. "U.S. Starts Dixie 'Open Door' Policy," *Jet*, May 18, 1961, p. 3; "Integrated Group Starts Freedom Ride," ibid., pp. 6–7. As African nations became independent and sent diplomats to the U.S., those traveling to Washington, D.C., from New York had been encouraged to fly rather than drive because of discrimination at rest stops in Maryland and Delaware. After one embarrassing incident in October 1957, President Eisenhower assigned Fred Morrow to bring Ghana's Finance Minister K. A. Gbedemah to breakfast at the White House to smooth over the VIP's having been refused service in a Howard Johnson's restaurant near Dover, Delaware. Simeon Booker, "Black Man in the White House," *Ebony*, Apr. 1961, pp. 77–86.

3. Simeon Booker, "Black Man in the White House," *Ebony*, Apr. 1961, pp. 77–86, at 80.

4. "Murrow Blasts U.S. For Bias Against Africans," *Jet*, Jun. 8, 1961, p. 4.

5. Raymond Arsenault, *Freedom Riders: 1961 and the Struggle for Racial Justice* (New York: Oxford University Press, 2006).

6. *Morgan v. Com. of Va.*, 328 U.S. 373 (1946).

7. *Mitchell v. Arkansas*, 313 U.S. 80 (1941).

8. *Henderson v. U.S.*, 339 U.S. 816 (1950).

9. *Boynton v. Com. of Va.*, 364 U.S. 454 (1960).

10. Simeon Booker, "*Jet* Leadership Survey Reveals How U.S. Negroes Feel About President Kennedy," *Jet*, Jun. 29, 1961, pp. 14–16.

11. Larry Still, "Rides Cost State $100,000 Monthly as Drive Continues," *Jet*, Aug. 17, 1961, pp. 14–18.

CHAPTER 16

1. "Races: Explosion of Hate," *Time*, Dec. 7, 1962; http://www.time.com/time/magazine/article/0,9171,829610,00.html.

CHAPTER 17

1. *Ebony*, Jan. 1963, p. 84.

2. Simeon Booker, Ticker Tape USA, *Jet*, Oct. 18, 1962, p. 12.

3. "Ole Miss Bars Negro Newsmen: 'Doesn't Discriminate,'" *Jet*, Oct. 4, 1962, p. 14.

4. Larry Still, "Negro Tells of Experiences at Ole Miss: Ex-GI Hopes His Actions Changed Course of Miss. History," ibid. at 17.

5. Simeon Booker, "Negro GI's, White Marshals Praised for Routing Miss. Mobs," *Jet*, Oct. 18, 1962, pp. 20–23.

6. Larry Still, "Meredith Attends Classes on Riot-Torn Ole Miss Campus," *Jet*, Oct. 11, 1962, pp. 14–17.

7. "Pulled from Oxford, Negro GIs Say: 'It's Our Fight, Too!'" *Jet*, Oct. 18, 1962, pp. 24–25.

8. Ibid.

9. Ibid.

10. Larry Still, "How Ole Miss Crisis Affects State's Negroes: Negroes Proud of Meredith, Plan Bolder Attack in Miss.," ibid., pp. 14–18, at 15.

11. Ibid. at 18.

12. *Ebony*, Jul. 1963, p.27.

13. "President Kennedy Entertains 1000 Negroes at White House," *Ebony*, May 1963.

14. *Ebony*, Nov. 1963, p. 29.

15. "March on Washington Was Largest Demonstration of Black Unity and Interracial Cooperation," *Ebony*, Jul. 1993, p. 124 *et seq*, at 126.

16. *Jet*, Oct. 31, 1963, pp. 6–8.

17. Simeon Booker, "Atty. Gen. Kennedy Explains Position on Civil Rights," *Jet*, Nov. 7, 1963, pp. 6–12, at 12.

18. Simeon Booker, "Roy Wilkins Disagrees with Views of Robert F. Kennedy," *Jet*, Nov. 14, 1963, pp. 8–14.

CHAPTER 18

1. http://millercenter.org/scripps/archive/presidentialrecordings/johnson/1963/12_1963.

2. Simeon Booker, "President Johnson's Rights Stand Praised by Leaders," *Jet*, Dec. 19, 1963, p. 6 *et seq*.

3. LBJ Telecon with Andrew Hatcher, Dec. 23, 1963. http://millercenter.org/scripps/archive/presidentialrecordings/johnson/1963/12_1963.

4. LBJ Telecon with Whitney Young, Dec. 23, 1963. http://millercenter.org/scripps/archive/presidentialrecordings/johnson/1963/12_1963.

5. LBJ Telecon with Roy Wilkins, Dec. 23, 1963. http://millercenter.org/scripps/archive/presidentialrecordings/johnson/1963/12_1963.

6. Simeon Booker, Ticker Tape USA, *Jet*, Jan. 30, 1964.

7. Memo, Carl Rowan to the president, January 28, 1964, [folder] "Ex HU 2 11/22/63-3/25/64," Box 2, White House Central Files Subject File, LBJ Library.

8. John H. Johnson, *Succeeding Against the Odds* (New York: Warner Books, 1989), pp. 281–82.

9. Ibid. at pp. 270–71.

10. LBJ Telecon with J. Edgar Hoover, Jul. 2, 1964. http://millercenter.org/scripps/archive/presidentialrecordings/johnson/1964.

11. LBJ Telecon with Roy Wilkins, Jul. 2, 1964. http://millercenter.org/scripps/archive/presidentialrecordings/johnson/1964.

12. Hatcher Telecon, *supra*.

13. LBJ Telecon with Geraldine Whittington, Dec. 23, 1963. http://millercenter.org/scripps/archive/presidentialrecordings/johnson/1963/12_1963.

14. LBJ Daily Diary, http://www.lbjlibrary.org/collections/daily-diary.html.

15. Ibid.

16. "Former Coed is White House Secretary," *Jet*, Jan. 9, 1964, p. 24.

17. Doris Kearns Goodwin, "Foreword," in *Lyndon Johnson and the American Dream* (New York: St. Martin's Griffin, 1991), p. xvii.

CHAPTER 19

1. Alvin Adams, "How a Movement Begins: With Scouts in Hard-Core Areas," *Jet*, Mar. 18, 1965, pp. 20–22.

2. John Britton, "Selma Woman's Girdle A Big Factor in Fight with Sheriff," *Jet*, Feb. 11, 1965, pp. 6–8; "Words of the Week," ibid, p. 30.

3. "Ala. Drive Spreads to Hometown of King's Wife," *Jet*, Feb. 19, 1965, p. 7.

4. "LBJ Speaks Up For Voting Rights," *Jet*, Feb. 19, 1965, p. 9 .

5. Alvin Adams, "Young Man Tried to Vote 5 Times Before Death," *Jet*, Mar. 19, 1965, pp. 14–19, at 18.

6. See Simeon Booker, "Untold Story: 7 Days of Crisis in Selma: Negroes Were Treated as Slaves, But Outnumbered Whites in Area," *Jet*, Mar. 25, 1965, pp. 14–25.

7. "Cleric Moved by Fellowship Before Selma Hoodlums Struck," ibid., pp. 26–29.

8. Simeon Booker, "50,000 March on Montgomery," *Ebony*, Apr. 1965, p. 46 *et seq.*

CHAPTER 20

1. *Jet*, Aug. 19, 1965, p. 14.

2. Simeon Booker, "Negro GI Heroes in the Vietnam War," *Jet*, Aug. 19, 1965, pp. 17–21, at 21.

3. *Ebony*, Aug. 1966, p. 44 *et seq.*

4. *Ebony*, Sept. 1966, p. 68 *et seq.*

5. *Ebony*, Oct. 1966, p. 37 *et seq.*

6. Ibid. at 42.

7. I interviewed Preston Bruce upon publication of his delightful memoir on his service at the White House over five presidential administrations; this incident is described in Preston Bruce, *From the Door of the White House* (New York: Lothrop, Lee and Shepard Books, 1985), pp. 133–134.

8. *Jet*, Feb. 22, 1968, pp. 20–21.

9. Jack Bass and Jack Nelson, *The Orangeburg Massacre* 2nd edition (Atlanta: Mercer University Press, 1984).

10. Bernard Garnett, "Orangeburg Tension High: Move to Form Biracial Group Stalled," *Jet*, Feb. 29, 1968, pp. 6–8.

11. *Jet*, June 20, 1968.

CHAPTER 21

1. Simeon Booker, "What Blacks Can Expect from Nixon," *Ebony*, Jan. 1969, p. 27, *et seq.*

2. "Constance B. Newman of VISTA," *Ebony*, Sept. 1972, p. 31, *et seq.*

3. Interview with Robert J. Brown, September 2010.

4. Hans Massaquoi, "A Battle the Army Can't Afford to Lose," *Ebony*, February 1973, p. 116, *et seq.*

5. Simeon Booker, "Untold Story of Black Hero of Watergate!," *Jet*, May 17, 1973, p. 20, *et seq.*

Selected Bibliography

Arsenault, Raymond. *Freedom Riders: 1961 and the Struggle for Racial Justice*. New York: Oxford University Press, 2006.

Bass, Jack, and Jack Nelson. *The Orangeburg Massacre*, 2nd ed. Mercer University Press, 1996.

Brinkley, Douglas. *The Wilderness Warrior: Theodore Roosevelt and the Crusade for America*. New York: HarperCollins, 2010.

Bruce, Preston. *From the Door of the White House*. New York: Lothrop, Lee and Sheperd, 1984.

DeLoach, Cartha D. *Hoover's FBI: The Inside Story by Hoover's Trusted Lieutenant*. Washington, D.C.: Regnery Publishing, 1995.

Deutsch, Stephanie. *You Need a Schoolhouse*. Evanston: Northwestern University Press, 2011.

Dubose, Carolyn P. *The Untold Story of Charles Diggs: The Public Figure, The Private Man*. Arlington, Va.: Barton Publishing House, 1998.

Eubanks, W. Ralph. *Ever Is a Long Time: A Journey into Mississippi's Dark Past*. New York: Basic Books, 2003.

Farmer, James. *James Farmer: An Autobiography of the Civil Rights Movement*. Fort Worth: Texas Christian University Press, 1998.

Henry, Aaron, and Constance Curry. *The Fire Ever Burning*. Jackson: University Press of Mississippi, 2000.

Johnson, John H., with Lerone Bennett, Jr. *Succeeding Against the Odds*. New York: Warner Books, 1989.

Lewis, John. *Walking with the Wind: A Memoir of the Movement*. New York: Simon & Schuster, 1998.

Morrow, E. Frederic. *Black Man in the White House*. New York: Macfadden Books, 1963.

Till-Mobley, Mamie, and Christopher Benson. *Death of Innocence*. New York: Random House, 2003.

Waring, James H. N. *Work of the Colored Law and Order League: Baltimore, Md., 1908*. See "The Capital and the Bay: Narratives of Washington and the Chesapeake Bay Region, ca. 1600–1925," http://memory.loc.gov/ammem/index.html.

Warren, Earl. *The Memoirs of Chief Justice Earl Warren*. New York: Doubleday, 1977.

Wilkins, Roy. *Standing Fast: The Autobiography of Roy Wilkins*. New York: Da Capo Press, 1994.

Williams, Juan. *Thurgood Marshall: American Revolutionary*. New York: Random House, 1998.

Wright, Simeon, and Herb Boyd. *Simeon's Story: An Eyewitness Account of the Kidnapping of Emmett Till*. Chicago: Lawrence Hill Books, 2010.

Index

CPSIA information can be obtained
at www.ICGtesting.com
Printed in the USA
LVHW092255240221
678869LV00005B/11/J